DICTIONARY OF PRINCE EDWARD ISLAND ENGLISH

EDITED BY T.K. PRATT

Dictionary of Prince Edward Island English

UNIVERSITY OF TORONTO PRESS
Toronto Buffalo London

© University of Toronto Press 1988
Toronto Buffalo London
Printed in Canada

ISBN 0-8020-5781-0

∞

Printed on acid-free paper

Canadian Cataloguing in Publication Data

Main entry under title:
Dictionary of Prince Edward Island English
   Bibliography: p.
   ISBN 0-8020-5781-0
   1. English language – Provincialisms – Prince
   Edward Island – Dictionaries. 2. English language –
   Dialects – Prince Edward Island – Dictionaries.
   I. Pratt, T.K. (Terry Kenneth), 1943–
   PE3245.P75D53 1988   427'.9717   C88-093351-8

This book has been published with the help of a
grant from the Canadian Federation for the Humanities,
using funds provided by the Social Sciences and
Humanities Research Council of Canada.

Contents

Acknowledgements

My primary debt is to the several hundred people, necessarily anonymous, who agreed to be interviewed or to fill out questionnaires, as typical Island speakers. These 'informants,' as they are called, gave of their time and knowledge freely, and they are the foundation of the entire work. A great many other people, especially some of my personal friends, took the trouble to communicate to me individual pieces of useful information.

Another fruitful source for me has been my linguistics classes at the University of Prince Edward Island. Every semester there was a new crop of students with whom I could discuss Island English, and from whom I could ask examples. The topic seems to interest almost every Islander who is asked to think about it. I am particularly grateful to those students who undertook term papers on subjects directly relevant to this project. They are Blaine Bernard, Margaret Carr, Charles Duffy, Shannon Flood, Anna Gojmerac, Wallena Higgins, Mark Jordan, Libby Kennedy, Lisa McCarvill, Joan MacDonald, Janet Macmillan, Claire Nantes, Anne Nicholson, Dawn Riley, Janice Robertson, and Anne Taylor-Murray. The familiar notion that research and teaching are a partnership has never been so clear to me as in working with these students.

My senior colleagues in the University also gave much help, especially in my own Department of English, in the Computer Centre, and in the Library. Two chairmen, Brendon O'Grady and Robert Campbell, and two deans, Frank Ledwell and Verner Smitheram, saw to it that I had space, time, and materials with which to work. I must also thank Frank Ledwell for his many personal contributions to these pages.

Other individuals as well contributed special support or knowledge. Murray Kinloch of the University of New Brunswick got me started; Jack Chambers of the University of Toronto kept me going. Both of these scholars, along with my immediate colleague, John Smith, read portions of the manuscript and gave valuable suggestions. I thank George Story of Memorial University not only for the example of the *Dictionary of Newfoundland English*, but also for one sentence of advice: 'Do not listen to counsels of perfection.' UPEI's David Weale made an extensive contribution in materials and observations. Other very helpful commentators and resource persons included Steven Connolly, the late Frances Dindial, Lawson Drake, Vivian Huizenga, C.W.J. Eliot, James Hancock, Keith Harrington, Keith Kennedy, Joseph Kopachevsky, James MacDougall, Harold MacLean, Harold Paddock, Frank Pigott, Layton Schurman, Bonny Suen, Ben Taylor, and Jonni Turner. I would like to single out Jennifer Shields for her strong encouragement in the final stages. And my parents, Audrey and Kenneth Pratt, were very supportive, as always.

Notwithstanding such generous voluntary help, the work would never have been completed without the many paid assistants, usually part-time or summer employees. Their salaries were funded chiefly by the Social Sciences and Humanities Research Council of Canada, in four substantial research grants. One of these grants also paid for a word processor, while another allowed me a term free of teaching, to work on the project full-time. In addition, the Council gave me a Leave Fellowship for 1986–87, to finish up the dictionary with the help of a sabbatical leave from UPEI. The Senate Research Committee of the University was also of major assistance. To this body I owe three handsome University grants and various smaller sums channelled from both SSHRCC General Grants and SSHRCC Small Universities Grants. The Island Studies Committee made five allocations, one of them sizeable. The English Department allowed me to spend the limit and more of its student assistant fund. And the Canada Employment and Immigration Program permitted me to hire three outside employees, each for several months part-time. I am grateful to these agencies both for their considerable help and for their faith in the project.

The assistants working on the dictionary formed a kind of pyramid. At the base were the fieldworkers. On their personalities and their knowledge of the Island, a great deal depended. They were Anne-Marie Arsenault, Sandy Beagan, Brenda Beagan, Lyle Brehaut, Phyllis Britten, Anne Cheverie, Rosemary Curley, Ann Dalton, Maura Green, Wallena Higgens, Annabel Hilchey, Carol Horne, Clara-Jean Howard, Peggy Howard, Larry Loveless, Heather MacDougall, Susan McManus, Bethany Murnaghan, Colleen Murphy, Ann Nicholson, Darlene Shea, Joanne Simmonds, Penelope Stuart, and Marion White. A special fieldworker was James Gormley, who single-handedly added or greatly strengthened more than two hundred words collected from primary Island industries.

The material gathered by these workers was subsequently manipulated in various ways, such as being punched into a computer or compared against other dictionaries. Here the premium was on concentration in the teeth of tedium. The staff in this case was mainly Linda Burke and James Gormley, assisted by Scott Burke, Barbara Ching, Carol Horne, Mark Jordan, Leslie Maclean, Lachlan MacQuarrie, Katy Palmer, Kant Sahajpal, Darlene Shea, and Frances Smits. I would also like to thank Carol Francis, the secretary of my Department, for her cheerful and speedy attack on many a set of foul papers.

Another, smaller group of assistants produced a different sort of primary material, by reading, and by listening to tapes. They worked on their own, and had to exercise considerable independent judgement. Their numbers included Phyllis Britten, Scott Burke, Barbara Ching, Frances Handrahan, Carol Horne, Effie Ives, Leslie Maclean, Norman St. Clair, and Anne Taylor-Murray. The latter was responsible for launching the reading program in the first place. The chief reader was Patricia Baldwin. Meticulous, hard-working, and clear-headed, she was responsible for the vast majority of the illustrative written quotations, probably the most entertaining part of this book.

In the project office, all the data had to be sorted, catalogued, and further dealt with. In these tasks I had the help over the years of four excellent research assistants, who stood at the second-last tier of the pyramid. They were, in chronological order, Claire Nantes, Carol Horne, Ann Boyles, and Annabel Hilchey. They brought to their jobs, particularly to the running of surveys, many various skills. I profited from discussions with each of them, especially the last, on matters of concept and theory far beyond the often humdrum tasks they were hired to do, and did well.

At the top of the pyramid stood Scott Burke, my editorial assistant. He joined me full-time early in the editing stage, and stayed almost to the end; his hand is in many places on every entry. He was resourceful, dogged, and quick. I have never worked with anyone with so much pleasure.

To all these people, and to Ron Schoeffel and his dedicated team at the University of Toronto Press, my warm thanks and again thanks. Any errors or omissions that remain are no one's fault but my own.

T.K. PRATT
University of Prince Edward Island

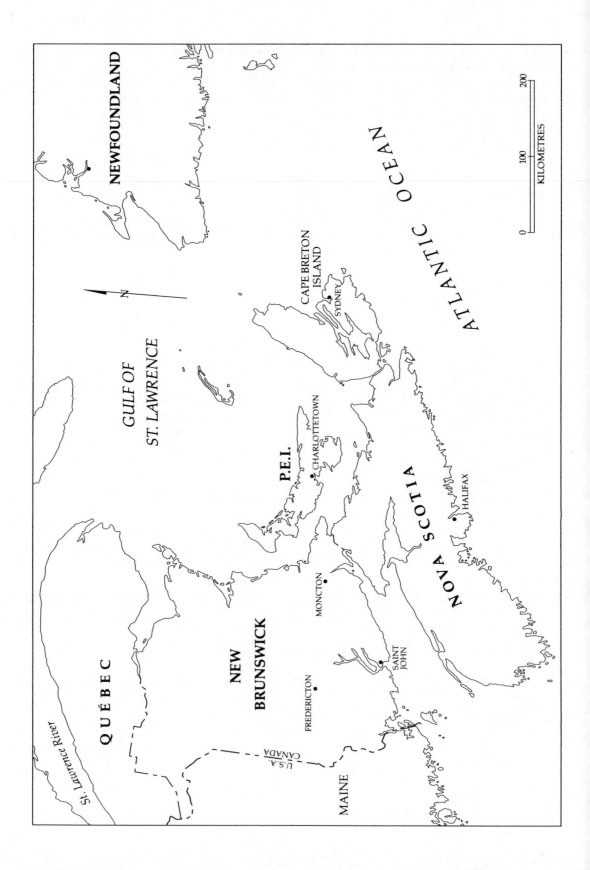

The Scope of the Dictionary

This dictionary is a record of non-standard words as used, or once used, on Prince Edward Island. The scope of the work can, in fact, be grasped fairly easily, simply by looking over a number of the entries. Nonetheless, the assumptions behind the choice of words must be made as clear as possible, and so it is necessary at the outset to be specific about the term 'non-standard.'

Most linguists are agreed that the term *standard* when applied to language means a form that is official and authoritative within a nation, used by the government and the courts of law, and for such functions as national news broadcasts and official ceremonies. It is the version favoured by the educated, and it is taught in schools and to non-native speakers. The standard is also associated with writing, especially print, and has a relatively fixed spelling system. Finally, it is the most widely accepted form of the language available, drawing least attention to itself in the widest variety of contexts. To some extent mastery of it is an ideal.

Non-standard language is the opposite. Far from being authoritative or official, its validity is sometimes questioned: purists may declare it incorrect, or out of date, or even non-existent. It is not taught in schools, but learned at home or in the local community, where it is transmitted orally. It is thus part of folk culture. When written, it is often found in hand-written forms, such as letters or diaries,

in which spelling can be quite variable. If it is printed, it is likely to be in material intended primarily for local circulation. Non-standard language is not an ideal; it is simply what people say. It is sometimes called 'the vernacular,' or 'folk speech,' or 'dialect.'

Inevitably, non-standard language also includes what some would call 'sub-standard.' An example in this dictionary is *slippy*, a popular, informal variant for *slippery* that many Prince Edward Islanders regard as incorrect. The *Dictionary of Prince Edward Island English* (hereafter *DPEIE*) has not especially sought out English of this kind, but neither was it refused when it came.

Standard language is normally quite uniform within a nation; indeed standard English is quite uniform internationally. But non-standard language is likely to be found in different forms in different regions, and these forms, of course, are known as *dialects*. It is tempting to think of, or perhaps even diagram, the relationship between standard Canadian English and its regional dialects as a central circle with smaller circles clustered around it. Prince Edward Island English would then be one of the smallest circles, perhaps partly contained by a bigger Maritimes one and close to a yet larger circle for Newfoundland. But such a diagram would be misleading for a number of reasons: what we now consider standard in Canada was itself developed from dialects in

England; much that we consider *non-*standard was once standard, now out of fashion; dialects merge almost imperceptibly into one another and into the standard – indeed, using *dialect* as a geographical boundary marker is merely a convenience, not to be taken literally; and the whole picture is more truly a continuum, from the most acceptable English nation-wide to the least. The continuum also fluctuates over time and space and social class. Thus, although the core ideas behind standard and non-standard Canadian English remain clear, isolating the dialect of any region, such as Prince Edward Island, sometimes requires arbitrary measures.

Yet there are a few obvious guidelines for the choosing of words for a dictionary of this kind. It is helpful to list some categories of words that *DPEIE* does *not* contain. (1) Proper nouns, except for a few traditional ones (*the Boston States*), names for the Island and its people (*North Sider*), and proper nouns within compounds (*Malpeque oyster*). (2) Foreign words from, say, French or Gaelic, unless used by native English speakers in an English context, like *rapure*. (3) Words for a special occasion, such as *Yankee Gale*, a particular storm in October, 1851. (4) Words judged to be transitory in Island speech, including most slang and other in-group vocabulary, like *rooney* 'a short fat carrot,' named after Mickey Rooney. (5) Non-standard words too well known to require further documentation, like *ain't*. (6) Multi-word expressions and folk sayings, such as *How's your belly where the pig bit you?* or *If you burn your ass you sit on blisters*. The decision to leave out such colourful sayings, not an easy one (there being several hundred in *DPEIE* files at time of publication), may disappoint some Island readers. However, folk sayings require such a special format for presentation, and their tone is such a bad fit with that generally adopted in this work, that in the end they had to be excluded. (7) Technical, scientific, or learned words, even if commonly used

in an Island industry; an example is *carapace* for a lobster shell. The same restriction applies to words for modern equipment, such as sonar equipment in fishing. (8) Words strictly confined to an occupation and understood only by the practitioners. At the same time, certain occupations centrally important to Prince Edward Island, such as lobster fishing and potato farming, have been singled out for special searches of their vocabularies. No account of Island English would be complete without close attention to these areas. Since they usually involve whole communities, or even the whole province, their terms normally fit within this guideline on occupational words. On the other hand, to the extent that these industries are practised elsewhere, the inclusion of such occupational words sometimes means a certain blurring of dialect lines, such as they are.

Even with such restrictions, borderline cases are inevitable. In many such cases, *DPEIE* has applied another guideline, through the editorial judgement of four dictionaries: *The Concise Oxford Dictionary of Current English* (1982), *Webster's New World Dictionary* (1970), *Gage Canadian Dictionary* (1983), and *Funk and Wagnalls Standard College Dictionary* (Canadian Edition, 1976). These dictionaries, one British, one American, one Canadian, and one Canadianized offspring of an American parent, attempt to capture three forms of standard English that are highly relevant for Canada. Thus most borderline candidates for *DPEIE*, other than occupational, have been rejected if they are found in any two of these dictionaries without a qualifying label. As for the label, the word *sonsy*, a typical example, is in three of the four dictionaries, but since it is labelled 'Sc. [Scottish]' by *Concise Oxford*, 'Brit. Dial.' by *Webster's*, and 'Scot and Brit dial.' by *Funk and Wagnalls*, its presence on Prince Edward Island is interesting, and thus it is included. This is a fairly rigorous test for a non-standard word to pass, and has cut down the number of entries, because some non-standard words make their way into such dictionaries unqualified, thanks to the elasticity of the concept of standard. They then serve to rule out the potential *DPEIE* entry.

With respect to the *Gage Canadian Dictionary*, the test has been even more rigorous. There is strong reason to believe that almost all the unlabelled words, or words labelled 'Canadian,' in this short, Canada-made dictionary are standard for this country. This being the case, any prospective word for *DPEIE* found in *Gage* has been subjected to a detailed search in many sources, to determine if there is any reason to include it in this collection of special Island vocabulary. By this rule, for example, *sea run* 'spawning run of fish up river from the sea' is not included here; neither is *rampike* 'tall, dead tree,' the latter labelled 'Canadian' in all three of the North American dictionaries. Yet both of these slightly unusual words are found on Prince Edward Island. As another example, *shell ice* 'thin ice over an air space' is also in *Gage*, marked 'Canadian,' but this label is itself qualified by 'in the North,' so the expression is included here on the grounds that readers might wish to know of its wider distribution. Finally, *glitter* and *silver thaw*, both meaning 'a glitter of ice on exposed surfaces after freezing rain,' are omitted from this dictionary because they are entered in *Gage*, while their synonyms *silver freeze* and *silver frost* are included.

A separate restriction has been applied to names for wildflowers, which, if unchecked, could easily sprout in profusion throughout the work. The rule has been to include only those *not* listed in Diane Griffin's *Atlantic Wildflowers*, 1984.

Notwithstanding the usefulness of these mechanical rules for the limitation of Island vocabulary, the editor has reserved the right – though exercised only occasionally – to break them, on the principle that it is better, after all, to err on the side of commission. A case in point is *breeze* 'a gale,' found unlabelled in *Webster's* and *Funk and Wagnalls* but identified in more specialized studies with the Atlantic coast, and so kept.

Questionable cases also exist at the other end of the scale, that is, words with so little evidence accompanying them that their authenticity could reasonably be doubted. Scores of words of this kind have been rejected; those retained have at least one written attestation or two oral ones. Even so, there can sometimes be suspicion, especially if the combination of spelling with meaning seems to contradict one's experience of the language. In such cases, the word has also been rejected.

These, then, are the principles by which words were chosen for this dictionary, from the much larger number that offered themselves through the research outlined in the next section. By now the reader will be forewarned that this is not a dictionary of 'Islandisms,' of words or meanings apparently unique to Prince Edward Island. There are indeed many such words and meanings: *Abegweit, board ice, crow piss, fox house, large day, Mcdonaldite, nosey weather, pin digger, sheep storm, slump, trap smasher*, and *weak*, to name a few. But a volume devoted to these alone would probably not be as useful as one that helps to show wider patterns of distribution, especially in the area of non-standard speech, which does not usually get the detailed attention that the standard does. The discovery is more interesting, not less, that Island words are shared by other dialects. These words include Maritime or New England terms not previously ascribed to Prince Edward Island specifically (*pung*), Newfoundland words not recorded outside that province (*baker's fog*), words of Canadian origin but uncertainly distributed across the country (*aboiteau*), Loyalist words (*barrack*), words from the British Isles showing early settlement patterns (Irish *bunyan*; Scottish *puckle*), and, as a sub-section of the latter, words from the British Isles used widely on Prince Edward Island but highly restricted elsewhere on this continent, where known at all (*stormstayed*).

It is undoubtedly one of the strengths of other dialect dictionaries in this hemisphere and in recent years – for example, the *Dictionary of Newfoundland English*, the *Dictionary of American Regional English*, the *Dictionary of Jamaican English*, and the *Dictionary of Bahamian English* – that they too show the links from dialect to dialect, and from dialect to standard, filling in the continuum for their respective catchment areas, and advancing our knowledge about the language as a whole. Together they complement the standard dictionaries of national and international English, as well as dialect dictionaries of the British Isles such as the *English Dialect Dictionary* and the *Scottish National Dictionary*. Finally, all regional dictionaries are also linked to the large and on-going dictionaries of record – the *Oxford English Dictionary* and *Webster's New International Dictionary* – since these are fed partly through researches at the local and non-standard level. The *Dictionary of Prince Edward Island English* is intended to take a place in this larger system.

The Making of the Dictionary

Compiling a dictionary is something like doing detective work. A number of investigations are started in different directions, in the hopes that one or more of them will turn up clues. One such clue may not seem very significant at the time, but put together with others from different sources it may show itself to be part of a pattern. As one famous detective remarked 'You [Watson] know my method. It is founded upon the observance of trifles.' This section outlines the various kinds of directed observance – the research – behind this dictionary.

OBSERVERS (O)

The first definite action taken on behalf of *DPEIE* was a letter sent in the summer of 1979 to about 500 Islanders considered to be informed observers of the local language. Their numbers included professors, teachers, librarians, journalists, lawyers, ministers, priests, speech therapists, and politicians. The letter listed several localisms that had come to the attention of the editor in previous years (many of them supplied by his students), and it asked for more. The response was extremely encouraging. The then premier, Angus Maclean, took the trouble to send in his observations, and two well-informed Island residents, Ben Taylor and David Weale, made available their own lists built up over several years.

After that first mailing, the contributions from observers continued unprompted. Thanks to generous media interest in the project, both local and national, the Island public was well informed about it, and words and comments about words continued to trickle in at a steady rate, by letter, telephone, and personal communication. Colleagues at the University of Prince Edward Island were particularly helpful, as was each new semester of students. The abbreviation 'O' is used in Dictionary entries to indicate a contribution from one or more of these observers. Other such abbreviations of research categories are explained below.

POSTAL SURVEYS (P1, P2, R)

After a few months, enough usable examples had been collected that it was time to put the research on a more formal footing. Postal surveys, although not reliable for every purpose, can bring in much information for relatively little expense. As a way of opening or closing a field of study, there is ample precedent for them in vocabulary searches elsewhere. The first such postal survey for *DPEIE* (P1) saw a questionnaire of 176 non-standard words mailed to 130 senior citizens across Prince Edward Island, through the member clubs of the Prince Edward Island Senior Citizens Federation. The questionnaire contained an additional forty-nine items on folk sayings and a multiple-choice section on standard words. The latter two aspects of the survey are not of further concern here. Senior Citizens were chosen as informants because it was assumed – on ample grounds from both observation and the evidence of other studies – that their speech retained more dialect than did that of any other age group. The later surveys (described below), with informants of all ages, clearly supported this assumption. The speech of seniors was a logical base line, then, for further research on Island English.

Seventy-two questionnaires were returned from the mail-out, a gratifying response. Informants were well distributed regionally, came from a full range of occupations, and matched the population as a whole in major ethnic backgrounds. Unfortunately, there were three times as many women as men. But this group was never taken as a representative sample of the Island population, or used for statistical purposes, in contrast to the sample in the fieldwork surveys undertaken later. Rather, the responses gave usage comments, new or fuller meanings, examples of words in context, reassuring confirmations of what was already thought, and, finally, new words.

A second postal survey (P2) was carried out in 1983–84. This study focused on seventy-two words gathered in previous fieldwork. These words seemed to be likely entries for the Dictionary, but there was too little evidence to include them with assurance. Thus a questionnaire containing them was sent again to elderly informants, this time to eighty-four residents in senior citizens' housing in the Charlottetown area. Cooperation was virtually universal, and in many cases, the assistant in charge was able to gain valuable additional data by administering the questionnaire in person. By this means, all of the seventy-two words were either cleared for entry or rejected.

A third survey of this kind was undertaken in the spring of 1986, after the first draft of the Dictionary was already completed. The seventy-four words under examination had been held back from that draft as rather unlikely candidates for various reasons; in fact, they were on the verge of being dropped. However, in a spirit of cleaning up, these words were put into a checklist with room for comment, and distributed to 100 informants, chiefly observers who had contributed significantly in the past. The responses numbered thirty-one. As anticipated, fewer than half of the words received endorsement, but these are now in the Dictionary with the research label 'R,' for Rare Words Survey.

FIELDWORK SURVEYS (I, II)

By the summer of 1980, the first postal survey and the observers had generated more than enough words to justify a larger and more scientific investigation, this time involving a cross-section of the whole population of the province. The first step was to determine how this cross-section would be selected. Four social factors, at least, were felt to be important: sex, age, class, and locality. For the first, it was easy to decide that the sample should contain equal numbers of men and women. For the second, however, it was not obvious that the study should exactly reflect the age distribution in the population at large. As mentioned, dialect studies of all kinds had demonstrated that traditional folk speech is less evident among the young. It was necessary to find a compromise between making statistical sense (so that labels could be attached to given words with some hope of accuracy), and finding the words at all. In the end, half the informants were chosen from speakers sixty and over, while the other half were spread fairly evenly from eighteen to fifty-nine, allowing a number of logical groupings. This decision turned out to be similar to that taken by the very successful *Dictionary of American Regional English*, then unpublished, for which people over sixty formed two-thirds of the informants. Nevertheless, it must be remembered that all generalizatons in *DPEIE* stemming from the surveys reported on here are based on a deliberately biased sample.

Social class is often a factor in linguistic differences, and it was thought necessary to achieve some kind of social spread in the sample. This was accomplished by establishing two broad groups, 'working class' and 'middle class,' using an eighteen-point scale of measurement that assigned a number to every informant's occupation, education, spouse's occupation, and father's occupation. As it happened, although this method probably ensured a sufficient variety of informant backgrounds, the vocabularies of the two classes did not differ very much in the results. Nor did any sub-classes emerge consistently within the two broad groups. Accordingly, judgements about word usage based on class measurement are infrequent in this dictionary.

In contrast, the differences between rural and urban speakers were marked, with the rural areas far richer in traditional dialect. Thus the sample had to include, at the very least, proportionate numbers from these areas. The tool for establishing this proportion was the federal Census for 1976, the latest available at the time. In that source (II, 27), urban dwellers are defined as those persons living in an area with a population concentration of 1,000 or more, and a population density of at least 1,000 per square mile. All others interviewed for this study were taken to be rural. The numbers finally chosen from each group are discussed below.

Another aspect of locality was also important, that of ensuring a spread of informants across the province. At the same time, if there were any dialectal divisions within the Island, it was necessary to create within the sample a workable number of areas that could reasonably be expected to show some such divisions in advance; it would then be necessary

to interview a sufficient number of Islanders from each designated area. For most purposes it is convenient to divide the Island by its three long-established counties, Prince, Queen's, and King's. But there was no reason on the face of it to consider the county boundaries, cutting arbitrarily as they do through the countryside, to be significant linguistically. Far better possibilities appeared in the then boundaries of the four federal ridings of Egmont, Malpeque, Hillsborough, and Cardigan. Here we have four areas with almost equal populations, divided naturally – from the point of view of possible dialects – by the bottleneck of Summerside, the urban concentration of Charlottetown, and the Hillsborough River. Moreover, helpful data was available for these ridings, from the Census. Accordingly, these were the areas chosen for dialect divisions in the Dictionary entries, with the exceptions that Hillsborough is renamed 'Charlottetown,' with which it is all but co-terminous, and Summerside is split off from Egmont to make a second specified urban locality, and thus five regions in all (see map on page xviii).

The funding available to the project in 1980 dictated a sample size of about 100 informants. Compared to other such projects to date, this was a very respectable number in relation to the size of the population under study. In order to come close to this number and yet involve all the factors outlined above in due proportion, a grid (see page xix) was created. Each cell was to be filled with the name of an appropriate informant. In the grid we see the four federal ridings with equal numbers of cells in each (reflecting the population numbers), except that Hillsborough is under-represented by half because of its thoroughly urban character. This was a second calculated bias in the sample, also based on the conviction that irreproachable statistics were not as important as going where the words were to be found. It can be seen that male (M) and female (F)

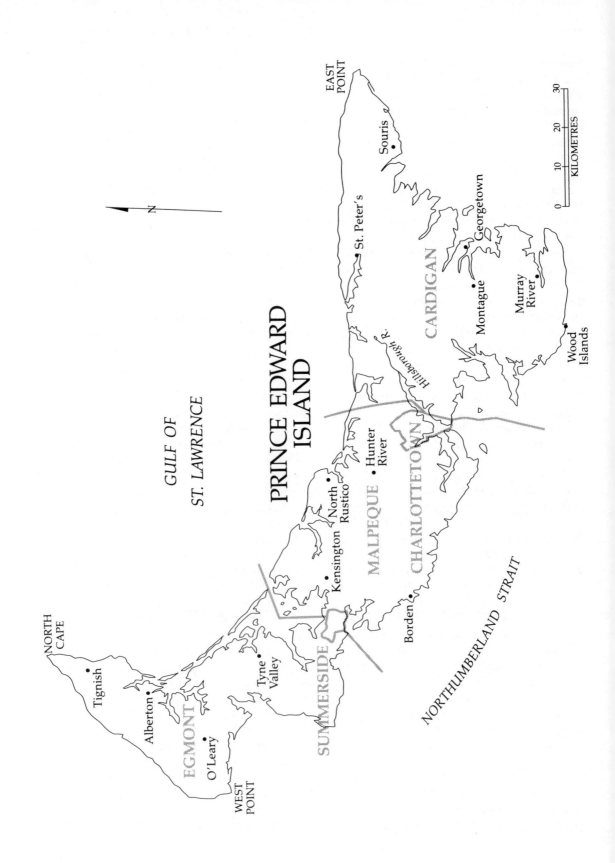

		Egmont		Malpeque		Hillsborough (Charlottetown)		Cardigan	
		M	F	M	F	M	F	M	F
U									
	WC								
R	Older								
	MC								
B									
	WC								
A	Younger								
	MC								
N									
R									
	WC								
U	Older								
	MC								
R									
	WC								
A	Younger								
	MC								
L									

informants are in equal numbers in every riding. Further, each riding except Hillsborough is split between rural and urban dwellers. According to the 1976 Census, it happened that in both Malpeque and Cardigan the proportion of rural to urban dwellers was almost exactly three to one (roughly 15,000: 5,000). This proportion was easy to reflect in the cell structure, as can be seen. Meanwhile, in Egmont, the balance was very close to 1:1, thanks to the town of Summerside; here, then, the numbers of rural and urban cells are the same. Finally, all areas are divided into equal numbers both of working class (WC) and middle class (MC) cells, and of younger and older cells (the latter being for informants sixty and over). When all the cells created by this grid are added up, they total 112, fairly close to the target number.

Zealous fieldworkers in the first round, however, overfilled some cells and raised this figure to 118.

It was the role of the fieldworker, usually a university student working part-time who came from a certain area and knew the people there, to take a subsection of the grid and to find willing Prince Edward Islanders to fill the cells. In Egmont all but two of the urban cells were deliberately filled from Summerside, to make a reasonable number for generalizations in the dictionary entries on this important town. One further bias of a sort was built in to the sample at this point: fieldworkers selected informants with a view to their being interested – or at least not uninterested – in the idea of talking about unusual 'Island' words. Once again it was assumed that without such a bias many hours and dollars might be wasted looking for data that simply was not there. However, the task of filling the cells was not a difficult one; word of mouth quickly supplied gaps among the students' acquaintances, and almost everyone was willing to participate.

The fieldworkers were armed with a questionnaire that listed most of the words collected to date in a logical flow within fields: weather, nature, fishing, farm, house, food, drink, special occasions, people, children, clothing, the body, places, and miscellaneous. There was also an open question at the end for new words. The questionnnaire suggested both *direct* ways of asking about each word ('Do you know a children's game called *leap*?') and *indirect* ones ('What children's games do you know?'). With practice the fieldworkers became quite independent of the questionnaire's wording, and conducted the interviews as they thought best, in a relaxed manner. The interviews took about two hours. The fieldworker made it his or her business to discover if the informant naturally used each word, or merely had heard it, or had never heard it. Those informants with

knowledge were encouraged to display it, to talk about the word, and, above all, to use it in context. No tape recorders were employed; the fieldworker wrote what he or she could, and made a fuller version immediately afterward. This version was later transcribed into *DPEIE* files, to be excerpted for Dictionary citations, definitions, synonyms, stylistic labels, and other matters. Meanwhile, each informant's background (age, sex, and so on) was coded and fed into a computer. The code included ethnic background, for the numbers of informants with identifiable Acadian, English, Irish, or Scottish ancestry were large enough that generalizations on these groups were possible, even though such determiners had not been built into the sample initially.

With the coding complete, the computer was able to put out statistics on which sub-groups of people within the general sample favoured which words. These statistics stand behind the labels on distribution in the Dictionary's head notes, as explained below in the 'Guide to the Dictionary.'

Survey I (One), consisting of 218 words investigated under this system, was completed by the end of 1981. Many informants had supplied new words. Together with those from other sources, the total was 224, enough, with new funding, for a whole new round of fieldwork (Survey II [Two]). This time the work was done in one summer, 1982, using largely the same informants as before but with some substitutions. The total number of words surveyed in this detailed manner, then, comes to 442.

COMMON WORD SURVEY (C)

Simultaneous with Surveys I and II was another kind of fieldwork relevant only occasionally to the Dictionary. The 'Common Word Survey' was chiefly about standard words, though the term *standard* was not in its title because some non-standard words were part of it also. The basis of this work was a multiple-choice questionnaire of 113 items, asking informants about such common choices in their speech as *serviette* over *napkin*, *chesterfield* over *couch* or *sofa*, and the possible times of day for *lunch*. Several *DPEIE* words were included among the choices, and some questions (for example, 'Do you have a name for a late spring snowfall?') were deliberately there to elicit dialect words (for example *sheep storm*). Thus it is sometimes possible in an entry for the Dictionary, using the results of this survey, to make a judgement about a word's popularity relative to other words, either standard (*spring storm*) or non-standard (*smelt storm*, *poor man's fertilizer*). There are also a few citations, marked 'C.'

The Common Word survey was conducted from 1980 to 1982. The questionnaire was administered to a sample of 196 Islanders, in a direct interview that lasted about forty minutes. There was no need to build into this sample the kinds of biases described above for the dialect surveys; indeed there was every reason to use as random a group of informants as possible. The method was to choose names from the electoral lists prepared for the 1979 federal election. It was decided that a sample of about 200 was financially feasible. Since there were approximately 80,000 voters on the lists, every 400th name was selected. This sampling method had the desirable effects of spreading informants across the Island and securing rural and urban areas in proportion. It also produced, fortuitously, almost equal numbers of men and women, and a representative spread both of ages and of ancestries.

SPECIAL LEXICONS (S)

A third and final kind of fieldwork focused on a number of occupations traditionally significant in rural life on Prince Edward Island. In order of investigation these were potato farming, lobster fishing, fox ranching, Irish moss harvesting, oyster fishing, and general fishing and farming. While various words from their special vocabularies had been gathered all along by the other means of research, it was felt towards the end of the collecting period that some concentrated attention should be given to these distinctive areas. The example of similar attention to cod fishing and seal hunting in the *Dictionary of Newfoundland English* was also instructive.

Two new sources were found for these 'Special Lexicon' words. In the first place, several of the fields were the subject of careful search and documentation by students at the University of Prince Edward Island and written up as their major papers for courses in linguistics. The students typically knew the areas first hand, and, with guidance, they planned their samples and methodology, conducted interviews, wrote dictionary-style entries including full linguistic descriptions, explained their procedures in an introduction, and drew conclusions. These essays are included in the Bibliography, and when drawn upon are referred to in the normal manner for written evidence.

The second source for information of this kind was in-house fieldwork conducted in the summer of 1986, to follow up the student papers, elicit citations, and find new words. The procedure in most cases was simple. With the words already on hand for a given field, a questionnaire similar to those used for Surveys I and II was drawn up. At least three informants not previously approached, but known to be expert in the field, were interviewed in each case. Their citations were recorded in the same manner as for the other fieldwork. Where used in the Dictionary, these are labelled 'S' for Special Lexicons Survey.

TAPES (T)

DPEIE researchers took advantage of whatever recorded dialect speech they

could find, which was not a great deal.
The Public Archives of Prince Edward
Island holds twenty-five tapes of interviews with senior citizens on the subject
of 'by-gone days,' compiled by the Belfast
Historical Society (here 'T B'). The University of Prince Edward holds 142 taped
interviews on folklore, compiled by students hired by Professor Wendall MacIntyre ('T M'). Finally, *DPEIE* was given
access to the tapes of eighty-nine locally
produced CBC radio programs on PEI
heritage, a series called 'Island Brew' ('T I').
All of the tapes from these three collections
were audited, and relevant quotations
extracted. On the whole, however, they
were not a strong source.

READING PROGRAM

Like other recent dialect dictionaries,
DPEIE is based on a mixture of oral and
written sources. All of the data mentioned hitherto have been oral, at least in
the first instance. But written sources
are traditional in dictionary-making, and
they are tremendously valuable, for they
add authority to what may seem transitory
in speech. Although this part of the research does not take many words to explain, it was the most extensive of all.

The bulk of the reading was done in a
programmed way over a two-year period,
1982–84, and again for some months in
1986. The entire 'Prince Edward Island
Collection' (books and manuscripts about
the Island or by Islanders) of UPEI's
Robertson Library was examined, and almost all of the works in it that promised
even remotely to contain the sort of words
delimited by 'The Scope of the Dictionary,'
above, were read and excerpted, as were
many books from the library's main hold-
ings. This collection, the fullest on the subject, was supplemented by that in the
(public) Confederation Centre Library. The

Public Archives of Prince Edward Island
also yielded about forty diaries, and some
other manuscripts. In addition, UPEI professor David Weale gave generous access
to his private collection of Island diaries
and his accumulated papers on social
history.

From these collections a total of about
900 titles was read, of which 360 yielded
one or more quotations that, having passed
through editorial selection, were used in
the Dictionary. The latter titles are listed
in the Bibliography. The major categories
are: (1) diaries, letters, autobiographies,
and reminiscences – 21%; (2) history, biog-
raphy, and folklore – 17%; (3) creative
works, especially those of Lucy Maud
Montgomery – 15%; (4) government and
other reports on the special occupations
– 14%; (5) community histories – 11%; (6)
geographical and social descriptions –
8%; (7) travelogues and non-fiction narra-
tives – 6%. The Bibliography also ac-
knowledges a number of quoted secondary
sources, chiefly on the English language.

CONCLUSION

These, then, are the various lines of investigation that were followed in the making
of the *Dictionary of Prince Edward Island
English*. Of course, it is always possible
to continue such lines or to start others: to
read one more book, or interview one
more informant, in the hopes of finding
something new. But the editor, and his
more than generous funding agencies,
must judge at some point that diminishing
returns have set in. This dictionary, like
others of its kind, has not been finished,
but merely ended. The number of words
presented in the main entries is 873, while
the alternate forms, many of them in their
own cross-referenced entries, bring the
total collection to over 1,000. Behind each
word is an average of about seven sources.

Guide to the Dictionary

The entries in this dictionary are meant to be as self-explanatory as possible. Very few abbreviations, or other such devices that are needed in more comprehensive collections, have been used here. Nevertheless, any reader who wishes to understand in full what *DPEIE* has to offer, or to see where decisions have had to be arbitrary, should read this brief guide.

Entries are of two kinds: cross-references and main entries. Cross-references simply take the form of *'rubber bread*: see *fog.'* Under the second word, *fog* in this case, is found the cross-referenced term, an alternate following 'Also' or 'Also spelled.' *Fog* is the head word for a main entry. All relevant information in any main entry applies equally to the alternate(s). A cross-reference is not supplied if the act of looking up the first word will inevitably produce the second (so *slumpy snow* automatically yields to *slump*).

The main entries, naturally, are the main interest. Each of them has potentially six sections. The first three of these are found in every case: head word, head note, and definition. The second three are options that depend on available information: citations, editorial note, and dictionary note.

HEAD WORD

The head word is the word proper, in the form judged by the editor to be the most common or basic. Nouns and verbs of the same basic form, like *snib*, are given separate entries, the noun first. Occasionally, two unrelated words can have the same form; these too are given separate entries, and marked arbitrarily '1' and '2.' The head word may also be longer than a single word, and take the form of a compound noun like *fox biscuit*, or a compact phrase like *on the lift*. Longer and looser phrases or sayings, like *There's one room in his attic not plastered*, are not a part of this work, as explained above in 'The Scope of the Dictionary.'

The head words are in alphabetical order, of course, and if they have more than one word within them the alphabetizing assumes that these are run together. Compound nouns and phrases should always be looked up under the first important word; *a shin of heat*, for example, is under 'S.' In cases where misdirection has seemed possible (say, to *heat* in the last example), there is a cross-reference.

In entries for which the evidence is wholly oral, the spelling of the head word or its alternates may be a matter of dispute. This is particularly true in the hyphenating of compounds. It is not possible to say for certain which is most correct: *down street*, *down-street*, or *downstreet*; the editor can only be guided by his instincts. Occasionally, as with *gomaug*, an alternate of *gommie*, the spelling is partly invented, by analogy. Capitalization, however, as in *Islander*, relies on written practice.

HEAD NOTE

The head note immediately follows the head word. Its function is to describe the perceived boundaries in the Prince Edward Island usage of that word and its alternates. The head note has potentially eight sub-sections: part of speech, pronunciation, alternate forms, alternate spellings, stylistic label, regional label, social label, and comparisons. Only the first of these is necessarily present; the others depend on the evidence at hand. It must be remembered that the judgements in the head note, while certainly open to mistake, are based on the complete *DPEIE* files and not simply on the illustrative citations in the entry presentation, which are usually selective.

(i) *Part of Speech*. This label has been kept as simple as possible, but in all cases it is based on current linguistic practice. Nouns usually used in the plural – *rabbit's candles* for example – are so noted. Verbs are marked 'transitive' if, like *card*, they habitually require an object, and 'intransitive' otherwise (for example, *mitch*). Other grammatical terms that may need explanation are: 'phrasal verb' (a verb forming a phrase with a particle, as in *fine up*); 'verbal adjective' (an adjective formed by adding *-ing*, *-ed*, or *-en* to a verb, as in *short-taken*); and 'verbal noun' (a noun formed by adding *-ing* to a verb, as in *scrimshanking*). The terms 'noun phrase' (*pork and jerk*), 'adjective phrase' (*charming likely*), and 'adverb phrase' (*up west*) merely indicate multi-word versions of the traditional parts of speech, while a 'prepositional phrase' is a preposition followed by a noun phrase (*in the round*). Compound nouns (*monkey fur*) and modified nouns (*poor man's weather glass*) are labelled simply 'noun.'

(ii) *Pronunciation*. In most of the entries pronunciation is not given, usually because it is thought to be obvious, but sometimes (with some words of limited currency like *nosic*) because it is not known.

Where it is given, it takes the form of a respelling, largely in the normal alphabet, between reversed slashes. Thus the pronunciation of *buss* is \boos\, with the double *o* signifying the same vowel as that of, say, *good*. A 'Pronunciation Key' explaining the respellings immediately precedes the entries. In some cases, such as *jigaree*, the pronunciation offered is an informed guess. In others, particularly words from Gaelic (*bodach*), certain sounds can be rendered only crudely by the symbols in the key. Occasionally, alternate spellings are labelled 'Also spelled and pronounced,' implying that it is possible to deduce the pronunciations from what has been already shown for the head word (as in *barachois*).

(iii) *Alternate Forms*. Following the word 'Also' are listed alternates that are close enough to the head word to be treated in the same entry. Thus, with *king hair* we find *king fur*. In this example, the alternate form is not cross-referenced from its own entry, since it is probably impossible to miss it where it is. In other cases, as explained above, a word following 'Also' may have been referred there from its own place in the alphabet.

(iv) *Alternate Spellings*. The *DPEIE* files sometimes reveal a number of different spellings for a word, not all of which necessarily appear in the selected citations. They are, however, listed in the head note at this point. An example is *slough*, also spelled *slew, sloo, slue*. Alternate spellings are entered as cross-references if they differ markedly from the head word.

(v) *Stylistic label*. Occasionally it is possible to judge that a word is restricted in its style to a certain context or level of speech. Thus, *five-gallon* is labelled 'humorous,' *scut* is 'impolite,' and *bare buff* 'informal.' Two of the labels chosen, 'archaic' and 'historical,' need special attention. Both of them apply to older words, but 'archaic' means that some informants still remember their use, while 'historical' means that in our time the word is found chiefly in written histories and in historical documents. An example of the former is *mussel mud*, and of the latter *holey dollar*. The label 'obsolete' is deliberately avoided, because in dialect study of this kind one can never be positive that a word is indeed finished with.

(vi) *Regional label*. As explained in 'The Making of the Dictionary,' the 1980–82 Fieldwork Surveys (I, II) of 112 to 118 native Islanders found it convenient to group these informants in five regions partly corresponding to the four Prince Edward Island federal ridings: Egmont, Summerside, Malpeque, Charlottetown, and Cardigan (see map on page xviii). The regional label judges the frequency of a given word in each of these areas, according to statistics derived from the surveys mentioned. Five levels of frequency are used: 'common' (70–100%), 'frequent' (50–69%), 'occasional' (30–49%), 'infrequent' (10–29%), and 'rare' (0–9%). These numbers refer to the percentage of users found in a given region, as against the total informants interviewed in that region. If the *overall* percentage for a word is 0–9%, it is not given any regional or social label except 'Rare.' A word lacking even this indication was not part of Fieldwork Surveys I and II.

(vii) *Social Label*. Since the surveys also classified informants according to age, sex, ethnicity, class, and rural or urban setting, labels within these categories are also possible for many words. For age, it has been found helpful to group informants variously as 'senior' (over sixty), 'older' (over fifty), 'middle-aged' (forty to fifty-nine), 'younger' (under forty), and 'under thirty.' The ethnicity labels are limited to 'Acadian,' 'English,' 'Irish,' or 'Scottish.' The only class label considered necessary is 'less educated,' which groups those informants with education up to and including grade ten but no further. The definitions of 'rural' and 'urban' are given above, in 'The Making of the Dictionary.'

Social labels are always preceded by one of two qualifiers, 'significantly' or 'especially.' The former means that the numbers have passed a chi-square test (in which $P < 0.05$), and that the distinction pointed at is very firm in the data available. The latter implies only a tendency, and is based on a spread of at least ten percentage points between the grouping created by the label and all other possible groupings.

The stylistic, regional, and social labels together can help the reader to a clearer sense of a word's place in the speech of Prince Edward Island, but they are not, of course, absolute. They go only as far as the *DPEIE* evidence at hand.

(viii) *Comparisons*. The final function of the head note is to refer the reader to complementary entries, signalled by the word 'Compare.' This referral is made even if the word in question is immediately adjacent. Complementary entries are generally in the same semantic field. It has sometimes been found necessary, however, to define such fields rather narrowly, to keep this section of the head note within reasonable bounds. Thus, the many kinds of sea ice are divided into three different fields: slushy ice (like *lolly*), flat ice (like *board ice*), and ice in pieces (like *drift ice*). Readers will undoubtedly break through the editor's boundaries to form their own comparisons.

DEFINITION

The writing of precise, simple, and nicely turned definitions is perhaps the most challenging task for any dictionary-maker. In general, the attempt here has been to use ordinary words in a natural way as far as possible. Yet non-standard words from *DPEIE* itself are occasionally used in definitions, between single quotation marks. At the other end of the formality scale, most plants are given their Latin names (for example *Hieracium aurantiacum* for *devil's paint brush*). Definitions of adjectives, and sometimes of other parts of speech, often have an unusual structure like 'Of butter or cheese, rancid or spoiled,' by which the opening phrase limits the application of the word so defined, in this case the adjective *windy*. Similarly, the definition for a transitive verb will commonly supply in parentheses a typical noun object that can follow such a verb: *twitch* 'to drag (logs) out of the woods by horse.'

Multiple definitions are listed in order of descending popularity, though the editor's judgement of this matter can be open to question. At times, the available evidence for a word runs two senses into each other in such a way that it is impossible to separate them in the presentation. In such cases there is only one definition, but the shift of meaning is marked by an interior semicolon: *cailleach* 'an old woman; also a hag or crone.'

Occasionally the definition reads simply 'See quotation,' referring the reader directly to the following section. In these cases, either there is a well-worded definition within the quotation itself, or the editor has no more information than what is presented, and that is inadequate as the basis for a full definition.

CITATIONS

The citations, that is, the selected quotations from various Island sources, are evidence that the words presented truly exist in the folk speech of the province. More than that, a citation is an example of a word in context, without which its definition can seem rather flat. The citations can also serve to justify the judgements of the head note. Finally, taken together, they make a unique anthology of Prince Edward Island social history.

Some citations, especially oral ones, explain a word but do not actually contain it. In other entries, there is no specific citation given, because there is nothing readily quotable in the data. In these instances, the authority for the word is given in parentheses immediately after the definition, using the abbreviations listed below and at the end of this guide, as in '*kye* ... A cow (O).'

The citations come in several possible forms. In order of presentation, these are from written works, fieldwork, tapes, postal surveys, and outside observers. Written citations are in chronological order, including the first and last on hand. They are followed by the name of the author, the title (always in italics), the date, and the page (or, in the case of some diaries, the day). A date in parentheses is the true date of the source, but not the one on the copy used by *DPEIE*. Full details on each title are given in the Bibliography.

The combined fieldwork (I, II, S, and C) yielded thousands of oral comments by informants, only some of which are actually used as citations. All have contributed to the accuracy of definitions and labels, and to the editor's sense of the subject. The informants are anonymous, according to promise, but they were numbered as interviewed, and are listed in that order. The speakers on tape (T B, T M, and T I) are similarly numbered, as are the contributors to the three postal surveys (P1, P2, and R). However, observers – those who volunteered information generously but haphazardly outside the directed research – are not numbered, so that all are grouped indiscriminately under the abbreviation '(O).' A single citing of this abbreviation can stand for many independent confirmations. Similarly, a single reference to any of the survey tools, when used (as noted) immediately after a definition, can cover several contributions from that survey.

If a citation happens to include a word that is itself treated in this dictionary, the word is put between single quotation marks, as another kind of cross-reference. Thus, under *pung* we find: 'And there was not room to sit down, so we would stand up on the pung sleigh and, of course, when there was "sloughs" we went out as often as we stayed in (T I54).'

It is not easy to explain fully the principles behind the selection of citations.

The reader may sometimes wonder that there are not more, and at other times, perhaps, wish that there were fewer. The only assurance that can be given is that the citations have been carefully chosen from the selection at hand, to round out every word as fully as possible within the bounds of what is readable.

EDITORIAL NOTE

The word *away*, as used by most Islanders in the phrase *from away*, is an excellent example of the need in some entries for an editorial note. In such cases there are too many subtleties of usage for all of them to be expressed conveniently within the earlier categories of the entry. As the only section in prose, the editorial note allows special interpretation in complex cases. These cases can involve anything within the scope of the work: definition, word history, distribution on the Island and in other dialects, relationship with standard words, secondary sources, and more. In short, the note attempts, briefly, to anticipate additional questions. It is marked by an asterisk (*).

DICTIONARY NOTE

The dictionary note is the last potential section of any entry, and often contains much information in compact form. Where present, it comes in two parts, the first optional. The *second* part lists by abbreviations other dictionaries that contain the word in question, or one like it. A simple reference with no quotation means that the definition in that dictionary is very close to the one supplied here. On the other hand, if a dictionary abbreviation is preceded by some parallel word, then any matter of interest in that dictionary pertains to the parallel and not to the *DPEIE* word as such. We may see these two conventions on either side of the period in the dictionary note for *kennebec ker*: '*ML. kennebunker: DA* 1895, 1902; *DAE*.' The abbreviations are explained in a list of 'Dictionaries Consulted' immediately following this guide.

The order in which dictionaries are noted is flexible, but generally they go from most useful to least, for *DPEIE* purposes. Quotations from them are highly selective, and the choice of these is governed solely by what is considered helpful to readers of this work. Dates of use in other dialects, for example, are frequently supplied, but quoted abbreviations are not expanded. In any case, no dictionary, of the large number consulted for every word, has been omitted if it has relevant information of any kind. As the most technical part of the whole presentation, this listing of parallel evidence elsewhere has been reserved for the final position in the entry.

The *first* part of the dictionary note is based on the second. When applied, it is a judgement on where the word in question came from. This judgement is not a full etymology, or word history, but merely a brief indication of which dialect or language possessed the word immediately before its use on Prince Edward Island, and was the probable source. The categories are of necessity sometimes very broad, as in 'British' or 'American' (modifying the word 'English' understood). This source is presented in square brackets, and is sometimes preceded by 'From,' sometimes not. In the latter case, which applies to several New World labels like 'Maritimes' and 'North American,' Prince Edward Island is within the circle where the word began, and it is not possible on the evidence to say that its citizens were not among the first users of it. Where there is no source given, but there are dictionary listings, it has not been considered safe to make a judgement. In a few cases where there is a source but no dictionaries, the latter are found with a similar word nearby (such as with a noun having the same form as a verb). Where there is neither source nor dictionary listed, the word may be special to Prince Edward Island.

Dictionaries Consulted

COD
The Concise Oxford Dictionary of Current English. Ed. J.B. Sykes. 7th ed. Oxford: Oxford UP, 1982

DA
A Dictionary of Americanisms on Historical Principles. Ed. Mitford M. Matthews. Chicago: U of Chicago P, 1951

DAC
A Dictionary of Australian Colloquialisms. Ed. G.A. Wilkes. Sydney: Sydney UP, 1978

DAE
A Dictionary of American English on Historical Principles. Eds. Sir William Craigie and James R. Hulbert. Chicago: U of Chicago P, 1936–44

DARE
Dictionary of American Regional English, Volume I: Introduction and A–C. Ed. Frederic G. Cassidy. Cambridge, Massachusetts: The Belknap Press of Harvard UP, 1985

DAS
Dictionary of American Slang. Eds. Harold Wentworth and Stuart Berg Flexner. 2nd supplemented ed. New York: Thomas Y. Crowell Company, 1975

DAusE
A Dictionary of Austral English. Ed. Edward E. Morris. Sydney: Sydney UP, 1898; rpt. 1972

DBE
Dictionary of Bahamian English. Eds. John A. Holm and Alison Watt Shilling. Cold Spring, New York: Lexik House, 1982

DC
A Dictionary of Canadianisms on Historical Principles. Eds. Walter S. Avis et al. Toronto: W.J. Gage, 1967

DGL
A Dictionary of the Gaelic Language. Eds. Norman Macleod and Daniel Dewar. Glasgow: W.R. McPhun, 1853

DJE
Dictionary of Jamaican English. Eds. F.G. Cassidy and R.B. LePage. Cambridge: Cambridge UP, 1967

DNE
Dictionary of Newfoundland English. Eds. G.M. Story, W.J. Kirwin, and J.D.A. Widdowson. Toronto: U of Toronto P, 1982

DOST
A Dictionary of the Older Scottish Tongue. Ed. Sir William A. Craigie. Chicago: U of Chicago P, 1937–77

DSAE
A Dictionary of South African English. Ed. Jean Brantford. Capetown: Oxford UP, 1978

DSUE
A Dictionary of Slang and Unconventional English. Ed. Eric Partridge. 7th ed. New York: Macmillan Publishing Co., 1970

EDD
The English Dialect Dictionary. Ed. Joseph Wright. Oxford: Oxford UP, 1898–1905; rpt. 1923

EDSL
An Etymological Dictionary of the Scottish Language. Ed. John Jamieson. Paisley: Alexander Gardner, 1879–87

ESI
English as We Speak It in Ireland. P.W. Joyce. London: Longmans, Green, and Co., 1910

FW
Funk and Wagnalls Standard College Dictionary. Canadian ed. Toronto: Fitzhenry and Whiteside, 1976

GCD
Gage Canadian Dictionary. Eds. Walter Avis et al. Toronto: Gage Publishing, 1983

GED
The Illustrated Gaelic-English Dictionary. Ed. Edward Dwelly. Glasgow: Gairm Publications, 1901–11

IED
An Irish-English Dictionary. Ed. Patrick S. Dineen. Dublin: Irish Texts Society, 1934

MED
Middle English Dictionary. Eds. Hans Kurath et al. Ann Arbor: U of Michigan P, 1956–84 [A–P]

ML
Maine Lingo: Boiled Owls, Billdads, and Wazzats. Ed. John Gould. Camden, Maine: Down East Magazine, 1975

ODEP
The Oxford Dictionary of English Proverbs. Ed.

F.P. Wilson. 3rd ed. Oxford: Oxford UP, 1970

OED
The Oxford English Dictionary. Eds. James A.H. Murray et al. Oxford: Oxford UP, 1884–1928; corrected reissue, 1933

OEDS
A Supplement to the Oxford English Dictionary. Ed. R.W. Burchfield. Oxford: Oxford UP, 1972–86

PEDGL
A Pronouncing and Etymological Dictionary of the Gaelic Language, Ed. Malcolm Mac-Lennan. Edinburgh: John Grant, 1925

SND
The Scottish National Dictionary. Eds. William Grant and David Murison. Edinburgh: The Scottish National Dictionary Association, [1931]–76

SSPB
The South Shore Phrase Book. Ed. Lewis Poteet. Hantsport, Nova Scotia: Lancelot Press, 1983

SSPB2
The Second South Shore Phrase Book. Ed. Lewis Poteet. Hantsport, Nova Scotia: Lancelot Press, 1985

W3
Webster's Third New International Dictionary of the English Language. Eds. Philip Babcock Gove et al. Springfield: G. and C. Merriam Company, 1976

WGE
A Word Geography of England. Harold Orton and Nathalia Wright. London: Seminar Press, 1974

WGUS
A Word Geography of the Eastern United States. Hans Kurath. Ann Arbor: U of Michigan P, 1949

WNW
Webster's New World Dictionary. Ed. David
B. Guralnik. Toronto: Nelson, Foster and
Scott, 1970

Abbreviations

Note: Abbreviations quoted from other dictionaries are not listed.

C	Common Word Survey, 1980–82	P1	First Postal Survey, 1979
I	Fieldwork Survey I (One), 1980–81	P2	Second Postal Survey, 1983–84
		R	Rare Words Survey, 1986
II	Fieldwork Survey II (Two), 1982	S	Special Lexicons Survey, 1986
n.d.	no date	T B	Tape: Belfast Historical Society
n.p.	no place of publication, *or* no publisher	T I	Tape: 'Island Brew'
		T M	Tape: MacIntyre Collection
n.pag.	no pagination given	UPEI	University of Prince Edward Island
O	observer(s)		
PAPEI	Public Archives of Prince Edward Island	*	signals editorial note
		\ \	signals pronunciation boundaries

Pronunciation Key

a	pat, pad, pan	ou	out, loud, cow
ā	date, paid, day	p	pan, nap
ah	father, far, saw, caught, cot	r	red, dare
b	bat, tab	s	sand, face, fuss
ch	chin, inch, fetch	sh	shall, lash
d	dab, bad	t	tip, pit, fatter
e	get, bed, bend	th	thin, bath
ē	be, beat, beet, piece, funny	<u>th</u>	then, smooth
f	fat, if, off	u	up, hug, money
g	go, dog	ur	fur, fir, offer, word, heard
h	hat, ahead, who	v	vivid, give
i	bit, bid, bin	w	we, away, when
ī	rye, ride, rice, lie, fine	y	yet, young
j	job, gem, judge	yo͞o	use, music, ewe
k	kind, cat, cook, tack, ache	z	zero, freeze
l	lip, pill	zh	azure, treasure, garage
m	mad, dam	ə	[unstressed vowels] vanilla, pavement, tonsils, ballot, focus
n	nap, pan	′—	indicates primary (strongest) stress on following syllable
ng	sing, sink, finger		
ō	go, gold, coat, hoe, low	,—	indicates secondary (medium) stress on following syllable
oi	boil, boy		
oo	good, put		
o͞o	boot, rule		

DICTIONARY OF PRINCE EDWARD ISLAND ENGLISH

A

Abegweit

Proper noun. \'a-bəg-,wīt\. Also spelled
**Abegweet, Epagweit, Epaigwit, Epay-
gooyat.** Compare **Island, Minegoo.**

   **Prince Edward Island (a Micmac Indian
name).**

He is presented with ... sundry plans,
surveys and grants, ... secured in a large
despatch box, on which are inscribed in gold
letters 'the *Epaigwit estate.*' It is a pretty Indian
word that, it means 'the home on the wave.' It
is the original name of that gem of the western
ocean, which the vulgar inhabitants have
christened Prince Edward's Island (*The Anglo-
American Magazine*, July 1855, 67). Although
such a tiny atom – among the larger divisions
of our fair Dominion, this charming bit of earth
– of old by Indian sage and warrior called
'Abegweit' – is by no means unknown to ...
pleasure seekers from the neighboring Repub-
lic ... (SMITH, R.E., *Where the Speckled Trout Doth
Jump*, 1899, 171). 'Abegweit,' cradled on the
waves, with its sweet pastoral scenery, its
fragrant groves, its almost tropical foliage, its
silvery beaches, its health-giving breezes from
the sea, marvellously clear atmosphere and [its
sky] blue as that of sunny Italy, is an ideal spot
in which to spend the summer holiday (*Prince
Edward Island: The Garden of the Gulf; its men of
action and its resources*, 1915, 29). Peace! You
never know what peace is until you walk on
the shores or in the fields or along the winding
red roads of Abegweit on a summer twilight
when the dew is falling and the old, old stars
are peeping out and the sea keeps its nightly
tryst with the little land it loves. You find your
soul then. You realize that youth is not a
vanished thing but something that dwells
forever in the heart. ... even if you are not
Abegweit-born you will say, 'Why ... I have
come home!' (MONTGOMERY, LUCY MAUD, *Prince
Edward Island*, 1939, 19). The Indians who lived
on the Island had it to themselves. One of
the names they gave to their homeland was
'Minegoo,' which simply means in our language 'The Island,' but lovelier by far than
'Minegoo' is the other name they used, 'Abegweit,' and that name means 'cradled on the
waves' (BLAKELEY, PHYLLIS, and MYRA VERNON,
The Story of Prince Edward Island, 1963, 13).
'Abegweit' cradled upon the waves – the
Micmacs called the Island. A more apt description would be hard to find, for by her very
nature, Prince Edward Island has always been
closely bound up with the sea that surrounds

it (RAMSAY, STERLING, *Folklore Prince Edward
Island*, [1973], 69).

[From Micmac: Algonkian] *DC* 1855–1962.

aboiteau

Noun; plural *aboiteaux*. \,a-bwah-'tō\. Also
spelled and pronounced **aboideau, abiteau**
\,a-bī-'tō\. Largely historical. Rare. Compare **bito.**

   **A dike on a tidal river equipped with a
sluice gate acting as a valve to hold back
the tide.**

No. 1699 William Howat, Senr., 100 £ / being
the balance of his contract for repairing the
Aboiteau at Tryon (PRINCE EDWARD ISLAND,
P.E.I. Legislative Assembly Journal, 1864, Appendix H, 24th November). Acts were passed in
1881, 1895, and 1898, for the appointment of
commissioners of sewers, and the reclamation
of the large tracts of marsh land that exist
throughout the province, for the purpose of
rendering the same available for cultivation. As
a result of such legislation, aboideaux (which
have been more or less successful) have been
constructed at the under-mentioned places: ...
Mount Stewart ... Fullerton's Marsh ... Dunk
River ... Pisquid River (CROSSKILL, W.H., *Handbook of Prince Edward Island: The Garden Province
of Canada*, 1906, 83). 'I remember hearing once
that there are the remains of an old French
aboiteau in Tryon. You should look it up, since
you are so interested in historical relics.' ... I
did. True – there were the remains of an old
dike which had been used to keep the water
back from the marsh. It did seem extraordinari-
ly well preserved for two hundred years of
wear and tear (CHAMPION, HELEN, *Over on the
Island*, 1939, 22). After the bridge was built to
span the river at the Abiteau, and the settlers
were taking up homesteads along the upper
part of the stream, gates were installed under
the bridge to hold back the tides so that the
farmers would be able to work on the marsh-
land which bordered the river on which their
farms fronted. ... This haying was carried on
until the Department of Highways built a new
bridge at the Abiteau in 1938 making it impossible to use the gates (*History of North Tryon*,
[1973], 10). The early French settlers had erected dykes or 'abiteaux' on the marshes of the
Tryon River so that the rich grasses could be
harvested for fodder for their cattle. Consequently, the bridge that now spans the river
by the United Church has always been called
the Abiteau Bridge. Residents of the area,
however, commonly refer to it as the 'Bito'

(CALLBECK, LORNE, *My Island, My People*, 1979, 138).

*This word, still extant in Prince Edward Island English according to the Fieldwork Surveys, is associated in other dictionaries only with New Brunswick and Nova Scotia, or simply labelled 'Canadian.' [From Canadian French] *DC* 1708–1960; *OEDS*; *W3*; *FW*; *GCD*.

across

Preposition serving as noun of locality. Usually in phrase **from across**. Also **over across**. Frequent generally, but infrequent in Charlottetown. Compare **away**, **other side**, **puddle**.
The mainland, Nova Scotia or New Brunswick.

Sometimes it was a horse-buyer, familiar figures then – one maybe 'from across the Strait,' come in to inquire where he might 'pick up a driver, and perhaps a low-set one for the mines,' to set my fancy adrift (DIXON, MARGARET, *Going Home: An Autobiography*, 1979, 90). The findings didn't surprize me a lot but I would imagine they would if I was to go to the other side of the Island or across and asked the same questions (*Unpublished student essay*, UPEI, 1981). People here definitely think that, that if someone is going to come from across, they've got to be better because they're 'from away' (T M73). I don't think, by listening to the bands across, I don't think it's going to be hard for me to get jobs (T M72). We bought one of these [hockey pads] across (O). 'Are these peaches from the Island?' 'No, they're across' (O).

*The Common Word Survey included the question 'If someone lives in New Brunswick or Nova Scotia he or she is from … ?' *Across* was favoured by 7% of the informants, chiefly rural users, over such choices as *the other side* or *the mainland*.

after

Preposition, used after *be* and before a verb with -*ing* to indicate either completion of the activity (*to be after doing* in this case approximates *to have done*), or the potentiality of the activity (*to be after doing* in this case approximates *to be likely to do*).
1. Indicating completion.

The main thing in training a horse, Jockie – and I have been after telling you many times – is to get the will of the horse (STIRLING, LILLA, *Jockie: A Story of Prince Edward Island*, 1951, 44).

Seamus was after staggering off the floor, following a session of 'old-time sets.' He had been dancing for the better part of the afternoon, and he wanted it known by everyone that he was a pretty fair stepper (MORRISON, ALLAN, *A Giant among Friends*, 1980, 89). We went to Annandale, was a 'concert' there. So when we got there, the concert, the baskets was after being sold. We stayed for the dance (T M63). I'm so old, I'm ninety-four, I'm after forgetting everything (T M74). 'I was going over to the lumber woods.' – 'What was your first impression of it?' – 'I'm near after forgetting' (T M88).

2. Indicating potentiality.

'What wud ye be after thinking if I told ye I'd find a tiny wee new baby there?' asked Judy, watching her sharply (MONTGOMERY, LUCY MAUD, *Pat of Silver Bush*, 1933, 17). Now, run up to yer room, and put off yer finery and we'll get to work. I belave we're after having a rainy night av it. The wind's rising and it's dark as a squaw's pocket already (*ibid*, 61). Grandfather's feet were braced. He was pulling her [a horse] back, holding her in until her hind feet were knocking the dashboard. 'I daren't hold her in any more. She'd be after slipping and break a leg' (STIRLING, LILLA, *Jockie: A Story of Prince Edward Island*, 1951, 2).

*Often in the context *to be after forgetting*, this usage, though not surveyed in the fieldwork, has been observed in several parts of contemporary Prince Edward Island.
[From Irish] *W3*; *ESI* 85; *EDD*; *DNE*.

alder mud

Noun. Archaic. Occasional in Egmont, infrequent elsewhere but rare in Charlottetown; significantly older, male; especially less educated. Compare **killkid mud, mussel mud, oyster mud, shell mud**.
Mud from alder swamps used as fertilizer.

Another winter task was the gathering of fertilizer. Since there was no such thing as commercial fertilizer, they resorted to alder or mussell [sic] mud. The alder mud was gotten from the swamps and then mixed with the manure from the stables before spread on the land (BLUE, ALEX et al, *History of Hopefield*, 1978, 70). It washes off the land, then gathers down by the brook (II 016). They called it black mud; it was mixed with straw to make fertilizer (II 019). It comes from alder swamps, usually with lots of alder trees around (II 024).

altogether
Adverb, especially in phrase **great altogether.**
    Completely, entirely, thoroughly.
    Then Hazel and I went to the 'Missionary Meeting' it was great altogether (OLIVER, GERTRUDE, *Diaries of Gertrude Hazel Meggison Oliver*, 1906, August 28). After supper I went to Club and had a great time altogether there was quite a number there too (*ibid*, December 1). Beautiful day altogether (MEGGISON, ELEANOR CARR, *Diaries of Eleanor Carr Meggison*, 1939, December 6). 'That is cheap' – 'Yes it was, terrible altogether' (T M79). Answer to 'How are you?' Fine altogether (O).

*What is non-standard is the position of this word immediately following an adjective: *altogether wicked* is standard, as is *wicked man altogether*; *wicked altogether* is not. On Prince Edward Island the word is often attested in answer to a greeting, as in the last citation.

amadon
Also spelled **amaden**. See **omadan**.

amberberry
Noun. Rare.
    Synonym for 'bakeapple': the edible amber berry of a low bog-dwelling plant with a single white flower, or the plant itself; the cloudberry (*Rubus chamaemorus*).
    An amberberry is low on ground like a cranberry bush. Found in boggy places (II 038). It resembles a knot on wood. Used to be used for medicinal purposes (O).

anchor
Transitive verb. Largely archaic. Compare **anchoring, banking²**.
    To store (lobsters) underwater in order to keep them alive until they can be processed.
    The packers do this. They anchor them in nice clean water and hold them for the market to get better before they ship them (S 4).

anchoring
Verbal noun. Largely archaic. See **anchor, banking²**.
    The act of storing lobsters underwater in order to keep them alive until they can be processed.
    Anchoring is the method used on really warm days to keep the lobsters alive until it is time to take them in to shore. The crates holding the lobsters are put under water and tied on to a buoy line (MACMILLAN, JANET, *The Language of Lobster Fishing*, 1985, 9). Anchoring used to be done constantly. They would have a line strung out with heavy anchors with forty or fifty crates tied to that line (S 5). Anchoring is not done anymore. They would anchor them in water to keep them alive (S 6).

andy-over
Also **anti-over, aunty-over**. See **leap**.

angishore
Noun. Also **hangashore**.
    A fisherman who is too lazy to fish.
    Critical term. Someone who didn't want to fish (II 083).

*In Newfoundland *hangashore* is a folk etymology from Irish Gaelic, the original being *aindeiseoir* 'a weak, sickly person.'
[From Irish Gaelic, probably via Newfoundland] *DNE*.

apron
See **digger apron**.

Aristotle's lantern
Noun. Compare **sea-thistle**.
    Synonym for 'whore's egg': a small, roundish shellfish with sharp spines, a sea urchin (I).

OED; *W3*.

armchair money
See **rocking-chair money**.

August gale
Noun. Occasional generally, but infrequent in Malpeque and Charlottetown; significantly older; especially male.
    Originally a specific storm on August 24, 1873; now any severe, late summer storm.
    My father, Capt Daniel Hemphill, was caught in the great August Gale, the time all the American vessels were lost on the North Shore of P.E.I. Capt Dan Hemphill ran from East Point to Pictou in the same gale, in a vessel called the Lily (HEMPHILL, JOHN, *Some of My Experiences at Sea*, 1982, 29). Throughout the latter part of the nineteenth and early

twentieth centuries, lobsters were much more plentiful in the Gulf of St. Lawrence than they are today. For example, the violent 'August gale' of 1873 tossed ashore so many live lobsters within five miles of one Island packer's factory that he could not process them all. There were estimated to be approximately one thousand lobsters for every eleven yards of shoreline and in piles of from one to five feet! (MORRISON, CLINTON, *Along the North Shore: A Social History of Township 11, P.E.I. 1765–1982*, 1983, 70). The August gale is associated with a bad August storm one time but now can be any time of the year (II 078). Watch out for the August gale. It doesn't have to be in August but it always comes just when you don't need it – when the harvest is ready perhaps (II 091). Tail end of a hurricane in late summer (II 101).

*The original August gale is sometimes confused with the 'Yankee Gale' of October 1851, which caused destruction among a nearby American fishing fleet. *SSPB* [gale] 'Around Little Harbour, people speak of the August gale, a reference to the high winds that come as the year's first hurricane from the South Atlantic sweeps up the coast, usually diminishing in force as it moves.'

away
Adverb serving as noun of locality.
Usually in phrase **from away**. Common.
Compare **across, foreign, foreigner, other side**.
   Any place other than Prince Edward Island or the Maritimes.
   First, it means that the folk tradition was vital enough in this area to make it worth Doyle's while to work within it, and second it shows Doyle preferring what is local and familiar to that which is 'from away' and 'new' (hence 'strange') (IVES, EDWARD, *Lawrence Doyle: The Farmer Poet of Prince Edward Island*, 1971, 247). You can see at once how that magnificent voice, those fast good looks, the casual good-humour carried an outsider from Ontario – someone from 'away' with no more than 18 years on the Island – to prominence in Party politics (LEDWELL, FRANK, and RESHARD GOOL, *Portraits and Gastroscopes*, 1972, 15). In such circumstances, many talented Islanders felt compelled to seek their fortunes 'Away' (ROBERTSON, IAN, *Notable Prince Edward Islanders*, [1973], 15). As she was a fond sister and extremely proud of all her brothers it was a joy to her to have one of them 'home from away' and available for one of her parties (STEWART, MARION, *Marion Stewart's Journal*, 1976, 20). One day in 1957 at Stanhope, ... it was reported a dead whale had come ashore. ...

Varied experts had come and had looked at it and decided, well, we could dig holes, we could drag it and bury it, but then an expert from away, meaning off the island, came down and said it was no problem at all, a few sticks of dynamite would do the job (ANDERSON, ALLAN, *Salt Water, Fresh Water*, 1979, 297–98). There are drawbacks in the cultural/social environment for anybody from away because the Islanders do not really accept ideas of people who are not born in Prince Edward Island (PRINCE EDWARD ISLAND MULTICULTURAL COUNCIL, *An Exploratory Survey of First-Generation Immigrants Living on Prince Edward Island*, 1980, 30). 'Mr. Beaton, we're going to give you a local anesthetic.' 'But Doc, the government's paying – why not bring in one from away?' (WRIGHT, WAYNE, *Wayne Wright's Prince Edward Island – A Selection of Comic Drawings*, 1980, n.pag.). Your Royal Highnesses – You are 'From Away' as we say, and I hope you don't try to change us. ... About ten years ago, Prince Charles, I tried to interfere with your mother's planting a tree. ... I still believe in a sort of 'dominoe' theory about outsiders; I think, 'today a tree, tomorrow what?' [message on a paper airplane thrown at Prince Charles and Princess Diana] (*The Guardian*, July 2, 1983, 4). They'll flock to see them, but then they won't pay any more than $1.50 to go see somebody who's probably better than the people who come from away (T M73). I know people from away, from down in the States, and they wouldn't come to your home unless they were invited at a certain time (T M110).

*This term has been informally observed in Newfoundland and the West Indies, as well as in Nova Scotia and Maine (see below). *DARE* gives users in Maine, Boston, Kentucky, and Georgia. On Prince Edward Island, the outer limit of *away* is not always fixed at the world but may be, in minority usage, North America or the rest of Canada only. People from Ontario are especially said to be *from away*. Non-native Islanders sometimes refer to themselves jokingly as *P.F.A.'s* 'people from away' or *C.F.A.'s* 'come from away.' Islanders who have moved elsewhere are sometimes *home from away*, as in the Stewart citation. In the Common Word Survey *from away* was the most popular answer (37.4%) to the question 'Someone not from the Island, say from Ontario, is ... ?' over such choices as *a foreigner, a stranger, a newcomer, a non-Islander*. *DARE* 'Any place other than the place considered home' 1888–1975 [citations all with *from*]; *SSPB* 'anyplace [sic] other than Nova Scotia, usually employed as the direct opposite of "around here": "Are you from *away*? Ye're not from around here"'; *ML* 'Any other place. To be *from away* is to be non-native [to Maine]. ... *from away* does suggest some effort to conform and belong. A man who has lived fifty years in your town and paid his taxes faithfully would hardly be called a *furriner*, and certainly not a *pilgrim*, but he will retain his non-Maine status of being *from away*.'

B

back, in
Adverb phrase. Archaic.
Inland, away from harbours and main settlements.
But then, in their heyday the Victorians themselves looked down on the people 'in back.' Those who dwelt inland were viewed as living in the boondocks: 'Crapaud was bad,' reminisces one partisan Victorian, 'Inkerman was worse.' That changed when shipping declined. ... Victoria itself became a backwater (TUCK, ROBERT, *Victoria: Seaport on a Farm*, 1979, 39).

back: W3 'distant from a centre of population or habitation or off the main routes of travel'; *DNE* 'Area inland from a harbour or settlement'; *DBE* 'the shore on the side of the island away from the settlement.' *in*: *DNE* 'Toward the interior; away from the coast or settled area.'

back door trots, the
Plural noun phrase. Frequent or occasional generally, but infrequent in Charlottetown; significantly older. See **blueberry run, flying axehandles, green apple quick-step, run outs and walk ins, short-taken, skithers.**
Diarrhea.
It's called that because of having to run out the back door to the outhouse (II 016).

The trots, as such, is common slang.
[From British] *OEDS* 1801, 1886; *SND* 1824–1932; *DARE* 1899–1970; *W3*; *EDD*; *DSUE*.

back end
Noun, usually in phrase **the back end of the year**. Infrequent generally, but unattested in Charlottetown; unattested under thirty.
The late autumn and early winter (O).

[From British] *OED* 1820–1860; *EDD* 1863–1895; *SND* 1920; *W3*; *EDSL*; *WGE*.

back kitchen
Noun. Also **harvester kitchen, summer kitchen**. Frequent or occasional generally, but infrequent in Charlottetown; significantly rural, older.
In older houses, a second kitchen, variously used as pantry, workroom, porch, or summertime kitchen with separate stove.
Their sink was in the back kitchen, and they used to prepare vegetables there (I 030). It was the second kitchen where utensils were kept and rough work done (P1–018).

DNE 'see *back house*: room in "outport" house leading off from the kitchen and used for storage, as an entranceway, etc.' *back*: *OED* 'Applied to a part of a house or building which lies behind, and is usually subsidiary to the front or main part bearing the name, as ... *back-kitchen* ...' 1535–1832; *DARE* 1916–1970. *kitchen back*: *DA*, *DAE*. *summer kitchen*: *OEDS* 'used for cooking in hot weather.'

backline
Noun. Compare **run line, trapline**.
A long rope, buoyed at both ends, to which a set number of lobster traps are attached by means of shorter ropes or 'snoods.'
The 'back-line' set by each boat is perhaps 9000 feet or over in length. This may be divided into three or more 'trawls,' and is carefully coiled in tubs or barrels, so that when the time comes it will run more freely. To both ends of each 'trawl' is attached a stone 'kellog' or anchor; and about twenty fathoms from the anchor a buoy line, to which is attached a buoy, is fastened to the backline. After the trawl line has been run or sunk on the place the fisherman selects, he proceeds to boat out his traps and attach them to the backline, allowing over 26 feet between each trap (*Running the Lines*, April 25, 1903, 2). The backline is the main line that the traps are attached to (S 5).

backswath
Noun.
See quotation.
Backswath: The swath that is next to the first one cut, that is cut in the opposite direction and that the tractor or horses have travelled over in cutting the first swath. It is nearly always the outside swath of the field. 'You may as well leave the backswath on the far side of the field. It's too damp that close to the woods' (DUFFY, CHARLES, *Lexicon of Beef Farming*, 1986, 7).

W3.

bagger
Noun. Compare **moss bag**.

In 'Irish moss' harvesting, a three-legged metal frame on which burlap bags are hung for packing with moss.

A burlap bag may be fastened by means of hooks which are placed so as to avoid injury to the hands of the packer. ... A 'bagger' ... facilitates the packing of burlap bags and allows a greater amount to be packed in a bag (MACFARLANE, CONSTANCE, *Irish Moss in the Maritime Provinces*, 1956, 15–16). They would use that bagger more down east where they grind it. When the moss is not ground up they use a baler (S 11).

bag needle
Noun.

A long needle with a curved end, used for sewing up bags of potatoes with binder twine.

Makes two ears on bag (S 1). A bag needle is six inches long and has a curl on the end. You hook it through the bag and it comes back up (S 2).

bait bag
Noun. Compare **bait box, bait cord, bait spear**.

A small mesh bag for holding bait in a lobster trap.

The traps are baited with readily available fresh or salt fish which are skewered whole on the 'bait spindle' or placed in mesh bait bags or wooden bait boxes (WILDER, D.G., *Canada's Lobster Fishery*, 1957, 16). The bait bag is a small bag that is sometimes used to hold the bait in a lobster trap, particularly if the bait is rotten or falls apart easily (MACMILLAN, JANET, *The Language of Lobster Fishing*, 1985, 9). They got to use bait bags where the perch is bad. The bait is shoved right into the bag so the perch can't get in to eat it (S 4). I didn't find the bait bag quite practical. With the perch around here now a bait bag would be a good idea (S 5).

bait box
Noun. Compare **bait bag, bait cord, bait spear**.

1. A container for storing bait on a lobster boat.

A plastic container designed to hold pickled bait such as herring or mackerel that has been preserved in a liquid (MACMILLAN, JANET, *The Language of Lobster Fishing*, 1985, 9). A bait box is something to stick your bait in, under the washboard, and it is snug and out of the way (S 4). A bait box is a wooden or aluminum box which usually holds one hundred to one hundred and twenty-five pounds of bait (S 5).

2. A small box for holding bait in a lobster trap.

The traps are baited with readily available fresh or salt fish which are skewered whole on the 'bait spindle' or placed in mesh 'bait bags' or wooden bait boxes (WILDER, D.G., *Canada's Lobster Fishery*, 1957, 16). The lobster is attracted by fresh or salted fish bait placed inside the trap on the spindle (a sharp stick) or in a bait box or bag. Herring is the most common bait used, but the type varies with fishermen's preferences or with availability (RUTHERFORD, J.B., D.G. WILDER, and H.C. FRICK, *An Economic Appraisal of the Canadian Lobster Fishery*, 1967, 37). They used those bait bags in some places to protect the bait, and bait boxes made of laths as well (S 6).

[sense 1]: *DAE* 1841–1871; *DNE*.

bait cord
Noun. Also **bait string**. Compare **bait bag, bait box, bait spear**.

A length of twine and a leather toggle in a lobster trap for fastening the bait in place.

The bait string served a dual purpose, as it was used to fasten the door, as well as the bait (PRINCE EDWARD ISLAND, DEPARTMENT OF FISH-ERIES, *Technical Report #175*, 1975, 1975, 2). A bait cord consists of two pieces of cord and a leather (S 4).

bait pin
See **bait spear**.

bait shed
Noun.

A small building on a wharf, used for storing bait.

During the 1970s and early 1980s, many harbour improvements have been carried out at Milligan's Wharf: a slip-way, enclosed inner harbour, unloading canopy, mechanical boat lift, electric cargo hoists and new bait-shed complexes have made the port one of the best-equipped along the Island's north shore (MORRISON, CLINTON, *Along the North Shore: A Social History of Township 11, P.E.I. 1765–1982*, 1984, 77). Years ago everyone salted their own herring and they needed bait sheds to store the bait in (S 4). I suppose you can still term it as a bait shed. These days we buy a little and fish a little (S 5). I had a bait shed up on the wharf. We had to build them. They were a great convenience (S 6).

bait spear
Noun. Also **bait pin, bait spike, bait spindle**. Compare **bait bag, bait box, bait cord**.

A spike for holding bait in a lobster trap.

A bait spear is a galvanized iron spike that is located in the middle of a lobster trap for the purpose of holding bait in place (MACMILLAN, JANET, *The Language of Lobster Fishing*, 1985, 10). Some people use a spike and a leather. They shove down the bait on a spike. We generally say bait spear or spear (S 4).

bait iron: DARE 'In lobstering: a needle-like tool used to insert small fish as lures in lobster traps.' 1975–1978.

bait spike, bait spindle
See **bait spear**.

bait string
See **bait cord**.

bakeapple
Noun. Also **yellowberry**. Infrequent in Egmont, rare elsewhere. Compare **amberberry**.

The edible amber berry of a low bog-dwelling plant with a single white flower, or the plant itself; the cloudberry (*Rubus chamaemorus*).

Fine and warm. Sowed the beans, fenced little garden in orchard, sowed cucumbers, pumpkin, squash – other garden seeds. John Joe here. Marcia Forscythe brought Gertie home. Bakeapple in blossom (MEGGISON, GEORGE, *Diaries of George Eden Meggison*, 1916, June 5). Your article on bakeapples stated they were found in Newfoundland, Labrador and northern Europe, but you failed to mention West Point, Prince Edward Island. The people in the area walk about a mile along the shores of Northumberland Strait and go to a real boggy area to get them. I'm not a native of West Point but I've gone picking them so I know all about the rubber boots and long walks. Everyone around here considers them a great treat (STEWART, GERALDINE, [Letter to the Editor] *Atlantic Insight*, December 1981, 88). One thing I was surprised to see on the Island were bakeapples, which we had seen in Newfoundland and learned to like but I hadn't known they grew in Canada. ... We took some bakeapples home as I thought they were a real treat. Mr. Allison didn't share my idea of them. He didn't say anything about not enjoying them, but remarked afterwards, 'Well, I'd never kill a man to get them from him' (JOHNSON, GEORGINA, *Life in the Parsonage*, n.d., 51).

*This word is a standard Canadianism, as several dictionaries indicate, and it is listed in Diane Griffin's *Atlantic Wildflowers*, 1984. It is included here to establish clearly its Prince Edward Island connections.
[Canadian] DC 1775–1936; DNE; SSPB; OEDS; W3; DA; GCD; FW. *baked-apple berry*: DARE 1889–1981.

baker's fog
See **fog**.

baking powder bread
Noun.
Bread made with baking powder as a substitute for yeast (II).

[North American] DC 1899–1957; DAE; DA.

baldy
Noun. Also **baldy cow**. Rare. Compare **mull, poley cow**.
A cow without horns.
Baldy Heifer got from M. Landry served this day by Mont. Young wht. Ayrshire Bull (MACDONALD, AUSTIN, *Diary 1881–1916*, 1905, September 15). A baldy cow is a cow without horns that can't hook (O).

*In the human context *baldy* is common slang. *baldies*: DSUE 'white Hereford cattle: Australian rural: C.20.'

ballast lath
Noun.
One of the strips of wood on the bottom of a lobster trap that secures the ballast.
The ballast lath goes on the bottom of the trap. You nail the ballast lath on the bottom (S 4). The ballast laths are the two central ones that are used for to hold the ballast (S 5).

band

Noun. Compare **band** (verb).

A short rubber band used to squeeze a lobster's claw safely shut.

The elastic band which is placed around the claws of a market lobster in order that it cannot crush the other lobsters (ROBERTSON, JANICE, *A Dictionary of Lobster Fishing in the Eastern Kings Area*, 1985, 4). Now we use bands instead of 'plugs.' We use pinchers to stretch the bands and then we put them over the claw (S 4).

band

Transitive verb. Also **rubber band**. Compare **band** (noun).

To secure a rubber band on (a lobster's claw).

Another thing that is not fully developed is banding the lobster. You have a band spread out and you have to hold the lobster. It is a tricky procedure (S 6).

bank

Transitive verb. Common. Compare **banking¹**.

To pile up seaweed, bales of hay, earth, spruce branches, or root vegetables against (a building) for insulation in winter.

Hauling sea weed and banking house (ROSS, DAVID, *The David Ross Diary 1836–1879*, 1841, 24). Cold – Freezing with high winds and snow, light showers. ... I banked the east-end of the barn and the W and N of the house (LAMONT, MURDOCK, *Diary, 1885–1888*, 1886, October 15). She fell sick in March, in June she was brought to Aunt Teresa's in Summerside where she rested for a while before going home. It was said she got cold because the school was not banked (CULLEN, TIMOTHY, *Some Pages from a Diary of T.P. Cullen, 1888–1889*, n.d., 10). Fine day. Banked the house. Gertie to Alberton. Zero in evening. Got an order from Eaton's (MEGGISON, GEORGE EDEN, *Diaries of George Eden Meggison*, 1916, November 17). I doing chores, hauled 2 loads of manure to back field took out a load of potato tops to bank around machine house (MACLEOD, ANDREW, *Diary: January 1, 1928–November 17, 1932*, 1928, November 6). Cold increasing. Lester Wallace here in evening and tells us that he 'banked his house with frozen turnips' (MEGGISON, ELEANOR, *Diaries of Eleanor Carr Meggison*, 1933, November 17). They hauled kelp from the seashore and spread it on their

land to fertilize it. They also hauled seaweed over this bridge and used it to bank their houses (MACDONALD, MARY, and MRS. CLINTON STEWART, *Historical Sketch of Eastern Kings*, 1972, 48–49). One of the major climatic factors that affected the Island, was the wind. At this time of year it would come swirling down upon the modest rural developments, cutting through the frame-work of most homes, and leaving a drafty dampness in its wake. One method of cutting down on this draftiness around a home, was by insulating the upper foundation, with one of nature's own products, seaweed. The process was commonly called 'banking a house' (MORRISON, ALLAN, *A Giant among Friends*, 1980, 57).

*The meaning here is more specialized than the standard, 'to heap up into a bank.' The types of banking are listed in the definition in order of popularity.
[North American] *DA* 'to protect (a cellar, house, etc.), esp. against the cold, by piling earth against it, usu. with *up*' 1720–1948; *DAE*; *DARE* 'chiefly n Eng' 1720–1952; *WNW*.

banking¹

Noun. Common. Compare **bank**.

Seaweed, bales of hay, earth, spruce branches, or root vegetables piled against a building for insulation in winter.

Fine, I took the last of the banking from the house and spread the dung for turnips and made a trough and took the sleighs apart (LAMONT, MURDOCK, *Diary, 1885–1888*, 1886, June 5). We resolved to climb out of this [upstairs window], slide down the roof and jump off on a pile of seaweed that had been used for banking in winter and hadn't been removed (CAVENDISH, MAUD [Lucy Maud Montgomery], *Our Charivari*, quoted in Francis Bolger, *The Years before Anne*, 1974 [1896], 148). Bears were a source of continual dread, though they rarely attacked men; they were so numerous that extreme watchfulness was required to preserve sheep or hogs from their claws. They would place their feet on the banking and look in through the window; but as the forest was cleared they gradually vanished (MACKINNON, JOHN, *A Sketch Book: Comprising Historical Incidents, Traditional Tales and Translations*, 1915, 46). We chatted. She would inquire as to the state of our farming: 'And is the plow put away now? And the banking tended to, and all made ready for the winter?' (DIXON, MARGARET, *Going Home: An Autobiography*, 1979, 23). In the early fall after the potatoes and vegetables were harvested I began hauling seaweed. With the help of Bill Chapman I hauled enough to bank our house for the winter. ... Most of the houses in the community had root cellars in lieu of full basements and banking around the foundation of a house to the top of the bottom row of shingles, with seaweed, helped immensely in keeping down the fuel bill (DALY, WHITMAN, *Daly: The Saga of a Family 1820–1926 and My Boyhood on Prince Edward Island*, [1969], 56–57).

[North American] *DARE* 'chiefly n Eng' 1872–1951.

banking²
Verbal noun. Also **crating up.** Rare. Compare **anchor, anchoring.**
   See quotation.
   'Banking' is storing caught lobsters in crates under water so they will be alive when it's time to take them in (I 045).

DC 'Maritimes the storing underwater of illegally trapped live lobsters until the opening of the season.'

bar
Noun. Compare **king hair, silvering, veiling.**
   A silver-white band on the hair of a silver fox pelt.
   Desirable fur characters – good density and length of fur, sharp, clear silver bars, clear-colored guard and underfur (DOMINION FOX ILLUSTRATION STATION P.E.I., N.S. AND N.B., *Progress Report, 1943–1947*, 1949, 31). That bar is on the silver fox. It is the silver section of the fox. On the hair you have the black top, the base, and in between is the silver bar. It can vary in length. You want the bar to be in proportion to the hair for a high quality fur (S 7). The bar is the silver bar that comes on the fur about an inch from the end of the fur and has a black tip on it (S 8).

barachois
Noun. \,bar-ə-'shwah\. Also spelled and pronounced **barasois, barashay, barashway, baraswa, barshwa.** Rare. Compare **blind pond.**
   A backwater near the mouth of a river; a marsh.
   There is a great extent of marsh land or Barachois on the islands [The Magdalens]. On those marshes grow immense quantities of cranberries and foxberries, for which a ready market is found in the Maritime Provinces (M'CORMAC, G.J., *The Kingdom of Fish*, 1901,

180). There are some barachois up near Nail Pond (I 014). It's a watery place. There was one at Union Corner. When I was a child I was told to keep away from it, as it was soft and marshy. A good fishing hole (I 030). From Darnley Bridge out to the point is the barachois. It was named by early settlers. Some pronounce it barashay (I 063). There's one at Malpeque, where the fishermen go, called the barachois (I 064). The Darnley River is the barachway from bridge to ocean (I 068). There's a bog in Traveller's Rest called the barachois (I 097).

[From Acadian French] *DC* 'Atlantic Provinces 1 ... They give the name *barachois* in this country to small ponds near the sea, from which they are separated only by a kind of causeway [1760 quotation]. ... 2 a narrow strip of sand or gravel rising above the surface of the adjacent water; a causeway. 1964'; *DNE* 'A shallow river estuary, lagoon or harbour, of fresh or salt water, sheltered from the sea by a sand-bar or low strip of land' 1778–1971. *Barasway*: *DNE* 1 'A sand bar 1766. ... 2 A shallow river estuary, lagoon or harbour of fresh or salt water, sheltered from the sea by a sand-bar or low strip of land' 1773–1971.

bar clam
Noun. Also **horse clam.** Common. Compare **piss clam.**
   A large, heavy clam with a distinctly corrugated shell, found on underwater sand-bars.
   Some foods were plentiful: bar clams, quahaugs, grandfather lobsters weighing ten pounds each ... (LEARD, GEORGE, *Historic Bedeque: The Loyalists at Work and Worship in Prince Edward Island*, 1948, 9). Some of our New Annan men drive to the Cove to fish. Others along with some women, go to Fish Island and Hog Island for bar clams (MOASE, LOUISE, *The History of New Annan, Prince Edward Island, Canada, 1800–1971*, 1971, 40). 'You stay here,' said the white seagull,'and I'll see what I can do.' And away he flew. But soon he was back with a great big bar clam filled to the brim with cool clear water (LAVIOLETTE, EMILY, *The Oyster and the Mermaid and Other Island Stories*, 1975, 17). At very low tide one can walk onto the flats and pick up quahaughs and large bar clams (MACLEOD, SALOME, *Memories of Beach Point and Cape Bear*, n.d., 14). They're dangerous if you happened to get your finger caught in the shell. Huge clams, not quahaugs. Just eat the muscle. Also called horse clams. We used a horse and cart to collect them (I 009). Bar clams are a hard-shelled clam on the

outside of big sandbars (I 058). They have a hard shell. You have to go in water to your knees to get them (I 065). Clams found on entrance to harbors, not on the shores (P1–018).

horse clam: DA 'a coarse clam of the north Pacific Coast.'

bare buff
Adjective. Informal. Frequent in Charlottetown and Cardigan, occasional in Egmont and Summerside, infrequent in Malpeque; especially male. Compare **bare pole.**
   Without clothes, naked.
   The women and girls 'put on' enormous garments called bathing suits and splashed around in the breakers. Further down the beach the men and boys 'took off' their clothes and went in barebuff (SELLICK, LESTER, *My Island Home*, 1973, 29). Yeah ... bare buff right out in the water ... the girls would always have a dress on (T M142).

*Buff as such is informal standard for bare skin.

bare pole
Adjective. Informal. Frequent generally, but occasional in Malpeque and Cardigan; significantly male; especially urban. Compare **bare buff.**
   Without clothes, naked.
   Caught going swimming bare pole (II 075). He was running around bare pole (O).

bar harbor
Noun.
   See second quotation.
   The Harbour of St. Peters, is situated on the North side of the Island. It is a bar harbour, and only admits schooners adapted to the trade carried on with Halifax and Newfoundland, and for the fisheries (HILL, S.S., *A Short Account of Prince Edward Island, Designed Chiefly for the Information of Agriculturist and Other Emigrants of Small Capital*, 1839, 11). It was raining hard and the wind was coming right off the Cape, the worst possible conditions for bringing a boat into the harbor. Murray Harbor has a bar harbor; a spit of sand crosses the mouth creating shoal water that is especially dangerous in high seas (HAMMOND, ELAINE, *The Sinking of the 'Thisisit,'* 1984, 32).

*Bar, as in *sand-bar*, is standard.
DC 'Maritimes' 1830–1871.

barkative
Adjective.
   Of a dog or fox, inclined to continual barking; sometimes applied to a talkative person.
   Answering yelps came from behind kennels and shoots. 'Listen to the barkative little rascals,' the girl cried delightedly. 'And see how beautiful their fur is growing,' she said, as a young pup left its mates and moved toward the door ... (HANSULD, EFFIE, *Effie's Rock: A Tale of Prince Edward Island*, 1980, 25). The barkative dog kept barking at me (P2–017). Used for wolves (P2–048). The baying of hounds (P2–057). The preacher had a barkative voice (P2–068).

barking sand
See **singing sand.**

barn sock
Noun. Occasional in Egmont, infrequent elsewhere, but unattested in Charlottetown; especially rural. Compare **hardwood sock, lumberman's sock, moccan, oversock.**
   A coarse, knitted sock worn for outside or barn work.
   They're coarse, up to the knee (I 009). Barn socks as opposed to school socks (I 040). Worn over overalls inside gum rubbers (I 051). For wearing during the week. You wouldn't wear them to church or to a dance (I 112).

barrack
Noun. Also **barracks, pole barn.** Archaic. Common in Cardigan, occasional in Malpeque and Charlottetown, rare elsewhere; significantly rural, older; especially male.
   A square structure of four long posts and a roof that is raised or lowered to cover straw, hay, or grain.
   Cutting and squaring logs for barracks (ROSS, DAVID, *The David Ross Diary 1836–1879*, 1838, 13). Put up barrack posts (MOAR, GEORGE, *Diary: February 1, 1881–July 31, 1881*, 1881, June 27). I went up afternoon for a load of wheat straw. A and I put what was left in the stack into the barrick [sic] and barn ... (LAMONT, MURDOCK, *Diary, 1885–1888*, 1885, March 12). 'Now look at the red point with the clump of spruce and the hay field with the three barracks in the center' (STIRLING, LILLA, *Jockie: A Story of Prince Edward Island*, 1951, 118). A full stook would be twelve sheaves placed on end

with butts down and heads up. These were left in the field a few days for the grain to harden, then they were loaded into wagons and put in barns, stacks, or barracks. A barrack was built with four long posts connected at the top by cross-pieces of timber and a roof. As the barrack filled the roof would be raised and held in place by iron pins. A floor, made of old rails or timber was placed under the sheaves (MACDONALD, MARY, and MRS. CLINTON STEWART, *Historical Sketch of Eastern Kings*, 1972, 2). The grain was harvested with a binder which made sheaves. The sheaves were then stooked and left in the field for a period of about ten days so the grain would dry and get hard. They were then hauled to the barrack and stored to await the threshing mill. The roof of the barrack rested on pins which were inserted through the four posts. The roof was raised or lowered as the barrack was filled or emptied. This allowed for threshing out-of-doors where the wind would blow away the dust. (MORRISON, A.L., *My Island Pictures: The Story of Prince Edward Island*, 1980, 30.)

Pole barn is standard for a building 'having a foundation made of piles or poles stuck into the ground' (W3), but is used additionally on PEI as a synonym for *barrack* and as a synonym for *loafing barn*.
[From northeastern United States] WGUS 'Barrack (14), an adaptation of Dutch *hooiberg* denoting a square hay stack with a sliding roof, is found in the valleys of the Hudson and the Mohawk and on Long Island' 24; *DARE* 'chiefly NY, C Atl' 1697–1973; *DA*; *DAE*; *DNE*; *OED*; *W3*.

basket
Noun. Compare **horse scoop**.
1. In 'Irish moss' harvesting from boats, a metal basket attached behind a rake to collect moss.
As the rake is towed it detaches the moss from the holdfast, and it collects in the rake teeth and in a metal basket attached to the rake (ANDERSON, NANCY, *Global Village? Global Pillage: Irish Moss from P.E.I. in the World Market*, [1977], 4). Partly from recommendations made by the [Marine Plants Experimental] station [in Miminegash], regulations have been put in force in 1978 that stop fishermen from using baskets behind their rakes which were blamed on hurting the beds and small lobsters (*The Guardian*, September 19, 1978, 5). A basket was a tool fishermen were using a few years ago. It was attached to the rake. They consisted of steel rabbit wire and would catch the loose moss behind the rake or drag on a boat (S 12).

2. A strong-framed, wire-mesh scoop on a handle, used by 'shore mossers' in collecting 'Irish moss.'
A basket consists of an iron frame covered with fairly open mesh and is about one foot high and two feet long, and it's got a handle of up to ten feet long made of wood. You chuck the basket away from you, then pull it towards you with the handle through the moss (S 10).

*Baskets, in the first sense, were declared illegal in 1977.

basket social
Noun. Archaic. Compare **box social**, **concert**, **pie social**.
A fund-raising entertainment, during which lunches in decorated baskets were auctioned off and then shared by donor and buyer.
Bad sort of night for 'Basket Social' in Bloomfield don't care I'm not going (OLIVER, GERTRUDE HAZEL MEGGISON, *Diaries of Gertrude Hazel Meggison Oliver*, 1910, Jan. 10). Gertrude trimming basket for basket social and practicing music for it (MEGGISON, ELEANOR CARR, *Diaries of Eleanor Carr Meggison*, 1923, March 6). After the building of halls in each community a popular form of entertainment was the basket social or pie social. All the girls and women in the district filled baskets with the best lunch they could prepare or baked a special pie. The baskets and pies were beautifully decorated and were sold by auction to the highest bidder. A young man was supposed to find out how his current girl-friend's basket was trimmed so he could buy it and they could eat their lunch together. If the crowd caught on that a young man was anxious to buy a certain basket they would bid it up and sometimes he had to pay outrageously high for it. The girl in question was greatly flattered if her basket brought a good price. ... These socials were favorite means to raise money for worthwhile community projects. There was always some local entertainment at those affairs and a witty auctioneer could add much to the fun and keep the bidding brisk (PENDERGAST, JAMES, and GERTRUDE PENDERGAST, *Folklore Prince Edward Island*, [1974], 19). Another annual event was the Thanksgiving Basket Social which was held in the hall. Those ladies who brought a lunch in their tastefully trimmed baskets were admitted free. Later in the evening these baskets were auctioned off. The music for the dancing was supplied by local talent. As years went by the Basket Social

was replaced by the Thanksgiving Chicken Supper. It is now being held in the basement of the new church but turkey is now in vogue (WELLINGTON CENTENNIAL COMMITTEE, *Immaculate Conception Parish Centennial, 1875–1975*, 1975, 24). They used to have basket socials too in the schools and the halls. We'd go there and buy a girl's basket and sit down and eat it with her. Them was good days. There's no days now, no. Somebody would run [a basket] up, you know. I remember one fellow over here in Wood Islands. He had a girl and he bought her basket and the other fellows run him up on it. Whether they wanted the basket or not I don't know, but they run it up. Of course, it wasn't run up much. You'd buy a nice basket for a quarter, you know. Yeah, they run that fellow's basket up to four dollars. But that was only a small price. You'd pay 15 or 20 dollars now at a 'concert' if you went there to buy a basket (HORNBY, SUSAN, *George Young: Horsing Around*, 1981, 29). They had what they called basket socials. They'd have a basket put up and the fella that bought it would have to eat with the woman that put the basket up (T M124).

DARE 'chiefly Upper MW, NW' 1895–1970. *basket*: *DA* '2. In combs. designating meals carried in baskets or gatherings at which meals so brought are partaken of, as ... (6) [basket] social.'

bauglan
Noun.
The common ragwort.
Such is the history of the 'Ragwort,' 'Tansy Ragwort,' 'Staggerwort'; botanists name it Senecia Jacobaea. More expressive, but less elegant in their diction, vulgar people call it 'Stinking Billy.' It is known as 'Bauglan' in the north-western districts of this Island, where it spread from seeds which rumor had it had been brought from Ireland in a bedtick, by a man named Ryan. ... It is an erect and very leafy, stiff perennial, growing from two to four feet high; with pretty twice-dissected leaves, – some of them fully eight inches long. The plant is crowned by large and handsome clusters (corymbs) of brilliant yellow flower-heads, each head like a golden daisy ... (WATSON, LAWRENCE, *Wolves in Sheep's Clothing*, 1900, 277).

*The name *stinking Willie* (or *Billy*) is recognized by Diane Griffin, *Atlantic Wildflowers*, 1984, and hence is excluded from this collection (see 'The Scope of the Dictionary').

bauken
Also spelled **bawken**. See **bocan**.

beal
Noun. Also **bealing**. Compare **beal** (verb), **bealing** (noun and verbal adjective).
An infected and festering sore.
A bealing is an internal infection drawn out by a poultice and then lanced (I 034). In the old days we wore skates that didn't fit and got a beal on the toe (I 050). A infected sore which is running (I 059). From a very foreign object in the skin that festers. Not the same as a boil (I 063). The boil has a hard core. The beal is a result of infection (I 104). A beal comes from a splinter. A boil comes to a head (I 107). Bealing – a sore with pus in it and inflamed (O).

[From British and Irish] *OED* 'Obs. or dial.' 1605–1703; *EDD* 1811; *SND* 1925; *DARE* 1824–1970.

beal
Intransitive verb. Also spelled **beel**. Compare **beal** (noun), **bealing** (noun and verbal adjective).
Of an infected sore, to fester and run.
When a fisherman's rubber raincoat would rub on his neck that had salt water on it, he would get an ulcer that would beal (I 056). A thorn will fester and beal. A boil has infection inside and a core (I 097).

[From British and Irish] *OED* 'Obs. or dial. ... Still in regular use in Scotland'; *EDD* 'Sc.Irel.Nhb.Yks.Shr. Amer.'; *DARE* 1895–1970; *SND* 'To fester; *fig.* to be filled with pain or remorse. Gen.Sc. and Uls.Sc.' 1705–1929; *MED* 'belen ... to inflame; become inflamed, fester'; *DOST* 'Bele, Beil, Bele. ... 2. To swell with morbid matter; to suppurate'; *W3*; *EDSL*.

bealing
Verbal noun. Also spelled **beeling**. Common in Egmont and Cardigan, frequent elsewhere; significantly older; especially rural. Compare **beal** (noun and verb), **bealing** (verbal adjective).
An infection.
The bealing has gone down (I 055). A stage of infection before it comes to a head. With modern medicine, bealing is not so common (I 114).

[From British and Irish] *SND* 1824; *W3*.

bealing
Verbal adjective. Also **bealed**. Also spelled **beeling**. Common; significantly older; especially rural. Compare **beal** (noun and verb), **bealing** (noun).
Of a part of the body, infected.

Francis very sick with a bad cold and bealing throat (LARKIN, ALEXANDER, *Diary: April 3,
1886–April 3 1890*, Sept. 29, 1888). And yet she
could not look upon pain. ... She would not
remove a splinter from a child's foot; the
operation was entrusted to an elder child. The
sight of blood made her faint. The simple
surgery which the Master might perform upon
the 'bealed' finger of a child filled her with
anguish (MACPHAIL, SIR ANDREW, *The Master's
Wife*, 1977 [1939], 14). Few of those old idioms
and catch-phrases seem to have survived; most
of them appear to have faded completely from
present memory. Many commonly used words
were legacies from our Scottish and Irish fore-
bears. Once, during my seafaring days, I
developed an infected finger, the result of an
imbedded splinter. When I remarked to our old
Scottish skipper that I had a 'beeling' finger,
he demanded to know where I had picked up
the word. When I assured him that it was a
commonly used word at home, he declared
that he had never before heard it outside the
Hebrides (DEVEREUX, JOSEPH, *Looking Backward*,
n.d., 117). I would use bealing for a sore on a
finger – a bealing finger (I 009). A bealing
throat – a bealing ear when you have quinsy
(I 042). Inflammation gathers but it doesn't come
to a head like a boil – a bealing ear (I 068).
Mostly used as an adjective for ears (I 069).
Bealed fingers from a splinter (I 106). Bealing
or bealed as adjective means it has been infected by a thorn, etc. It is a soft infection
(I 108). Soft infection. A boil has a hard core
(I 116).

[From British and Irish] *SND* 'Sc. and Uls.' 1879–
1929; *OED* 'Obs. exc. dial.'; *EDD bealed* 1790, *bealing*
1895; *DARE bealed* 1903–1982.

bear's match
Noun. Usually in plural. Also **devil's
match**. Rare.
    **One of the bright red nodules of a
lichen that grows on rotting logs and
stumps (*Cladonia cristatella*).**
    Pine stumps used to be used for reading
portents, especially at a certain part of the
moon. Forerunners (II 003). Phosphorus top.
Devil's matches (II 039).

bear's head: W3 'an edible fungus growing on trees in
irregular masses.' *devil's match*: *DNE* 'British soldier,
a type of lichen.'

beater digger
Noun. Archaic.

**An early potato digger with revolving
prongs that beat the earth, spreading
potatoes for the pickers.**
    Later dad used a beater digger which not
only exposed all the potatoes but also scattered
them over a wide area (*The Journal Pioneer*,
November 9, 1981, 4). By the 1890's black-
smiths and machinists were manufacturing a
number of potato diggers. ... These were
probably the forerunners of the beater diggers.
A beater digger consisted of a steel shear
which went under the row of potatoes and the
beaters which spread the potatoes and clay
behind it. The first beater diggers had only one
prong at each spoke with eight to ten spokes.
An improved model had two prongs at each
spoke and these could throw the potatoes and
dirt much farther (FREETOWN HISTORICAL
SOCIETY, *Freetown Past and Present*, 1985, 45).
It's a wheel with six inch rubber hoses on the
end of the prongs (S 1).

bed
See **digger bed**.

bedlunch
Noun.
    A snack or light meal at bedtime (O).

*Lunch, as such, is standard for 'a light meal at any
time of the day.'

bed money
See **rocking-chair money**.

bedroom
See **parlour**.

berried
Verbal adjective. Compare **spawn**.
    Of a lobster, egg-bearing.
    Witness has noticed that there are very few
'berried' lobsters this year (CANADA, DEPART-
MENT OF MARINE AND FISHERIES, *Report of the
Commissioners ... to Enquire Into and Report Upon
the Lobster and Oyster Fisheries of Canada*, 1887,
38). Q. Is the practice of stripping or washing
the eggs from the female lobster followed here?
A. Only when the manager of the factory tells
the fisherman he will not take the berried
lobsters. Then it is done (CANADA, HOUSE OF
COMMONS, *Lobster Fishery Evidence Taken before
Commander William Wakeham, M.D., Officer in
Charge of the Gulf Fisheries Division, in Quebec
and the Maritime Provinces*, 1910, 21). The sale
of egg-bearing or berried lobsters has been

prohibited by law in Canada since 1873. In the early days of the fishery when lobsters were large and plentiful this regulation was almost completely ignored and most of the berried females that were caught were canned or sold alive. When the catch began to drop fishermen became more and more conscious of the wisdom of protecting berried lobsters and observance of this regulation gradually improved. At the present time berried lobsters are rigidly protected in most areas. In a few places, particularly where such lobsters are plentiful, fishermen continue to sell them after removing the egg (WILDER, D.G., *Canada's Lobster Fishery*, 1954, 14). 'Berried' or spawning and soft-shelled lobsters were not allowed to be landed (MORRISON, CLINTON, *Along the North Shore: A Social History of Township 11, P.E.I. 1765–1982*, 1984, 67–68). A berried lobster is a spawn lobster. They have thousands of them little black specks on their body. They turn as they get ripe to a dark brown and then they let them go at sea. I've seen the little lobster berry in the belly of a cod and you could see the shape of the lobster already (S 4). A lobster that has spawn is a berried lobster. The spawn is sort of a light brown or even a bluish brown. Maybe the bottom has something to do with it (S 6).

OED 1868; W3; GCD; FW; WNW; COD.

betimes
See **by times**.

beulah
Intransitive verb. \'byoō-lə\. Informal.
   To vomit.
   To beulah upwind (P2 013). He beulahed up all night (P2 017).

beyant
Preposition. \bā-'yahnt\.
   Beyond.
   I knew ould Larry Gordon whin he lived on the Taylor farm beyant the store. He's a skim milk man, that he is (MONTGOMERY, LUCY MAUD, *Pat of Silver Bush*, 1933, 80). They lived in a House at the Harbour Head, and I was living there, too, on a bit of a farm, beyant the barrens. It was just after I'd married my second, worse luck. The way the men get round you! (MONTGOMERY, LUCY MAUD, *Jane of Lantern Hill*, 1936, 167). I slipped through the haystacks and I wint right over an acre of sparrow grass wid no bumps to speak av – and thin up looms a spruce hedge and a wire fince beyant it. And I did be knowing I had a few

minutes to spare (MONTGOMERY, LUCY MAUD, *The Road to Yesterday*, [pre–1940], 202).

[From Irish] W3; EDD; SND *beyont* 1724.

bicken
Noun. Informal. Rare.
   The penis (O).

*This word has been reported from parts of Nova Scotia, especially Cape Breton. It is said to be Gaelic.

big head
See **centre head**.

Billy Button
Noun.
   A parlour game.
   Our women spun the yarn and wove it into cloth and then we had a jolly pulling frolic, and when the web was out, we put a bench across the kitchen, in front of the fire-place, and had our web-ends sewn together and had the web soaked in soapy water, and had about a dozen boys and girls around the bench raising the web up and down around with the sun for about an hour or more to thicken it, singing their love songs. When it was done we had a roast goose and tea, and when it was over we played Billy Button to get some forfeits, and then sold them for a good price in kisses, kissing each other. Then the boys took the girls home (AUTUMN, GENE, *My Life in Crapaud*, 1929, 14).

button: DAE 'A guessing game in which forfeits are exacted of those who guess wrong' 1773–1860.

bin-piler
Noun. Also **bin-loader**.
   A machine having a conveyor belt running up a boom, usually used to pile potatoes for storage.
   Each year the firm produces new equipment. Special care is taken to protect the potato from damage of any kind. One of these is a first on the Island, a special bin piler, which deposits potatoes from the warehouse into the potato planter (*Journal-Pioneer Annual Farm Issue*, 1975, 15). The bin piler should be equipped with a dirt remover and be moved as frequently as possible to prevent the formation of soil cones (LINKLETTER, GRAEME, *Potato Storage Important*, 1982, 6–7). It's a machine that is used to pile potatoes that will be loaded from the end of a bulk truck. It has an hydraulic control to adjust the height and position of the

boom (S 1). A bin-piler is an elevator with slats on it, with an hydraulic hoist. You must keep it just above the pile (S 2).

bito

Noun. \'bī-tō\. Also **abito, vito**. Largely historical. Rare. Compare **aboiteau**.

A contraction of 'aboiteau': a dike on a tidal river equipped with a sluice gate acting as a valve to hold back the tide.

The general store of 'Preacher George' (as he was called) was situated in Tryon, on the left hand side of the hill past the 'Bito Bridge' towards Augustine Cove (HASLAM, DORIS, *The Wrights of Bedeque, Prince Edward Island,* 1978, I, 80). He was a seaman and owned the *William and Charlotte,* a 44 ton brig he built in Tryon (below the Bito, on the south side of the bridge and on the west side of the river) and launched in 1845 (*ibid,* 140). It's a corrupted version of aboiteau. Originally the gate in a dike. The Bito Bridge in Tryon is not an aboiteau but it was an aboiteau in Acadian times (II 055). A dam to keep sea water off land (II 101).

*Like *aboiteau,* the word survives most strongly as a place-name.
[From French] DC 1896–1957 'Once a tidal stream, the creek had been brought into subjection by what the country people called a "bito," built across its mouth to shut out the tides …' [1896 quotation].

black ice

Noun. Occasional in Cardigan, infrequent elsewhere, but rare in Charlottetown; especially rural, male. Compare **glib ice, shell ice**.

1. A thin layer of ice formed on a body of water, appearing dark because of its transparency.

A thin spot on the ice over water. The river would be used as a winter road. You had to beware of black ice (II 008). You can see through right to the bottom (II 039). In a bay, thin ice shows up black where a mussel bed is located (II 063). The ice over a pond that wouldn't be safe to walk on (II 066). Usually in spring. Danger when we used to travel the ice (II 075). New ice that is fairly thin and smooth. Too thin to travel on (II 076).

2. A thin, almost invisible, coating of ice on pavement.

Black ice is smooth ice on pavement (II 004). A thin layer of ice over the road (II 016). On the road after a freezing rain (II 094). Ice over the pavement. You can't see it until you're on top of it (II 095). It is the same color as the highway so it is unnoticeable (II 108).

[sense 1]: *DC* 1829–1961; *DNE; DARE* 1944–1979.
[sense 2]: *DC* 1964; *DARE* 1967–1980; *OEDS; COD.*

blackleg

Noun. Compare **hollow heart, spindle tuber**.

A bacterial disease of potatoes.

The most readily visible symptom of blackleg is the moist, black appearance of the stem of the plant. Further inspection usually shows the black rot to extend downward to the stem-end of the seed piece where rot is also present. … The soft rot associated with blackleg is unmistakeable. Blister-like lesions form on the tubers which when incised release a watery ooze of bacteria and dead tissue. Infested areas vary from light to dark brown (*Prince Edward Island Potato Handbook,* 1980, 39–40). The bacteria that cause blackleg are usually present on the surface of tubers. When conditions are right, the organism becomes active and causes the decay of the seed piece before the emergence of the plant. Under other conditions the organism may invade the stem of the plant causing it to decay into an inky-black, wet breakdown that usually results in the death of the plant. The leaves of infected plants become yellowed, young leaves roll and the plant is dwarfed. Some tubers from infected plants show decay at the point where the stolon is attached to the tuber. In advanced stages the decay extends into the center of the tuber leaving only an outer shell (ADVISORY COMMITTEE ON POTATOES, *Atlantic Canada Potato Guide,* 1984, 29). Blackleg goes from the stalk to the potato which goes to mush when stored. You can't tell by looking. It's very smelly. You can't use the basement for years after (II 056). It's called blackleg because it creeps up the stalk (II 112). The stem rots right at the ground, and the potatoes rot and stink (S 2).

black moss

Noun. Compare **bleach moss, moss**.

'Irish moss' that has been harvested and dried, but not bleached.

In 1941 this price was almost doubled and the export price for high-grade 'bleached moss' has not since fallen much below 20c per lb., with, of course, much lower prices for 'black moss' (dried but not bleached) (CANADA, FISHERIES RESEARCH BOARD OF CANADA, *Irish Moss Industry in the Maritime Provinces,* 1947, 2). When dried, the plant darkens so that unbleached dried moss is known to the trade as 'black moss' (MACFARLANE, CONSTANCE, *Irish Moss in the Maritime Provinces,* 1956, 5). The moss after it is harvested and dried turns black. That is black moss. When it is first harvested it is green (S 11).

W3, *DARE* 'Spanish moss' [in this case, a plant that hangs in tufts from trees in the southern U.S. and West Indies].

black robin
Noun. Rare.
   The red-winged blackbird (*Agelaius phoeniceus*).
   Some blackbirds have a little tint of red on them like a robin (I 039). They are blackbirds with red wings (I 065).

*According to R.W. Tufts in *The Birds of Nova Scotia*, 1961, p. 411, *black robin* is a colloquial name in Nova Scotia for the rusty blackbird (*Euphagus carolinus nigrans*).

black snow
Noun. Compare **sheep storm, smelt storm**.
   1. A late spring snow-storm (II; R).
   2. Old, dirty snow (R).

DC 'North drab, greyish snow soiled by dust in the atmosphere' 1946.

blainey
Adjective. Rare.
   Of a field, bare in patches where frost has killed the roots.
   Their land sown out with grass-seed, for what they call upland hay, is not generally so well covered in the bottom as in Scotland; even that which has been under the scythe several years, where the snow has been swept from the surface, and the frost has had free access to it, is so strong as actually to destroy some of the roots of the grass. I have often examined these blainey places, and found the old grass lying withered in the bottom, and little new springing up (JOHNSTONE, WALTER, *A Series of Letters, Descriptive of Prince Edward Island*, 1822, 12).

[From Irish and Scottish Gaelic via Irish and Scottish] *SND* 1808–1929; *EDD*; *EDSL*; *IED*.

blank head
Noun. Also **blind head, end head**. Compare **head** (noun).
   One of the two pieces of twine mesh that form the ends of a lobster trap.
   The lobster trap was made up of three parts, viz. 'fishing head,' 'parlour head,' and 'blind head' (MACDONALD, MARY, and MRS. CLINTON STEWART, *Historical Sketch of Eastern Kings*, 1972, 51). The blank heads are at the ends of the traps. Some traps are lathed in instead of having blank heads (S 5).

bleach moss
Noun. Also **bleached moss**. Compare **black moss, moss**.
   'Irish moss' that is bleached white as a first step in the extraction of carrageenin.
   At the plant the moss is bleached by salt water while being dried either by mechanical dryers or by sunlight. The latter process is the traditional method, but it is being supplanted rapidly by the mechanical process. Upon completion of the drying process the bleached moss is then baled and shipped to the extraction plants. Frequently, the minor processors sell their dried moss directly to industry (e.g. beer industry) without any further processing (FFRENCH, A., *A Current Appraisal of the Irish Moss Industry*, 1970, 26). Bleach moss was more profitable to sell, because supposedly, the extraction was easier to do (BERNARD, BLAINE, *Dictionary of Irish Moss*, 1986, n. pag.). Once Irish moss has been dried to a certain point and then wet with fresh water it bleaches white. This is what we call 'bleach moss' (S 10). Bleach moss is processed to a certain degree. Some of the things that are not carrageenin are taken out and then they bleach it by sunlight. Sometimes we used a lime solution and it bleached quicker (S 11).

blind head
See **blank head**.

blindman's snow
Noun. Rare. Compare **May snow**.
   A late spring snow-fall thought to have curative properties, especially for the eyes.
   A snow in May (Mary's month), when put in the eyes, will cure blindness (II 009). Good for failing sight, in folklore (O).

blind pond
Noun. Also **hidden pond**. Occasional in Egmont, infrequent elsewhere, but rare in Charlottetown; significantly older; especially rural. Compare **barachois**.
   A pond with no apparent inlet or outlet.
   There's Little Peter's Blind Pond in Darnley (II 068). It's dry most of the time but fills up in a heavy rain (II 100).

blind: DA 'designating depressions, bodies of water, etc. having little or no inlet or outlet'; *DSAE* 'Of or pertaining to an estuary, lagoon, or river mouth which lacks access to the sea, except in times of flood: as in Blind River (East London).' *blind slough*: DC 'a narrow, meandering, sluggish side-channel of a river, usually shallow and often coming to a dead end.'

blink
Noun. Compare **michaud, short**.
   A small mackerel; occasionally a lobster below the legal length for fishing (S; O).

[From American] *DAE* 'A mackerel when about a year old'; *DA* 1856–1888.

blueberry barrens
Noun. Also **blueberry plains**. Common generally, but frequent in Charlottetown; significantly rural, rare under thirty; especially male. Compare **cranberry barrens, fire barrens, spruce barrens**.
   A tract of untillable or burnt-over land where blueberries grow.
   The picturesque appearance of Charlottetown in its early years when the principal features were log houses, blueberry barrens, spruce trees, and an old earthwork fort, has not been very much improved during its subsequent history (*The Examiner – Weekly Edition*, 1881, n. pag.). The August evening was so hot and close that the crowded cars were stifling. Nobody ever knew just why trains stopped at Millward siding. Nobody was ever known to get off there or get on. There was only one house nearer to it than four miles, and it was surrounded by acres of blueberry barrens and scrub spruce trees (MONTGOMERY, LUCY MAUD, *Rilla of Ingleside*, [1920], 256). There are great sand-hills or 'dunes' between the lakes and the sea. ... Along here the early settlers landed. There are great cranberry and blueberry barrens a little distance from the shores (MELLICK, HENRY, *Timothy's Boyhood: or Pioneer Country Life on Prince Edward Island*, 1933, 14). Over eighty years have passed, and the tiny province's growth accelerates with every passing year, and today we look over its many 'Highlights': red earth and sandstone, green fields and undulating farmland, ... wondrous potato fields and heavy-yielding blue-berry barrens (WARREN, EVANGELINE, *Andy the Milkman*, 1957, 6). One of the earliest forces released by the settler was fire. About 1738, when the North Shore was only a base for drying fish, fire burnt from Tracadie eastward to East Point, devastating the entire north-eastern peninsula. It must have spread easily in the dry spruce and pine forest. One result of this burning was the encouragement of the heath shrubs; the resulting blueberry barrens of Tracadie have been perpetuated by accidental and deliberate use of fire ever since. The fire of 1840 in central Prince produced a great blueberry barren at Conway which persisted for over thirty years (CANADA, DEPARTMENT OF AGRICULTURE, *The Plants of Prince Edward Island*, 1960, 19). John Doughart, who lived halfway between the north and south of the Cundall estate, states: 'I have lived there 30 years. I am in the very centre of the blueberry barrens. There are blueberry barrens there if the berries upon the bushes are any indication' (PAYNTER, RUTH, *From the Top of the Hill: The History of an Island Community*, 1977, 20). Barlow road lies between Ellerslie and Lot 11. It passes by the barrens known as the 'blueberry plains.' Tradition says that the region was once swept clean by a terrible fire from which it did not recover for over a century and a half (MACARTHUR, F.H., *The Ghost of Barlow Road*, n.d., 15).

*Barrens, as such, is standard in North America for any tract of wasteland supporting only low vegetation, 'sometimes with defining terms prefixed, as *pine-barrens*' (*DAE*).
[North American] *DARE* 1937–1969. *barrens*: DC 'in the Atlantic Provinces, an elevated tract of exposed land that nourishes only scrubby trees, shrubs, berries, etc. and resembles a moor'; *SSPB* 'usually a northern word for "tundra," this word is used in Nova Scotia to describe bogs in which blueberries, cloudberries, low stunted spruce, and mosses grow'; *OED* 'In Nova Scotia and New Brunswick ... an open marshy space in the forest, sometimes so soft as to be almost impassable, at other times composed of good solid hard peat.'

blueberry grunt
See **grunt**.

blueberry run
Noun.
   1. A heavy rainfall in blueberry season.
   A blueberry run meant you lost all the blueberries in a rainstorm (P2–003). It can be a rain to wash the blueberries (P2–018).
   2. [With *the*] **Diarrhea from eating blueberries** (P2). Compare **back door trots, flying axehandles, green apple quick step, run outs and walk ins, short taken, skithers**.

blunt cow
See **mull**.

boarded
Verbal adjective.
Of a fox pelt, stretched on a 'pelting board' to dry.
After you skin the fox you put the pelt on a board and stretch it to its size. This is what is known as a boarded pelt. We have two standard sizes (S·8). When the pelt is on the board it is boarded. It is usually a pine board of forty-eight inches long (S 9).

fox board: DNE 'wooden board on which a fox pelt is stretched to dry.'

board ice
Noun. Occasional in Egmont, infrequent elsewhere, but rare in Cardigan; significantly older, male. Compare **field ice**, **shore ice**.
Solid, flat, sea ice attached to shore and extending out to broken ice or open water.
Board ice began to move from the shore (4 months on shore). … Board ice all gone but a lot of floating ice in the gulf and a lot still aground out on the ledge square off here (Nail Pond) (LARKIN, ALEXANDER, *Diary: April 3, 1886–April 3, 1890*, 1887, April 28,30). Went up to try the board ice and see if they could haul a house round the Cape. … Charlie and George at home in forenoon, went to finish their road on board ice after dinner only to find that the wind had taken the ice off shore and spoiled the hauling entirely (WOODMAN, SUSAN, *Diary: January 1, 1885–December 31, 1896*, 1895, March 27, 29). Finally she persisted in going out to the extreme point of the solid ice in that part of the field. It was low – typical board ice – and we investigated the wide lane that ran on two sides of it (HICKMAN, ALBERT, *The Sacrifice of the Shannon*, 1903, 198). For a distance of about one mile on each side of the strait, the ice is attached to the shore and is known as 'the board ice.' This leaves only seven miles for the ferry; but owing to the tide, which runs about four miles an hour, carrying with it the ice fields, the distance travelled by the boats is considerably increased. Teams carry the passengers from the edge of the board ice to the railway stations. A trip by The Capes is a unique experience (CROSSKILL, W.H., *Handbook of Prince Edward Island: The Garden Province of Canada*, 1906, 94). It was the work of brave and stalwart men thus to launch, or drag out of the icy water these boats heavily laden with baggage and mail-bags. Often it was difficult to effect a landing from the rushing tide full of tumbling bergs to the solid ice – board-ice so-called – which extends out from either shore. Often after or during a storm the treacherous snow covered up and concealed open water beneath, and the otherwise luckless strap passenger plunged to the armpits in the chilly slush and water, and was dragged out by his fellow toilers … (McCREADY, J.E.B., *Traditions of Prince Edward Island*, 1923, 207). Along each shore in winter there usually extends an immovable border called the board-ice; on arrival here the boats are hauled to a building where before a good fire all the equipments are made perfectly dry. When not in service the boats are kept in this building (CARLETON WOMEN'S INSTITUTE, *A History of Carleton, Prince Edward Island*, n.d., 14). Board ice is a broad flat area of solid ice (I 031). It's heavy ice, not piled up (I 042). Heavy ice frozen solid offshore that could be driven on. It went out to open water where ice floated around (I 049). The smooth ice you walk over to get to the rough broken stuff (I 070).

*The relatively high use of this term in Egmont may be connected to the former employment of 'ice boats' across the Northumberland Strait.
[Maritimes] DC 1904 [PEI citation]–1923.

bocan
Noun. \'bah-kən\. Also spelled **bauken, bawken, bocain, boccan**. Often used with children. Rare.
A bogeyman.
Witches, ghosts and fairies were so common they excited little interest. Bocans were a more serious menace. A bocan might leap upon a boy in the dark at any moment. Lights were seen; bridges would quiver in sign of an approaching funeral. There were interpreters of dreams and omens; and … persons with the gift of second sight (MACPHAIL, SIR ANDREW, *The Master's Wife*, [1939], 108). They [the Scotch pioneers] also had weird stories about ghosts and hobgoblins and bocain (big ghosts) and what not from the old country. Hair-raising stories of the antics of an unearthly bocain, called 'Colunn gun ch'eann,' held the young breathless and often caused an uncomfortable shifting of chairs nearer to the company on the part of their elders too (MACDONALD, HUBERT, *The Lords of the Isles and Their Descendants*, 1944, 97). The bocan used to frighten children from going places they

should not go (O). A sort of a ghost (O). 'The bawkens will get you' – a threat to little children (O).

*This word is often found in British English dialects to mean 'scarecrow' (see Harold Orton and Eugen Dieth, *Survey of English Dialects* [Leeds: E.J. Arnold, 1962]).
[From Irish and Scottish Gaelic via Irish and British] *EDD* 'Mothers frequently frighten their children away from dangerous wells by saying, "Doan'ee go there, my dear; there's a bawker in that will"'; *PEDGL; GED; DGL; IED; boggard -art: OED* 'a spectre, goblin, or bogy.'

bodach
Noun. \'bō-dahk\. Impolite. Rare.
An old man.
An old fella who's past it (II 101). Old man. Used in derogatory fashion (O).

[From Irish and Scottish Gaelic via Irish and Scottish] *SND* 'an old man. ... often used in a more or less contemptuous way. ... [Gael. *bodach*, an old man, a churlish old man, a mutchkin. O.Sc. has *boddoch*, a mutchkin, early 17th cent. (*D.O.S.T.*).]' 1887–1934; *OEDS* 'Ir. ... a peasant, churl' 1814–1903; *W3* 'Scot. & Irish: 'a boorish old man'; *PEDGL* 'an old man, a churl or niggardly fellow'; *EDD; EDSL; DGL; GED*.

bollock
See **kellick**.

book
Noun, usually in phrase **a good book**. Archaic. Compare **script**.
See quotations.
The ration book came about after the Second World War and was available to anyone over the age of twenty-one for a fee of two dollars. Before that, a doctor's prescription was required to buy alcohol. The 'book' permitted four purchases per month, but for heavy drinkers that was never enough and they would have to get a friend who had a 'good book' to make a purchase for them. Just as we now hear 'Hi – how are you?' the salutation often heard then was 'Hi – gotta good book?' (P2 084). 'Have you got a good book?' – when you ask someone if he has any 'scripts' left in his monthly book (o).

borrowed day
Noun. Rare. Compare **freshet, gosling day, pet day**.
A day of unseasonably good weather.
'G'day, boys,' he says, 'Borrowed day, ain't she? ... If she keeps up, the clay roads'll be all

dried up 'fore you know it' (BOYLES, ANN, *Living in Harmony*, 1983, 93). It is a May day in April or a November day in December (O).

EDD '(a) the last three days of March (old style); (b) the first eleven days of May'; *SND* 'Gen Sc.' 1728–1918. *borrowing days*: *W3* 'the last three days of March, Old Style'; *DARE; SND*.

Boston States, the
Proper noun. Also **Boston**. Archaic. Infrequent generally, but rare under thirty.
1. New England.
Social integration with their fellow Canadians was slow to be achieved as well. When Islanders looked abroad, they looked not to Upper Canada, but to the 'Boston States' (MACKINNON, WAYNE, *A Short History of Prince Edward Island*, 1976, 121). It was an era [early 1900s] when the population of Prince Edward Island was declining dramatically, as thousands of Islanders left for central Canada, or, more frequently, 'the Boston States' (ROBERTSON, IAN, Introduction to *The Master's Wife*, 1977, x). A healthy shipping industry had added hundreds of thousands of pounds annually to the Island economy. The dislocations caused by the decline were severe; the loss of employment opportunities, for example, giving an added impetus to the migration of skilled tradesmen to the 'Boston states' and elsewhere (FISCHER, LEWIS, *The Shipping Industry of Nineteenth Century Prince Edward Island: A Brief History*, 1978, 21).
2. The United States or a portion of it.
There was scarcely room at home for all the new arrivals by the cradle route – the families were large – so a constant stream of young people kept leaving the island for Boston. Boston was a general island name for the whole United States (KELLEY, FRANCIS, *The Bishop Jots It Down: An Autobiographical Strain on Memories*, 1939, 10). In comparatively recent times, in the early 1900s, a large migration of young people took place to United States or as some called the destination, the Boston States, where Island boys and girls were in strong demand (SHAW, WALTER, *Tell Me the Tales*, 1975, 30). Going to Boston meant a destination anywhere / from Rumford, Maine, to Dayton, Ohio. / Just as to the Yankee, that amorphous mass / on the Atlantic Coast of Canada – the Maritimes / and Newfoundland – was known as Nova Scotia, / so to the Maritimers and Newfoundlander, anything / north of the Mason-Dixon line and east of the Mississippi

/ was the Boston States (LEDWELL, FRANK, *The North Shore of Home*, 1986, 20).

*When used today, the expression is sometimes deliberately humorous (I 015, 048, 089; O). [Maritimes] DC 'Maritimes New England' 1948. *Boston*: ML 'To quite an extent *Boston* means Massachusetts and sometimes anything in that general direction. ... In Nova Scotia, the United States of America are the *Boston* states, and Maine shares something of this down eastism; no doubt it is a holdover from the coasting days when *Boston* really had a maritime importance to the region.'

bottle lamb
See **bummer**.

bottom sill
Noun. Compare **sill, top sill**.
   One of the heavy pieces of wood that form the bottom frame of a lobster trap.
   The bottom sill, that'd be the two outside shoes that the 'bows' are inserted into (S 4). The bottom sill is usually three-quarters of an inch material two and one-half inches wide or so, or mine are anyway (S 5). The bottom sills are the bottom pieces that she sits on (S 6).

bottom up
Transitive phrasal verb.
   To turn over (potatoes).
   You bottom your potatoes up before harvest to kill the blight (P2–038).

bow
Noun. \bō\ Also **bowstick, trap bow**.
   A curved wooden strut forming part of the frame of a lobster trap.
   A man came here in the evening with bows for lobster traps and stayed all night (WOODMAN, SUSAN, *Diary: January 1, 1895–December 31, 1896*, 1895, January 21). Will in Warehouse in forenoon. Went to H. Hunter's woods for bowsticks after dinner. Judge McLeod came up tonight (*ibid*, 1896, March 2). Mild but wind raw. Seymour hauling ice for Tom in forenoon; went for sticks to make more bows in afternoon (*ibid*, March 31). Basically the popular trap is in the form of a half cylinder with three or four curved wooden bows fitted into a rectangular wooden base (WILDER, D.G., *Canada's Lobster Fishery*, 1957, 15). Conventional semicylindrical wooden lobster traps were also employed. These were constructed with a rectangular flat base which held cement ballast. Anchored on each side of the base were wooden bows which served as the semi-

cylindrical frame. The bow-frame was covered with laths except for the ends and tunnel entrance which were covered with poly mesh (PRINCE EDWARD ISLAND, DEPARTMENT OF FISHERIES, *Offshore Lobster: Technical Report #175*, 1975, 2). They [lobster traps] have been unchanged in design since the turn of the century, with the exception that laminated bows, nylon nets, and polypropylene warps usually replace fir bows, cotton, Manila, and cedar (BOLGER, FRANCIS, *Memories of the Old Home Place*, 1984, 17). The bows are curved pieces of the trap. They are usually hardwood; in a lot of cases people are using oak (S 5). We made our own bows. Elm is the best, but we usually got spruce (S 6).

DNE.

bow trap
Noun. Also **four-bow trap, three-bow trap**.
   A conventional, semi-cylindrical lobster trap, built chiefly on a framework of three or four curved pieces of wood or 'bows.'
   Methods of capturing had to be changed as fishing by hand, spear, or hoop net could not bring in enough lobster to supply the factories. The European settlers were not short on ingenuity and bow traps soon evolved, similar to traps used in their homeland; then fishermen were able to increase their catches (JENKINS, J.B., *Lobstering in the Maritimes*, 1978, 7). [Jim Reggie MacDonald] builds approximately 60 traps per year and fishes about 300 traps. He said he now builds four-bow traps because they fish better than the three-bow variety (*The Guardian*, March 26, 1984, 5).In other areas fishermen using three bow lathe traps would only face an expense of less than $100 since only one lathe piece would have to be removed and replaced with an escape lathe (*The Guardian*, January 6, 1986, 5). It is the bow trap we use. The box trap is square. The bow trap won't pack as nice as the square, but we can pack more on because they are smaller (S 4).

box sleigh
Noun. Also **box sled**. Compare **pung**.
   A horse-drawn sleigh with a box-like body.
   The winter roads with their series of 'pitches,' or winding through the fields often behind houses and barns. Going to school in winter, riding in a big box sleigh, pulled by Mallet's trained ox (BROWN, IRA, *Sketches of*

the First Settlers of Little York, 1967, 33) To be part of this outing was adventure indeed and I was sure to be in a state of shivery excitement when I joined my cousins in the cosy box sleigh – layers of straw underneath and fur robes tucked securely around us (STEWART, MARION, *Marion Stewart's Journal*, 1976, 56). When the snow came, people used large two seated box sleighs piled high with blankets and buffalo robes for warmth. Some families kept wood sleighs, with sides and ends, so passengers could be hauled when work was done. In addition to these, the jaunting sleigh, light box sleigh and pung sleigh was used by couples for travelling to rink, church and other distant places (FREETOWN HISTORICAL SOCIETY, *Freetown Past and Present*, 1985, 18).

[North American] *OED*; *DC* 1896–1960; *DAE*; *DA*.

box social
Noun. Archaic. Compare **basket social, concert, pie social.**

   A synonym for 'basket social': a fund-raising entertainment, during which lunches in decorated baskets were auctioned off and then shared by donor and buyer.
   Yesterday was the 14th and St. Valentines day so there was a box social in the school last night. I spent all evening decorating my basket. ... Then for the contents, I made cakes and valentine cookies, along with sandwiches. John was teasing me about who would be the lucky fellow. Claude put the highest bid on my basket – $2 (BUSHEY, SARAH, *Memoirs of Sarah Bushey*, 1893, February 15). Another source of entertainment during the winter was the box-social auctions held in the Murray Harbour village hall with the proceeds going to some church fund or charity. The women of the neighboring area displayed their fine talents by baking fancy cakes, cookies and other goodies which were packed in a hand-decorated box or basket to be auctioned off to the highest bidder. The auctioneer would announce the name of the donor and the bidding would begin. The average box usually went for around two dollars but many of the younger men would try to outbid each other for a certain lady's basket and the price frequently paid topped four dollars. One fellow in particular, Elly Williams, often had to pay seven or eight dollars for his girl friend Carrie Carson's basket, after some of the other fellows would try to outbid him. Carrie was our schoolteacher and she usually did an exquisite

job in decorating a basket. After the auction, tea was served and the purchaser of a basket had the privilege of sharing the contents with the lady who donated it (DALY, WHITMAN, *Daly: The Saga of a Family 1820–1926 and My Boyhood on Prince Edward Island*, [1969], 51). Entertainment was simple. ... In winter the fellows would take the girls sleigh-riding and skating and bring them home from quilting parties and 'box socials.' The box social was an interesting and very profitable form of entertainment. The young women of the community would pack lunch boxes containing sandwiches and every imaginable kind of delicious pie, cake, squares and cookies. The boxes were then decorated with pretty paper and ribbon. The fellows and girls would gather at an appointed place, usually the school and after an evening of entertainment an auctioneer would be appointed who would sell all the boxes to the highest bidder. It was the rule that the buyer of the basket would eat its contents with the girl who had prepared it (MACDONALD, BERTHA, *Through All the Days Gone By*, [1983?], 43). We'd pack a lunch, you know, and trim our baskets all up nice and put our lunch in, we always had enough lunch for two people. Well then whoever bought the basket, they'd bid on them, you know – whoever bid the highest, that's who'd get the basket. Well usually our boyfriends bought the baskets and then we'd sit down and eat our lunch (T M36).

[North American] *DC* 1908–1966; *W3*; *DARE* 1928–1969; *DA*. box supper: *DA*, *WNW*.

boxty
Noun. Rare.
   Bread made of grated raw potatoes and flour.
   A potato bread (II 098). A bread like bannock (O).

[From Irish] *EDD* 1874–1890; *OEDS* 1880–1969; *ESI*.

boxy
Adjective.
   Of wood, tough, gnarled, or crooked (O).

[Probably from Newfoundland] *DNE* 1915–1965.

breachy
Adjective. Also spelled and pronounced **breacy.**

   1. Of livestock, apt to breach fences and other barriers.

Most farms had at least one animal that refused to respect man-made barriers. ... Such an animal was usually fitted out with a wooden yoke. ... Another method of foiling breachy stock was to hang a board or a burlap sack in front of the eyes of the offending beast. Either remedy would usually keep cattle or sheep within their proper pasture (KNOX, GEORGE, *Island Fences*, 1980, 25). But never a word of a quarrel / Have we had in many a year; / Except when his garden patch was tramped / By a breachy beast of a steer (ROGERS, WEBSTER, *Abegweit and Other Poems*, n.d., 13).

2. Of a wife, unfaithful or ungovernable.

Now, when Crapaud was young, I knew a young man who fell in love with a strange, good-looking girl. He married her without courtship, and after a short time, he could not keep her at home. She strayed away at nights from him. His friends pitied him and tried to get her back, but she said no. She wanted to be a free girl again. They both wanted to be parted forever. The law at this time was to advertise a breacy wife and put a halter on her neck and lead her to town to the Market Square, and sell her by public auction. He sold his wife and got ten shillings and some goods for her (AUTUMN, GENE, *My Life in Crapaud*, 1929, 2).

[From English] *DARE* 1780–1969; *DAE*; *W3*; *OED*; *OEDS*; *EDD*.

bread and point
Also **bread and think**. See **potatoes and point**.

breeze
Noun.

A gale at sea.

The captain would come fored and say boys give her more cable, we are going to have a breeze of wind. When you would think it could blow no harder (HEMPHILL, JOHN, *Some of My Experiences at Sea, Part One*, 1982, 29–30). A fair breeze is really bad weather – not fit to take a boat out in (II 095).

[North American] *DARE* 1842–1945; *DJE*; *DBE*. *breeze up*: *WGUS* 'Along the Atlantic coast, from New Brunswick to Cape Fear in North Carolina, the wind is said to *breeze up*, *breeze on* (less commonly simply to *breeze*) when it gets stronger. This is one of a number of seafaring terms that are current the full length of the Atlantic coast but known only to those who live within easy reach of the sea'; *SSPB* 'a way of saying that the wind is rising. According to Ruth Lewis

("Why did you say that?", *Nova Scotia Historical Quarterly*, Dec., 1980) it was used as early as 1752 in Washington's diaries and widely used in New England in the 1800's and in England'; *DNE*; *DAE*; *W3*; *OED*; *FW*; *WNW*.

bridle
Noun. Compare **haul-up**, **snood**.

A length of rope secured to two sides of a lobster trap, to which a second rope or 'snood' is attached for hauling.

The bridle is the piece that goes from one 'bow' to the other 'bow' and then the 'snood' attaches on to the 'backline' (S 5).

W3 'a length of rope or cable with the ends secured to different parts or sides of an object (as a ship) and with a second rope or cable attached to the bight to which the force for hauling, lifting, securing is applied.'

brogue
Transitive verb. Archaic. Compare **broguer**, **broguing**.

To puncture and re-solder (a hot can of lobster meat), to release steam believed to contain contamination.

I filled a can and didn't brogue it and laid it up on a beam in the cookhouse and it stayed there from that summer and all winter until the next summer; and when the wardens came over I said, 'Look, I got a can that I didn't brogue, and there was no need of "broguing".' And the can was rusty, you know. It laid there all that time, over a year, I think. And I went in and got the can and opened it and the meat was just as bright and nice as ever was. I never 'brogued' a can after. I guess I was the first that stopped, I think. Some of them 'brogued' for a year after, maybe. All that work for nothin'! They didn't know the difference (MORRISON, CLINTON, *Along the North Shore: A Social History of Township 11, P.E.I. 1965–1982*, 1983, 74).

[From Scottish] *brogue hole*: *W3* 'a vent in a tin can for the escape of steam and air while in an autoclave.' *Brog*: *OED* 'To prick, prod; to push an awl through.'

broguer
Noun. Compare **brogue**, **broguing**.

A worker in a lobster cannery who 'brogues,' or punctures cans of lobster meat.

The 'broguing' process was carried out by two workers, one to puncture the tins and one to resolder them. Vernon H. Boyle of

Conway recalled that 'broguers' such as 'Dry' Hart from Alberton and Danny Inglis from Conway could 'brogue' as many as twenty-eight cases of lobster in sixteen hours depending upon the size of the cans being used (MORRISON, CLINTON, *Along the North Shore: A Social History of Township 11, P.E.I. 1765–1982*, 1983, 74).

[From Scottish.]

broguing
Verbal noun. Compare **brogue, broguer**.
   The process of puncturing and re-soldering a hot can of lobster meat, to release steam believed to contain contamination.
   'Broguing' began early in the history of lobster packing. There were arguments that some of the 'flux' from soldering the tins during the sealing process contaminated the contents and that 'broguing' released the pent-up gaseous contaminate after the can had been partly 'bathed.' But the most logical reason for 'broguing' undoubtedly resulted from the fact that frequently excessive quantities of fresh lobsters were landed, especially during the beginning of the season, and often the meat became stale before it could be canned. 'Broguing' released the inside pressure from the hot, 'bathed' cans, resulting from expanding gases which were believed to contain bacterial contamination. 'Broguing' released these gases and when the contents of the can cooled a partial vacuum was created which tended to preserve the meat better over an extended period of time (MORRISON, CLINTON, *Along the North Shore: A Social History of Township 11, P.E.I. 1765–1982*, 1983, 74). They used to punch a little hole in the can with a wooden mallet with a nail in the end and then resolder the can after the moisture came out. This is what was known as 'broguing' (S 6).

[From Scottish.]

brook, the
See **puddle**.

brookie
Noun.
   A brook trout.
   'I see you've had good luck, my boy – a catch to brag about! / Red fins, green sides with polka dots – looks like a mess of trout.' / 'Yes sir, they're Island brookies,' was my

prompt and proud reply. / 'I got them all on worms. Can't afford to use a fly' (DOCKERTY, MALCOLM, *Rhymed Reminiscences of a Pathologist: His Life's Story*, 1980, 12). The mile and a half stretch from Alley's Bridge to Beaton's Dam and back was full of thrills for me, if not for my dad. We had about a dozen sea-run brookies on my 'gad' as we arrived back at the bridge (DOCKERTY, MALCOLM, *Streamside Reminiscences: Selected Instant Replays*, 1981, 5). Hundreds of years ago, a giant spruce tree had blown over into its deepest end, and underneath its still preserved stubs of branches, one could see, on a clear day, dozens of big brookies cooling themselves off in its 50-degree water. An old cow trail, a quarter of a mile long, led down from my father's back pasture to the big spring, and standing in one spot near the base of the ancient windfall, one could catch a line of trout in an hour without moving (*ibid*, 46).

[North American] *DC* 'Informal' 1958–1963; *DARE*; *DAS. brook*: W3 'brook trout.'

buck, the
Noun phrase. \book\. Rare.
   A fit of bad temper.
   I went to see Malcolm Madison today but when I asked his wife where he was she told me Malcolm took the buck today. Apparently Malcolm sat on the edge of a washtub (wooden, three feet across) and of course the tub tipped and he fell into the water. Well then, he took the buck (II 041).

[From English] *EDD* 'Wm. Let's hev nin o' thi buck, but gang on wi' thi wark.'

buggerlugs
Noun. Informal. Occasional generally, but infrequent in Egmont and Charlotte-town; unattested under thirty.
   An insult, sometimes affectionate, sometimes contemptuous.
   It's a swear word, an epithet. You don't necessarily like the person you say it to (II 002). You call anybody in a friendly or familiar way a buggerlug (II 003). Look at old buggerlugs going by (II 010). Almost an endearment, 'Little buggerlugs' (II 027). Not someone of high standing, a lay-about (II 055).

*The ambiguity in this term is similar to that in standard *bugger*.
DSUE.

bull trawl
See **dog trawl**.

bummer
Noun. Also **bottle lamb**.

A motherless lamb that is raised by hand.

Chester is feeding the lambs by hand because their own mother could not feed her triplets. Gigi, Baba and Sooty became orphans, often called 'bottle lambs' or 'bummers'; but now they consider Chester their mother. They would follow him around all day if he didn't keep them penned (CLIMO, LINDEE, *Chester's Barn*, 1982, 23). The bummer was usually the result of a triple birth. The mother could only accommodate two at one time so rather than share, she would abandon one. The responsibility of feeding the bummer usually fell on a child in the family and it was a pleasure to have your very own pet (P2–084).

[From English] *DARE* 'west of Missip R' 1931–1968. *bottle lamb*: *EDD* 'Used with regard to lambs, and sometimes, though rarely, to foals'; *DARE*.

bunch
Noun. Compare **dog trawl, dump**.

A group of lobster traps tied to the same 'backline.'

The traps were set out four to a bunch, usually in a straight line or a T formation (PRINCE EDWARD ISLAND, DEPARTMENT OF FISHERIES, *Offshore Lobster: Technical Report 175*, 1975, 1975, 3). A bunch of traps is the number of traps on one 'backline,' collectively. Used in phrases such as 'three-trap bunch,' 'twelve-trap bunch,' 'fishing a bunch,' 'hauling a bunch' (MACMILLAN, JANET, *The Language of Lobster Fishing*, 1985, 12). Hauling one bunch or two bunches is the same as hauling dumps or dog trawls (S 5).

*The terms *bunch*, *dog trawl*, and *dump* are synonymous, but vary from port to port.

bunk
Noun. Frequent in Egmont, rare elsewhere; especially older, less educated.

1. A crossbeam on a lumbering sled that takes the weight of the logs.

My team started getting very restless and I didn't know what was wrong with them. The voice in the woods was getting nearer and nearer, and the team was getting more and more hard to hold. As I unloaded the last log the team bolted and I just had time to jump onto the hind sled. As I landed on the bunk of the bob, I looked back and saw the yay-ho just coming out of the woods. I'll never forget it. It

was about eight feet tall, covered with long black hair, but it did not have the features of an ape: it had the features, feet and hands of a man (GREEN, ALICE, *Footprints on the Sands of Time*, 1980, 260). It's part of sled for hauling lumber (II 006). Pieces of wood placed on a sleigh to keep it from sinking in the snow (O).

2. A lumbering sled with such crossbeams. Also **bunk sleigh, bunk sled**. Compare **double runner**[2].

They used a double sleigh for lumbering. They threw the logs into the bunk (II 003). A bunk sleigh was homemade (II 055). There are two sets of runners (II 062). Of course I should have told you before he had bob sleighs, of course, to haul these logs, and you have to extend them. There were two sleds – you know what they're like – what they call a fore and back bunk, and they had to extend them possibly ten or twelve feet (T I14).

[From American] *DA* 1770–1907; *DAE*; *DARE*; *OED*; *W3*; *DNE*.

bunyan
Noun. Rare.

1. A suckling pig.

As a boy I imagined that all who spoke English called a suckling pig a 'bunyan' as we did. When I discovered that it was restricted to certain parts of the Island, I began to seek for its origin, but with little success. I did come across the word 'bonyeen' in the *Irish Folklore Journal*, and with that hint I discovered that the Gaelic for a suckling pig was something like 'bonaheen,' which very easily fell into English 'bunyan.' So the Gaelic left its trace in many ways, more than I can measure (CAMPBELL, ALPHONSUS, *The Heritage of the Highland Scots in P.E.I.*, 1975, 53). The mother pig and bunyan (I 095).

2. An unweaned baby.

An unweaned baby. 'Look at the little bunyan' (I 033).

*Informal indications are that this word is chiefly found in the eastern part of the Island among older, rural residents. In the Common Word Survey *bunyan* was chosen over *piglet* or *weaner* by 3% of informants.
[From Irish Gaelic via Irish] *banbh*: *IED* 'a young pig; a suckling pig.'

buoy line
Noun. \'bo͞o-ē\.

A rope attaching a buoy to one end of a line of set lobster traps.

To both ends of each trawl is attached a stone 'kellog' or anchor; and about twenty fathoms from the anchor a buoy line, to which is attached a buoy, is fastened to the backline (*Running the Lines*, April 25, 1903, 2). We have a buoy line on each end of the trapline with a buoy on each end. We use twenty to twenty-five fathoms of unsinkable rope (S 4). The buoy line is the section between the first trap and the buoy itself (S 5).

DNE 'rope leading from float to net.'

bush
Transitive verb.
To mark a safe road across (winter ice) with bushes or small trees set at intervals.

Vickerson bushing ice up river and some are continuing it down (ROSS, DAVID, *The David Ross Diary*, 1838, February 5). We drove along the frozen surface of a river, our track 'bushed,' as it is called, with pine-branches on either side, placed at equal intervals, to denote the safe portions of the ice (SLEIGH, B.W.A., *Pine Forests and Hacmatack Clearings; or Travel, Life, and Adventure, in the British North American Provinces*, 1853, 142). No. 1399, Charles Haszard, 3£ 10s od being his account for bushing the ice from Gallas Point to Belle Vue (PRINCE EDWARD ISLAND, *P.E.I. Legislative Assembly Journal* 1865, Appendix L). Dear Sir as there is a grate deal of traveling don on the ice and it and it [sic] wants to be bushed as it as it [sic] is dangerous if it is not bushed it can be dun for a bout six dollars let me know if I will have it dun please send word by return of mail Yours, Wm McArthur road master (PRINCE EDWARD ISLAND, ROADS CORRESPONDENCE, *Letters. 1913*, Record Group 11, 1912, December 30). And always, along the well-bushed roads across the vast expanse of frozen harbour and bays, heavy farm-sleighs loaded with produce or trim 'cutters' with the care-free jingle of bells were travelling to and from the town (WARREN, EVANGELINE, *Andy the Milkman*, 1957, 22). In placing the trees in the ice, one man would chop a small hole through the ice, then step off sixty yards, while the man with the loads of bushes would put a bush in the hole, and so on, until the job was finished. The river was laid off in zones, so quite a number of men got contracts. This work was known as 'bushing' the ice. The bushes were to guide people in case of a storm or at night, as there were many 'spring holes,' that a man or horse could drop into. ... The bushing of the ice was paid for by the P.E.I. goverment (MACDOUGALL, ARLENE, and VIOLET MACEACHERN, *The Banks of the Elliott*, 1973, 51–52). Tne river in winter was a convenient but often dangerous passage

of transportation and a very important precautionary measure after the ice formed was marking a safe route by setting small evergreen trees into the ice. This was called 'bushing the ice' and if it was not done properly a grave danger existed because of areas of thin ice where large beds of mussel mud, rising beneath the surface, kept the ice from forming to a safe thickness (PAYNTER, RUTH, *From the Top of the Hill: The History of an Island Community*, 1977, 29). I started bushing the ice as a boy. I'd go with my father, best part of 75–80 years ago. We got paid around $2 a mile. It was about one mile across Salutation Cove and from there to Summerside about three miles. We cut the spruce trees about six feet high and cut a little hole through the ice so the water would come up and freeze the bush in solid: between 50 and 60 yards apart. If you got in a storm you could get to one bush and then go a piece and see another bush (STEWART, DEBORAH and DAVID, *Winter Travel*, 1979, 19). In the following year occurred the tragedy of the Robins family, who, returning to Bedeque frem a visit in Summerside over the unbushed ice, and bewildered by falling snow, drove into an opening at the mouth of the harbour (MAC-LEOD, ADA, *Roads to Summerside: The Story of Early Summerside and the Surrounding Area*, 1980, 42–43). I got on the road and left George-town; the ice was bushed you know, and when you left Georgetown you could just see the first one but you couldn't see the next one (T B8).

[Canadian] *DC*; *W3*; *GCD*.

busker
Noun.
An energetic, hard-working woman (O).

DNE 'A vigorous, energetic man.'

buss
Noun. \boos\. Also spelled **boos**, **boose**. Often used with children. Infrequent except rare in Charlottetown.
1. The mouth of an animal or person.
A number of words we used were taken from the Gaelic and changed a bit. ... The farmers will still refer to the mouth of an animal as a 'boos.' This is a Scotch Gaelic word, and there is a Gaelic turn of phrase, 'Tha bus mor aige' – literally, 'There is a big boos at him (or to him).' The word was transferred to a sulky expression: 'He had a big boos on' (CAMPBELL, ALPHONSUS, *The Heritage of the Highland Scot in Prince Edward Island*, 1984, 5).

2. A sulky look or pursing of the mouth.

Get that buss off you (I 048). You've got an awful buss on you (I 052). Get that buss off your face (I 116).

[From Scottish Gaelic via Scottish] SND '...to have a buss on one, "to be disappointed and slightly sulky in consequence"'; EDD; DARE. bus: GED 'pouting of the lips in anger'; DGL. busach: PEDGL 'pouting-lipped, sulky.'

but

Adverb, when used at the end of a sentence.

All things considered; though, however.

'We had a very good time but,' means in spite of, or clear of that, or all things considered (R 20). He lost the lantern in the snowstorm. He found it in the spring. It was out but (R 27). We had a good time but (O).

*The more standard use of *but* in sentence-final position suggests that the speaker could say more but tactfully will not: 'John is all right but ...' EDD; DAC; DSUE.

button

Noun.

See second quotation.

A door or hatch, hinged with leather and kept shut with a wooden button, is built into the trap to allow the fisherman to remove his catch (MORRISON, CLINTON, *Along the North Shore: A Social History of Township 11, P.E.I. 1765–1982*, 1983, 77). This is used to hold a door shut. You take a piece of wood and drive a nail through the middle of it and when the door closes you put the thing down. This is a small piece of wood that rotates on the nail and falls into place. The little square piece of wood is the button (O).

W3.

by times

Prepositional phrase. Also spelled and pronounced **betimes**. Frequent generally, but infrequent in Summerside; especially rural, male.

From time to time; occasionally.

'What about Milton and Shakespeare? And the poets of the Bible? They tell me Milton could not get along with his wife, and Shakespeare was no more than respectable by times' (MONTGOMERY, LUCY MAUD, *Rainbow Valley*, 1923, 77).

The day had been cloudy by times but now the sun suddenly came out and performed its usual miracle (MONTGOMERY, LUCY MAUD, *A Tangled Web*, [1931], 268). Tue. 19. Warm day, I am in bed had Dr. Moyse to see me my temperature is over 102. ... Sat. 23. I am up by times (CAIRNS, SCOTT, *Diary: January 1, 1932–March 31, 1939*, April, 1938). But don't think the winter days were all work and no pleasure. Apart from a bit of loneliness by times, Andy was really enjoying his new experience (WARREN, EVANGELINE, *Andy the Milkman*, 1957, 58). It would get pretty cold by times but we were dressed warm and we were young and active and kept ourselves warm (CAMPBELL, FRANK, *As the Fella Says ...*, 1983, 75).

*This usage is reported from Lunenburg County, Nova Scotia. Historically, *by times* is an alternate of *betimes* (DARE).
[From British and Irish] OED 'Obs'; EDD; SND 1824; DARE 1841.

C

cailleach

Noun. \'kāl-yək\.

An old woman; also a hag or crone.

'Certainly Morag,' said Joseph, 'we can talk as I walk you home, lest a bear gets you.' 'Oh Joseph, a wee bit of humor after a long day is as refreshing as the heather in bloom, and what may I ask would a bear do with an old cailleach like me now?' 'Sorry Morag, I don't quite follow.' 'Oh, forgive me, my lad, the Gaelic tongue is a habit hard to break. Cailleach is an old woman.' 'It's been my experience, Morag, that bears are not inclined to ask your age before they attack' (MILLIGAN, DORIS, *Shipwreck: A Novelette*, 1983, 12).

[From Irish and Scottish Gaelic via Irish and Scottish] OED; W3; EDD; SND; ESI; GED; IED; DGL; PEDGL.

cake bread

Noun. Common in Egmont, occasional in Summerside and Malpeque, infrequent in Charlottetown and Cardigan; especially middle-aged and older.

Biscuit bread resembling bannock, leavened with baking powder or soda rather than yeast, and baked in cakes.

This is also called baking powder bread. Less shortening than in biscuits. It is flat like a cake. Sometimes made with sour or buttermilk. Less

rich than a biscuit. It can also be called buttermilk bannock (II 009). Sort of a bannock, like
biscuit dough not cut out (II 020). Cake bread is
bannock dressed up a little with sugar and
raisins (II 021). My father lived on cakebread (II
056). Biscuit dough all in one. People also called
it a bannock. They fed it to their minks (II 057).
My mother-in-law used to make it, one loaf at a
time. It's higher than bannock and has eggs in
it. Sort of yellow-ish. Like a coarse pound cake
but not sweet (II 097). My grandfather used this
term for biscuits (O).

[From British] *OED* 1377–1882; *W3* 'now dial. Brit';
EDD. *cake*: *SND* 'Specifically used in Sc.) an oatcake.
Gen. used in *pl*. Also *attrib.* with *breid*. 1715–1924. …
In phrs.: (1) *cyaks o' breid*, oat-cakes'; *COD*. *cake of
bread*: *DNE* 'hard, rounded, dry ship's biscuit' 1772–
1955.

cake ice
See **ice-cake**.

calm out
Intransitive phrasal verb. Often \kam\.
**Of the wind or the sea, to quieten,
become less rough.**
I think she's going to calm out (O).

canner
Noun. Compare **market, michaud, short**.
**A small but legal-sized lobster, used for
canning.**
In some areas the legal-sized lobsters are
divided into two categories – the 'canners,'
about seven to nine inches long which are
canned or prepared as chilled, fresh lobster
meat, and the 'markets' (WILDER, D.G., *Canada's
Lobster Fishery*, 1957, 16). Fishermen can't understand the difference in market lobsters
where they are shipped to market live – a
pound is a pound. If the difference in canners is
small, perhaps the packers will be embarrassed
into paying a better price (*The Guardian*, May
21, 1977, 1). A canner is a lobster that measures
2 1/2–3 3/16 from the eye to the end of the body
(MACMILLAN, JANET, 'The Language of Lobster
Fishing,' 1985, 13). A canner is the smaller
lobster in the carapace measurement system
(S 4). A canner is a small lobster between the
short and market size (S 6).

OEDS 'A beast fit only for canning. Chiefly U.S.'
1880–1892; *DA*; *DAE*.

card
Transitive verb. Also **card out**. Frequent in

Egmont and Summerside, infrequent elsewhere; unattested under thirty. Compare
carding, read, skivver.
To scold or criticize.
After Mary's death, one of her sisters came to
keep house for Larry, and while Larry had
thought a great deal of his wife, he did not care
for her sister at all. Charlie Gorman remembers
a letter that Larry wrote home to his sister Ellen
in which he described the woman and his
troubles with her. 'I wish I had that letter now,'
he said. 'Everybody was laughing over it, it was
so comical. He really carded her to a peak' (IVES,
EDWARD, *Larry Gorman: The Man Who Made the
Songs*, [1964], 84).

[From Scottish and northern English] *OED*; *EDD*
1859; *EDSL*.

carding
Noun. Common in Egmont and Summerside, frequent in Malpeque and Cardigan,
infrequent in Charlottetown; significantly
older. Compare **card, raking[2], reading**.
A scolding.
They come right in and say, you know, give
you an awful carding that you won't give them
any work (T M17). You jaw a fella right hard – a
good carding or raking (P1 010). Give him hell.
Like, the wife gave him an awful carding when
he got home (P1 119). She is giving him a
carding (P1 079).

[From Scottish and northern English] *EDD*; *EDSL*.
cardail: *IED* 'a scolding.'

cat
Noun, usually in phrase **cat of gin**. Rare.
Compare **kitten**.
A quart container (O).

DSUE 'a quart pot'; *EDD* 'Lon. slang' 1851.

cat and clay
Noun phrase. Also **cob and clay**. Archaic.
Compare **cob**.
**1. Straw and clay worked together and
laid on a wooden frame to make a primitive chimney.**
The chimney or fireplace was built of stones
… and the remainder of the flue was constructed of a frame-work of sticks of the same
shape as the chimneys now in use. Each side
had battens across it like rungs of a ladder and
the spaces between these battens were filled

with straw and clay mortar. These chimneys
were called cat and clay or cob chimneys
(ALLEY, JUDGE, *Prince Edward Island 100 Years
Ago*, [1890?], 8). Stone fireplaces for heating
and cooking had chimneys made of 'cat-and-
clay' on frames of wood (LEARD, GEORGE, *Historic Bedeque: The Loyalists at Work and Worship in
Prince Edward Island*, 1948, 10). The upper
portion of the chimney was probably constructed of a mixture of wood and clay mixed with
straw and known in 'the old country' as 'cat
and clay.' A story has been passed down to the
author about the time Robert's brother, Hugh,
constructed his first chimney for his house in
this manner about 1845. Hugh's proud young
bride, Johannah, exclaimed with satisfaction:
'You n'er were beat!' However, several weeks
later when the clay and wood had thoroughly
dried Hugh's handiwork contained flaws
which caused the chimney to catch on fire. Not
wishing to indicate any lack of faith in her
young husband Johannah loudly bemoaned:
'tis a trap from the devil to burn the house!'
(MORRISON, CLINTON, *Emigrant from the Highlands: Robert W. Morrison, Sr. and His Descendants*, 1978, 57). The first schoolhouses were
little log huts without any floor, except the
native earth. For a chimney two logs standing
upright … about three feet apart, served as
jambs between which the fire was built. … On
top of these perpendicular logs of about four
feet in height was constructed cob and clay
work, namely; a mixture of mud and ferns
between sticks, with the ends of each crossing
those of the other like the walls of a log house
(SAGE, MARY, *The Lord Selkirk Settlers in Belfast,
Prince Edward Island*, [1973], 21).

**2. Straw and clay worked together to
form a primitive house wall.**

Two long, low houses built of clay (commonly
called cat and clay houses) extended from
Mrs. Findley's corner west along Kent Street.
The walls were thick and bore the appearance
of some of the rude structures which existed in
England in the time of the Druids (TANTON,
JOHN, *Memories of the Past – Continued*, 1899,
351).

[From Irish and Scottish and northern English] *DC*
'Obs.'; *OED*; *W3*; *EDD*; *SND*; *DARE*; *DAE*; *ESI*;
DOST 'of obscure origin.'

catawampus
Adverb. \‚ka-tə-'wahmp-əs\. Humorous.
Askew, out of order.
No, no, calm yourself, Mrs. Doctor, dear.
Something has happened, though. Dear me,

everything has gone catawampus this week. I
spoiled the bread, as you know too well – I
scorched the doctor's best shirt bosom – and I
broke your big platter … (MONTGOMERY, LUCY
MAUD, *Anne's House of Dreams*, 1917, 308).
Knitting is something you can do, even when
your heart is going like a trip-hammer and
the pit of your stomach feels all gone and your
thoughts are catawampus … (MONTGOMERY,
LUCY MAUD, *Rilla of Ingleside*, [1920], 84).

*OED calls this word 'A humorous formation, the
origin of which is lost,' and 'A high-sounding
word with no very definite meaning.'
[North American] *OED*; *OEDS*; *DARE*; *DA*; *DAE*.

cat ice
Noun. Compare **double ice, top ice.**
**Synonym for 'shell ice²': A thin layer of
ice, under which the water has retreated.**
Cat ice is only fit for a cat to walk on (C 118).

OED 1884; *EDD*; *W3*; *DARE* 1950–1979; *COD*.

cat spruce
Noun. Compare **line tree, pasture spruce.**
The white spruce (O).

[North American] *DC*; *W3*; *DARE* 1894–1966; *DA*; *ML*
'A spruce with attractive bluish tinge, but having
an odor suggesting a kitty pan. … Botanically it's the
white spruce. … Sometimes called a skunk spruce';
SSPB 'short scrub evergreen growing along shore
where taller trees can't survive. – Liverpool. See also
mink spruce. People in Cape Sable Island say the
name *cat spruce* was applied because if you "bring one
into the house for a Christmas tree, in a few days it'll
smell like you've let a tomcat in!"'; *DAE* 'The black or
the hemlock spruce.'

caubeen
Noun. \kah-'bēn\.
A man's hat or cap.
Sometimes a caubeen was passed around at
Irish parties in order to give a donation to the
piper, who played on the flute (R 9).

[From Irish Gaelic via Irish] *OED* 1831–1874; *EDD*;
W3; *DNE*; *IED*.

ceilidh
Noun. \'kā-lē\ Also spelled **calidh, caly,
cedilliah, kalee, kaylee, kaylie.** Frequent
in Charlottetown and Cardigan, occasional
in Egmont and Summerside, infrequent in
Malpeque; significantly older. Compare
ceilidh (verb).

1. A social gathering for traditional Irish or Scottish music, storytelling, or dancing.

We should expect then that Lawrence Doyle's songs and the satirical and local pieces of others would be more likely to be sung in the informal context of the ceilidh, the 'time,' the 'spree,' the 'frolic,' than in the concert with its suggestions of 'culture' (IVES, EDWARD, *Lawrence Doyle: The Farmer Poet of Prince Edward Island*, 1971, 235). The Ceilidhs were indeed an important institution, cementing friendship and goodwill, joining together old and young with mutual respect and happiness all centered on a community social structure of great significance (SHAW, WALTER, *Tell Me the Tales*, 1975, 43). In the evenings, as they gathered together for a 'cedilliah' (pronounced kaley) many were the tales that were told of the dear days of their childhood in Scotland. Stories of strange happenings in the old land, doubtless exagerrated by many repetitions and guaranteed to give the listener a shiver up the back, were told as they sat around the chimney enjoying the 'cup of tea' poured by the kind hostess (MACDONALD, BERTHA, *Through All the Days Gone By*, [1983?], 21). As mentioned earlier when the first settlers arrived their only entertainment was visiting one another, telling stories or singing songs they brought with them from the old country. In the Scottish and Irish districts a visit was called a Ceilidh (pronounced 'caley') (PENDERGAST, JAMES, and GERTRUDE PENDERGAST, *Folklore Prince Edward Island*, [1974], 16).

2. A casual evening visit.

'That's what they call visiting to another person's house,' Jack Farrell said. 'They'd say that was going on a kaylee' (IVES, EDWARD, *Lawrence Doyle: The Farmer Poet of Prince Edward Island*, 1971, 230). Fluent in Gaelic, odd words fell naturally, among the studied English she spoke. They talked of the farming, and as well, of current interests in the community, of mutual friends and relatives. Then after what she chose to call her 'wee ceilidh,' she would take her leave, always blessing Mother, and all, at parting, and promising to 'come over the way again, before the leaves will fall' (DIXON, MARGARET, *Going Home: An Autobiography*, 1979, 116). There was also a 'ceilidh' (kaylie) when neighbors dropped in of an evening, made a semi-circle in front of the blazing logs on the hearth, recited their several experiences, regaled the latest gossip and foreign news (MACFADYEN, JEAN, *For the Sake of the Record*, n.d., 2). I remember hearing the word ceilidh (kaylie)

for the first time during those summers in Kinkora. It is a Gaelic word and was used to refer to any outing or social affair. The question, for instance, might be asked, are you going on a ceilidh tonight? It was used recently as the title for a television program emanating from Cape Breton Island (MURPHY, ELMER, *A Newspaperman Remembers*, [1980?], 108). Make your ceilidh means to stay awhile (I 020). Any visit – 'I'm going on a ceilidh to see some neighbors' (I 110).

*This word has been used since the beginning of settlement on Prince Edward Island for almost any social gathering from a quick visit to a planned entertainment. The division into senses here is somewhat arbitrary. Constance Cullen, in 'Dialect Research on Prince Edward Island,' 1971, finds *ceilidh* better known in Scottish-settled Belfast than in three other communities of different backgrounds. The word has been popularized by television 'ceilidhs,' beginning in Cape Breton in 1958.
[From Irish and Scottish Gaelic via Irish and Scottish] OEDS 1875–1965; SND; W3; DGL; GED; PEDGL; IED; ESI; GCD; COD.

ceilidh

Verb, usually intransitive. \'kā-lē\. Also spelled **calidh**, **kalee**. Compare **ceilidh** (noun).

To visit.

The agricultural history of Prince Edward Island naturally divides itself into three periods. In the first place there is the period of settlement coming down to 1850. ... Roads were laid out, schools opened, and churches erected. The wants of the farmer were few, and the means of supplying them limited in proportion. The neighbour kaleeing with neighbour, of a winter evening, enjoying a friendly chat before the fire of blazing logs; the young men and maidens combining the stumping and spinning 'frolics' in the summer, and the thickening 'frolic' in the early winter, constituted the social enjoyment of the people (FERGUSON, DONALD, *Agricultural Education: A Lecture, Delivered before the Young Men's Christian Association*, 1884, 27). Cloudy, cold – when I went to see the cattle this morn the horses were no where to be found. I guess they are off calidhing (LAMONT, MURDOCK, *Diary, 1885–1888*, Dec. 1, 1885). During the long winter evenings young and old gathered in neighboring homes to 'ceilidh,' drawn by the genial atmosphere that pervades certain homes in every community. There they told stories and sang folk songs. These were in Gaelic (MACQUEEN, MALCOLM, *Skye Pioneers and 'The Island,'* 1929, 32). Since there were no automobiles,

TV's or even radios for many years, people often 'went ceilidhing.' This involved social visits with the neighbors complemented with musical entertainment. Whole families would join together in conversation and laughter. They would share news, tell stories, play games, perform on musical instruments and enjoy dancing (MORRIS, MARY, *The Way It Was: A Brief Social History of the Boughton River Area 1890–1930*, 1981, n. pag.). Oh she's out ceilidhing – she's out calling on a neighbor (I 001). To go ceilidhing was to visit neighbors. You'd go one night and they'd come back another. One visit per night (I 098). There'd always be someone coming. Your relatives would be coming and the neighbors, they'd arrive, you know, beating the cans and if they came here some night to ceilidh you, you'd have to pay the whistler (T B14). Years ago there was more people and they came in visiting or ceilidhing; that was a Scotch name. You know, they visited more (T M134).

*See notes for *ceilidh* (noun).
[From Irish and Scottish Gaelic via Irish and Scottish.]

centre cake
Noun.
A decorated cake, often a fruit-cake, placed as the centrepiece of a public supper, and sometimes auctioned off at the end.
Usually a centre cake is a fruit cake decorated and placed on a pedestal cake plate in the centre of a table. When outdoor church suppers were held there would be several of these cakes at various places on a long table. After the supper was over these cakes would be auctioned off and proceeds went for church work (R 7). Sometimes it was a dummy cake like at a wedding. It remains uncut. The fruit cake is sliced and wrapped beforehand to be passed around (R 12). The main cake, the real show piece (R 20).

centre head
Noun. Also **big head, funnel head, parlour head**. Compare **head** (noun).
The funnel of twine mesh in a lobster trap that separates the first chamber the lobster enters, or 'kitchen,' from the second or 'parlour.'
The centre head is the funnel shaped mesh found in the middle of the trap which leads the lobster into the back of the trap where he cannot escape (MACMILLAN, JANET, *The Lan-*

guage of Lobster Fishing, 1985, 13). A centre head is the one with the funnel in and it is up high on a slant, and the lobster drops through and can't get out (S 4). What we call the big head or the centre head is the head that separates the 'kitchen' end and the 'parlour' (S 5).

chain sweep
Noun. Compare **teeth sweep**.
In scallop fishing, a net made of chain links, dragged along the sea bottom by boat.
Chain sweep: a bag made of rings (chain links) that drags behind the boat and scoops up the ground fish or scallops. This type is usually used in rocky bottomed areas (KENNEDY, LIBBY, *A Visitor's Guide to the Language of the Wharf*, 1985, 8). Those here scallop fishermen use chain sweeps. I believe it is the links they make the bags with (S 13).

chamberdish
Noun. Also **dish**. Polite. Frequent in Egmont and Summerside, infrequent in Malpeque and Cardigan, rare in Charlottetown; especially older, female. Compare **charlie, dish², thunderjug, thundermug**.
A chamber-pot.
A chamberdish can be made of the finest pottery (II 002). The dish (II 009). We used this term when there was company around (II 066). She came down to the store and bought a chamberdish (O).

chamberwork
Noun. Infrequent generally, but rare in Egmont and Summerside; especially rural, senior.
The work of a chambermaid; also ordinary housework around bedrooms.
I'm tired of this goddamned chamberwork (I 033). Making beds and cleaning bedrooms (O). Chambermaids clean in chambers. They do chamberwork (O).

OED 1621–1884; *DARE* 1870–1950; *DAE*.

charlie
Noun. Also **charlie pot**. Informal. Occasional generally, but infrequent in Cardigan, rare in Charlottetown; especially older. Compare **chamberdish, dish², thunderjug, thundermug**.
A chamber-pot.

This word comes from World War Two. We never use it around home (II 003). Another name for a chamberpot (O). Charlie's under the bed (O).

DARE 1968.

charming likely
Adjective phrase. Sometimes sarcastic.
   Very likely; certain.
   I've heard the saying for something that could happen, something that you're pleased about (P2 044). This was used when the person wanted to emphasize that the event certainly did happen without any doubt (P2 084).

*One informant (P2 066) called the usage both 'sarcastic' and 'a woman's expression.'

chiard
See **rapure**.

chocolates
Plural noun, usually in phrase **to get chocolates**. Informal. Occasional in Egmont, rare elsewhere. Compare **fudge** (noun and verb).
   A severe scolding; occasionally a beating.
   To get chocolates means to get hell (P1-021). To get chocolates means you'd be in for a rough time from your parents for doing something wrong. Same as a bawling out or getting 'fudge' (P1-036). He's sure to get chocolates. More like a licking (P1-039).

DSUE: 'chocolate without sugar, give (a person). To reprove: military' 1785–1890.

choke
Transitive verb. Occasional in Egmont, infrequent elsewhere; unattested under forty; significantly male; especially less educated. Compare **choke rope**.
   To rescue (a horse that has fallen through the ice) by choking with a rope, so that air will be trapped in the horse's lungs and it will float.
   We got her out. Choked her. They put a rope right around her neck. Pulled her out on the ice, jumped out on her feet. We took her up to Finley MacDougall's barn in Belle River there, put her in there. … Put her out on the mail the next morning, didn't bother her any (HORNBY, SUSAN, *George Young: Horsing Around*, 1981, 29–30). Digging 'mussel-mud' was a cold, hard job in the midst of winter on the open ice. And it was a dangerous job for the careless or inexperienced digger. Occasionally a hapless farmer or his struggling horse would have to be plucked from the icy water in minutes if tragedy was to be averted. A common practice on the Island for rescuing a drowning horse was to choke it with a noose while several farmers and their teams pulled the terrifed beast from the freezing water. The choking procedure caused the horse to bounce or float up and hence it was easier to extricate it from the hole in the ice (MORRISON, CLINTON, *Along the North Shore: A Social History of Township 11, P.E.I. 1765–1982*, 1983, 128). Arriving at the scene, McInnis found an argument in progress as to the best method of rescuing the horse. The majority were of the opinion that the horse should be choked, thus causing him to float and lessen the danger of plunging hooves (NICHOLSON, MRS. ANGUS, *A Story of Early Days in Belfast*, n.d., 40). People in Southport did it delivering milk in Charlottetown (II 009). You choke him. His body fills up with air and then he'll float (II 106).Once in a while in the spring of the year, when the ice'd get thin, a horse went through the ice. You know, the only way you can get a horse out of the ice – the easiest way, is to put a rope around his neck and choke him. You gotta choke him stiff and then he'd float. He'd float then – he'd come up (T B23).Commonly used on rivers with tides, especially in spring to rescue a horse from drowning (O).

[Canadian] *DC* 1820.

choke rope
Noun.
   A length of rope used in 'choking' a horse.
   You use a choke rope or one of the reins to stop a horse from struggling (II 075). You use a choke rope or plug the horse's nose with your hand (II 076).

[Canadian] *DC* 1795–1955.

chowder
Noun.
   Irish moss mixed with other matter in order to raise the weight and price.
   Chowder: blending pure Irish moss with impurities in order to get a better price for the moss. [1] In the old days, most buyers just wouldn't take any chowder. [2] Some fishermen make a moss chowder before they sell it so they will have a heavier load and get more money

(BERNARD, BLAINE, *Dictionary of Irish Moss*, 1986, n. pag.).

clapper-claw
Transitive verb.
To criticize, scold, abuse.
Now you know, Anne, I always take the ground that we women ought to stand by each other. We've got enough to endure at the hands of the men, the Lord knows, so we hadn't ought to clapper-claw one another, and it isn't often you'll find me running down another woman. But I never had much use for Rose Elliot (MONTGOMERY, LUCY MAUD, *Anne's House of Dreams*, 1917, 105–6). Ilse called me a sneaking albatross to-day. I wonder how many animals are left to call me. She never repeats the same one twice. I wish she wouldn't clapper-claw Perry so much. (Clapper-claw is a word I learned from Aunt Nancy. Very striking, I think) (MONTGOMERY, LUCY MAUD, *Emily of New Moon*, 1923, 300).

[From British] *OED* 'arch. or dial.'; *W3* 'dial Eng'; *EDD*; *SND*; *DARE* 1834–1939; *WNW*; *COD*.

clart
Noun. Rare.
A dirty, untidy person.
This is a very negative disagreeable word, a Baldwin's Road expression. Irish (I 077). 'Clart' is bits of shit on sheep's fleece. Therefore, a clart would have to be an abominable housekeeper (I 092). If you drop a dishcloth you are a dirty clart (I 110). A dirty untidy housekeeper (O).

*This word is especially used of women as housekeepers. As in I 092 above, the original British and Irish meaning is 'sticky dirt, filth.' Constance Cullen, 'Dialect Research on Prince Edward Island,' 1971, finds that 50% of her Kinkora Irish informants recognize it, and that no other informants do. The word's vitality is well attested by observers, and in the first postal survey it was chosen by 8% of those tested, over words like *sloven* and *slouch*.
[From British and Irish] *OED* 'Now Sc. and north. dial.' 1808–1877; *W3* 'dial. Brit.'; *SND* 1866–1877; *EDD*; *EDSL*.

clay road
Noun. Common.
An unpaved road, a dirt road.
Now all we want is Justice: / At least we'd like fair play. / When others drive on pavements, / Why should we drive on clay? (MACDOUGALL, ARLENE, and VIOLET MACEACHERN, *The Banks of*

the Elliott, 1973, [1935], 20). The clay roads were narrow and curving, slippery in rain, dusty in dry weather, and muddy and rutted in the Spring (INDIAN RIVER WOMEN'S INSTITUTE, *History of Indian River*, 1973, 24). Have you ever been away down in Fernwood? You leave the paved road and go down a lovely little red clay road – some people call it a dirt road, but not I. I like to think of it as part of the beautiful red earth that hasn't yet been covered with pavement (LAVIOLETTE, EMILY, *The Oyster and the Mermaid and Other Island Stories*, 1975, 11). The numerous streams, rivers and coastal waters were unquestionably the fastest and most economical form of transport by 1841 even though Island roads, though quite rough, were usually passable for most of the year with the exception of spring and summer when the rains turned the clay roads into quagmires (MORRISON, CLINTON, *Emigrant from the Highlands: Robert W. Morrison, Sr. and His Descendants*, 1978, 68). Mrs. Reid later acknowledged there are still people in the district living on clay roads, but she pledged a Progressive Conservative government re-elected to power will continue to work towards providing a hard surface highway for all (*The Guardian*, August 28, 1982, 12). This word is used even if it is more sand than clay. 'Dirt roads' came later (II 009). All roads were clay roads until they were paved (II 019). Soil is not dirt on P.E.I. – there are no dirt roads (II 101). Visitors called them 'dirt roads' (C 018).

Clay, as such, is standard, but is used here to refer to earth that is not necessarily clay-like. In the Common Word Survey, choices were: *dirt road* 50%, *clay road* 42%, *mud road* 1%, and 'other' 7%.
[North American] *DARE* 1856–1970; *DAE*.

cleaning drum
Noun. Also **drum**, **spinning drum**. Compare **drum** (verb), **drumming**, **shaker²**.
In fox ranching, a revolving cylinder in which fox pelts are cleaned.
The work is done in large factories where an expert handles every department and machinery does most of the tramping and beating. … Besides the engine or motor which supplies the power, the following apparatus is used: … cleaning drums, which, with an exhaust air arrangement, remove the sawdust or corn starch from the skins (JONES, WALTER, *Fur-Farming in Canada*, 1914, 123). Custom pelters and some ranchers have cleaning drums which tumble the pelts in slightly damp sawdust or corncob meal together with a solvent that

removes grease and generally cleans up the pelts (*Fox-Tales*, October 1982, 7). The second stage is cleansing. The pelt, skin side out, goes into a spinning drum – Thompson's is about seven feet in diameter – filled with sawdust or corn grit. Keith Milligan mixes his grit with hot water, a cleaning solvent and, to give the pelt 'a little extra sheen,' an Amway detergent. He puts 15 pelts into his drum at a time and spins them for 15 minutes (BRUCE, HARRY, *Silver into Gold: Alchemy in Action on Prince Edward Island's Booming Fox Farms*, 1985, 66). The drum is used in cleaning pelts. It is usually four feet around and about two feet deep. You put eight or ten pelts in at a time and run them so many minutes (S 8). Most farmers would not have a drum. It actually involves a rotating drum and the fur would be placed in the drum with sawdust. Fox furs would roll in a mixture of sawdust (S 9).

drum: W3 'a revolving cylinder in which hides are tumbled during processing into leather (as for washing, pickling, tanning, dyeing) or in which furs are cleaned (by tumbling with fine sawdust).'

cleaning iron
Noun. Compare **oyster knife**.
  In oyster fishing, a metal device, usually axe-shaped and often attached to 'oyster tongs,' for cleaning oysters as they are harvested.
  The best way to have cleaning irons is to fasten them right on to the tongs. Cleaning irons are just a flat piece of iron sharpened on the end that is used to clean the shells (S 14). We used to use cleaning irons. They were a device with a wooden handle with a hatchet like object on the end. You had to hit the shells to clean them off (S 15).

cleaver
See **cracker**.

clever
Adjective. Rare.
  Hospitable; agreeable, pleasant.
  Hospitable about giving things. Not scrounging every penny or expecting to be paid back (I 064). Very hospitable. People who use others well in their home (I 090).

*This sense of this word has been reported by field-workers in Nova Scotia and New England, including Henry Alexander in 'Linguistic Geography,' 1940, 8. [From British] *OED*; *W3*; *EDD*; *DARE*; *DAE*; *DSUE*; *GCD* 'Informal'; *FW*; *WNW*.

clobber
Noun. Rare. Compare **clobber** (verb).
  Mud, dirt; a piece of such.
  A clobber of dirt (I 003). 'Clobbers of mud' is very common in this area (I 056).

[From Irish and Scottish Gaelic via Irish and Scottish] *OED* 1824–1880; *SND*; *EDD*; *PEDGL*; *GED*; *IED*; *EDSL*; *DNE* 'Untidy state; sloppy or cluttered remains of some activity' 1955–1968.

clobber
Transitive and intransitive verb, sometimes with *up*. Rare. Compare **clobber** (noun).
  To muddy, dirty, make a mess.
  Don't clobber all that mud in here (I 009). Clobber up – to make a mess (I 015). He clobbered across the floor. Maybe walking across the floor in a rough way with dirty boots (I 029). Clobbering all over the floor (I 077).

*See notes for *clobber* (noun).
[From Irish and Scottish Gaelic via Irish and Scottish]

clout
Noun. Rare.
  A baby's diaper.
  'Clout' was a common word years ago (II 032). Mostly it means a diaper but any diaper or old rag. We still use dish clout for dish cloth (II 055).

*In the general sense of 'cloth' or 'rag' and in combinations like *breech clout* and *dish clout, clout* is known in many dialects.
[From British and Irish] *OED* 'Obs. or dial.' 1200–1826; *W3*; *EDD* 1790–1887; *DARE* 1733–1970; *MED. clouting diaper*: *DAE* 'Obs.' *cloutheen*: *ESI* 'Cloutheens is specially applied to little rags used with an infant.'

cloutie
Noun. \'kloo-te\ Rare.
  A plum pudding steamed in a bag.
  The bag itself of fine unbleached cotton was the cloutie. Now the pudding is called the cloutie (II 021). Now called 'pudding in a bag' (II 054).

club
See **cradle hill**.

clucker
Noun. Also **clucky**. Common generally, but occasional in Summerside and Charlottetown; significantly rural, older, male; especially less educated.

1. A hen that is ready to sit on eggs, a clucking or broody hen.

I also call a clucker a sitting hen (I 021). Setting hen. Biddy (I 098). A hen that is clucking – which means she wants to sit on eggs to bring chickens out (P2-016). Clucking hens were useless, so there were many ways to get them back into production, such as dropping them in water or turning a bucket upside down over them for a night (P1-051).

2. A person who is anxiously looking for something (O).

[From northern English] *DARE*; *WGUS. cluck hen*: W3 'a broody fowl.' *clucking hen, clocker*: *OED* 1804–1871; *DJE. cluck* (adj.): *EDD* 'Pem. Dor.' *clucky*: *DAC* 'pregnant.'

clumpet
Noun. Frequent in Egmont, rare elsewhere; significantly rural, especially older. Compare **drift ice**, **ice cake**, **raft ice**, **running ice**.

A large chunk of floating sea ice.

One day we were working along off the low snow-covered beach at Tracadie. The lagoon inside was frozen, and the 'board-ice' extended well out into the Gulf. The wind was northwest and stinging cold, and the clouds hung low and grey. Outside it was clumpets, – clumpets everywhere, coming down from the north, – and big clumpets too (HICKMAN, ALBERT, *The Sacrifice of the Shannon*, 1903, 130). Around the *Duncrieff* was piled some of the heaviest ice I had ever seen inside the Gulf. The whole body of the pack was made up of clumpets which had been driven together by the gales of the last few weeks and had been frozen into place until they formed one great field without a lane of open water in sight. The surface was so rough that it would have needed almost superhuman efforts to drag even a light broad-runnered 'ice-boat' over it, and to have taken across such boats as the *Duncrieff* had was beyond the power of men (*ibid*, 137). The pans and clumpets, white and green, were melting fast, the latter in all sorts of queer hour glass shapes, with tops like the tops of big mushrooms, breaking off, coming down with a crash and sliding *plup* into the water. Little lone clumpets were navigating around by themselves, with the ripples insulating them by washing clear over their peaks, – peaks which used to be so high that the big black ice-crusher, that now roared over them without even feeling the shock, would turn aside when they showed up ahead and try another path

(*ibid*, 278). But I was kept busy keeping up with the boat, for the crew kept going at a good clip. We worked and toiled around 'clumpets' and 'hummocks,' as they call ice where the tide has thrown it up, til I was about ready to drop, when I heard shouting and on looking up we were about to make the 'board ice' on the island side (LEARD, GEORGE, *The George Leard Files*, 1977, reel 5). Big 'junks' out at sea (II 072). You get 'moss' from them. They drag the bottom of the sea (II 098).

[From Newfoundland] *DC* 1835; *DNE*. *EDD* 'A clod of earth' Brks. Hmp.

cob
Noun. Compare **cat and clay**.

Straw and clay worked together for a building material.

The chimney or fireplace was built of stones … and the remainder of the flue was constructed of a frame-work of sticks of the same shape as the chimneys now in use. Each side had battens across it like rungs of a ladder and the spaces between these battens were filled with straw and clay mortar. These chimneys were called cat and clay or cob chimneys (ALLEY, JUDGE, *Prince Edward Island 100 Years Ago*, [1890?], 8).

[From English] *OED* 1602–1889; *EDD*; *COD*.

cobbler
Noun. Frequent in Egmont, occasional in Summerside, infrequent elsewhere; significantly male.

A brown scavenger fish having a large head surrounded with spurs, a sculpin (family Cottidae).

We used to think it was fun to put the cobbler on the washboard in the sun. He'd swell up and we'd chuck him over and he couldn't go down because he'd be full of air and he'd die (II 063). The cobbler has an ugly big mouth. You don't want them on the hook (II 020).

*In a number of localities around the world, *cobbler* is used to name various other fish.

cod
Transitive and intransitive verb. Also **coddle**. Infrequent in Malpeque and Cardigan, rare elsewhere; unattested under fifty. Compare **codding, joust**.

To tease or kid; to trick.

To pull someone's leg. 'You're not codding me are you?' (I 052). I'd be saying things I didn't believe myself, and I'd say, 'I'm only codding you' (I 087). 'You're just codding me' means lying or pretending, rather than physical teasing (I 091). Are you trying to coddle me? (O).

[From Irish and Scottish and northern English] *OED* 1873–1889; *OEDS*; *EDD*; *W3*; *DARE* 1890–1950; *DSUE*; *DAS*; *SSPB*; *COD.*

codding
Verbal noun. Infrequent in Malpeque and Cardigan, rare elsewhere; unattested under fifty. Compare **cod**.
   Teasing, kidding.
   Codding is like kidding, verbal rather than physical (I 024). Quit your codding (I 065).

[From Irish and Scottish and northern English] *EDD*; *OEDS* 1933–1966.

coggly
Adjective. Also **cogglesome**. Occasional in Egmont, infrequent or rare elsewhere; significantly rural, older; especially less educated.
   Of people or things, shaky, unsteady, wobbly.
   If a person drinks too much we'd say he's getting pretty coggly (I 063). A person who's unsteady on his feet, especially because of illness or old age (I 090). Used for some loose, not tightly put together, thing (I 093). Out of balance (I 095). Coggly means unsteady on one's feet (P1 016). It could be a boat that is easily upset (P1 063). A weakened condition following illness, perhaps (O).

[From Irish and Scottish and northern English] *OED*; *W3*; *SND* 1890–1934; *EDD*; *DARE*; *EDSL.*

coil
Noun. Often \kīl\. Also spelled **quile**. Archaic. Compare **coil** (verb).
   A small rounded pile of cut hay.
   Fine open the coils to dry, bad hay, wet (*Meggison Family Diary, 1809–1950*, 1833, August 20). August 5th [1888] A little damp today; have a lot of good hay out in quile (coil) (CULLEN, TIMOTHY, *Some Pages from a Diary of T.P. Cullen, 1888–1889*, 9). If she wrote a poem – if it was whispered that she had been seen dancing alone by moonlight among the coils of a New Moon hayfield – it was all because she was temperamental (MONTGOMERY, LUCY MAUD,

Emily's Quest, 1927, 133). After the hay was raked, it was all piled in coils by hand and was left in coil overnight to sweat. If the next day turned out to be a good drying day, the coils were spread out to dry in the late morning, and loaded by hand on wagons with hay racks to be taken to the barn in the afternoon. This method continued for many years until hay loaders came on the market (FREETOWN HISTORICAL SOCIETY, *Freetown Past and Present*, 1985, 34). Hay was put in coils which would shed rain when there wasn't time to get it in (II 047). In my childhood not everyone could make good coils. They must be good for appearance and protection from rain (II 104).

[From British and Irish] *OED*; *W3* 'dial.'; *EDD*; *PEDGL*; *EDSL*; *FW*; *GCD.*

coil
Transitive and intransitive verb. Compare **coil** (noun).
   To pile (cut hay) into 'coils.'
   Morning thick mist, p.m. sunny we coiled hay in Brookfield and below road in W. farm (MCEACHERON, JOHN, *A Diary or Memorandum, of Weather, Work and Other Incidents Connected with the Farm and District*, 1875, August 7). Beautiful day very warm. Papa started to make his hay. I helped coil a 'bit' in the evening. 'great sport.' (OLIVER, GERTRUDE, *Diaries of Gertrude Hazel Meggison Oliver*, 1909, July 31). Gathering up a handful of the fallen [hay], he would twist it tightly, to find out by appraising the water content, whether or not it was in a condition to coil (DIXON, MARGARET, *Going Home: An Autobiography*, 1979, 48). There were spinning and weaving songs, but I also remember relatives singing while hoeing turnips and coiling hay and, most particularly, while milking (HOWATT, BETTY, *History Begins at Home*, 1981, 24). Get hay coiled before it rains. You forked it into piles so rain would run off it (II 064).

[From British and Irish.]

comber
Noun. Compare **handpicker, handscoop, mosser.**
   A person who harvests 'storm-tossed Irish moss' at the shore with a hand rake.
   Some of them ['mossers'] are combers and they don't care if they comb your gates or your fields [to steal moss] (S 11).

come-all-ye
Noun. Occasional in Egmont, infrequent or rare elsewhere.

1. A folk song or ballad beginning with these words of invitation.

Whiskey began to circulate freely. Very soon almost all the men were partly drunk. Those in the porch and outside around the door began howling 'come-all-ye's' and continued to howl them (MONTGOMERY, LUCY MAUD, *The Blue Castle*, 1926, 129). Then there were the songs, ballads as a rule which began 'Come all ye' (KELLEY, FRANCIS, *The Bishop Jots It Down: An Autobiographical Strain on Memories*, 1939, 11). Sometimes on such evenings neighbors were welcomed and jokes and merry witticisms were bandied back and forth. News of the neighborhood and the current trouble of the day were discussed. Ballads of by-gone days, come-all-ye's of more recent composition, and sweet songs with melancholy harmonies, were sung with peculiar ecstasy and abandon (BAGNALL, MARGARET, *The Red Fox*, 1956, 38). For his model, Larry took the well-known come-all-ye pattern in which a girl dons men's clothing to follow her lover; then he kidded the corners off it (IVES, EDWARD, *Larry Gorman: The Man Who Made the Songs*, [1964], 66). Of the five pieces that I can attribute to him at present, three are come-all-ye's – long, perfectly traditional ballads making full use of the broadside style and morality (*ibid*, 153).

2. A party at which such folk songs are performed.

Pronounced 'comeallya' – a dance at someone's home (II 038). A party where come-all-ye songs are sung (II 095). No special invitation. Sing and dance (II 112).

[From Irish] *OEDS* 1878–1965; *W3*; *EDD*; *DARE* 'A commotion'; *EDD*; *DSUE*; *ESI*; *GCD*.

concert
Noun. Archaic. Compare **box social, pie social.**

A 'basket social,' a fund-raising entertainment during which lunches in decorated baskets were auctioned off and then shared by donor and buyer.

Well, that's what they called concerts; 'basket socials' – there'd be singing and such like (T B18). We went to Annandale, was a concert there. So when we got there, the concert, the baskets was after being sold (T M63). And maybe there would be a box concert – a social – and each one would make something, and the young fellows, if they had a girl there if they knew the girl's cake they'd buy it (T M64).

cooligan
Intransitive verb. Archaic. Rare. Compare **striking party.**

To scrape the outside walls or windows of a house as a prank, in order to startle those inside.

Going out cooliganing means taking a spool of thread notched, and rubbing it against a window (II 095). It is a very old word used when people would be knocking underneath windows in homes (II 107). On New Year's Eve, people came to the house in St. Peters to cooligan – the real object was to get invited in for lunch (O). I recall someone doing it at my house when I was young (O).

cooper
Transitive and intransitive verb. Also **cooper up, crouper (up)**. Rare.

To repair temporarily; to clean.

You could say you were going to crouper something if you were repairing it (II 019). To cooper – a rough job of sewing in a hurry – any repair in a hurry (II 022). Also spelled crouper it up. Clean it up (O).

OED 1829–1833.

corduroy
Transitive verb.

To prepare (a bed for oysters) by laying down logs side by side on the bottom.

Some people build their oyster beds with logs and shell. This is corduroying the bottom (S 14).

[Canadian] *DC* 'surface or bridge a swampy place with logs laid side by side at right angles to the way'; *GCD* 'surface or bridge with logs laid crosswise.'

cork
Noun. Also **corker**. Rare.

A hired hand on a fishing boat, especially a lobster boat.

At one time most fisherman fished alone but there were some double boats as they were called with two men in them. In later years, after the fishermen started buying their own boats and having their own gear, each fishermen [sic] usually had a hired man or a 'cork' as he was called. A woman was not allowed near the boat as it was supposed to bring bad luck. However, it is now becoming a common practice for women to act as cork for their husbands (MACDONALD, ROSE MARIE, *Those Were the Days: A History of the North Side of the Boughton River*, [1980?], 24). This is the helper on a lobster boat, but not a larger boat (I 100). This is what the men in Murray Harbour area call their hired men (O).

*Observers identified this word with eastern PEI; all seven of the Survey informants came from Cardigan. [Perhaps from Scottish] *OED* Sc. colloq. 'A small employer or master tradesman, an overseer or foreman'; *W3*; *EDD* 'Sc. colloq. from 1830.'

cotton bread
See **fog**.

couchy
Adjective. \'kŏŏ-chē\
   Infested with couch grass.
   We hoeing couchy late potatoes in Norman's old place all this week (MCEACHERON, JOHN, *A Diary or Memorandum of Weather, Work and Other Incidents Connected with the Farm and District Being a Continuation of Such since 1839*, July 26, 1873). Couchy ground – it goes right through potatoes (P2–035). I wouldn't put potatoes there, its too couchy (P2–036). The ground has to be worked up with plows and harrows so it won't be couchy (P2–044).

cow grass
Noun.
   Perennial red clover.
   The grass most commonly used in the country is the timothy. It is usually sown mixed with cow grass, which is a perennial red clover. This mixture, with the thick native white clover, which the land every where spontaneously produces, forms a most luxuriant meadow, and yields under favorable circumstances about three tons per acre (HILL, S.S., *A Short Account of Prince Edward Island, Designed Chiefly for the Information of Agriculturist and Other Emigrants of Small Capital*, 1839, 37). White clover and timothy, which had been the basis of the cultivated hay fields since the late eighteenth century, were finding increasing competition from 'cow grass' (perennial red clover) (CLARK, ANDREW, *Three Centuries and the Island: A Historical Geography of Settlement and Agriculture in Prince Edward Island, Canada*, 1959, 74).

W3; *OED*; *EDD*; *DARE*; *COD*.

cow-mare
Noun. Also **cow-horse**. Derogatory.

   A foolish person, supposedly unable to tell a cow from a horse.
   Then up steps 'MacPherson' so straight and so tall / Like the rest of the Cow Mares he knows it all. / And with strictest regard to his pronunciation / He gave a long talk on Incorporation (*Come Listen My Friends*, n.d., n.pag.).

*This word has been associated by several informants with south-eastern Prince Edward Island. According to oral tradition in this area, the term originated in the Hebridean island of Skye, when a dead horse washed up on the beach and was allegedly eaten by the local inhabitants in the belief that it was a cow. The compound is still a very potent insult in Prince Edward Island.

cow's breakfast
Noun. Informal.
   A large straw hat.
   Wheat straw was braided and rolled flat between two wooden rollers turned by a hand crank and sewn together to make everyday hats, these were called 'Cows breakfasts' (JOHNSTONE, MRS. ANDREW, *Making Cloth*, [1964], 4). 'Sarah – could you find me a big straw hat?' She recognized the gleam of mischief in his eye and asked 'Now Donald, what are you up to this time?' He said, 'Oh nothing – nothing at all – just give me the hat.' After some hesitation, she produced a hat of the kind we used to call Cow's Breakfast (PRINCE EDWARD ISLAND HISTORICAL SOCIETY, *Folklore of Prince Edward Island*, n.d., 34).

[Canadian] *DC* 'slang' 1900–1959; *DSUE* 'Canadian: C. 20.'

crack¹
Noun. Rare.
   A conversation, especially gossip.
   We had a good crack (I 039).

[From northern Irish and Scottish and northern English] *OED*; *SND* 1773–1929; *W3*; *EDD*; *EDSL*; *FW* 'Dial. or Scot'; *WNW* 'Brit. Dial'; *COD* 'Sc. & North.' *crak*: *DOST* 'A talk or gossip' 1570. *craken*: *MED* 'To utter ... say; speak, talk.'

crack²
Noun. Infrequent; especially older, female, less educated.
   An anal emission of gas, a fart.
   Was that a crack I heard? (II 017). To let a crack go (II 052). To make cracks (O).

OED 'Obs. exc. dial' 1387–1611. *crak*: *MED* 'a fart.' *craken*: *MED* 'let a fart.'

cracker

Noun. Also **cleaver**. Compare **knuckle-picker, shaker**[1].

A worker in a lobster factory who cracks open lobster knuckles and claws.

The legs and claws went to the cleavers. One person noted that 'Cass Blaisdell was the best cracker (or cleaver) that ever entered a factory' (CHEVERIE, LEO, *Johnson's Lobster Factory, 1935–1945*, 1982, 6). The processing of the lobsters involved the combined efforts of several persons, each with his or her own specialized job to perform. ... The 'cracker' split the knuckles lengthwise and cracked the claws in two. He then passed the cracked shells to the 'shaker' whose job it was to shake the meat from the shells and then pass it along to the 'knuckle-picker' who had the unenviable task of picking the meat from all the knuckles while the legs were squeezed between rollers to extract the meat and the remaining bodies were discarded. Usually the 'cracker' performed the job of 'shaker' as well, especially if he was a fast worker or if it was not too busy at his table (MORRISON, CLINTON, *Along the North Shore: A Social History of Township 11, P.E.I. 1765–1982*, 1983, 73). The cracker is the fellow that cuts the claws in two to get the meat out of them. He uses a cleaver and a block; that's the cleaver (S 4).

cradle hill

Noun. Also **club**. Frequent generally, but infrequent in Summerside and Charlottetown; significantly rural, older, male. Compare **cradle hollow**.

A small mound of earth, with a cradle-shaped hollow at its foot, usually formed by the felling or uprooting of a tree.

But there is another impediment to travelling in the woods: many of the trees have been torn up by the roots with high winds, which have raised little hills of earth, which the natives call cradle hills (JOHNSTONE, WALTER, *'Letters' and 'Travels' Prince Edward Island, 1821*, 1955, 102). As I hinted above, the greater part of the land here must be turned to pasture, before it can be stumped, and some of it is only fit for pasture all the time, and often it is not even good for this purpose, for the cradle-hills I spoke of, where they are high (and they are not equally high everywhere), cause all the good earth to fall down into the hollow parts, and the higher parts produce nothing but moss or sorrel (JOHNSTONE, WALTER, *A Series of Letters,*

Descriptive of Prince Edward Island, 1822, 26). They passed through Happiness where all the little cradle hills were sound asleep (MONTGOMERY, LUCY MAUD, *Pat of Silver Bush*, 1933, 101). This [uneven ground] results from cradle hills which are stumps of trees that have died and fallen over. In time they become covered with soil and vegetation to form mounds. If the land had once been cultivated these cradle hills would have been plowed out (BAGLOLE, HARRY, *Readings in Prince Edward Island History*, 1976, 203). In her hand she held a huge hoe with which, when we came upon her, she had been smiting the cradle hills to unearth potatoes (HARRIS, ROBERT, *Some Pages from an Artist's Life*, n.d., 33). A cradle hill is a depression in a wooded area, not necessarily where a tree was uprooted. It could also be a natural depression in cleared land (I 002). Cradle hills are mounds and hollows that people had trouble with in the woods. The tractor wouldn't go over the cradle hills (I 009). A lot of snow in the cradle hills yet (I 032). Any rough ground is 'full of cradle hills' if the field is rolling and bumpy (I 065). It can also occur where a tree is rotted out (I 093).

[North American] DC 1820–1955; OED 'U.S.'; DARE 1887–1969; DA 'Obs'; DAE; OEDS; GCD 'Cdn.' *cradle knoll*: W3 'a small knoll (as on a logging road) that requires grading'; DARE; DAE.

cradle hollow

Noun. Compare **cradle hill**.

A cradle-shaped depression in the earth, usually formed by the felling or uprooting of a tree.

His leap, however, too vigorous, carried him headlong over board where he fell in a cradle hollow, with the pig on top (SHAW, WALTER, *Tell Me the Tales*, 1975, 82). All went well until one wheel of the wagon went into a cradle hollow and the top of the load, fork, and children all tumbled off (PENDERGAST, GERTRUDE, *A Good Time Was Had by All*, 1981, 8). I used to see it in the woods. It's the hollow and the hill all smoothed over with moss on it (I 095). A sudden dip or hollow in a clay road – especially in winter time (O).

[North American] *cradle hole*: DC 1826; OED 'U.S.'; DAE; DA; OEDS.

craithar

Noun. Rare.

1. A sieve for separating husks and bran from flour.

This [hand-mill] crushed or ground the grain when properly dried, after which the meal or flour was separated from the husks and bran by the 'craithar' (sieve) (MACDONALD, HUBERT, *The Lords of the Isles and Their Descendants*, 1944, n.p.).

2. A small amount of liquor.

A drop of the craithar every morn (II 002). 'Will you have a drop of the craithar' means will you have a spot of liquor to drink (O).

[From Irish and Scottish Gaelic] *crihir: IED* 'a particle, a small portion.' *criathar: GED* 'sieve, riddle, cribble.'

cranberry barrens

Noun. Compare **blueberry barrens, fire barrens, spruce barrens**.

A tract of untillable or burnt-over land where cranberries grow.

There are great sand-hills or 'dunes' between the lakes and the sea. ... Along here the early settlers landed. There are great cranberry and blueberry barrens a little distance from the shores (MELLICK, HENRY, *Timothy's Boyhood: or Pioneer Country Life on Prince Edward Island*, 1933, 14). If he be weary of the haunts of men and long for 'the way of the wilderness,' there is the west with its secluded rivers and unbroken forests, or its cranberry 'barrens,' where one may lounge for a day on the dry, springy heath by the shores of the Straits and hear no sound but the twittering of the bank swallows and the booming of the waves on the cliffs below (MCLEOD, NEIL, *Prince Edward Island*, n.d., 766).

*Barrens, as such, is standard in North America for any tract of wasteland supporting only low vegetation, 'sometimes with defining terms prefixed, as *pine-barrens*' (*DAE*).
[North American] *barrens: DC* 'in the Atlantic Provinces, an elevated tract of exposed land that nourishes only scrubby trees, shrubs, berries, etc. and resembles a moor'; *SSPB* 'usually a northern word for 'tundra,' this word is used in Nova Scotia to describe bogs in which blueberries, cloudberries, low stunted spruce, and mosses grow'; *OED* 'In Nova Scotia and New Brunswick ... an open marshy space in the forest, sometimes so soft as to be almost impassable, at other times composed of good solid hard peat.'

crating up
See **banking²**.

creep
Noun.

A small pen used for feeding or sheltering young farm animals.

The Department of Agriculture has come up with a project which cuts the electrical costs of heating new born pigs. It is the construction of insulated creeps (*Journal-Pioneer Annual Farm Issue*, June 1, 1978, 7). To minimize starvation and chilling [of piglets], a warm clean, dry draft-free creep area close to the sow, but outside her danger area, is essential (*The Corner Post*, April 1982, 18). To make sure the lambs get their own feed, Chester will put it into a special little pen called a 'creep.' The pen's opening is too small for the ewes, but just the right size for the lambs to creep through (CLIMO, LINDEE, *Chester's Barn*, 1982, 22).

W3; OEDS. OED 'an opening in a hedge or other enclosure, for an animal to creep or pass through.'

cross-lots
Prepositional phrase, often modifying *road* or *path*. Also **across lots**. Infrequent generally, but rare in Malpeque and Charlottetown.

Across adjacent lots or fields, as a short-cut.

The road we took was a beautiful one, for we went 'cross-lots,' and we enjoyed it (MONTGOMERY, LUCY MAUD, *The Golden Road*, [1910], 260). She hurried home by the cross-lots road – the little old road over which the vagabond wandered and the lover went to his lady ... the road that linked up eventually with the pasture field (MONTGOMERY, LUCY MAUD, *Emily's Quest*, 1927, 232). Joscelyn, coming home across lots from an errand to the harbour, paused for a moment at the little gate in Simon Dark's pasture that opened on the side road leading down to Bay Silver (MONTGOMERY, LUCY MAUD, *A Tangled Web*, [1931], 269–70).

[North American] *OED* 1633–1879; *W3; DARE* 1825–1968; *DAE; DA; OEDS.*

crottle
Noun. Also spelled **crotal, crotle, kronthal, krotle**. Archaic. Rare.

A lichen growing on hardwood trees, formerly used in dyeing and occasionally as a tonic.

Her dye-pot was always on the stove. She was an expert in home-made dyes. No 'bought' dyes for Judy. They faded in a year, she averred. Crottle and lichens and barks ... elderberries that gave purple dyes ... yellow from Lombardy poplars (MONTGOMERY, LUCY MAUD, *Pat of Silver Bush*, 1933, 110). The next operation was coloring or dyeing, using home-made dyes which were made from crottle and barks gathered from the woods. Crottle is a fungus that grows on rock maple trees and produces a fawn shade (ALEXANDRA WOMEN'S INSTITUTE, *A Short History of the District of Alexandra, Prince Edward Island*, 1965, 14). A number of words we used were taken from the Gaelic and changed a bit. For instance, the moss of the rock maple tree was used by my parents for two things: to make a spring tonic, and to make a kind of brown dye. This was called 'kronthal,' a word which, I have found out, is used in the Hebrides for moss or shells on a rock. I don't know whether anyone on the Island still uses kronthal for a tonic or dye, but it is good for both (CAMPBELL, ALPHONSUS, *The Heritage of the Highland Scots in P.E.I.*, 1975, 53). Hooking and braiding rugs is one of her main hobbies, and every winter there are two or three mats in the frames, and beautiful hooked rugs are produced from scrap rags and discarded articles of clothing. These were often dyed with the 'Krotle' or moss from the hardwood trees in the woods. This must be a Gaelie [sic] word, as I cannot find it in the English dictionary. As children we were sent to collect it. The cloth and the krotle were boiled together in a big pot and beautiful non-fading green colors were produced (DEWAR, LLOYD, *A History of My Family and the Family Farm at New Perth, Prince Edward Island*, 1975, 42). He drank crottle instead of something else and someone said that it would color his water for sure (I 064). That's a thing that grows on the tree and you boil it. We dyed socks. Men when they went to the woods took a bag and picked it off. Sort of an orange color (I 095).

[From Irish and Scottish Gaelic] *SND.* '*crotal*, a gen. name for the varieties of lichen, more especially those used in dyeing' 1825–1941; *EDD*; *OED*; *OEDS*; *W3*; *EDSL*; *DGL*; *PEDGL*; *IED.*

crouper
See **couper**.

crow piss
Noun, usually in phrase **to be up at crow piss**. Also **crow piss time**. Informal.
   A very early hour in the morning.
   My father was always up at crow piss (O).

crumbcloth
Noun.
   A covering to protect a carpet from food droppings, usually laid under a table.
   In the exact centre of the room and over the carpet was a rug about ten by ten feet in size which they called a 'crumbcloth.' This particular one was a real beauty, with cream colored centre, black edge and decorated with 'raised' roses in pink and reddish shades and green leaves and ferns. At each door and before the organ were small mats about three quarters of a yard by a half yard in size. These matched the 'crumbcloth' in design and color and were called 'door mats' (BAGNALL, RUTH, 'When I Was Very Young,' [1964], 5).

OED 1843–1864; *DAE* 1838–1863; *EDD.*

crunnick
Noun. Rare.
   A dry, weathered stick of wood (O).

DNE 1894–1969; *DC*; *IED. crannock*: *EDD* 'Pem. Dor.'

crusher claw
Noun.
   The larger claw on a lobster.
   The first pair of legs are large and armed with strong claws, one of which, the crusher claw, is usually considerably heavier than the more slender biting claw. … The heavy crusher claw looks like an excellent tool for crushing hard-shelled shellfish but it is doubtful if it is actually used for this purpose (WILDER, D.G., *Canada's Lobster Fishery*, 1957, 5, 7). The crusher claw, that's the big claw, and if he gets a hold of you with that claw, you have to wait until he decides to let you go (S 4). The crusher claw is the big claw, and you'll know if you get your finger caught in it why they call it a crusher claw (S 5).

cuckle
Noun.
   The cocklebur or burdock (genus *Arctium*).
   Used in the western end of the Island, from North Cape to Alberton at least (O).

[From English] *W3* 'dial. var. of *cockle*' [cocklebur]; *OED*; *EDD*; *SND*; *DARE.*

culling board
See **tonging board**.

cup oyster
Noun.
   See quotation.
   A cup oyster is a choice or fancy oyster. It has a cup shape to the shell (S 15).

D

dammer
Noun, often with **little**.
   A bad child, a brat.
   This word is usually used for a younger child: 'He's a regular little dammer' (P2 026). 'He's a dammer' – they said it about us children (P2 063). You might say, 'The little dammer made an awful noise' (P2 068).

dead man's overcoat
Noun. Informal.
   A coffin.
   There once lived a man in Crapaud – his name was Big John, an old bachelor from the Old Coutry [sic], who made carts and truck wheels, and also made our coffins, which he called dead men's overcoats (AUTUMN, GENE, *My Life in Crapaud*, 1929, 24).

wooden overcoat: *OEDS* 'a coffin. slang.'

denning box
Noun.
   A synonym for 'whelping den': in fox ranching, a box sometimes placed inside a fox kennel as a shelter for the female to whelp in.
   A denning box is a little box in the back of the big box. It has a hinged roof. The denning box is probably three feet by two feet. It is an annex of the room for darkness for the nervous animals (S 9).

devil
Noun. Archaic.
   A synonym for 'sloven': a long, horse-drawn wagon with the platform slung lower than the axles and close to the ground, formerly used for hauling heavy or awkward loads.
   A devil is used for dragging things around (II 083). It's a dropped-axle wagon mostly used to haul barrels from the farm and city (R 29).

W3 'a drag for clearing plowed ground'; *EDD* 'an instrument used for harrowing chalk into the soil.'

devil's egg
See **whore's egg**.

devil's jews' harp
Noun.
   See quotation.
   When the line was completed in September, 1914, there was placed in the home of each shareholder who requested it a large crank style telephone which had a mouth-piece at the end of a long black projecture and which cost twelve dollars. ... Some Brae residents, who felt the community would be kept in a turmoil by the new and easy means of spreading gossip, objected strongly to the building of the telephone line and named the telephone the devil's jews' harp (MACNEVIN, MRS. LORNE, *Past and Present: A History of Brae*, 1979, 145).

devil's matches
See **bear's matches**.

devil's paint brush
Noun. Also **devil's carpet, Indian paint brush**. Frequent; significantly rural, older.
   A weed with a bright orange and black flower, a species of hawkweed (*Hieracium aurantiacum*).
   Common in central upland and uplands of Kings, local in Western Prince. Naturalized from Europe. J.A. Clarke (1904) noted that an untended cemetery in Kinkora had acted as a focus for its naturalization in East Prince; it is even now more abundant there than anywhere else in the county. Open grassy places: fields, old pastures and borders of woods (CANADA, DEPARTMENT OF AGRICULTURE, *The Plants of Prince Edward Island*, 1960, 264). The devil's paint brush is an undesirable weed because it chokes hay (I 002). It is a kind of orange hawkweed (I 040). An orange weed that grows in late summer (P1 016). I have been and am cursed with them. Also called devil's carpet (P1 024). A very prevalent plant like a dandelion (O).

*The name *paintbrush*, as such, is included in Diane Griffin's *Atlantic Wildflowers*, 1984, but without a modifier.
[North American] *W3*; *DA* 1907–1947; *WNW*.

devil's picture book
Noun, usually in plural. Also **devil's prayer book**.
   A playing card.
   Self-disciplined, they had no time for such useless activities as dancing or playing with cards, 'the devil's picture-books' (THOMSON, WINNIFRED, *Vernor Had Vision: A Tribute to Vernor Wilberforce Jones*, 1976, 11). Sunday 'doings' were very strictly controlled by the older people in the community: there were no games, no cards (Devil's picture books), only religious books might be read, and all work

possible was done on Saturday (STANHOPE WOMEN'S INSTITUTE HISTORY COMMITTEE, *Stanhope – Sands of Time*, 1984, 187). It happened to be the notorious game called 'Three Card Monte,' which I had never heard of. It seemed strange that this should have caused me any trouble as up to that time I had never had a play-card or 'Devil's Prayer Book' in my hands, even the simplest game of chance being forbidden (ANDERSEN, MAUDE, *Under Our Own Roof Tree: A Saga of the Lane Family*, n.d., 14).

W3; DSUE. *devil's books*: OED 1729–1861; EDD; W3; DSUE. *devil's painted books*: EDD. *devil's picture gallery, devil's playthings*: DSUE.

dickering
Noun. Rare.
   A sprinkling of salt, pepper, or other seasoning (II).

digger apron
Noun. Compare **digger bed, elevator digger, picking table**.
   A conveyor belt on a potato digger that lifts potatoes from the earth, allowing the soil and stones to fall back.
   It's the chain that carries the clay and tubers from the shears to the digger (S 1). The apron is made out of rods which sift the clay through. It runs right in behind the shear and right into the box (S 2).

digger bed
Noun.
   The framework for a 'digger apron' on a potato digger.
   Increase the main bed speed when the soil moisture is high. Agitate only the front of the main digger bed and agitate it only when necessary (ADVISORY COMMITTEE ON POTATOES, *Atlantic Canada Potato Guide*, 1984, 11). The apron is on the bed, and the bed is the frame (S 2).

digger rod
Noun.
   A metal bar that forms one of the sections of the 'digger apron' on a potato digger.
   Metal bars run lengthwise to make up the digger apron (MCCARVILL, LISA, *A Potato Farming Lexicon from Kinkora, P.E.I.*, 1986, n. pag.). Each link of the apron chain is a digger rod (S 3).

dilly
Noun. Also **dilly bar**. Common in Egmont, infrequent in Summerside, rare elsewhere; significantly rural; especially male.
   A roadside canteen, usually one selling ice-cream.
   Canteens are dillies up west, Alberton area (II 056). A dilly refers to any small canteen, ice cream parlour, etc. Common in West Prince. May have originated from the Dilly Bar, an early soft ice cream stand (O).

dilsey
Noun. Rare. Compare **kippy, trappy**.
   A good-looking young woman.
   A young girl of courting age (O).

dip net
Noun.
   A small fishing net with a long handle.
   Finally my Father arrived with a dip net. … He selected a narrow place in the waterway, placing the net there, and had me hold the handle while he frightened the smelts down the narrow stream, and into the net (MACDOUGALL, ARLENE, and VIOLET MACEACHERN, *The Banks of the Elliott*, 1973, 55). In the 1860s lobsters were very plentiful and were easily caught with dip nets, poles or simply by picking from the rocks (PRINCE EDWARD ISLAND, NATURAL HISTORY SOCIETY, *Winds of Sea and Wood*, 1975, 28).

[From English] OED; W3; EDD; DAE; DNE; COD.

dipper
Noun. Common generally, but occasional in Charlottetown; significantly female; especially rural.
   1. A small, long-handled saucepan, a type of cooking pot.
   I can remember the thrill of hanging to a low branch with one hand reaching far out with an old dipper (does anyone remember the word) and pouring and splashing without interruption, and without – amazingly – falling in (STEWART, MARION, *Marion Stewart's Journal*, 1976, 10). Used for dipping water out of a bucket. Relatively small. Later it became an all-purpose word meaning pot (II 027). I would use the word to describe both a water dipper and a long-handled saucepan (II 095). A saucepan with no cover and a handle (II 099).
   2. A bottle of home-made liquor.
   In Johnson's River area, 'get the dipper' meant a bottle of moonshine was coming

around. A fellow told me he bought a new set of dippers (II 079).

*Dipper is standard in the sense of 'a long-handled cup for dipping up water.'
DNE.

dirt¹
Noun.
Stormy weather with snow, sleet, or rain.
Mild W.S.W. some dirt forenoon, hauling wood (MACLEOD, ANDREW, *Diary: January 1, 1928–November 17, 1932,* 1931, January 1). But that very nite just before dusk a bank of 'dirt' came slowly over the western horizon. It hung there close to be consumed by a great red glare that swooped up from the departing sun, spread almost to the zenith and bathed the surface of the sea in an infernal blaze of lurid light (JOHNSTON, LORNE, *Recollections of an 'Ole Salt,* 1982, 84). 'So it looks like we may be in for a bit of dirt' [CBC weatherman] (O). The dirt's starting (O). Are we getting some dirt out there, boy? (O).

*Dirty, said of weather, is standard.
[From English and Irish] *OED* 'dial'; *W3*; *EDD.*

dirt²
Noun. Compare **monkey fur, shoe-string**.
In 'Irish moss' harvesting, other varieties of seaweed that must be picked from the moss.
Dirt: any impurity in Irish moss. [1] The dirt which should be cleaned out of moss is anything which would choke a cow! [2] the toughest part of the industry is picking the dirt from the moss (BERNARD, BLAINE, *Dictionary of Irish Moss,* 1986, n.pag.). Dirt in moss is the impurities in it. There is usually a lot of kelp and other rock weed and all that stuff that they won't buy. It has to be picked out (S 10). The dirt in moss is other kinds of moss (S 11).

dish¹
Noun. Infrequent in Egmont and Cardigan, rare or unattested elsewhere; significantly rural; unattested under fifty. Compare **gillock, pup, teddy**.
1. A bottle of liquor of large but indefinite size.
A dish might be a gallon or keg (I 009). He had a dish at the party (I 052). A dish is a two and one half gallon square container from Miquelon containing pure French liquor (I 056).

Bring a dish with you (I 065). I guess I'll get a dish for Christmas (I 118). 'Bring me home a dish from town.' That's not a serving at the table (I 121).
2. A small amount of liquor, a snort.
I think this deserves a cilibration. Would you like a dish? ... Whin I say 'dish' I mane something stronger than tay (HARRIS, ELMER, *Johnny Belinda: A Play,* 1956, 15). Have a little dish of something. We would use 'snort' instead of 'dish' now (I 042).

*In standard English, dish (usually in *dish of tea*) is used for a small quantity of any liquid for drinking, but the term is becoming archaic.

dish²
Noun. Rare. Compare **chamberdish, charlie, thunderjug, thundermug**.
A chamber-pot.
The chamberpot was called 'the dish under the bed' since her family didn't want to say 'chamber' in public (I 017).

dizzy block
Noun. Humorous.
The central block of downtown Charlottetown, bounded by Grafton Street, University Avenue, Kent Street, and Queen Street.
People went around dizzy block so fast they got dizzy. You'd get dizzy too, just watching them (O).

doghouse
Noun. Also **spray house, spray shield**.
The small, three-sided wheel-house on a lobster boat.
Doghouse is a slang word for the wheelhouse or cabin of a boat. It usually refers to the three-sided structure on a smaller boat (ROBERTSON, JANICE, *A Dictionary of Lobster Fishing in the Eastern Kings Area,* 1985, 6). A doghouse is a shelter amidships. You are in out of the rain and spray while you are steaming (S 4).

OEDS 1961; *W3*.

dog trawl
Noun. Also **bull trawl, trawl**. Compare **bunch, dump, string**.
A group of lobster traps tied to the same line or 'backline.'
Approximately 12 traps are on a dog-trawl and these are placed on the 'washboard' until the whole trawl is hauled. ... Because of the large number of traps on each line, storm

damage was never as great as it is now since the line was so heavy and it took a lot to move it. The trend towards the shorter dog-trawls occurred in the 1940s as haulers on boats were installed. Because these are so light, they are very vulnerable in even a small storm (*The Guardian*, June 16, 1975, 3). A dog trawl is a group of traps which are tied to the same backline, with a buoy at each end. Fishermen at North Lake tend to use 8, 10, or 12 trap dog trawls (ROBERTSON, JANICE, *A Dictionary of Lobster Fishing in the Eastern Kings Area*, 1985, 6).

*The terms *bunch*, *dog trawl*, and *dump* are synonymous, but vary from port to port. In standard English *trawl* is a fishing line having attached to it many short lines with baited hooks.

dog trawl board
Noun. Also **dog trawl chart**, **scoreboard**, **tallyboard**.
   A chart or board used by lobster fishermen to show which of their lines have been fished.
   A dog trawl board is a board with numbered leather pieces attached to it, each number corresponding to a dog trawl. As the trawls are hauled, the corresponding pieces are turned down on the board, enabling the fisherman to keep track of which trawls he has hauled. These are not used by all fishermen (ROBERTSON, JANICE, *A Dictionary of Lobster Fishing in the Eastern Kings Area*, 1985, 6–7). That'd be a board with the numbers of your buoys and buttons over each number to show which dog trawls you had hauled that day. Everybody had a board and had from one to thirty-eight on the board and buttons to tally up what trawls they hauled that day (S 4).

doings
Noun. Also **doings piece**. Infrequent generally, but rare in Charlottetown. Compare **jigamirandee**.
   A person or thing whose name cannot be recalled at the moment.
   A doings piece is a part of something (II 034). 'Doings piece' is used when you can't think of the name or don't know the name of the part you need (II 058). Baked everything, all sweets, never went to the store for anything sweet. You'd have a big doings of kerosene oil since there was no electricity at that time, that is, when we were kids. You'd get kerosene oil perhaps you'd get a big what-ya-call-it ... of molasses (T M17). Word used to refer to someone or something when you can't think

of the right word – a whatchamacallit (O). Bernadette has all the doings out of the trailer (O).

doing: OEDS 'Applied to any concomitant, adjunct, or "etcetera," or anything that happens to be "about" or to be wanted. orig. war slang.' doings, the: DSUE 'The thing (*any* thing); esp. what is at the moment needed or otherwise relevant; from 1912.'

doozy up
Intransitive phrasal verb.
   To smarten up in appearance.
   He was doozied up with spats on his shoes (BUSHEY, SARAH, *Memoirs of Sarah Bushey*, 1893, July 4).

*A meaning of *dude* may be relevant: 'a man who is over-fastidious in dress' (OED, W3). A *doozy* 'anything outstanding' is common slang (GCD, WNW).

doty
Adjective. Also **dozey**, **dozy**. Also spelled **dotey**, **doughty**. Common in Egmont and Cardigan, frequent elsewhere, but infrequent in Charlottetown; significantly rural, middle-aged and older, male.
   Of wood, rotten, spongy, or decaying.
   Dozy wood is wet and rotten and won't burn (I 032). A bad spot in a plank is a doty place (I 063). Old houses sometimes have doty wood (I 089). Sort of dozy wood, spongey. Had taken water (I 095). It's used of wood, crumbly (P1–024). Say a sheet of plywood was used in a potato warehouse as a divider; if it got all full of moisture from the potatoes and started to rot it would be called doty wood (O).

*A standard sense of *doty* is feeble-minded. The origin for both senses appears to be the standard verb *dote*, 'to be feeble-minded from old age,' which can also mean 'to rot or disintegrate' (EDD, MED, FW). [From English] W3; EDD; SSPB. dozed: ESI.

double boat
Noun.
   See quotation.
   At one time most fishermen fished alone but there were some double boats as they were called with two men in them (MACDONALD, ROSE MARIE, *Those Were the Days: A History of the North Side of the Boughten River*, [1980?], 24).

double ice
Noun. Compare **cat ice**, **shell ice**, **top ice**.
   Synonym for 'shell ice': a patch or layer

of thin ice over thicker ice, with an air space in between, caused by refreezing or by freezing rain; or a thin layer of ice, under which the water has retreated; or ice that is pocked like a honeycomb.

In the spring of the year it was bad because you had times of double ice and there were times of single ice. All of the ice looked good on the top, and as you cut through it got all honeycombed. You might have two feet of ice in one place and six inches in another (STEWART, DEBORAH, and DAVID STEWART, *Winter Travel*, 1979, 24).

double runner[1]
Noun. Archaic. Occasional in Charlottetown, infrequent in Summerside, rare elsewhere; especially middle-aged and older. Compare **spring skate, stock skate**.

A child's skate with two blades, a bobskate (I; O).

[From New England] *W3*.

double runner[2]
Noun. Infrequent in Charlottetown and Cardigan, rare elsewhere. Compare **bunk**.

A home-made bobsled consisting of two short sleds fastened at the ends of a heavy board, used for hauling wood or for pleasure sledding.

There was another thing we had at the time; what they called a double runner. It was two small bobsleds with a long board between the two. The board would be about ten feet long by about one foot wide. Now the front sleigh was rigged with a steering mechanism on it and the fella in front, he done the steering. Now the back sled had a 'bunk' on it about fourteen inches high, so you could sit comfortable on this. Now this would hold about ten or twelve young people and when that thing would start downhill you could gain fifty to sixty miles per hour at the bottom of the hill (CAMPBELL, FRANK, *As the Fella Says ...*, 1983, 75). A double runner was two sleighs with a platform on them. You could steer by the front one (I 035). A sleigh made of two separate sleighs really. Extendable, used for hauling logs for example (O).

*The term *double runner* was used by many Fieldwork Survey informants interchangeably with *bobsleigh* or with *bobsled*.
[North American] *WGUS* '*Double runner* is current in

the entire coastal area from Narragansett Bay to New Brunswick, including Worcester County in Massachusetts and all of New Hampshire except the northern third. ... None of these New England terms seems to have survived west of the Hudson'; *DAE* 1883–1905; *OED*; *W3*; *DA. double ripper*: FW.

double seated wagon
Noun. Also **double seated buggy, double seater**.

See quotations.

Had a dandy supper then after that was over we all went to church. Mr. Smallman took us in the double seated buggy (OLIVER, GERTRUDE, *Diaries of Gertrude Hazel Meggison Oliver*, 1908, November 19). Two vehicles were sent to convey the members of the family to church on Sunday mornings in summer, a single riding wagon, and a double seater (BAGNALL, RUTH, *When I Was Very Young*, [1964], 1–2). A beautiful day friends and relatives came from near and far in buggies and double seated wagons to celebrate with them (BALTIC LOT 18 WOMEN'S INSTITUTE, *History of Baltic Lot 18*, n.d. 43).

double sled
Noun. Also **double sleigh**.

A heavy sled drawn by two horses.

White frost. Slightly cloudy. Will and Seymour off for 'mussel mud' with one double sled and two single ones, so taking all the horses (WOODMAN, SUSAN, *Diary: January 1, 1895–December 31, 1896*, 1895, January 30). Everybody was hunting the mud ['mussel mud']; the whole country turned out to load single sleighs and double sleighs (WALLACE, LESTER, *Hunting the Mud*, 1977, 57).

DNE.

dough dolly
Noun.

A pancake made with bread dough.

Bread that was rising from the night before. It was sliced off and fried. It rises in the pan. My sons still ask for this for breakfast when they come home (II 095).

dough cake: *DAE* 'a flap jack or a kind of cake made with bread dough.'

down east
Adverb phrase. Common. Compare **down west, out east, up east, up west**.

1. In or to any part of Prince Edward Island east of Charlottetown.

While it is true that there are often winter conditions that prevail throughout the whole 140 miles of the Island, there are days in which it is much milder down east (SELLICK, LESTER, *My Island Home*, 1973, 81). Roads used to be the traveller's greatest problem. Rain, of course, magnified the problem and if you were caught 'up west' or down east in the spring before the roads were properly dry and it rained you were lucky to get home without either getting stuck and having to be pulled out or sliding into a ditch (MURPHY, ELMER, *A Newspaperman Remembers*, [1980?], 118). For the early Gowan Brae days I recall a good many differences from the folkways and mores of Victoria and environs. 'Down East' there were always more children about. It was the pre-pill era in both places but family planning was more obviously coming into vogue in the community farther west (MACQUARRIE, HEATH, *Recollections of His Early Childhood and Society on Prince Edward Island*, 1985, 2). Souris and Montague (I 011). *In, up, down, over,* are all used interchangeably for going places. *In* to town, and *up* to Summerside, but *over* to Southport, and *down* to Vernon (I 020).

2. In or to any part of Prince Edward Island east of one's habitual location.

Going to Souris is going *down east* when you are in Charlottetown. Going to Souris is going *over east* when you are in Montague (I 022). East of where you are at the time (I 063). If in Montague, would mean Souris (I 085).

*The standard Canadian sense, 'in or to the Maritimes,' is also commonly known, but generally expresses the point of view of someone in, or coming from, central Canada (see the *Dictionary of Canadianisms*). Similarly the dominant sense above (no. 1) is really an imposition from the point of view of Charlottetown. The prepositions *down, up, over,* and so on are extremely variable in expressions of this kind.

downstreet

Verb. Also spelled **down street**. Common generally, but frequent in Malpeque, occasional in Charlottetown. Compare **upstreet**.

In or to the centre of a town; the shopping district, or the main street.

Went downstreet and waited for Papa he got the horse shod (OLIVER, GERTRUDE, *Diaries of Gertrude Hazel Meggison Oliver*, January 5, 1907). Cousin Jimmy's method of looking after her was to take her to a restaurant down street and fill her up with ice-cream (MONTGOMERY, LUCY MAUD, *Emily of New Moon*, 1923, 54). 'Going

downstreet' to centre of town (I 011). It is used in Montague more than anywhere else (I 031). I've heard downstreet used in Souris to mean going downtown (I 043). It would be used only in small towns to mean downtown (I 060). Going to the centre of town, where the bank, post office, etc., are (I 077). It's Water Street in Summerside (I 106). You go downstreet, you don't see as many people standing talking to one another as they used to. They don't have time (T M119).

[From English] *W3. DAE* 'Down, or in the direction regarded as down, the street'; *EDD* 'the lower part of a town'; *OEDS* 'One goes *down city* only if he is going to the business centre; if he is going no farther than the nearest grocery store or shopping centre, his destination is *downstreet.*'

down west

Adverb phrase. Compare **down east, out east, up east, up west**.

In or to any part of Prince Edward Island west of Charlottetown.

And I know fellas who come in all the way from Souris and Tignish just to see them play a game. Too bad they don't run special trains in from up east and down west any more, like they used to when the Junior Royals were playing. That'd fill the old Forum like it used to then (LEDWELL, FRANK, and RESHARD GOOL, *Portraits and Gastroscopes*, 1972, 74). People from up west (Alberton) say 'down east,' but the people from Souris say 'up east' and 'down west' (O).

*This term was generally used by informants living 'up east.'

dozy

See **doty**.

draft rug

Noun.

A quilted bedspread.

If heavier yarn were needed it would usually be the task of the children to make it into two or more ply yarn using the small spinning wheel to twist it, after which it would be knitted into heavier garments, hooked into rugs, or used for pattern weft in 'draft rugs' as the overshot coverlets are called. These are the most interesting and colorful pieces of weaving remaining, and the names of the patterns and their distribution are almost as fascinating as the coverlets themselves (BURNETT, MARY, *Handwoven and Homespun*, 1973, 21).

drag
Transitive and intransitive verb. Compare **dragger, dragging**.

To harvest ('Irish moss') with a rake dragged behind a fishing boat.

The boats which drag moss have seriously hurt the lobster fishing in West Prince (BERNARD, BLAINE, *Dictionary of Irish Moss*, 1986, p?). If you drag for moss you are using a boat and are dragging behind the boat (S 10). When you drag you use the same system as they use to catch fish except with rakes instead of nets (S 11).

W3 'to fish or search with a drag'; *OED*; *FW*.

dragger
Noun. Compare **drag, dragging, mosser**.

An Irish moss harvester who 'drags' for moss behind a fishing boat.

Dragger: a 'mosser' who generally drags rather than scoops. [1] Since the draggers have been mossing, the area has been pretty well 'raked off.' [2] Draggers make more money, but have more bills to pay (BERNARD, BLAINE, *Dictionary of Irish Moss*, 1986, n. pag.). A dragger is one who drags rakes in his boat (S 12).

W3 'one that drags: specif: a fishing boat operating a trawl or dragnet'; *DA*.

dragging
Verbal noun. Compare **drag, dragger, drag rake**.

Synonym for 'raking[1]': the harvesting of 'Irish moss' by rakes dragged behind a fishing boat.

Dragging: harvesting the Irish moss by cutting the plants using a boat-drawn rake. [1] The most hateful and dangerous thing about dragging is having to clean the sharp teeth in the rake after every load (BERNARD, BLAINE, *Dictionary of Irish Moss*, 1986, n.pag.).

drag rake
Noun. Also **rake**. Compare **dragging, pole rake, raking[1]**.

In 'Irish moss' harvesting, rakes for pulling up moss from the sea bed.

The western P.E.I. moss rakers found they could harvest Irish moss more effectively by dragging rakes over the sea bottom behind their boats – and so the drag rake was developed to sweep the bottom more quickly and thoroughly (SCARRATT, D.J., *Rocks and Rakes: Lobsters vs. Irish Moss*, 1977, 56). The term *rake*

today usually refers to the mechanical rake that draggers use (BERNARD, BLAINE, *Dictionary of Irish Moss*, 1986, n. pag.).

drag sled
Noun.

See quotation.

A drag-sled, ox- (or horse-) drawn, made by nailing slabs or plank over unshod runners, was the first type of sleigh in Lot 9 (MACNEVIN, MRS. LORNE, *Past and Present: A History of Brae*, 1979, 63).

dreep
Intransitive verb.

Usually of rain, to fall in drops, to drip (O).

[From British and Irish] *W3* 'dial Brit.'; *OED*; *EDD*; *SND. dreeping*: *DOST* 'Dripping moisture'; *SND*.

dress
Transitive verb. Occasional in Egmont, infrequent elsewhere.

To make (a bed), especially in an elegant manner.

Making the bed for company with a bed-spread and everything (II 075). 'Get all the beds dressed' (II 105).

*Dress has a wider sense in standard English: 'put in order, make ready.'
DNE 1888.

drift ice
Noun. Compare **clumpet, ice cake, raft ice, running ice**.

Loose masses of ice driven by wind and current.

We lost no time in launching the boat into a surging mass of broken drift-ice (SLEIGH, B.W.A., *Pine Forests and Hacmatack Clearings*, 1853, 124). The appearance of the ice floating about the rivers, with here and there a patch of snow, is almost the only trace of winter now discernable in this quarter. ... The Straits are full of soft drift-ice, and the mails unable to cross to Pictou (BAGSTER, BIRTH, *The Progress and Prospects of Prince Edward Island*, 1861, 103). You know that these harbours and bays in the Gulf freeze in winter, and the drift-ice comes down from the north and helps to fill the whole of Northumberland Strait (HICKMAN, ALBERT, *The Sacrifice of the Shannon*, 1903, 24–25). Drift ice accumulating in the Gulf circulates through the Northumberland Strait and, more especially, around the northern shores of the Island before finding its exit at Cabot Strait (CANADA, DEPART-MENT OF AGRICULTURE, *The Plants of Prince Edward Island*, 1960, 11). There was a lot of ice, all 'board ice' along the shore and drift ice out farther (*Bedeque Area Multicultural Family Tree Report*, 1978, 8). In the early spring of 1864 an exciting and almost tragic seal hunt took place on the drift ice that had been carried in from the open sea by a long period of east wind. A large field of ice had been stranded between East Point and Red Point and the seals were easily heard bawling in the calm of an April morning (*East Point United Baptist Church 1833– 1933 Historical Record*, 1983, 82). Open water areas are constantly changing as the drift ice is moved by wind and tide conditions (*The Guardian*, April 2, 1985, 3).

OED 1600–1820; W3; DC; DNE; COD.

droghey
Adjective. Compare **peevish, snotty**.
Of weather, rainy, drizzly (O).

[From Irish] EDD.

drop
Transitive verb, in phrase **drop sets**. Archaic.
To plant (potato 'sets').
The planting is generally done with the plough, the sets being dropped, every third round, from 12–18 inches apart in the row (ROSS, THEODORE, *Potato Growing*, 1915, 335). A common method among farmers is to open the furrows, drop sets by hand and close the furrows with an ordinary plough. ... The potato planter ... plants or drops the sets (MACOUN, W.T., *The Potato in Canada: Its Cultivation and Varieties*, 1918, 7).

drop trap
Noun.
A lobster trap fished on its own line, or with only one or two other traps.
A single trap, a one trap 'dump' that is a drop trap. They are usually bigger traps. They use a lot of them out in the Atlantic (S 4). A drop trap is a term they use in some areas of the south side. It is a single trap or two trap 'dog trawl' (S 5).

drum
Transitive verb. Compare **cleaning drum, drumming**.
In fox ranching, to clean (fox pelts) in a revolving drum.

After the drying, Thompson puts his pelts through a fourth and final process. He drums them all over again, fur side out, using two grades of sawdust (BRUCE, HARRY, *Silver into Gold: Alchemy in Action on Prince Edward Island's Booming Fox Farms*, 1985, 67).

W3 'to clean (fur) by prolonged shaking with fine sawdust in a revolving drum.'

drumming
Verbal noun. Compare **cleaning drum, drum**.
In fox ranching, the act of cleaning fox pelts in a revolving drum.
The average fur merchant is quite capable of judging the quality of the fur without its having been put through any cleaning process. Some even go so far as to say that thay prefer to have the pelt presented in its uncleaned, natural greasy state. But when the pelt is cleaned by combing or drumming, it looks more like the finished product, and naturally the inexperienced observer can more readily see and judge of its quality and beauty (ALLEN, J.A., and CHESTER MCLURE, *Theory and Practice of Fox Ranching*, 1926, 203). Auction companies have cleaning drums but by the time the pelts arrive there, the damage is already done and the grease is so set that it is difficult to remove completely. Drumming at the time of pelting is the answer (*Fox-Tales*, 1982, 7). Only after that final drumming does he box them for shipment (BRUCE, HARRY, *Silver into Gold: Alchemy in Action on Prince Edward Island's Booming Fox Farms*, 1985, 67). Drumming is a cleaning process. It has that name because the facility is a type of drum on a shaft. It rotates and is driven by an electric motor. Within the drum there are handles drilled and fastened into the interior. You put a mixture of hardwood sawdust of a medium to fine grade in the drum and twenty to twenty-five pelts. This cleans the oil off the pelts (S 7).

dump
Noun. Compare **bunch, dog trawl**.
A group of lobster traps tied to the same line or 'backline.'
A line with eight or ten traps on it. Where a fisherman might have used only three or four lines, they now use up to forty individual dumps (KENNEDY, LIBBY, *A Visitor's Guide to the Language of the Wharf*, 1985, 7). A dump is a bunch of six to ten traps (S 4). The boys up in French River call a dog trawl a dump (S 5).

*The terms *bunch*, *dog trawl*, and *dump* are synonymous, but vary from port to port.

dump cart
Noun. Archaic.
   A cart built for tipping its load easily.
   I also made several trips to the Harbour with the horse being hitched to a two-wheeled dump cart. This type of vehicle was used extensively thruout the Island and was the principal means of conveyance for the farmer (DALY, WHITMAN, *Daly: The Saga of a Family 1820–1926 and My Boyhood on Prince Edward Island*, [1969], 55).

[North American] *W3*; *DAE*; *DA*; *FW*.

dunch
Noun. Rare.
   Heavy, soggy, or crusty bread.
   It's a piece of bread put into milk, dunking it. It's made from homemade flour (I 050).

[From English] *OED* 1842–1879; *DNE* 1896–1941; *EDD*; *SND* 'A hunk of bread.'

dye pot
Noun.
   A chamber-pot reserved for urine that is to be used in making dye.
   Don't forget to piss in the dye pot (O).

[North American] *OED*; *DAE*; *DA*.

E

easy
Adjective, usually in phrase *to make easy*. Often in command to a child. Infrequent generally, but rare in Malpeque and Charlottetown.
   Calm, quiet, well-behaved (O).

Egg Circle
Noun. Archaic.
   A collective for the marketing of eggs.
   Fine and mild, wind northeast. Roads very soft. Annual meeting of the Egg Circle in Temperance Hall tonight. Trade very good (MCGAUCEN, MRS. JOHN, *Diary of Mrs. John McGaucen [1914–1916]*, 1914, March 6). Mr. L. brought in our mail. Got rebate from Egg Circle (MEGGISON, ELEANOR, *Diaries of Eleanor Carr Meggison*, 1926, February 26). A feature that

reminds one of rural Denmark is the development of agricultural co-operation: the *egg circles*, especially, have been very successful (TRICOCHE, GEORGE, *Rambles through the Maritime Provinces of Canada*, [1931], 138). For the first time in the history of farming in this part, farmers were getting cash for their eggs. In a year or more Senator J.E. Sinclair got Mr. J.A. Benson, the Government Poultry Representative, to come and organize Egg Circle No. 26. … A covered van drawn by two horses went on the road four days a week. The eggs were shipped to Montreal and Boston the week they were gathered and paid for in full the following month (SPRINGFIELD WOMEN'S INSTITUTE, *Springfield 1828–1953*, 1954, 36). The first Egg Circle was organized in Long River but others got into production first. A covered wagon was bought for the Summer months to keep the eggs cool. Each farmer was given a number and a chart was attached to each egg crate, in this way the candling station could tell the owner and number of dozens. Eggs were paid for according to grade; producer and consumer both benefited (THE LONG RIVER WOMEN'S INSTITUTE, *A History of Long River*, 1967, 52). I hauled eggs for a lot of years for the Egg Circle. … I got eggs in cases and I shipped them from four different stations to Charlottetown and they were graded in here and I got the report back (T M104).

elevator digger
Noun. Compare **beater digger**, **digger apron**.
   A potato digger that uses a conveyor belt to lift potatoes from the earth.
   Also by the late 1940s the 'beater diggers' were being replaced by a type of elevator digger built by Hoover, John Deere and other companies. The first elevator diggers would elevate the potatoes on a chain which passed over cogs designed to shake out the dirt. The potatoes were deposited on the ground and gathered by potato pickers using baskets. The baskets were dumped into a barrel or, by the late 1940s into bags. The elevator digger soon had an addition called a bagger which eliminated potato pickers and baskets. With the new system, bags were eit from the bagger on to a trailing tractor and wagon or placed on the ground for later pick up (FREETOWN HISTORICAL SOCIETY, *Freetown Past and Present*, 1985, 49).

end head
See **blank head**.

Epagweit
Also **Epaigwit, Epaygooyat**. See **Abeg-weit**.

escape ring
Noun. Also **escape hatch, escape
mechanism**.
   **A hole in a lobster trap that allows
undersized lobsters to escape.**
   The proposal to introduce escape mechanisms into the lobster trap is designed by the
federal department as a conversion measure to
ensure small lobster can escape back into the
environment. The regulation requires that
either a plastic or wooden escape hole be
constructed into the trap to provide a 1 3/4 inch
diameter hole to allow small lobsters to escape
(*The Guardian*, December 14, 1985, 3). Mr. White
estimates the price of the escape rings alone (at
35 cents each) will cost Southern Kings fishermen almost $700 to install since the most
common trap here is a knitted parlor on both
ends. ... It took 36 minutes to install the four
escape rings necessary on both ends of [one of]
his 300 traps (*The Guardian*, January 6, 1986, 5).
The new regulation will require round holes to
be 1 3/4 inches in diameter on escape mechanisms. ...' The escape mechanisms, usually
allowing lobsters five years old or less to get a
quick exit [from] the trap, are not used merely
for limiting the catch' [Mr. Siddon] explained.
'It allows for larger lobsters in the future, and
helps ensure future incomes for the fishermen'
(*The Guardian*, January 27, 1986, 1). An escape
mechanism is a wooden lath which has three
holes in it to let undersized lobsters out of the
trap. Located the back end of the trap on each
side (MACMILLAN, JANET, *The Language of Lobster
Fishing*, 1985, 15). We are supposed to have
them on now. They are laths with holes in them
to let the small lobsters out of the trap. Some
have got three holes and some have got two
holes. One of the best ideas that ever struck
was the escape hatch (S 4). An escape hatch is
the rig here on the side of the trap with three
small holes in it so lobsters can get out. Some
people are starting to use a lath that is spaced
so the lobsters can get out (S 6).

evening
Noun. Rare. Compare **forenight**.
   **The period from noon or the midday
meal to nightfall.**
   We hitched her up in the evening around
four o'clock and we were home around half

past six (HORNBY, SUSAN, *George Young: Horsing
Around*, 1981, 28). Long before dark. Latter part
of day rather than beginning of night (I 051).
It's about twelve or two p.m. Once you head
towards night (I 095). Any time after noon (O).

[om English] *W3* 'chiefly South and Midland'; *DAE*
'dial' 1790–1904; *DNE* 1874–1970; *OEDS* 'dial. & U.S.
local.'; *EDD*; *DJE*; *DBE*; *FW* 'Dial.'; *WNW* 'in some
parts of the South, in rural areas, and in parts of
England.'

F

faigarie
See **flagarie**.

fall herring
Noun. Compare **spring herring**.
   A coastal herring taken in the fall.
   We are inclined to believe that what are
called Fall herring, is as much a different
species of herring from the 'Spring herring,' as
Winter wheat differs from Summer wheat. It
is in all respects a better article, and we do not
see why merely because it is apparently more
grown, it should be considered the same as the
'Spring herring,' when there are more marked
differences, not to be so easily accounted for
or reconciled. The Fall herring, scored and
rubbed in oatmeal, and nicely fried, make a dish
that all lovers of fish must consider a delicacy,
and worthy of commendation (BAGSTER, BIRCH,
The Progress and Prospects of Prince Edward Island,
1861, 96).

[North American] *W3*; *DAE*; *DA*; *DNE*.

falling weather
Noun. Occasional in Egmont and Cardigan,
infrequent elsewhere; significantly rural;
unattested under forty; especially male.
   **Anticipated rain or snow; damp, foggy,
or drizzling weather.**
   It's mainly used for fun but not always.
Hearing a blue jay is a sign of falling weather
(II 001). A fisherman's term in reference to the
barometer (II 009). Any kind of birds flocking
together would be a sign of falling weather
(II 017). Falling weather is fog. It was so thick I
couldn't get to the barn (II 038). Falling weather
is the same as heavy weather (II 058). You look
at the clouds and say, 'We're going to have
falling weather' (II 066). Falling weather is

weather about to be nasty or to worsen. It's just before precipitation (II 082).

[From English] *W3* 'chiefly Midland'; *DAE* 1732–1919; *OEDS* 'dial. and U.S.'; *EDD*.

farewell summer
Noun.
A late-blooming aster.
It's a pearl of a day and the old hill road is lovely. Just now it is scarfed with a ribbon of golden rod and airy smoke blue asters – so beautiful and yet suggestive of sadness in that they are forerunners of autumn. In fact the country people hereabouts call asters by the pretty poetic name of 'farewell summers' (MONTGOMERY, LUCY MAUD, *Spirit of Place*, [1908], 70). Emily was just turning to go back when she caught sight of a magnificent spray of farewell summer, growing far out on the edge of the bank. She must get it – she had never seen farewell summers of so dark and rich a purple (MONTGOMERY, LUCY MAUD, *Emily of New Moon*, 1923, 271). My, but he was fond of flowers ... hated to mow down the buttercups. No matter if the wheat crop failed as long as there was farewell-summers and golden-rod (MONTGOMERY, LUCY MAUD, *Anne of Ingleside*, [1939], 110).

OED; W3; EDD; DAE; DA.

farmer's blessing
Noun. Compare **May snow, million-dollar rain**.
A synonym for 'poor man's fertilizer': a late spring snow-fall.
A wet snow which covers the ground well (no drifts) and then slowly soaks into the ground. Sometimes it is plowed into the ground if spring plowing has started (R 3). Supposedly helped to draw the last remaining frost from the ground (R 13). Moisture from snow sinks into the ground as a rule, while rain tends to run off, especially a heavy shower (R 27).

farmer's fertilizer
Also **farmer's manure**. See **poor man's fertilizer**.

feather-white
Adjective. Also **feathery**. Frequent in Egmont, rare elsewhere; especially older, less educated.
Of the sea, rough, foaming, having many whitecaps.

It's breaking feather-white (II 019). It's when big breakers are all over the sea (II 072). 'The sea is feather-white' means the sea is wild (II 112).

[From English] *OED* 1883; *EDD* 1896.

feeler
Noun.
A single lobster trap, or a small number of traps, used as a test for a good fishing ground.
A feeler would be a test trap. Sometimes you would use a whole 'trawl' as a feeler (S 4). Sometimes now they have a part of their gear in four-trap 'bunches' used as feelers (S 5).

fence horse
Noun. Also **fencing horse**. Archaic. Rare.
A quiet old horse.
It was probably used in earlier days when fencing was quite common in spring and there were smaller fields (II 069). These horses had patience when working at hauling logs in the woods (II 107).

*The term probably originated in the patience required of a waiting horse while its owner repaired fences, formerly a constant occupation.

fernenst
Also **fernent**. See **fornenst**.

fiddler
Noun.
Any small fish.
Any little fish (II 058). Too small to fiddle with. Not big enough to take home. As near as I can come to size it is a finger, maybe smaller (R 12). About two or three inches long (R 29).

DC 'Maritimes an Atlantic salmon weighing less than 8 pounds' 1964.

field ice
Noun. Also **flow ice**. Compare **board ice, shore ice**.
A large, flat field of floating ice.
Then we would come to a patch of field-ice about a hundred feet broad: each man stepped from the stern towards the bows, and, assisted by those who had first jumped on the ice, one by one we stepped on the frozen surface. ... It was a strange feeling, when drawing the 'ice-boat' along on the runners, and proceeding at the rate of three miles an

hour, to know that the field upon which we stood was passing with the current away to the south at the rate of five miles an hour (SLEIGH, B.W.A., *Pine Forests and Hacmatack Clearings*, 1853, 124). Then the surface frequently freezes over, and the danger of being caught by a nip is carefully guarded against. The 'lolly,' which now boils and bubbles, will before night become a congealed consistency, and form field-ice (*ibid*, 131). Wind still N. × E. and has been so since Good Friday. We are blocked up with field ice tho' the harbour is clear. There is a large quantity of ice outside (DYER, ROBERT, *Diary, 1859–1883*, 1877, April 13). Hard frosts for four or five days had filled all the bays with field-ice. A westerly gale lasting for a day had driven the fields off shore, then an easterly gale had smashed them up and the pans had blown together and frozen into big 'clumpets' (HICKMAN, ALBERT, *The Sacrifice of the Shannon*, 1903, 93–94). Found the harbour blocked by a piece of field ice made fast on outside of ice (MACDONALD, EDWARD, *Diaries of Edward MacDonald, Vol I, June 30, 1910–Dec. 31, 1910*, 1910, item 1).

[North American] DC 1850–1954; DA 1796; OED; W3; DNE; FW.

fine up
Intransitive phrasal verb. Common.
Of the weather, to clear, become fine.
'Are you really from Boston? If'n yuh are why in the world would you travel at this time of year?' Without waiting for my answer he said 'I thinks mee-self if'n I was in Boston at this time of year I'd stay there at least until the weather fined up' (JOHNSTON, LORNE, *More Recollections of an Ole Salt*, [1983?], 33). It'll fine up in the afternoon (I 065). It's a typical fishing expression (I 099).

EDD 'Wor'; OEDS 'Australianism' 1966. *fine* [verb]: OED 'rare' 1888; W3 'often used with *off*.' *fine off, out*: DNE.

finger
Noun.
In commercial fishing, a device that kicks a rope out of the 'gurdy' or winch, to prevent jamming.
A finger is what runs the rope out of the groove or block, and makes room for the next trap (S 4).

fire barrens
Noun. Compare **blueberry barrens, cranberry barrens, spruce barrens.**

A tract of burnt-over land where only scrub or berries grow.
This word may refer to burning blueberry barrens each fall or spring for a more prolific crop (O).

Barrens, as such, is standard in North America for any tract of wasteland supporting only low vegetation, 'sometimes with defining terms prefixed, as *pine-barrens*' (DAE).
[North American] DC 'Maritimes.'

fire line
Noun. Archaic.
A line of people passing buckets of water from hand to hand to fight a fire, a bucket brigade.
As early as 1858, an Act was passed by the Legislature authorizing the people of Summerside to meet yearly and appoint seven man [sic] as 'fire-wardens and assessors.' This act also required that every householder 'must keep one leathern bucket, capable of containing not less than two gallons, with the owner's name printed thereon, hung up in the entry of every house,' and also ladders sufficient to carry water to all parts of the building. In case of fire, a 'fire-line' was to be formed from the wells or water-front and these leather buckets passed from hand to hand (MACLEOD, ADA, *Roads to Summerside: The Story of Summerside and the Surrounding Area*, 1980, 61–62).

fish duck
Noun. Occasional in Egmont, infrequent elsewhere; significantly male.
A salt-water duck that feeds on fish, a cock-a-wee or merganser.
With this brief and general description in mind, let us now classify the ducks that visit our waters under the three heads [mergansers, seaducks, river ducks] as given above. In the first, that is, the fish ducks, we can place two only; the American merganser and the red-breasted merganser (MCSWAIN, JOHN, *Our Feathered Friends*, 1905, 5). Fish duck is used by the average person to mean any diving duck that eats fish (II 002). Ducks other than fresh water ducks (II 101). It has a pointed serrated bill. No one bothers to shoot it because it tastes fishy (O).

[North American] W3; DAE 1858–1917; DA.

fishing end
Noun.
A synonym for 'kitchen': the first,

**baited chamber in a lobster trap, where
the lobsters enter.**

The fishing end is where the 'fishing heads'
are, and the 'bait spear' (S 4).

fishing head
Noun. Also **side head**. Compare **head**
(noun), **hoop**, **squinteyed head**.

**One of the two funnels of twine mesh
on a lobster trap by which lobsters
enter the trap.**

The head in the 'fishing end' of the trap,
holding the rings where the lobster enters
the trap (ROBERTSON, JANICE, *A Dictionary of
Lobster Fishing in the Eastern Kings Area*, 1985,
8). The fishing heads funnel into the middle
where the bait is. They force the lobsters
towards the bait. The fishing heads have a
wooden ring in them from four to five inches
(S 4).

side head: DNE.

five-gallon
Adjective phrase. Humorous. Compare
ten-gallon.

**Of a social occasion, especially a wake
or funeral, moderate in size.**

You'd come in and get your drink, there'd be
five-gallon and 'ten-gallon' funerals. The ten-
gallon funeral'd be the big one. You wouldn't
want to miss that one. But you had to get an
invitation (T B14).

five-stack marsh
Noun.

See quotation.

The importance of the marsh is reflected in
the many old deeds that designated parts of
it as belonging to certain farms. Dykes were still
in existence when my mother-in-law helped
her father make marsh hay. She recalls that the
marshes were named by the number of stacks
they were expected to produce, such as a 'three
stack marsh' or a 'five stack marsh' (HOWATT,
BETTY, *History Begins at Home*, 1981, 24–25).

flagarie
Noun, usually in plural. \flə-'gā-rē\. Also
spelled and pronounced **faigarie**, **flega-
rie**, **frigarie**. Occasional in Egmont and
Summerside, infrequent or rare elsewhere;
especially middle-aged and older. Compare **jigaree**.

**A fancy piece of trimming or orna-
mentation.**

On a dress, car, anything with lots of fancy
trimming (II 017). All kinds of faigaries:
houses, decorations, food, dresses (II 040).
Fancy decoration on dress or hat (II 071). I
heard an elderly neighbor woman refer to a
fancy trim on her verandah (II 075). Orna-
mental trim for cupboards (O). Any unusual
trimming on something: 'He made a nice fence
and put some flegaries on it' (O).

*SND relates this word to *vagary* in the sense of 'a
play of fancy, an extravagant notion.'
[From Scottish] SND 1728–1893.

flake
Noun. Also **flanke**. Compare **make**.

**A long platform or frame on which fish
or 'Irish Moss' is dried in the open air.**

Charlie putting out codfish on the flankes to
dry in forenoon (WOODMAN, SUSAN, *Diary:
January 1, 1895–December 31, 1896*, 1896, June
8). 'Irish moss' is sold by the collector either
wet or dry, according to the region. In either
case, it is necessary that drying begin immediately. Otherwise the moss heats and spoils
rapidly. It should be spread out in a thin layer
in a clean spot. ... Flakes made of laths nailed to
two side rails are easily made, inexpensive and
satisfactory. They are light and easily portable.
A quarter-inch space between two successive
laths allows for circulation of air and hastens
drying, and at the same time is narrow enough
to prevent loss of small pieces of moss (MACFAR-
LANE, CONSTANCE, *Irish Moss in the Maritime
Provinces*, 1956, 11). In earlier days fishermen
sought the codfish which filled the Gulf of St.
Lawrence. However, it was found that the
Island sun 'burned' cod drying on flakes, and
that on the north coast, blowing sand ruined
the dressed fish (HOCKING, ANTHONY, *Prince
Edward Island*, 1978, 30). After passing through
the various stages – icing, splitting, deboning,
salting, and pickling – the cod is normally dried
in the open air on flakes. These flakes are
constructed of wood, and the cod to be dried is
placed on frames covered with nylon netting.
Since the best grade of fish is produced by
sunshine and low temperatures, most of the cod
is dried on the flakes in early fall (BOLGER,
FRANCIS, *Memories of the Old Home Place*, 1984,
8). They used to make their own flakes. One or
two men would drive stakes in the ground and
then place boards two or three feet off the
ground. The fish would be laid on that to dry
(S 13).

[From Newfoundland] *DNE*; *DC*; *OED*; *EDD*; *W3*;
GCD; *WNW*; *COD*; *FW*.

flamer

Noun. Informal. Occasional in Egmont, infrequent in Malpeque and Cardigan, rare elsewhere; significantly older, especially rural.

1. A rough-tempered person, usually a woman.

She was as red as a lobster, but she couldn't keep hold on the pupils. You'd think, with that red hair, she'd be a flamer. But they just about run her out of the school (LEDWELL, FRANK, *The North Shore of Home*, 1986, 38). A flamer is a cross between a 'streel' and a battleaxe (I 012). A flamer is a bitchy kind of a woman (I 034). A flamer would use her tongue on you (I 049). Oh, she's a real flamer, that one (I 090).

2. A high-strung or wild-acting person or domestic animal.

In my father's generation a flamer was a horse or cow that was not easy to control (I 005). 'Real flamer' is used with cattle that are wild and miserable (I 017). A regular outlaw, whether man or woman. They'd stop at nothing (I 095). Full of tricks or the devil, and hard to get ahead of. You can't be up to them, in other words (I 097).

DSUE 'a person, incident, or thing very conspicuous, unusual, or vigorous' 1808–1900; *OED* 'slang.'

flanke

See **flake**.

flat calm

Noun phrase. Also **flat-arse calm, flat-arsed calm, flat-ass calm.** Frequent in Egmont, infrequent elsewhere; significantly male.

Of the sea, completely still; dead calm.

You could hear them clear back to the wharf. O'course, it was flat calm, and that might of explained it (BOYLES, ANN, *Living in Harmony*, 1983, 64). Flat-arsed calm and the wind's south is an ideal situation (I 010). Fishermen around Tignish say 'flat-arse calm' now, and they'd even say it to the Governor-General (I 014). It is flat-ass calm out there (I 116).

[From English] *OED* 1651–1880; *ML*.

flat skin

Noun.

See quotation.

When the under fur is not sufficiently dense to properly support the 'guard fur,' the pelt is spoken of by the trade as a flat skin (ALLEN, J.A.,

and CHESTER MACLURE, *Theory and Practice of Fox Ranching*, 1926, 53).

fleet

Noun.

1. The total number of traps fished by a lobster fisherman in a season.

Short seasons do, however, lead to a keen race among the fishermen, each trying to catch as big a share of the lobsters as possible in the limited time available. To do this they have built such large fleets of traps that in many areas far more traps are fished than are actually needed to harvest the available lobsters. This practice greatly increases the cost of fishing and so reduces the net profit (WILDER, D.G., *The Lobster Fishery of the Southern Gulf of St. Lawrence*, 1954, 14). Licences are issued in relation to the two maritime lobster zones in which the island falls. Each permits the operation of one boat and one fleet of traps – 300 in the northern zone and 250 in the southern zone (HOCKING, ANTHONY, *Prince Edward Island*, 1978, 30–31).

2. All the equipment and gear owned by a lobster fisherman.

The entire traps and boat and engine and fish house and nets are what we call the fleet (S 4). A fishing fleet would include everything: the boat, the traps, everything (S 6).

*OED, EDD, and one Prince Edward Island informant use *fleet* in reference to fishing nets, but not lobster traps.

flow ice

See **field ice**.

flushing

Verbal noun.

The process of preparing foxes for breeding by increasing and improving their food.

The process of switching to the high energy diet on January 25th, and feeding a little more heavily for ten days is known as 'flushing' and is done to bring the fox females into heat in a more uniform and compact mating period than if they were left to mate when the spirit moved them. Of course if your foxes are too fat during January, this 'flushing' action cannot be initiated (*Fox-Tales*, January 1982, 3). On February 5th the low energy diet of 20% tripe, 40% cod and haddock racks and 40% meal replaces the high energy diet, bringing the 'flushing' period to a close (*ibid*, February 1982, 3). You would keep your animals maybe a bit on the thin side and then in breeding season you give them extra nutrition. I am very skeptical of the whole theory of flushing. I heard it used more in relation to sheep farming (S 7). Flushing would be a means whereby the cheapskate farmer would only feed foxes expensive horse meat or fish in certain periods of the year (S 9).

flush: W3 'to prepare (sheep) for breeding by improving the rations for a time before turning the rams and ewes together'; *OEDS* 1764.

flying axehandles, the
Plural noun phrase. Also **slippy axe-handles, throwing axehandles, wild axehandles**. Humorous. Occasional in Egmont, infrequent in Summerside and Cardigan, rare elsewhere; significantly rural, male. Compare **back door trots, blueberry run, green-apple quick-step, run-outs and walk-ins, short-taken, skithers**.
   Diarrhea.
   You used this term after you had Ex-lax or forced physic (I 056). Flying axehandles is used in the Tignish area (I 077). So and so has the flying axehandles (I 099). My husband used this in connection with the summer flu which kept him in the bathroom (P1-016). A quick run for the toilet (P1-049).

*This term is also reported in Newfoundland and Nova Scotia. No satisfactory origin has been suggested.
DARE 'Nth.'

fog
Noun. Also **baker's fog, cotton bread, ghost bread, plastic bread, puff, rubber bread**. Humorous. Infrequent generally, but rare in Summerside and Charlottetown; especially middle-aged and older, less educated.
   Commercially produced white bread.
   That bought bread is only fog (I 032). You may as well be chewing fog (I 038). My husband says, 'Bread from the store is nothing but fog' (I 050). It's like eating fog off the breakwater (I 099). Baker's fog doesn't stay with you (I 100). Most people made their own bread and felt store bought bread inferior, especially commercial white bread. 'I hope the missus doesn't start buying that awful plastic bread' (P2-055). Due to the chemicals in the bread, we called it plastic bread (P2-056). We also called it cotton bread. It was like cotton batting (P2-066).

baker's fog: DNE 1972. *puff*: EDD 'A piece, esp. a piece of bread' 1889.

footer
Intransitive verb, usually followed by *around*. \'foos-tur\. Rare. Compare **footer, fustle**.
   To act in a hasty but purposeless way; to fuss, dither.
   Foostering around means wasting a whole morning on little things (I 011). An old person not accomplishing a lot is foostering (I 024). Stop foostering around and get busy (I 038). Needless fussing (O).

*Constance Cullen reports in 'Dialect Research on Prince Edward Island,' 1971, that *footer* was known to 20% of her Kinkora (Irish) respondents and to fewer than 10% of the respondents in other non-Irish communities (p. 53).
[From Irish] W3; OED; EDD; EDSL.

foosy
Noun. \'foo-ze\. Also spelled **fussy, fosie**. Rare.
   A special treat of food.
   It was a fancy cake for special company when you didn't have much money for that sort of thing or to tempt someone who was ill (I 031). Any little treat (I 095). A special treat of candy, etc. Fort Augustus term (O).

footer
Intransitive verb, occasionally transitive, and usually followed by *around*. \'foo-tur\. Also spelled **foother** \'foo-thur\. Rare; unattested under fifty. Compare **fooster**.
   To putter, trifle, waste time.
   Don't footer away your time (I 019). Footer means sitting down with the feet up (I 026). Footering around is killing time (I 036). Footering around is going around but not accomplishing anything (I 090).

*One-third of Constance Cullen's Kinkora (Irish) respondents knew *footer* (or *foother*); it was unknown to respondents in three other, non-Irish communities that she surveyed ('Dialect Research on Prince Edward Island,' 1971, p. 53).
[From British and Irish] SND 1880–1930; OED; EDD; W3; IED.

fore-and-aft carriage
Noun.
   A horse-drawn carriage with two seats back to back.

Each summer our parents would take the whole family two or three times to the shore. We had a fore-and-aft carriage (that was what they called it, back to back) and some of us piled into it. The excitement was terrific (STANHOPE WOMEN'S INSTITUTE HISTORY COMMITTEE, *Stanhope – Sands of Time*, 1984, 243–44).

*This term is normally used only in the strict nautical sense, 'running lengthwise on a ship.' Other transferred senses are 'Applied to a field service cap' (*OEDS*), and in *fore-and-aft wagon* 'a prairie schooner' (*DA*; *DAE*).

foreign
Adjective. Sometimes humorous. Compare **away**, **foreigner**, **imported**.

Of a person or object, not from Prince Edward Island.

The relative isolation of Prince Edward Island causes many of its sons to think they live in a little world by itself. This turn of mind is detected, for instance, in the way Islanders speak of things coming from the mainland: objects shipped from other provinces are 'imported'; correspondence from the same source is 'foreign mail' (TRICOCHE, GEORGE, *Rambles through the Maritime Provinces of Canada*, [1931], 171). My first experience of coffee was in the Minister's house. His wife was a foreign woman, that is, from Nova Scotia. She gave me a cup; and the strange exotic flavour and fragrance gave entrance into a new world (MACPHAIL, SIR ANDREW, *The Master's Wife*, [1939], 72). As we are visitors from the mainland, like the 'foreign' mail, and are planning to see as much of the Island as time will permit, an excellent plan is to sit down for a while with a large-scale map (BURPEE, LAWRENCE, *Prince Edward Island*, 1946, 193). Only an Islander, for example, would refer to New Brunswick as 'foreign soil' (MACDONALD, EDWARD, *The Great Adventure: Travel Letters of William MacDonald*, 1985, 25). The inspector told a farmer to pick the foreign objects from his potatoes. Someone asked him what he was doing. He said, 'Picking tourists out of my potatoes.' The words were synonymous (I 064). Any car without P.E.I. plates, even if from Nova Scotia or New Brunswick, was called a foreign car (I 065). When we were kids, we'd see tourist cars and call them foreign cars. It used to mean from off the Island, now it means from another country. The foreign mail came off the ferry boat (I 091).

foreigner
Noun. Sometimes humorous. Frequent

generally, but infrequent in Charlottetown; especially rural. Compare **away**, **foreign**, **imported**.

A person not from Prince Edward Island.

You ask in your letter if 'Cavendish has become a place of pilgrimage for my admirers?' Alas, yes. And the chagrin expressed in that alas is not affectation at all but genuine regret and annoyance. Cavendish is being overrun and exploited and spoiled by mobs of tourists and my harmless old friends and neighbors have their lives simply worried out of them by car loads of 'foreigners' who want to see some of Anne's haunts (MONTGOMERY, LUCY MAUD, *My Dear Mr. M.: Letters to G.B. Macmillan from L.M. Montgomery*, [1928], 130). 'You a foreigner? – 'If Nova Scotia is foreign, I am.' – 'Any place off this Island is foreign,' he shot back (BIRD, WILL, *These Are the Maritimes*, 1959, 195). I was trembling in my shoes at confronting such an august person as a Supreme Court Judge. With his glasses on the end of his nose he looked over them and said, 'So you are a foreigner, are you?' I was astounded. Previous to that I had been abroad for several years and wondered what mannerisms I might have picked up that I would be thought a foreigner. Drawing myself up to my full 5 feet, 3 inches, I said, 'Why no! I am a Canadian!' Then came his deep ho ho chuckle with the explanation that anyone who isn't Island-born is considered a foreigner (DALEY, HARTWELL, *Volunteers in Action*, 1981, 59). This was the era of the Prince Edward Island Development Plan with its proposed restructuring of Island economics and, consequently, of Island society. References to 'foreigners' – especially of the government variety – in Bernard's narrative reflect the flavour of Island attitudes at the time (BOYLES, ANN, *Living in Harmony*, 1983, iii). Foreigner is a fooling term (I 006). Foreigner refers to people who live in other places, even Toronto or Montreal (I 077). A surgeon was formerly resident here. They didn't treat him well because he was a foreigner. I found out later the man was from Montreal (O).

*In the Common Word Survey, this word was the first choice of 16% for 'someone not from the Island, say from Ontario.' *Foreigner* in the general sense of 'a person regarded as an outsider or stranger' is standard.

forenight
Noun. Rare. Compare **evening**.

The time between twilight and bedtime; the evening (I 119; O).

[From Scottish] *OED* 1513–1865; *W3*; *SND* 1761–1950; *EDSL*; *DOST*; *MED*.

for fair

Adverb phrase. Occasional generally, but infrequent in Charlottetown and Summerside; significantly rural, older.

For sure, for certain.

Definitely final (I 059). For good and forever (I 098). He's stuck for fair (I 120). He was going for fair (O).

OEDS 'U.S. slang' 1900–1957; *EDD* 'Northumberland' 1824–1869.

fornenst

Preposition. \fur-'nenst\. Also spelled and pronounced **fernenst, fernent, fornent**. Rare.

In front of, opposite to, facing; next to, beside.

The tiny window was resplendent with red geraniums and right 'fernent' the door, a huge rose bush flourished (BAGNALL, MARGARET, *The Red Fox*, 1956, 38). I've heard, 'I never went fernent her,' from a man protesting a charge of paternity (I 038). Right fornent your eyes (I 084). That house is going up right fernent the river (O).

[From Irish and Scottish and northern English] *OED* 1524–1864; *W3*; *EDD*; *SND*; *DOST*; *ESI*.

four-bow trap

See **bow trap**.

four-headed trap

See **two-headed trap**.

fox

Transitive verb. Compare **fox horse**.

In fox ranching, to kill (a horse) for fox meat.

'Ya, well father,' said Seamus, on a more solemn note, 'we have ta fox that old mare, she's gettin' old and snappy' (MORRISON, ALLAN, *A Giant among Friends*, 1980, 61). Some old people wouldn't part with them though. They'd have to find out what you were going to do with them, whether you were going to fox them or trade them off or give them to somebody that would ill-use them you know. And, if you did, you had to be dang cute to tell them what you were going to do with them. Because if not, you weren't going to get them, no (HORNBY, SUSAN, *George Young: Horsing Around*, 1981, 31). In the early years of [fox] ranching, if a horse got old or crippled, the owner would say I guess I'll fox him, that is have him slaughtered and a fox rancher would buy the meat for his foxes (S 7). We took our old mare, Bob, to be foxed (O).

fox biscuit

Noun.

In fox ranching, a large round biscuit, made of flour and bran or fish meal or cod liver oil, for feeding penned foxes.

Fox biscuits: a perfect fox diet can be secured in the patent dog biscuits. These are made with various kinds of food content, so that balanced rations can be provided. The biscuit medicines have also been proved excellent, and are easy to administer. It is possible that the manufacture of biscuit with meat or fish fibre will be an industry that will develop contemporaneously with fur-farming. The meat can probably be best preserved in this way and feeding made easier and pleasanter (JONES, JOHN, *Fur-Farming in Canada*, 1914, 45). The use of milk and a suitable fox biscuit during winter would tend to counteract some of the dietary deficiencies. Such a biscuit might advantageously contain several cereals, such as whole wheat flour, rolled oats, rice flour, corn meal, etc., but it is advisable that they should be ground to a fine powder before being introduced into the biscuit. It should contain also 8 to 10 percent of fat, cod liver oil being preferable, and at least 8 to 10 per cent of edible tankage or bone meal (ALLEN, J.A., and ENNIS SMITH, *Fox Ranching in Canada*, 1929, 40). The newcomer is often amused at signs in show windows or in newspaper advertisments concerning foxes, such as: 'Fox Biscuits for Sale' (TRICOCHE, GEORGE, *Rambles through the Maritime Provinces of Canada*, [1931], 158). Hired an express wagon and horse and went out to Tiplin's ranch with some biscuit boxes. In the ranch the foxes were going around in circles (LEARD, GEORGE, *The George Leard Files*, 1977, n. pag.). Fox biscuits are a real biscuit formulated and produced for fox feed. They are not made anymore. Now we have fox cubes or fox pellets (S 7). During World War I they sent them overseas and they looked like hardtack and they ate them in the trenches (P2-004). In Charlottetown they were made in Jenkins' old transfer building (P2-059). They were usually made out of fish meal, commercially, and old flour and bran if baked at home. We never used any raising in the home biscuits (P2-066). I remember watching my husband's grandmother make the biscuits – usually in the morning – to be fed to the foxes (O).

fox horse
Noun. Compare **fox**.

In fox ranching, an old horse intended for fox food.

There was fox ranches would buy them for fox meat, you know. In my young days they just simply died and buried [sic]. But, in later years (1920's) when the foxes was around, a good fat horse would be 20 dollars. I and another fellow went away one day, we bought 14 fox horses (HORNBY, SUSAN, *George Young: Horsing Around*, 1981, 31). Horses with broken legs (P2-020). An old horse that was no more good on the farm and they'd kill him for fox food (P2-026). Old or sick horses even when they were not used for feed. 'That looks like a regular fox horse' (P2-066).

fox house
Noun. Also **fox home**. Frequent in Egmont and Summerside, infrequent elsewhere. Compare **fox money**.

A large, ornate house built from the profits of fox ranching.

Our pioneer fox men were all prospering. Many had expanded their operations to include several ranches while others had sold large chunks, if not all of their stock, for phenomenal amounts. The fact that many fast approached the million dollar mark in 1913 and 1914 is not at all surprising when one considers that sales over the $30,000 mark for a pair of mature breeders was not uncommon. It was the period of the 'fox homes' as they were referred to, homes built not in terms of dollars but in terms of fox pelts (GUNN, PAUL, *The Silver Fox Industry on Prince Edward Island*, 1973, 69). However, by the end of the period some Victorian details had returned and houses became more elaborate. On Prince Edward Island these are sometimes referred to as Fox Houses, meaning houses built by persons engaged in the fox industry (ROGERS, IRENE, *Island Homes*, 1976, 9). The house was known as a 'fox home' because it was built during the fox fur boom on the Island around the turn of the century and had a grand and luxurious style. ... The so called fox houses were built in the Alberton area just before the First World War from the large profits of the sale of foxes. In some cases the sale of one pair provided enough money to construct the large houses. ... The houses were built in the best

possible style of the day with little expense spared. Stained glass windows and marble fireplaces are common. Trim is of top quality and fancy in places. The fox houses were generally of three floors built over a full basement. Even the size of the wood used in the construction of the homes would be hard to find today (*The Guardian*, January 21, 1983, 2). They were ornate, with big posts, pillars, and large grounds (II 002).

fox money
Noun. Compare **fox house**, **moss money**, **pelt cheque**.

Money earned from fox ranching.

In different places, farmers having 'fox money' decided to lease barren rivers, and, without any expert guidance, stocked them carelessly during the summer with imported seed oysters (TRICOCHE, GEORGE, *Rambles through the Maritime Provinces of Canada*, [1931], 139). The first quarter of the 20th century was a remarkable time for some Prince Edward Islanders. Thousands of people made the kind of money they had never seen before and never would again, for 1910 to 1935 were the years when the silver fox enterprise dominated the economy of Canada's smallest province. For many families it was a period of extraordinary wealth. Very few, however, benefited in any lasting way from the millions of dollars which enjoyed a brief stay in their midst. But if the money is gone, and the foxes are gone, there is one phenomenon which remains, perhaps to haunt some, in the now obscure area of west Prince County. In desolate spots, dotting the countryside of the most remote part of the province are the handsome houses built with 'fox money' (WELLS, MARLENE, *The House That Fox Built*, 1974, 56). Fox money was money that was quickly made. Many fur ranchers had literally barrels of money, tons and tons of money coming out of their ears (S 9).

fox phone
Noun.

See quotation.

One of the more interesting items of equipment was known as a 'fox phone.' It consisted of a microphone and listening post installed in each kennel to allow the rancher to tune in on any one of them and to listen to the slightest sound, even the breathing of the foxes. Like the watch tower, the fox phone was used primarily during the critical periods, in this case particularly at whelping time. The listener could tell from the sounds picked up at the listening post exactly when pups were born in a kennel and, if there appeared to be trouble, could go right to the rescue. The Research Station at Summerside had such an installation and for a time a number of ranchers on Prince Edward Island used fox phones. The cost of the equipment was listed as $75.00 for fifteen pens and with a bit of experience a caretaker could distinguish quite readily what was taking place in the kennel at any given moment. With careful listening, one rancher told us, you could even tell how many pups were in the nestbox (FORESTER, JOSEPH and ANNE, *Silver Fox Odyssey: History of the Canadian Silver Fox Industry*, 1980, 52).

fox wire
Noun. Also **fox netting**.

In fox ranching, wire used in the construction of fox pens.

Fox Wire – the wire used in building fox enclosures – is similar in structure to ordinary chicken netting wire, but of heavier gauge. Netting wire manufacturers now provide a special wire for this purpose. The weight usually recommended varies from 14 to 16 gauge, and the mesh varies from 1 to 2 1/2 inches. This wire is marketed in various widths – from 2 to 6 feet – and in rolls of 150 feet in length (ALLEN, J.A., and ENNIS SMITH, *Fox Ranching in Canada*, 1929, 7). In a sense, fox wire is simply a wire fabric that was manufactured specifically for fur ranching. We used to be able to get old English metal. Today it is welded fabric (S 7). You can get different gauges. Fox wire was made especially for fox ranching. The first wire came from England. You would use a smaller mesh on the bottom of the pen (S 8). At the very beginning, all the fox wire was imported from England. It consisted of hexagonal mesh of various gauges. It was galvanized and allowed them to economically create fox ranches. Roger's Hardware really got into fox wire (S 9).

French fence
Noun. Compare **longer fence**.

A fence made without nails, in which horizontal poles interlock with each other to form a zigzag pattern.

I went to peter Finly's to get french fence stakes and found him yarding wood (LAMONT, MURDOCK, *Diary, 1885–1888*, 1886, 4). A zigzag fence seen in Quebec (R 29).

Frenchman's turkey
Noun. Also **Newfoundland turkey, poor man's turkey, Rustico steak, sea turkey**. Humorous. Infrequent in Egmont and Summerside, rare elsewhere.

A fish dinner, usually herring.

Frenchman's turkey is a fish meal referred to as turkey (II 033). Poor man's meal. The French were poor fishermen (II 075). Blue potatoes and salt herring (O).

freshet
Noun. Compare **borrowed day, gosling day, pet day**.

An unseasonably warm day in winter or early spring.

It's the same as a borrowed day. Comes after certain signs in nature (II 065). In the winter or early spring, a warm day that causes extensive melting with running water and really sloppy conditions. A kind of thaw (R 20). The term 'freshet' used in this area means a big thaw in the spring (R 22).

*The sense here is related to the more common one of 'a rush of fresh water.'
fresh: SND 'A period of open weather, a breaking of a spell of frost, a thaw.'

fricko
Noun. \'frē-kō\. Also spelled and pronounced **frickle**. Common in Egmont and Summerside, infrequent elsewhere.

Chicken stew.

It's an Acadian dish (II 029). It's chicken and dumplings, heard up west. It's always a big deal after card parties (II 098).

*'The fricot, a favourite dish, was made by frying chicken with pork. To this was added shallots, diced potatoes, and a thickened batter' (ARSENAULT, AUBIN, *Memoirs of The Hon. A.E. Arsenault*, [1951?], 5). [From French *fricot* 'stew, food.']

friendship cake
Noun. Also **thirty-day cake**.

A cake containing fermented fruit, an extra portion of which is given away to start another cake.

1 1/2 c. starter juice, 2 1/2 c. white sugar, 1 28 oz. can sliced peaches and juice. Stir daily for 10 days. On the 10th day, add: 2 1/2 c. white sugar, 1 19 oz. can pineapple chunks and juice. Stir daily for 10 days. On the 20th day, add: 2 9 oz. bottles of red and green cherries (cut up without juice). Stir daily for 10 days. On the 30th day, there is enough fruit for 3 cakes. Drain juice from fruit. Save 1 1/2 c. for yourself.

Give the rest away (P2-068). A cake with peaches and apples and pears. A lot of work to make (P2-044). It's around today. You get a starter from a friend, and when you finish your mixture you keep one cup for yourself and keep two cups to give away to friends. A cake made with fruit including pineapple and cherries in liquid slightly fermented. Several cakes are made and given to friends, and the base is kept going, much like sourdough (P2-055). So called because you have to share in order to make the cake and have to pass the starter on to someone else (P2-079).

frigarie
See **flagarie**.

frolic
Noun. Also spelled **frolick**. Historical.

In pioneer days especially, a community gathering at a farm, consisting of a day of communal work followed by an evening of partying; a bee.

In raising this first habitation, if any where adjacent to a settlement, abundant assistance is voluntarily contributed by the neighbours, under the denomination of a *frolic*, and is afforded at the price merely of a few regales of meat, fish, potatoes, and rum, being often thus accomplished in a single day (BOUCHETTE, JOSEPH, *The British Dominions in North America; or a Topographical and Statistical Description of the Provinces of Lower and Upper Canada*, 1832, II, 175). June 11 – Hauling down old house & digging cellar by way of frolic. 25) The cellar completed. 26) Hauling frame on to cellar by frolic. 30) Shingling frolic (ROSS, DAVID, *The David Ross Diary 1836–1879*, 1846, 33). We have had a 'stumping frolic,' that is, a gathering together of friendly neighbors to help Critchlow clear a piece of Bush land from stumps, etc., and make it ready for the plough. We had twelve (including Critchlow) to dinner and Tea, so you may think we were rather busy, for of course they had to be well entertained. I made all the pies and cakes the day before, the dinner hour being half past twelve. ... One old man said he had been on the Island 23 years and it was the best frolic he had ever been to (TUCK, ROBERT, *The Island Family Harris*, 1983 [letter of 1858], 73–74). Sunny, Dougald to McRae mud frolic, travelling bad on the ice (MCEACHERON, JOHN, *A Diary or Memorandum of Weather, Work and Other Incidents*, 1873, March 25). Mrs. MacAulay and I went to a quilting frolic at Mrs. John Dan's. We had a great day and everyone

had plenty of time to get their talking done. The quilting frame had two long poles which the canvas was wrapped around, then attached to a shorter pole at each end. When we finished one row which didn't take too long, with so many hands, we'd pull the canvas over and start again. The quilt turned out beautiful (BUSHEY, SARAH, *Memoirs of Sarah Bushey*, 1893, September 14). Cool and windy. Digging frolic at Kinches (O'CONNOR, MAURICE, *Diary: January 1–December 31, 1895*, 1895, 17). The waulking, or 'thickening frolic' was the happiest day of the year. These frolics were common in the winter time. When the web of cloth, containing generally from fifteen to thirty yards, according to the needs of the family, was ready for thickening word was sent through the settlement (MACQUEEN, MALCOLM, *Skye Pioneers and 'The Island,'* 1929, 31). Frolics were the order of the day whether it be the felling of trees, stumping, cabin building, fire place construction, quilting or feasting around a great fire of burning stumps (MORRISON, A.L., *A History of Grand Tracadie*, 1963, 9). The pioneers believed that many hands make light work and a frolic which combined work with pleasure was called for any task from stumping a field to fulling (shrinking) a web of wollen cloth. Usually at a stumping, barn raising, or other outdoor frolic home brew supplemented water as a thirst-quencher (MACNEVIN, MRS. LORNE, *Past and Present: A History of Brae*, 1979, 70). They [the early settlers] had a unique method of combining work and pleasure in the community system of 'frolics.' Was there a frame to be raised or wood to be hauled, or a piece of ground to be stumped or plowed? The accepted method of getting it done was by gathering neighbors to a 'frolic.' Most popular of all, perhaps, was the 'fulling-frolic,' at which the homespun cloth was 'fulled' or thickened by hand (MACLEOD, ADA, *Roads to Summerside. The Story of Early Summerside and the Surrounding Area*, 1980, 117). Stumping frolics, used to have lots of stumping frolics ... yeah, we'd have a piece of land, you know, do a lot of work too and they'd have a dance in the night. That was before my time (T B21). If a farmer lost his barn, maybe through fire or it just deteriorated, would they have a barn building frolic or whatever they called them, you know, where everybody came and helped to build (T M61).

*Commonly the word *frolic* is preceded by a modifier signifying the type of work: *fulling, hooking, knitting, quilting, spinning, thickening, waulking, weaving* (for domestic work, usually by women, indoors); and

barn, building, chipping, chopping, digging, hauling, logging, mud, ploughing, raising, seaweed, shingling, stumping, threshing, wood (for farm work, usually by men, outdoors).
[North American] *OED* 'U.S.'; *DC* 1822–1964; *W3* 'dial.'; *DAE* 'Obs.'; *DA* 'Obs.' 1775–1845; *GCD* 'Historical.'

from across
See **across**.

from away
See **away**.

fudge
Noun. Occasional in Egmont, rare or unattested elsewhere. Compare **chocolates**.
A scolding.
I gave him fudge (I 010). It's used in Tignish (I 021). 'You're going to get fudge or 'chocolates' means you'll get a hard time for being bad, you'll get bawled out (I 036). I would use it 'up west.' It means any bad time. Used for adults as well as kids (II 098).

full kilter
Adverb phrase.
1. At full speed, headlong; full tilt.
It's also used to describe walking fast (I 032). Used to describe riding a horse really fast (I 035). The highest speed, for example, of a bicycle (I 050).
2. Of a dial, at the maximum setting.
Also used in reference to a radio: at the highest volume (I 050). A thermometer on full (O).

*The standard *kilter* 'good working condition' is now usually found only in the informal phrase *out of kilter*. The origin of *kilter* (formerly *kelter*) is unknown. [From British] *EDD kelter*: 'Sc. Yks. eAn. ... 4. sb. Rate, pace; headlong speed.'

fun money
See **rocking-chair money**.

funnel head
See **centre head**.

fur house
Noun.
1. In fox ranching, a wholesale company that buys pelts from ranchers.
Recently, fur houses have made certain improvements in the method of presenting the goods to the busy merchant or manufacturer. Formerly, the prospective buyer of silver fox furs was compelled to wade through a maze of skins in order to make his selection. A thousand pelts might be examined before a skin suitable for his needs was reached. This process was so tedious and time-consuming, that the busy merchant would tire before he completed his inspection, and often he never saw the pelts that would have interested him most. A partial system of grading silver fox skins is now in force, and some of the inferior pelts are bunched. All the high grade skins are arranged according to color classification (ALLEN, J.A., and CHESTER MCLURE, *Theory and Practice of Fox Ranching*, 1926, 206). Fur houses are mostly people like Hudson's Bay who we sell our furs to and they sell them wholesale on commission (S 8).
2. A building for presenting fox pelts.
Fur houses: ... Buildings in which fox pelts are graded (FLOOD, SHANNON, *Fox Farming*, 1986, 11). A fur house is usually a facility where furs are assembled for marketing to the trade (S 7).

[sense 2]: *DC* 1900.

fur out
Intransitive phrasal verb. Also **fur up**.
Compare **green**, **Samson**.
Of a fox, especially one raised on a fox ranch, to grow a winter coat of fur.
The priming process follows a definite pattern and proceeds from the belly up to the sides and along the back towards the head. The last area to be covered with the winter fur is the middle line of the back and at the nape of the neck. So when the area at the nape of the neck is prime, the rest of the pelt will be prime as well. Of course, both the underfur and the 'guard hairs' have to be fully grown and the former takes longer to develop, but once the hide of the animal no longer shows any trace of pigment, the process of furring out for the winter is complete and the fur is prime (FORESTER, JOSEPH, and ANNE FORESTER, *Silver Fox Odyssey: History of the Canadian Silver Fox Industry*, 1980, 90). Furring out – shedding an old coat of fur and growing a new one (FLOOD, SHANNON, *Fox Farming*, 1986, 12). When a fox is furring out it is the same thing as a prime fox (S 7). A fox that is furred up is a fox in its prime. It would fur up in its tail first, belly next and head next. The fox was furred up usually by late November or December. To be furred up meant that the fur had reached its optimum point (S 9).

*The alternate form, *fur up*, is especially used for foxes ready to be killed and pelted.

furring shed
Noun. Also **pelting shed**. Compare **pelting pen**.
   In fox ranching, a building housing individual pens for foxes.
   Proper ventilation in a shed is essential to the production of good fur texture. If the furring shed is placed on high dry ground, especially in dry windy climates, and exposed to the wind, the fur on the foxes will become too dry. Therefore, it is advisable to build a fox shed in a north-south direction unless the prevailing winds would indicate otherwise. ... Size of the individual pens in a furring shed is important because this can affect the general well-being of the fox pups (DOMINION FOX ILLUSTRATION STATION P.E.I., N.S. AND N.B., *Progress Report 1943–1947*, 1949, 16). A good size for individual pens in a furring shed is 90 × 90 × 150 cm. long. Use 2.5 × 3.7 cm, 14-gauge galvanized wire for the floors, and bevel the cross beams under the wire to avoid collecting droppings (CANADA, AGRICULTURE CANADA, LIVESTOCK DIVISION AND ANIMAL PATHOLOGY DIVISION, *Fox Farming in Canada*, 1979, 8). Breeding foxes should be moved out of pelting sheds, or other light reduced areas, into open pens before the pelting season. They should not be allowed into the 'whelping den' or nest box until just before whelping. Overly fat foxes sleep a lot and do not see as much light as do properly fitted active animals. They breed late and not too satisfactorily (*Fox-Tales*, January 1982, 2). A furring shed is a part of the ranch equipment. It is a shed that is designed for housing foxes and it protects them from the weather (S 7). A furring shed is where you put your foxes mostly that you are going to pelt or show to keep them out of the weather – the sun, the wind and the rain (S 8).

fussy
See **foosy**.

fustle
Intransitive verb. Occasional in Egmont, infrequent or rare elsewhere; especially rural, middle-aged and older, less educated. Compare **fooster**.
   To hurry, bustle; to fuss.
   Fustling about the house too much (II 096).

[From British] *OED* 'dial'; *W3* 'dial. Brit'; *EDD. fistle*: *SND* 1786–1900.

G

gad
Noun. Common in Cardigan, occasional elsewhere, but rare in Summerside; significantly rural, male.
   A stick passed through the gills of a fish for ease in carrying; a number of fish thus carried.
   The sky was overcast, and this time no trout were rising. However, I wasn't more than halfway down the marsh when my alder gad became so heavy with trout that I decided to turn back. My night crawlers had performed for me (DOCKERTY, MALCOLM, *Streamside Reminiscences: Selected Instant Replays*, [1981], 3). A dozen or so is a good gad (I 010). We'll cut down a gad when we get to the lake (I 026). Gad refers more to the number of fish than to the stick they are on (I 070). You'd put a gad of fish on a forked alder (I 087). It's a willow you thread fish on (I 092).

[From Scottish Gaelic via Scottish and northern English] *DNE* 1894–1972; *GED* 'a number of fish, as carried home on a string or withe.' *gad* 'fishing rod': *W3* 'chiefly Scot'; *OED* 'dial'; *EDD* [Scottish and northern English citations] 1788–1891; *EDSL*.

gaff
Transitive verb. Frequent in Egmont, occasional in Malpeque, infrequent elsewhere; significantly rural. Compare **gaffle**.
   To take or steal; to grab or grapple with (someone).
   It was 10:00 and the wedding was set for 11:00 with Fr. MacDonald officiating. ... Doug stepped through the door, just as the two ladies came down the stairs and into the parlour. 'Top of the morning to ya, ladies. I must say, my younger brother has managed to gaff the finest lookin' woman in the community' (MORRISON, ALLAN, *A Giant among Friends*, 1980, 87). He gaffed something. He didn't steal it, he took it (II 016). My husband remembers someone who went by the name of 'Gaff' because he stole (II 067). He was walking by and just gaffed a hammer and put it in his pocket (O). To gaff is to grab hold of someone as he goes by (O).

*To gaff 'strike or land (a fish) with a gaff' (a pole with a hook) is standard. The meaning here appears to be a figurative extension.
DNE 'To steal or pilfer.'

gaffle
Transitive verb, often followed by *on to*.

Synonym for 'gaff': to take or steal; to grab or grapple with (someone).

To gaffle something is to take it, but you wouldn't call it stealing (II 020). He gaffled on to it means he took it. He gaffled right on to it means he really grabbed it (II 058). If someone gaffled on to you he grabbed you and threw you on the ground (II 065). I'll gaffle on to him and he'll get what's coming to him (O).

DNE speculates that this word is influenced by *grapple*.
DNE 'To set to (something) with force and vigour; seize hold of; heave.'

gallows
Adjective. Also spelled **gallous, gallus.** Often applied to children. Common in Egmont and Summerside, occasional elsewhere.
   Wicked, villainous, born to be hanged.
   It describes someone with a devilish or guilty look, from the word gallows, because they might end up there (II 003). Someone who needs to be watched (II 009). Gallows-looking (II 042). Gallous bastard that fella is (II 065). Evil-looking, jealous, sneaky, conniving. He's a gallous bugger (II 075). The priest would come to our house when I was a child and say in fun to us children, 'You've a gallous look on your face' (O).

[From British] *OED* 1425–1892; *W3* 'now dial.'; *EDD*; *SND*; *EDSL*; *DSUE*.

gam-stick
Noun.
   A crooked stick used for hanging up slaughtered animals.
   A two-pronged stick used to hold up pigs by the legs every fall (I 037). It cut the tendon on the hind foot (I 053). A gam-stick was made of ash wood (I 070).

Gambrel 'the hock of a horse' is also the standard term for such a stick, because the two are similar in shape.
[From British] *gambrel-stick*: *EDD*.

gansey
Noun. Dialectal variant of *guernsey*.
   A thick, knitted vest or sweater.
   He then changed from John's loose lumberman's garb into a neat pair of britches and a gansey; then he went down the road to wait for his brother (BAGNALL, MARGARET, *The Red*

Fox, 1956, 46). It's like a jersey, a short vest. An inner garment (O).

*The garment is named after its island of origin.
[From British] *W3*; *OEDS*; *EDD*; *SND*; *DNE*; *SSPB2*.

gate
Noun.
   A driveway or laneway.
   Roads drifted up in just a few places. Seymour had to shovel the gate out and then we got over to afternoon service without any further difficulty (WOODMAN, SUSAN, *Diary: January 1, 1895–December 31, 1896*, 1895, 5). I remember I left home and I said, 'I don't want to be around when the mare leaves.' So I stayed away for quite a while. I was just driving in the gate when they were taking her out (T M135).

[From Scottish and northern English] *OED* 'Sc. and north dial.'; *W3* 'archaic'; *SND* 'A way, road, path'; *WNW* 'Obs. or Dial.'

ghost bread
See **fog**.

gib
Transitive verb. \gib\.
   To clean (fish).
   Fishing being the chief occupation [of the Magdalen Islands], it is not uncommon to see in front of a fisher's house a pile of fish, with women 'gibbing' at one side of the heap and pigs eating out of the other (M'CORMAC, G.J., *The Kingdom of Fish*, 1901, 178). It's a job done by the fishermen's wives (P2–015). To gib you open the fish out and take the inside out, then you salt or dry them for the winter (P2–031). Gibbing is taking the insides out, with a knife or fingers (P2–051). The fish are all gibbed and ready for cooking (P2–085).

DNE 'To remove the gills and entrails of a herring'; *OED* 1883-1893.

gillock
Noun. \'ji-lək\. Also spelled **jillic, jillick, jillock, jullic**. Rare. Compare **dish**[1].
   1. A small quantity of liquid, usually alcohol.
   Come over and have a wee jillick with me (I 099). Music, dance, and song, with a good jillic in every glass (O).
   2. A container for such liquid.
   A small measure used with any liquid. A woman in the hospital said, 'I want to make

my gillock' [to urinate] (I 020). A little bottle, less than a quarter of a pint (I 071).

[From Scottish] *EDD*; *W3*. *gill*: *OED* 1275–1862.

gimp
Noun. Compare **jam**.
   Courage, spirit.
   'You little cuss! I didn't think you'd gimp enough for that,' said Ilse. ...' I don't think it was gimp,' said Emily, too honest to take a compliment she didn't deserve. 'I was too scared to stay in that room' (MONTGOMERY, LUCY MAUD, *Emily of New Moon*, 1923, 117).

OEDS 'slang'; *W3*; *WNW* 'colloq.'

girn
Intransitive verb. \gurn\ Rare.
   To whine or complain.
   Don't be girning (II 068).

[From northern Irish and Scottish and northern English] *SND* 1725–1924; *OED*; *EDD*; *W3*; *EDSL*.

glib
Adjective, usually in phrase *glib ice*. Also **glebe**, **glibby**. Common generally, but occasional under thirty. Compare **black ice**.
   Of a surface, especially ice, very slippery, smooth, and hard.
   If the ice be smooth and glibby, and if the wind blows across the carriole, it is frequently turned round, bringing the horse up at the same time with it (MACGREGOR, JOHN, *British America*, 1833, 561). I passed on, calling at Mr. D's; had my horse shod in order to go down the ice, home. It was well that I did, for, it being so hard a frost last night and no snow about, hardly anywhere, the ice would be like one sheet of glass. Went on to Colonel Duvar's ... and then started for Alberton, down the ice and sure enough, the ice was glib. Having got the horse and sleigh on it, I was obliged to drive as hard as I could to keep the horse on his feet, for 4 or 5 miles. Thank God, I got home safely about 4 o'clock p.m. (DYER, ROBERT, *Diary, 1859–1883*, 1874, January 6). Skating and hockey were favourite winter pastimes over the years in this area. ... The pond at Bristol was also used and other areas where glib sheets of ice afforded an opportunity for this sport (*Morell: Its History*, 1980, 67). The Cove Head track with a grand-stand for 2,500, became a legend in Maritime racing, being dubbed the parlor track because of its glib surface. 'It was the fastest piece of dirt

on Prince Edward Island,' said Ingham Palmer, the voice of EPR who visited the track as a youth (*Atlantic Post Calls*, November 17, 1982, 11). Travel on the glib, frozen surface of rivers, bays and harbours was marvelously easy, and for Islanders along the shoreline and the rivers, many destinations became far more accessible in winter than at any other time of the year (WEALE, DAVID, *The Emigrant: Life in the New Land*, 1985, 7). Since 1885 each [ice-]boat carried a compass, two paddles, some food and the means of making a fire. On smooth water or glib ice a sail can be used (CARLETON WOMEN'S INSTITUTE, *A History of Carleton, Prince Edward Island*, n.d., 14). It could also be a thin unsafe coating of ice over a bay or river (I 025). You could hardly stand up on glib ice (O).

*In the first postal survey, *glib ice* was chosen by 83%, over the alternatives *glare ice* and *black ice*, for 'slippery, icy patch on road.'
[From British] *OED* 'Now rare exc. dial.' 1559–1888; *DC* 'Now rare' 1837, 1952; *W3* 'archaic'; *EDD*; *SND*; *EDSL*.

go-devil
Noun. Historical.
   A primitive cart.
   When the footpaths were widened into roads, the inventive resources of the settlers were drawn upon to produce some means of conveyance. The first vehicle consisted of a box with a pole or shafts and mounted on an axle with a pair of wheels. The wheels were made of plank nailed crosswise and were made fast to the wooden axle which turned with the wheels. The axle was kept in place by wooden pins that were driven through the sills of the box on either side of the axles. The make-up was called a go-devil (READY, J.A., *Lot Twenty: From Forest to Farm*, II, 1899, 194). The first carts were a crude affair called a go-devil, the wheels were made of plank nailed together crosswise to make a solid wheel four inches thick, axle was wood and sills of box was kept in place by wooden pins on each side of axle (THE LONG RIVER WOMEN'S INSTITUTE, *A History of Long River*, 1967, 16).

*In other dialects, chiefly in the United States, a *go-devil* is a sled (see *DC*, *OEDS*, *W3*, *DA*, *FW*, *GCD*, *WNW*).
[North American.]

gommie
Noun. Also **gomaug**, **gommach**. Rare. Compare **kittardy**, **nosic**, **omadan**, **oshick**, **stouk**.

A foolish or silly person, a simpleton.
You sit there like a gommie and don't say a word (I 112). Get that gommie look off your face (I 116).

[From Irish and Scottish Gaelic via Irish and Scottish] *gomach*: SND 'A fool, a simpleton.' *gommach*: EDD 'Sc. Irel. also Cor.'

gooseberry
Noun, especially in phrase **to play gooseberry.**
A chaperon, or one who interferes with a pair of lovers.
Ken wanted to see *her* – to see her *alone*. That could be easily managed. Shirley wouldn't bother them, father and mother were going to the manse, Miss Oliver never played gooseberry, and Jims always slept the clock round from seven to seven. She would entertain Ken on the veranda – it would be moonlight – she would wear her white Georgette dress and do her hair *up* (MONTGOMERY, LUCY MAUD, *Rilla of Ingleside*, [1920], 136–37). Anne had seen a good deal of Terry that spring, for Hazel had insisted on her playing gooseberry frequently (MONT-GOMERY, LUCY MAUD, *Anne of Windy Poplars*, 1936, 174).

OED 1837–1889; DSUE.

goose-boat
Noun. Also **sneak boat**. Occasional in Summerside, infrequent elsewhere; especially older.
A boat used for approaching geese unobserved.
Just consider how the 'honk, honk' of the wild-goose operates upon the men of your acquaintance. It reminds some that they are run down after their Winter's work, and that they will surely be victims of La Grippe if they do not have a holiday. Forthwith they excuse themselves from their business, and with a gooseboat and a bag of ammunition – among which is usually included a Canadian Club ... they travel to Cascumpec or to St. Peter's Island (*Prince Edward Island Magazine*, 1903, 56–57). When the geese and brant re-turned, before the ice left the river and straits, a 'goose-boat' was used. This was a flat-bottomed boat, like a small scow, decked over at the front for camouflage, and moved by hand-operated side paddlewheels. The whole thing was paint-ed white so it would look like an ice flow to the rafts of feeding geese. My husband's uncle told how, as a boy, he brought home a cart-load of geese as a result of a foray in a goose-boat (HOWATT, BETTY, *History Begins at Home*, 1981, 26). They were used in the spring hunt that ended in 1917. They were low to the water and paddle driven. The hunter would lie flat and paddle himself to the middle of a goose colony (II 055). We also called them 'sneak boats.' They could be used at any time of the year and are illegal now. You paddled it with your feet while lying down (II 058).

sneak boat: OED 'U.S.'; OEDS; W3; DAE; DA 1853–1949.

gosling day
Noun. Rare. Compare **borrowed day, freshet**.
A fine spring day.
Mother Goose takes out her young goslings (O).

gosling blast: EDD 'a sudden squall of rain or sleet ... freq. occurs in April or early May about the time the young geese are beginning to run about.'

gossoon
Noun. Rare.
A clumsy young fellow.
It's just a silly boy. We called the dog a gossoon too (I 010).

Gossoon 'a servant boy' is standard, though archaic, from an Irish alteration of French *garçon*.
[From Irish] EDD; DSUE. [standard meaning]: OED 1684–1896; W3; ESI 'gorsoon'; COD; FW; GCD; WNW.

government man
Noun. Compare **stamp collector**.
A man who receives government assis-tance, such as Unemployment Insurance (R; O).

graip
Noun. \grāp\, sometimes \grip\. Also **graip hoe**. Archaic. Rare. Compare **graip** (verb), **three-prong drag**.
A short-handled fork with three to six tines at right angles to the handle, used for digging potatoes.
A graip hoe was used for digging potatoes in the fall. It had five prongs at right angles to the handle (I 056). It was used for digging potatoes and had five or six tines turned at right angles to the handle. ... It's used for clams now (I 102). Three prongs bent backward, like a hoe. I've not seen one for forty years (O).

*The number of tines, their angle, and the uses of this fork vary in different dialects. The spelling *grape* is common in the British Isles.

[From Irish and Scottish Gaelic via Irish and Scottish] *W3*; *OED* 1459–1894; *EDD*; *SND*; *GED*; *DGL*; *PEDGL*; *IED*; *EDSL*; *MED*; *DOST*; *WGE*; *ESI*; *COD*.

graip
Verb, usually followed by *out*. \grāp\, sometimes \grip\. Archaic. Compare **graip** (noun).
> **To dig up (potatoes).**
We graiped out potatoes, pulled them out sideways in the row (I 102).

[Probably from Scottish] *SND* 'To grope, to search with the hands' 1773.

grass colt
Noun. Rare.
> **An illegitimate child.**
It's like a colt born out on the pasture, where no one sees it, rather than at home in the barn (O).

grasshopper land
Noun. Occasional in Egmont, infrequent or unattested elsewhere; unattested under forty.
> **Unproductive land.**
A grasshopper would have to carry a lunch to get across (II 016). Originally grasshoppers swarmed and cleaned the land. After that a rabbit would have to take his lunch to get across (II 039). Land so poor you couldn't raise an umbrella (II 113).

grayback
Noun. Rare.
> **A large ocean wave.**
'Yes, indeed, the Lord does provide, because here we is, floating on the sea, as calm as that sea ... where Jesus stilled them big grayback rollers' (BOYLES, ANN, *Living in Harmony*, 1983, 65). It rolls like a blanket and the whole top comes off before it hits the boat, you hope (I 056).

[Maritimes] *DC* 1916–1964; *W3* 'dial'; *DSUE* 'nautical coll. late C. 19–20.'

grease leg
Noun.
> **A disease affecting the heels of horses.**
This horse was naturally slow, a trait made worse by a severe case of 'grease leg,' caus-

ing one hind leg to be twice its normal size (PAYNTER, RUTH, *From the Top of the Hill: The History of an Island Community*, 1977, 51).

grease: *OED* 'A disease which attacks the heels of a horse' 1674–1865.

green
Adjective. Compare **fur out**.
> **Of a ranch-raised fox, having a coat that is not yet ready for pelting.**
A green fox is a fox that is not 'furred up.' It is a common term in live fox shows. A judge would realize it was a good fox but that it was green (S 7). A green fox is a fox that is not prime, not ready for pelting (S 8).

green apple quick-step, the
Noun. Also **green apple trot**, **green apple two-step**, **sour apple quick-step**, **two-step**. Occasional in Egmont, infrequent or rare elsewhere. Compare **back door trots**, **blueberry run**, **flying axehandles**, **run-outs and walk-ins**, **short-taken**, **skithers**.
> **Diarrhea.**
After eating green apples you'd be stepping pretty quick (II 038).

Green apple polka is attested in Cape Breton (O).

greening
Verbal noun. Compare **greensprouting**.
> **Discoloration of potatoes that occurs when they are exposed to light.**
The very fact that a potato can be kept for this length of time ... and still be firm and free from sprouting plus any appreciable greening, is exceptional (MCCABE, WAYNE, *Potato Wash and Wax Test*, 1974, 4). Potatoes should always be kept in darkness to prevent greening (ADVISORY COMMITTEE ON POTATOES, *Atlantic Canada Potato Guide*, 1984, 12). Indirect or artificial light will cause greening of the potatoes (S 3).

greensprouting
Verbal noun. Compare **greening**.
> **The sprouting of seed potatoes deliberately exposed to light in order to decrease growing time.**
Tubers warmed and sprouted in the presence of light form short, compact, tough green sprouts. These short sprouts are less subject to damage than are the longer white sprouts formed in the dark. Greensprouting will give

earlier emergence, tuberization, sizing and maturity. The greatest advantage of green-sprouting occurs with early harvest particularly in early frost-prone areas and diminishes as the crop is allowed to grow to maturity (ADVISORY COMMITTEE ON POTATOES, *Atlantic Canada Potato Guide*, 1984, 3). Greensprouting is increasing the temperature of the seed potato so that it will incorporate well into the ground when planted (MCCARVILLE, LISA, *A Potato Farming Lexicon from Kinkora, P.E.I.*, 1986, n. pag.).

gridley grinder
Noun.
   A severe storm.
   A gridley grinder is a hell of a storm (P2-032). A bad storm that made you scared and sounded like a grinder. It's old fashioned. 'Here comes a gridley grinder' (P2-066).

grist
Noun.
   A large quantity or amount.
   A grist of fish (II 002). Scads would be the same thing (II 021). A whole grist of things (II 081).

*This sense of *grist* must be distinguished from the standard sense in *a grist of grain* 'grain that is to be ground' or 'an amount of such grain.'
[North American] *OED* 'U.S.'; *DAE* 1833–1906; *DA*; *W3*; *OEDS*.

groik
Noun. Rare.
   1. An awkward or clumsy person, a bungler.
   A person who is untidy or awkward (II 028). 'He's some sort of a groik' means an awkward clumsy person who can't do his work right. 'A groik of a thing' also refers to a person (II 107). Gaelic for a person not doing work properly (O).
   2. A finicky person, especially with food (O).

[From Scottish Gaelic via Scottish] *SND* 'Gael. *groig*, an awkward, bungling man' 1931–1954; *DGL*; *GED*; *PEDGL*.

ground-dried
Verbal adjective.
   Of 'Irish moss,' dried on lawns and driveways, before being sold (S).

growl
Transitive verb, sometimes followed by *out*. Compare **growling**.

   To scold; to quarrel with.
   My father would growl me for not being able to make the horses go (O). Barb growled me out for taking off my coat. It was such a nice day … I said, 'What are you growling me for?' (O). She'll growl me out (O).

growling
Verbal noun. Compare **growl**.
   Quarrelling; scolding.
   We collided. … I took five spokes out of his new wagon wheel and he was going to sue me for it. … The girls got out of the wagon and walked home. We were doing the growling there on the road (HORNBY, SUSAN, *George Young: Horsing Around*, 1981, 28). I've heard 'a growling' used to mean a scolding (II 058).

grunt
Noun. Also **blueberry grunt**. Infrequent generally, but rare in Egmont; significantly female; especially older.
   A steamed pudding made with berries, especially blueberries (I, O).

[Maritimes and New England] *DC* 1894–1964; *W3* 'so called fr. the noise it makes when steaming.'

guard hair
Noun. Also **guard fur**. Compare **king hair**, **veiling**.
   The long, glossy hair that protects the underfur of a fox reared for pelting; a single strand of this hair.
   For the purpose of description the fox's coat may be said to be made up of two types of fur: the underfur or that fine, soft silky down which constitutes the body of the pelt, and which is the first to grow on the animal, and the guard fur or 'king fur,' as it is sometimes called. It is to this long guard fur, which does not reach to maximum growth until the coat is reaching maturity, that the fox owes its intrinsic value, and beauty, so rare in fur-bearing animals (ALLEN, J.A., and CHESTER MACLURE, *Theory and Practice of Fox Ranching*, 1926, 53). Guard fur is an extremely important factor, because without it the skin is practically worthless. The fur expert lays great stress on this point, and his judgement and decision is largely based on the quality of this fur. Guard fur, then, may be taken as the outstanding factor, because its presence or absence decides the value of the finished product. The guard fur should be long, dense, and should cover the entire body or coat of the fox. It should be longer on the top of the

neck and shoulders than on the rest of the body. Such a coat is to be preferred to one having guard fur of uniform length and density over the entire body, even though the top fur in this case is fairly long. In color, the guard fur should be glossy black, almost purplish-blue black. The silver guard hairs or fur should be of equal length and quality to that of the black guard hair, and it should be of a bright metallic color, free from chalky or whitish appearance and equally distributed on both sides of the body, with the white-ringed guard hairs preferable to the all-white sprinkling of silver (*ibid*, 54). There are two kinds of fur on a fox. The guard hair fluctuates and creates the appearance of a much larger animal than a ten to twelve pound fox. The guard hair is more prominent and protects the underfur and creates the 'veil' effect (S 9).

W3 'any of the long coarse hairs forming a protective coating over the underfur of a furred mammal'; *DC*.

gulch
Noun. \gulch\, sometimes \gulsh\, \kulch\.
   Unappetizing or non-nutritious food.
   Any prepared dish in which the ingredients are not easily identified and appear unappetizing (R 8). My mother would use it, for example, in reference to junk food (R 10). Food of poor quality or poorly prepared. 'The worst mess of gulch I ever tasted' (R 13).

gully
Noun.
   See quotation.
   On we went, speeding miles on the pans of ice until we came to a large outlet of a lake through which we drove the horse and sleigh and got up again, journeying on until we came to turn in for land. But to get on shore we had to cross what the people call a gully, a deep ravine of water which had become all broken up, except a narrow part, just enough to pass the horse and sleigh over (DYER, ROBERT, *Diary, 1859–1883*, 1862, April 21).

*The meaning here is an extension of the standard one: 'a ditch or small ravine worn by water.'

gullywasher
Noun. Rare. Compare **sod-soaker**.
   A severe storm that causes soil erosion.
   It has to move clay. A heavy rain in any time but winter (II 002). We don't get gullywashers like we used to when we had more snow in winter (II 091). High wind and lots of rain, an 'up west' word (II 105). A really furious storm. It could be any time, but mostly spring or fall. It would wash right up to the Cape (O). I use it in natural speech: 'It'll be a real gullywasher.' I picked it up from fishermen in Egmont, and assume it relates to tide being whipped into gullies along the cape, eroding them (O).

[North American] W3 'dial'; *DA* 1923–1948.

gurdy
Noun. Also spelled **girdie**. Compare **nigger-head**.
   A winch for hauling lobster traps, nets, or lines aboard a fishing boat.
   The vessel was equipped with a trap hauler, consisting of a girdie and a 'nigger-head' powered by a 4 h.p. Briggs and Stratton gasoline motor (PRINCE EDWARD ISLAND, DEPARTMENT OF FISHERIES, *Offshore Lobster: Technical Report #175, 1975*, 1975, 3). A piece of hydraulic equipment resembling two discs placed back to back. When a boat comes up to a buoy, the buoy line is gaffed and wrapped around the wedge that is formed between these two discs. As the gurdy rotates, the line is wedged tighter and tighter, and this pulls the traps up from the bottom (MACMILLAN, JANET, *The Language of Lobster Fishing*, 1985, 16). I never seen a gurdy. Mostly it's used when a fellow is fishing alone. The trap comes right up to the washboard. It saves a man who is fishing alone (S 4). A gurdy is like two saucers put back to back. This thing rotates and hauls the traps up (S 5). A gurdy is a set of tapered discs that act as a trap hauler (S 6).

*This word is an abbreviation for *hurdy-gurdy* 'crank or windlass,' derived in turn from the musical instrument of the same name that produces sound by a turning wheel (*OED*).
DNE 1924–1971; *DC*; W3.

gurry-butt
Noun.
   See quotation.
   'Gurry-Butt' was another term used by fishermen. It was a barrel in which the livers were placed for rendering. This process was accomplished by the heat of the sun. There were two plugs, one a short distance above the other, on the barrel. The lower one was to drain the water and the upper one to drain the oil. Cod and hake livers were placed in this container, and the oil, when drained off was sold (MACDONALD, MARY, and MRS. CLINTON STEWART, *Historical Sketch of Eastern Kings*, 1972, 37).

Gurry 'fish offal' originated in the Atlantic provinces, but has not been attested in this study, as such, on Prince Edward Island (see *DC*).

gut pudding
Noun.
   A sausage stuffed with cornmeal and suet (O).

OED 'Obsolete.' *gut sausage*: *DC* 1958.

guzzle
Transitive verb.
   To grasp by the neck, to throttle.
   The other day he told me, with his characteristic put-on philosophical mask, 'Women ought occasionally to be guzzled!' On that occasion he was a safe distance from his wife, who can look sometimes as if she could happily 'guzzle' him (LEDWELL, FRANK, and RESHARD GOOL, *Portraits and Gastroscopes*, 1972, 23).

[From British and northern Irish] *OEDS* 'slang and dial.'; *EDD*; *SND*; *DNE*; *DAS*.

H

haley-over
See **leap**.

half
Intensifier. Informal. Infrequent.
   Extremely, very.
   You could say, 'it's half windy' or 'it's half cold' (O).

*In other dialects, *half* is so used with *not*.

half a look
See **look and a half**.

half line
Adverb phrase following verb *to fish*; sometimes **on the half line**.
   (To fish) for half the catch.
   Wages for lobster fishermen and factory workers invariably remained low. In addition to hiring workers to operate their canneries, local lobster packers often owned their own small fleet of fishing boats which they rented out to many fishermen for the season. These 'hired' fishermen were also supplied with the necessary equipment, including gasoline, bait and board and lodging. In return for his investment the factory owner received one-half of the season's catch from each boat. This arrange-

ment was commonplace and in some localities was referred to as 'fishing half line' (MORRISON, CLINTON, *Along the North Shore: A Social History of Township 11, P.E.I. 1765–1982*, 1983, 70. If I owned a boat and gear, in order to give you a good break I would fish on the half line with you. That is, we would halve up the catch between the two of us (S 4). Half line is when two guys fishing together get half the catch each (S 6).

handpicker
Noun. Compare **comber**, **handscoop**.
   1. In 'Irish moss' harvesting, one who gathers 'storm-tossed moss' by hand at the shore.
   After a good storm, you might see 100 handpickers on a single stretch of beach (BERNARD, BLAINE, *Dictionary of Irish Moss*, 1986, n. pag.). Handpickers are the people who go down with a bucket or pail and pick out moss, out of the water. There is not much money in this type of mossing (S 12).
   2. A person who removes impurities from harvested moss.
   Somebody who is good to handpick is good at sorting the 'dirt' out of the moss. If they are good handpickers they can clean a fork-full on the back of the wagon as fast as you can fork it up to them (S 10). A handpicker, he would pick on the shore. He would pick the dirt out of the moss (S 11).

To handpick 'to pick by hand as opposed to a machine process' (*W3*) is standard.

hand scoop
Noun. Compare **comber**, **handpicker**, **man drag**.
   In 'Irish moss' harvesting, a wire net on a pole, used for gathering 'storm-tossed moss' by hand at the shore.
   The advantage of a hand scoop over a rake is that one can collect moss, dump it, turn the scoop over, and collect again (BERNARD, BLAINE, *Dictionary of Irish Moss*, 1986, n. pag.). They use a hand scoop on the shore. They have like a 'dip' net generally made with w with a handle on it to pull towards them or they use a rope (S 11). A hand scoop is a tool used by mossers who instead of hauling behind a horse do it by hand (S 12).

hand socks
Noun.
   Mittens, especially if oversized.

They were home knitted mittens lined with a roll of carded wool to keep your hands warm, and used for driving to Charlottetown or for long trips. They were worn rarely because they were clumsy (P2-002). They were mitts especially made for fishermen to wear (P2-009). You made them bigger so that when you got them wet in salt water they still fit when they shrank (P2-054).

hand stocking: EDD.

handy
Preposition. Common.
Close to, near.
'Well, Anne Shirley,' said Marilla as soon as she could speak, 'if you must borrow trouble, for pity's sake borrow it handier home. I should think you had an imagination, sure enough' (MONTGOMERY, LUCY MAUD, *Anne of Green Gables*, 1908, 167). Got lost on the ice one time out on Malpeque Bay and the only way we could find our way back from the 'mussel mud' diggers was to follow the tobacco juice along the ice where the old farmers spit. Where they squirt, it was sometimes handy the road (STEWART, DEBORAH, and DAVID STEWART, *Winter Travel*, 1979, 22). Now this fella lived right handy me in town, so when he arrived home ... the first thing he done was went into my place (CAMPBELL, FRANK, *As the Fella Says ...* , 1983, 172). We recommend all policyholders, especially those using woodburning appliances, install smoke detectors and keep a fire extinguisher handy the woodburning appliance (P.E.I. MUTUAL FIRE INSURANCE COMPANY, *Annual Report, 1983*, n. pag.). Our base camp is situated on the seashore in Lot 28, handy the spot where my great, great, great, great grandfather, Belcher Muttart, one of the very first settlers on the Island, carved a homestead out of the wilderness (MILLER, LLOYD, *Our Forefathers Builded Wisely*, n.d., 2). You always have the garden handy the house (II 077). We wouldn't go handy the table because the 'mickeram' might get us (O). My sunflowers are handy the barn (O).

*In other dialects, *handy* is commonly followed by *to*, *for*, or *by*, or is used as an adverb meaning 'convenient': 'The store is handy.'

hangashore
See **angishore**.

hank
Noun. Rare.

A quantity (of fish) looped on a string.
What a beautiful hank of trout (O).

SND 'As in Eng., a loop, coil. Hence ... *hank o' fish*, half-a-dozen fish looped on a string.'

Hannah
Noun.
A fussy older woman, especially if unmarried.
One of those fussy old maids, a Hannah (P2-031). Hannah was an expression for fussy women used by the people of Rustico in olden times (P2-044). A lady in the country community who did good deeds for her neighbors. The name is taken from Hannah in the Bible who sacrificed her son to God's work (P2-054). Used for a fussy woman. She's fussy because she has no family like the one in the Bible. 'She's a regular Hannah today' (P2-066).

*The biblical reference is to 1 Samuel 1:2.

hardwood sock
Noun. Rare. Compare **barn sock, lumber sock, moccan, oversock**.
A heavy woollen sock usually worn inside a work boot (II; O).

harvester kitchen
See **back kitchen**.

haul-up
Noun. Compare **bridle**.
Synonym for 'snood': in lobster fishing, the rope that connects a lobster trap to the 'backline,' or main fishing line.
A trap's coming up, we see the haulup real clear / We 'washboard' the trap, the first one this year (FLEMING, RICHARD, *Lobstering*, 1985, n.p.). A short piece of rope that connects the trap to the 'backline.' On 'bridle' traps it is tied on to the middle of the 'bridle' (MACMILLAN, JANET, *The Language of Lobster Fishing*, 1985, 17).

head
Noun. Also **heading**. Common in Egmont, frequent in Summerside and Cardigan, occasional in Malpeque and Charlottetown; significantly rural, male. Compare **blank head, centre head, fishing head, head** (verb), **squinteyed head**.
Any of the knitted pieces of twine mesh in a lobster trap.

Charlie home in afternoon putting heads in traps and loading sleds with them (WOODMAN, SUSAN, *Diary: January 1, 1895–December 31, 1896*, 1896, March 9). The trap at the end, as a general thing, has heads that are knit with quite a large mesh and a large number of the small lobsters work through anyway (CANADA, HOUSE OF COMMONS. *Lobster Fishery Evidence Taken before Commander William Wakeham, M.D., Officer in Charge of the Gulf Fisheries Division, in Quebec and the Maritime Provinces*, 1910, 342). A good fisherman ... has all his traps fixed in the winter. I remember when my father and I – and my brother helped too – made a thousand traps in the winter. We went to the woods, got the spruce, sawed the laths, cut the 'bows,' knit the heads, made the rings all ourselves. Today you can buy most anything for a trap (STIRLING, LILLA, *Jockie: A Story of Prince Edward Island*, 1951, 65). Then you'd buy twine and you'd knit all your headings yourself. I suppose you could make outright, with your headings and everything, about three or four traps a day, that's about all (ANDERSON, ALLEN, *Salt Water, Fresh Water*, 1979, 77). 'We didn't locate any of the missing traps except for the eight attached to a buoy,' confirmed fisheries investigator Boyd McMaster. 'On these traps the doors had been removed, the heads were cut out and some were smashed (*The Guardian*, May 17, 1985, 1). We used to make the heads. It is the same stitch that is used for tatting (P1-016). Fishermen pay so much per head for knitting (P1-024).

DNE; ML.

head
Transitive verb. Compare **head** (noun).
    To knit 'heads' for (lobster traps).
    Agnes washing, Charlie at home heading traps in forenoon (WOODMAN, SUSAN, *Diary: January 1, 1895–December 31, 1896*, 1896, March 23).

SSPB.

heading lath
See **rigging lath**.

heading needle
Noun. Also **twine needle**.
    A flat, wooden or plastic needle used for knitting the 'heads' or mesh pieces on lobster traps.
    Heading needles are what we call twine needles. We had to make them out of wood,

out of clean maple straight grained and cut out a notch for the twine (S 4). Heading needles were knitting needles something the same as they used for mending nets (S 6).

head stick
See **rigging lath**.

heat
See **shin of heat**.

hidden pond
See **blind pond**.

high boat
Noun.
    In lobster fishing, the boat with the largest catch in a day or season.
    In the best producing areas the high boat will catch up to 25,000 pounds in a good year but this is unusual. The general average for a fleet of boats is considerably less than half this amount (WILDER, D.G., *Canada's Lobster Fishery*, 1957, 17). Most factories had fishermen competing for a 'high boat' prize (CHEVERIE, LEO, *Johnson's Lobster Factory 1935–1945*, 1982, 3). A boat that fishes real well. 'He was high boat today' (S 4). A high boat is the boat with the high catch for the day or season (S 6).

high dory: DNE 'the dory crew with the largest catch of cod' 1960.

hiller
Noun. Also **potato hiller**. Archaic.
    A machine with two rotating discs used to hill or pile soil around potatoes.
    George Bishop assumed management of the foundry about 1878, and by 1890 was successfully manufacturing the popular 'Western Boy' plows, mud-diggers, hay forks, 'scufflers,' and potato hillers, as well as performing general blacksmithing jobs for local residents and ships in port (RANKIN, ROBERT, *Down at the Shore: A History of Summerside, Prince Edward Island [1752–1945]*, 1980, 85). Two discs with a concave shape; as the discs turn they throw the dirt up (S 1). It had two discs on each side or two moldboards for each row. There were a lot of different types of them (S 2).

W3 'an attachment to a cultivator or plow for hilling plants.'

hips
Plural noun.
    Hip-waders.

Coveralls made of waterproof plastic fabric which is worn above the hip. I wear waders [rubber boots] when 'mossing' close to shore. When I wanted to go in deeper because of incoming moss, I had to go home to get my hips (BERNARD, BLAINE, *Dictionary of Irish Moss*, 1986, n. pag.). When the weather is cold in the spring and fall we wear hips. All you need when it is warm is a pair of sneakers to save your feet because you are going to get wet anyway (S 10).

hip: DAE 'a rubber boot reaching to the hips' 1893; *DA*.

hire with
Transitive phrasal verb.
To get a job with (some person).
He was a native of Suffolk, England, and came to the Island alone in 1831 when a very young lad. He hired with a farmer, and on cold winter nights could see ranks of stars through the gaping roof above his head in the attic where he slept (MACLEOD, ADA, *Roads to Summerside: The Story of Early Summerside and the Surrounding Area*, 1980, 68).

SND 'To engage oneself as a servant, to take service.'

hitherie-hie
Adjective. Rare.
Disorderly, in confusion.
Everything is hitherie-hie in my house today (O).

hog back
Noun.
Anything resembling the back of a hog in outline.
There was quite a knack in building sleighs. You take a stick with a hump in it – they'd call it a hog back – it would never run well, had no life to it. A good runner needed to have life in it to run well; it could straighten out and have bounce to it (STEWART, DEBORAH, and DAVID STEWART, *Winter Travel*, 1979, 23).

W3.

hoikster
See **oxter**.

holey dollar
Noun. Also spelled **holy dollar**. Historical. Informal. Compare **John Joy Token, leather dollar, merchant's forgery, Sheaf of Wheat, tree cent.**

A Spanish silver dollar with a hole punched out of the centre.
It is also ordered that Spanish Dollars, limited to the amount of One Thousand, shall be cut at the Treasury, by having a circular piece taken out of the center of each – the Dollars so cut, are to be issued from and received at the Treasury at the rate of Five Shillings Currency each, and the piece so taken out to be issued from and received at the Treasury at one shilling currency each (*Weekly Recorder of Prince Edward Island*, 1813, 375). A Canadian coin collector in Vancouver has a specimen of the 'holey dollar' with the center piece. The coin is very rare and far above the purse of the average coin student to possess (BREMNER, BENJAMIN, *An Island Scrap Book: Historical and Traditional*, 1932, 149). In recent years the rarity of the holey dollar and plug has attracted fakers. About 1961 a rash of holey dollars suddenly appeared on the market. Some were undoubtedly unimpeachable, but too many were of recent and not very careful manufacture. The perforation was not always perfectly round and the cut edge was a little new for the age of the coin. Sometimes the countermark was carelessly made and misapplied, and sometimes the range of dates on the coins was too wide (WILLEY, R.C., *Early Coinages of Prince Edward Island*, 1979, 354). Here, win ye want to sell, the only money to be had is Spanish Pieces ov Eight … Pirate Money. Now I hear they're cuttin' the middle out ov them. What kind ov money is that I'm askin'? A hole in the middle indeed! … They're after callin' the outside a 'Holy Dollar' an' its the centre that's called a 'dump' (TOWNSHEND, ADELE, *For the Love of a Horse*, 1985, 2–3). In 1813, the Executive Council of P.E.I. under Governor Smith, authorized the punching out of the centre of the Spanish dollar – the dollar to retain its value, the punched out centre, called a 'plug,' valued at one shilling. This was the 'holey dollar.' The idea of the project was to make more plentiful silver pieces of smaller value (PRINCE EDWARD ISLAND HISTORICAL SOCIETY, *Pioneers on the Island, Part 2*, n.d., 45).

*The same coin and name were used in Australia at about the same time (*OED, W3, DSUE, DAC, DAusE*).
DC 'P.E.I., Hist.'

hollow heart
Noun. Compare **blackleg, spindle tuber**.
An abnormal condition of potatoes that have grown too fast, characterized by an internal cavity.

Netted Gems grown for processing require specific management practices which are very important to ensuring a good yield of tubers with the quality characteristics required by the processor, namely, large, undamaged, mature tubers with a high specific gravity reading free from hollow heart (WHITE, R.P., and H.W. PLATT, *Hints on Growing Netted Gems for Processing*, 1980, 1). These disorders are associated with tubers which size very rapidly. Tubers may size rapidly when a rainy period follows a drought, through the improper placement of fertilizer or in fields with poor plant stands. Varieties vary in their susceptibilities to these disorders. Kennebec is very susceptible to hollow heart (ADVISORY COMMITTEE ON POTATOES, *Atlantic Canada Potato Guide*, 1984, 32). Heat, warm soil, and moisture can mean rapid growth and can cause hollow heart or growth cracks. A 'V' that is healed is an indication of a growth crack, caused by less than ideal growing conditions (S 1). Hollow heart is a thing that they never got a solution for (S 2).

W3; OEDS.

home boy, home girl
Noun.
1. A mentally handicapped boy or girl who stays at home.
Mainly a slow, shy person who cannot or does not want to leave home (R 12). Today this is not necessarily true, but in olden times it was considered a disgrace to have a retarded child and they were kept at home (R 15). In my part of the country a home-girl was thought of as often rather feeble-minded (R 21). Refers to a boy (mentally retarded) who would always be around home probably all his life (O).
2. A boy or girl from an orphanage, a foster child.
A boy from a home in England who was sent to Canada to farm homes where he worked and finished growing up and going to school. They were sort of 'hired boys' for room and board. Many were not very well treated (R 5). A boy taken from an orphanage (home) to live with a family where he was expected to earn his keep. Often abused and over worked and treated little better than a slave. 'We got a home boy to help with the chores' (R 13). A girl from the Nova Scotia Home. I suppose like Anne of Green Gables (R 21).

*For many Canadians, sense 2 applies specifically to *Barnardo boy*, a boy from Dr. Barnardo's Homes, a charitable institution in England.
[Canadian] DC 1913–1932; OEDS; DSAE.

hoop
Noun.
In lobster fishing, the circle of wood or plastic in the 'fishing head' of a trap, through which lobsters enter.
Q. Do you not think your entrance hoops are so small that large lobsters cannot get into the trap? – A. Well, if some of these chaps had to make a hoop to suit them every lobster would go out. Q. What is the size of your hoop? – A. Four and a half inches (CANADA, HOUSE OF COMMONS, *Lobster Fishery Evidence Taken before Commander William Wakeham, M.D., Officer in Charge of the Gulf Fisheries Division, in Quebec and the Maritime Provinces*, 1910, 241). The hoops were of wood or plastic construction measuring 5 inches (PRINCE EDWARD ISLAND, DEPARTMENT OF FISHERIES, *Offshore Lobster: Technical Report #175, 1975*, 1975, 2).

horn
Noun. Occasional in Summerside, infrequent elsewhere; significantly male. Compare **horn up** (verb).
A drink of liquor, sometimes specifically as used for a bribe during an election campaign.
From open vote days. There could be a keg in front of the polling station. You went up and got your drink in a horn cup (II 009). It's used in the country. 'Would you like a little horn?' (II 058). He likes to have his horn (II 083). Let's go out and get a horn (II 091). Any kind of a drink for a bribe. The mayor would give me a horn (O).

*A horn elsewhere is a drinking vessel made of horn; the term is here extended to the contents of the vessel.
[From British] OED 1000–1868; W3; EDD; SND; EDSL; DNE 1866–1976; DSUE; WNW.

horn up
Intransitive phrasal verb. Compare **horn** (noun).
To take a drink of liquor, especially as a bribe during an election campaign (O).

horribles, the
Plural noun phrase. Archaic.
Costumed clowners who would parade on New Year's Day.
This used to be when I was young. Adults dressed up in outlandish garb, often with weird masks on or with a blackened face. They rode in the New Year's parade (R 20). In Summerside at one time, an annual New Year's

parade was held with sleighs, wagons, horses, and clowns all decorated, called the horribles parade (R 23). The horribles were costumed clowns that appeared on New Year's Day in Charlottetown at the horse races on University avenue each year, from the Soldier's Monument to Gallows Hill (R 27).

*DARE reports the phrase *antiques and horribles*, a humorous variation of *ancients and honorables* (i.e. 'the Ancient and Honorable Artillery of Boston'), for clowners who paraded in or near Boston on the Fourth of July; the phrase was often shortened to *horribles* (1907–1940). In Canada, the custom apparently died out during the First World War.

horse clam
See **bar clam.**

horse mosser
Noun. Compare **horse rake, mosser, moss horse, shore mosser**.
  An 'Irish moss' harvester who uses a horse and rake at the shore to collect 'storm-tossed Irish moss.'
  Many horse mossers have lost their horses because of depressions in the sea-bed (BERNARD, BLAINE, *Dictionary of Irish Moss,* 1986, n. pag.). There are no horse mossers here [in north-east PEI] but they do it up west. It is like a sleigh affair, you go out from the shore to where the moss is and then circle back through the moss. The rake gets quite full and heavy but the water helps to float it. Then when they get to the shore somebody else trips the rake and dumps the moss and they go out again. The rake used is like an old hay rake (S 10). You might say that they are all horse mossers around here [Anglo]. The horse mosser gets the moss in the landwash before it gets to the shore (S 11). A horse mosser uses a horse to drag a scoop to collect 'storm-tossed moss' (S 12).

horse rake
Noun. Compare **horse mosser, horse scoop, moss horse**.
  A large rake pulled by a horse for harvesting 'storm-tossed Irish moss' at the shore.
  You would go out on horse back and rake for moss. The horse rake would probably be pretty big, say about four to six feet wide (S 10).

W3 'a horse drawn rake.'

horse scoop
Noun. Also **scoop.** Compare **basket, horse rake**.

  A strong-framed wire-mesh basket pulled by a horse for harvesting 'storm-tossed Irish moss' at the shore.
  An implement used to collect Irish moss which is somewhat shaped like a small hockey net. A horse scoop is able to collect fifteen pound of moss per load (BERNARD, BLAINE, *Dictionary of Irish Moss*, 1986, n. pag.). There is considerable drama associated with the gathering of moss. Very often the harvesting is a family affair, with women and children flocking to the beaches with the men after heavy weather has sent the waves rolling in with fronds torn from the bottom. While the moss on the shore is being gathered up by rakes and forks, horses with scoops harnessed behind them trot or canter – often to the urging of children – along the ebb waters to salvage the moss floating out of reach (BOLGER, FRANCIS, *Memories of the Old Home Place*, 1984, 1). A horse scoop would be a large basket of wire with an iron frame and two runners on the bottom so the wire would not get ruined on the bottom. They would have two guys, one on the horse and one on the shore, to dump the scoop (S 11).

hot-ache
Noun.
  Pain caused by rapid warming of the body after extreme cold (II).

[From British and Irish] *OEDS* 1917; *EDD*.

hot-jacket
See **wrap-jacket.**

hum
Noun. Compare **humming**.
  A smell of perspiration, especially on clothing.
  That old coat has quite a hum to it (P2-055). There's an awful hum in this room (P2-056). That is quite a hum on that sweater (P2-067). It could mean strong odor emanating from any source (P2-072). There is an awful hum from him (P2-082).

[From English] *DSUE* 'low: from ca. 1890'; *COD* 'sl.' *hum* [verb]: *EDD* 'To stink'; *OEDS* 'To smell disagreeably' 1902–1970.

hummer
Noun. Rare.
  1. A child's sleigh.
  Speed sleigh on ice made humming sound (II 039). Grandpa said, 'I had a nice hummer

when I was a kid' (II 093). A child's sleigh that would go fast (O).

2. The act of sleighing.

We had a 'big old' time at dinner hour; snow falling and we made a snow man too poor Pearl is quite a piece to roll snow. Claude was out also. Grand Hummer (OLIVER, GERTRUDE, *Diaries of Gertrude Hazel Meggison Oliver*, 1907, February 11).

humming

Adjective. Compare **hum.**

Of clothing especially, smelling of perspiration.

The shirt was humming (P2-052). They used to be humming, some of them that visited us at the store (P2-053). It's said of dirty, smelly socks which were worn around the neck for a cold cure: 'Those socks is hummin'' (P2-066).

hundred-year storm

Noun.

A storm so severe that it is said to occur only once in one hundred years.

A common expression: 'Yes, they've only had one like this in a hundred years' (P2-026). A storm which is the worst one can remember for a long period of time (P2-069).

husher

Noun. Rare.

A cover for the lid of a chamber-pot.

A complete set of bedroom china, consisted of a large wash basin, and enormous pitcher to hold cold water, a smaller one for hot water, a soap dish with a cover, a vase-like dish to hold ones tooth brushes, and a chamber mug complete with cover. This cover was further adorned with a crocheted cap securely fastened in place. This cap was called a 'husher.' Chamber pot, cover, husher and all reposed in a little cupboard with a door underneath the commode (BAGNALL, MARGARET, *When I Was Very Young*, [1964], 4). Something that was knit and put over the cover so the cover wouldn't rattle as it was replaced (II 019). A crocheted top for the cover – to muffle the noise of putting the cover back on the pot (II 062). People did have cloth coverings for the covers to subdue the noise of taking it off or putting it on the pot in the middle of the night (II 089).

I

ice-boat

Noun. Compare **strap.**

One of the amphibious boats that plied across the Northumberland Strait in winter before the establishment of powered ferries.

On inquiring whether the mail from Prince Edward had arrived, I was answered in the negative; and though two days over-due, it had not made its appearance; from which it was justly argued that the 'ice-boat' had not been able to cross the Straits (SLEIGH, B.W.A., *Pine Forests and Hacmatack Clearings*, 1853, 116). The ice-boat was being rushed along at a great rate. Every man seemed to be doing his utmost, and, as they came nearer, we could see Wilson still on the bow strap, now pulling the boat toward him and hanging on to the gunwale as she rushed down a sharp slope, and now putting his broad back under the bow and jamming it over into some new path. They came to a widening crack we had not noticed before. He plunged into it waist deep on the shelving ice, and we could hear him shouting to the men to get in the boat. A moment afterward he climbed in, streaming with icy water, only to leap out on the pan on the other side of the crack a moment later. The men jumped out, ran the boat over the pan to the next crack, and splashed in again (HICKMAN, ALBERT, *The Sacrifice of the Shannon*, 1903, 165). The earliest regular crossing began in 1828, the couriers getting $16 per trip. At the outset the trips were only monthly, then weekly, and for many years daily when the weather allowed (MACKINNON, JOHN, *A Sketch Book: Comprising Historical Incidents, Traditional Tales and Translations*, 1915, 53–54). The last trouble of the kind happened in 1885; a party of several ice boats carrying mail with 15 crew and 7 passengers, had to spend the night in the middle of the Strait. Three of the boats were so arranged as to provide shelter; and the tin was ripped off the fourth to make cooking utensils. The wood of that craft was used to make a camp fire, which was kindled with newspapers taken out of mail bags. The marooned party reached land the next day at 3 p.m., with a man badly frost-bitten and another one that had become de-lirious, and died soon afterwards (TRICOCHE, GEORGE, *Rambles through the Maritime Provinces of Canada*, [1931], 133). Winter transportation to the mainland for much of the ninteenth cen-tury was carried out exclusively by ice-boats. An ice-boat was approximately 5 1/4 meters in

length by 1 1/4 meters in width with a hull especially designed so that it could be navigated
easily among and over the ice floes in the
Northumberland Strait. The exterior of the craft
was sheathed with metal to prevent damage
by the ice and the boat was propelled by sails,
oars, and paddles. Quite often the male passengers, as well as the crew of four or five men,
n and row or push. Either side of the bottom
of the hull had runners which enabled it to slide
more easily over the solid ice in the strait.
Long, leather straps attached to chains were
fitted to the gunwales on one end and to a
harness on the other end. These were used by
the crew to propel the boat over the ice.
More than once these straps served as life-lines
when some unfortunate crewman or passenger
fell through the ice into the freezing waters.
Passengers who paid $2.00 or its equivalent
in British pound sterling were obliged to help
transport the boat and Royal Mail. However,
if they paid a fee of $4.00 or its equivalent in
pound sterling they did not have to assist unless an emergency developed (MORRISON,
CLINTON, *Emigrant from the Highlands: Robert
W. Morrison, Sr. and His Descendants*, 1978, 70).

[Canadian] *DC* 1853–1939.

ice cake

Noun. Also **cake, cake ice**. Compare
clumpet, drift ice, raft ice, running ice.
   A large chunk of floating sea ice.
   The weather, which has been so mild for a
week that the frost in some places has all
gone out of the ground, has turned colder
today. There is not a spot of snow, however,
on all the autumn-like landscape, nor a cake of
ice on the river (BAIN, FRANCIS, *Notes in Natural
History – Prince Edward Island, 1868–1877*, 1870,
January 1). The Island Province, the smallest
of the confederation, is sometimes called the
Garden of Canada. It is separated from New
Brunswick and Nova Scotia by Northumberland Strait, whose ice in winter sometimes shuts
off the Island from communication with the
rest of the world. Such intercourse as is then
irregularly achieved is carried on with
difficulty and danger by means of open boats,
which are alternately dragged over the ice-
cakes and pushed through the loose ice for a
distance of 9 miles between Cape Traverse
on the Island and Cape Tormentine on the New
Brunswick shore (ROBERTS, CHARLES, *The
Canadian Guide Book: The Tourist's and Sportsman's Guide to Eastern Canada and Newfoundland*, 1892, 192). The leather harnesses served

a double purpose. The shoulder strap was for
heavy pulling across pressure hummocks, or
even over miles of rough, broken ice cakes. The
waist belt was to hold one up when the ice
gave way, or a cake tipped and dropped the
passenger into the frigid water (CALLBECK,
LORNE, *Sagas of the Strait*, 1959, 58). I saw Ice
cakes while crossing [the Northumberland
Strait] that were from eight to ten feet thick.
They must have come clear from the Arctic
(LEARD, GEORGE, *The George Leard Files*, 1977,
Reel 5). The 'spring break-up' of the ice was
always a thrilling spectacle, and everyone
gazed at the ice and the tide as it raced
through like a swift and terrible river. Everyone
had a good laugh when Raymond Sweeney
said (as if speaking to the ice cakes), 'Take your
time, boys, ye'll all get out' (JOHNSTON,
LORNE, *Recollections of an 'Ole Salt*, 1982, 28).
'But in between you cut a cake and float it
out but the mud stuck out of the water on the
low tide (T M123). These are flat pieces of ice
piled up along the shore (P1-001). We used to
go stumping cakes. Hopped or poled around
on them like a raft (P1-046).

[Canadian] *DC* 1870–1953; *OED*; *OEDS*.

ice kill

Noun.
   **In oyster fishing, the destruction of
oyster beds by winter ice.**
   If oysters are on a hard bottom in the winter
time, the ice kills the oysters. It sets on them
and either freezes them or picks them up and
drags them up. This is ice kill (S 14). Some
years you get ice kill and some years you don't.
The ice lies on the oysters, and depending
on the bottom it can crush them. Sometimes the
ice freezes them or smothers them or crushes
them (S 15).

ice pole

Noun. Also **spar buoy**. Archaic.
   **A marker for the end of a line of lobster
traps, used in ice conditions instead of,
or in combination with, a buoy.**
   An ice pole is a long slender piece of wood
used to mark the ends of a 'trawl' instead of
a buoy during the time when there is ice on the
water. They're not used much now, since
the Department of Fisheries will delay the
opening of the season during ice conditions
(ROBERTSON, JANICE, *A Dictionary of Lobster
Fishing in the Eastern Kings Area*, 1985, 9). An
ice pole was a pole about three inches in
diameter on the bottom and fifteen to twenty

feet long. You would set your gear in the ice and the ice pole would not be crushed or broken off like a buoy would be (S 4). An ice pole is a pole maybe three or four inches in diameter and about six feet long or so with a hole in one end to attach to the buoy. It goes under the ice instead of getting caught (S 5). An ice pole is just a long pole, maybe sixteen feet or so, that tied on in place of a buoy. They slide underneath the ice instead of getting smashed off (S 6).

ignorant
Adjective.
Rude, ill-mannered.
As the years pass, common courtesy declines, and it becomes more and more acceptable to be ignorant to other people (*Unpublished student essay*, 1983, n. pag). Very ignorant if you say something you don't usually say to other people (but might think it!) (I 011). If you said something rude to me about my answers I'd say you were ignorant (I 079). It means more than knowledge. It's behavior, not education. It's used more this way than the right way on the Island (I 087). And I said 'Did you have anything to eat?' And he said 'No.' So I said, 'Look, I want to tell you something; you were at my door the other night and I says I've had other people come to my door and I know them. And I know you, but you're just plain ignorant and I am just not going to open the door for you' (T M17). It's used often to mean rude or insensitive, i.e., 'It was an ignorant thing to do,' or, 'Don't be ignorant.' In these usages it has nothing whatever to do with knowledge (O).

[From British and Irish] *SND; SSPB* 'used for a wide range of insulting judgments, not just of someone who lacks information'; *EDD; DNE; DJE*.

imported
Adjective. Compare **away, foreign, foreigner**.
From outside Prince Edward Island, from 'away.'
The relative isolation of Prince Edward Island causes many of its sons to think they live in a little world by itself. This turn of mind is detected, for instance, in the way Islanders speak of things coming from the mainland: objects shipped from other provinces are *imported*; correspondence from the same source is *foreign mail* (TRICOCHE, *Rambles through the Maritime Provinces of Canada*, [1931], 171).

Indian paint brush
See **devil's paint brush**.

Indian pear
Noun.
A purple or red berry from a bush of the genus *Amelanchier*, a June-berry or saskatoon berry.
The far greater part of the Island is in its original wild and uncultivated state, covered with groves of various kinds of trees. ... There are also wild cherries, gooseberries and currants. ... A fruit in this Island, called the Indian Pear, is very delicious (*A Description of Prince Edward Island in the Gulf of St. Laurence, North America; with a Map of the Island and a Few Cursory Observations* ..., 1805, 4).

[North American] *DC* 'Esp. Eastern Canada' 1818–1872; *W3*.

inside
Adverb. Compare **outside**.
In commercial fishing, close to shore.
This year I heard some of my outside fishermen say those that fish outside get more than those that fish inside – that if they had known they had to fire them away they would not have come to the shore at all (CANADA, HOUSE OF COMMONS, *Lobster Fishery Evidence Taken before Commander William Wakeham, M.D., Officer in Charge of the Gulf Fisheries Division, in Quebec and the Maritime Provinces*, 1910, 297). The best wind for lobsters here on the 'north side' is ... south west for inside fishing (inside of six fathoms) (*The Guardian*, June 16, 1975, 3). Inside is shallow water; close to land. E.g. 'I'm fishing inside today' (MACMILLAN, JANET, *The Language of Lobster Fishing*, 1985, 18). When the fish move inshore they fish these waters. The inside ground is water of two or three fathoms deep (S 4).

*The boundary between *inside* and *outside* is variable from port to port.

in the round
Prepositional phrase. Also **on the round**.
Of fish, not gutted, salted, or otherwise prepared for market; whole.
Selling on the round: another way of saying selling them green or not salted (KENNEDY, LIBBY, *A Visitor's Guide to the Language of the Wharf*, 1985, 9). A fish in the round has no gut out. It is not dressed (S 6).

W3.

Irish curtain
Noun, usually in plural. Derogatory.
  A spider's web indoors, a cobweb (C).

Irish draperies: ML: 'Mainers took part in the general
laughter of the times about the Irish. *Irish* draperies
are cobwebs, perhaps a bit of one-upmanship with
"lace-curtain" *Irish*.'

Irish moss
Noun. Compare **black moss**, **bleach moss**,
moss, **mosser**, **mossing**, **rake moss**,
shore moss, **spring moss**.
  Either of two edible seaweeds
(*Gigartina mamillosa* or, more usually,
***Chondrus crispus*) harvested from the sea**
bed near the land, or from the shore after
being washed up by storms, and sold for
their extract, carrageenin, a stabilizing
or thickening agent in a variety of foods
and pharmaceutical products including
ice-cream and toothpaste.
  Irish moss is a seaweed, called carrageen in
Ireland and Scotland, barallawr in Wales, and
laver bread in England; it is also found off
southwestern Nova Scotia and western P.E.I.
It is a relative of the edible reddish-brown New
Brunswick seaweed known as dulse, a delicacy
for some cultivated palates (SCARRATT, D.J.,
Rocks and Rakes: Lobsters vs. Irish Moss, 1977,
56). The sea plant industry is of major importance on the west and north-eastern coasts.
Irish moss can be dried and refined to produce
the substance carrageenin, used as a stabilizer
in food processing and other industries. The
moss, light green to purple in colour and in
appearance something like parsley, grows
attached to rocks in depths of up to ten metres.
Each storm washes Irish moss ashore, and it
is gathered by local families and transported to
drying plants. From there it is eventually
exported to refineries on the mainland. There
are no restrictions on gathering this 'storm-
tossed' weed, but restrictions do apply to
harvesting Irish moss still growing on the
rocks (HOCKING, ANTHONY, *Prince Edward Island*,
1978, 32). There's horses in the water / And
horses on the road / And here comes old Russel
Aylward / And he's hauling up another big
load. / And the party lines keep ringing / And
the word keeps passing on / You can hear them
roar from the Tignish Shore / There's moss in
Skinner's Pond. / On old Prince Edward Island /
There's one big hullabaloo / The boys and the
girls and the old folks / They're going to make
a few bucks too. / Getting wet to the neck in
the ocean / Where the waves all turn and toss /

But it's a free-for-all, and they're having a ball /
They're bringing in the Irish Moss (CONNORS,
TOM, *Song of the Irish Moss*, 1967). So far this
year the price for mixed Irish moss is 25 cents
per pound dry and six cents per pound wet (*The
Guardian*, April 25, 1986, 3).

*Although this term is found in standard dictionaries,
it is included here because of its central position in
a cluster of words that form the special lexicon of the
Irish moss industry on Prince Edward Island.
Carragheen is a town in Ireland, near which such
moss grows abundantly.
OED 1845; W3; EDD; GCD; FW; WNW; COD.

Irish moss pudding
See **sea-moss pudding**.

Island, the
Proper noun. Common. Compare **Abeg-
weit**, **Islander**, **Minegoo**.
  Prince Edward Island.
  Now here is a man who had tried both
countries [Scotland and Prince Edward Island],
and who gave the preference to the Island
(JOHNSTONE, WALTER, *'Letters' and 'Travels'*
Prince Edward Island, 1821, 1955, 149). We feel
like the old Scotch Islander in Winnipeg did.
He said he was from 'the Island!' What Island?
queried a listener. 'What Island,' repeated our
honest countryman, in amazement? 'Why Prince
Edward Island, man? What other Island is
there?' (MONTGOMERY, LUCY MAUD, *From Prince
Albert to P.E. Island*, 1891, 1). As everyone
knows who knows anything about this province, its true and proper name is that by which
the people who live there call it, and that is
simply 'The Island.' That is what Island-born
people, whether at home or abroad, call it
(MCCREADY, J.E.B., *Traditions of Prince Edward
Island*, 1923, 204). Has any other district in
the world aquired so many descriptive names?
Prince Edward Island; St. John's Island; Isle
St. Jean; Spud Island; *The* Island; Canada's
Garden Province; The Cradle of Confederation; The Million Acre Farm; The Home of the
Silver Fox Industry; 'Epagweit'; 'Minegoo';
P.E.I.; The Garden of the Gulf (CHAMPION,
HELEN, *Over on the Island*, 1939, 25). Wher-
ever an Islander may travel he remains an
Islander. He speaks of his home as 'The
Island' without explanation or qualification,
and he uses the term as if less to describe a
body of land surrounded by water than a state
of life (GREENHILL, BASIL, and ANN GIFFARD,
Westcountrymen in Prince Edward's Isle, 1967,
14–15). Since I'm Island-born home's as precise /
as if a mumbly old carpenter, / shoulder-straps
crossed wrong, / laid it out, / refigured to the

last three-eighths of a shingle. / ... In the fanged jaws of the Gulf, / a red tongue. / Indians say a musical God / took up his brush and painted it; / named it, in His own language, 'The Island' (ACORN, MILTON, *I've Tasted My Blood*, 1969, 37–38).

Island cent
See **tree cent**.

Islander
Proper noun. Compare **Island**.
1. A person born on Prince Edward Island.
'Jim Armstrong came from New Brunswick,' said Rebecca Dew. 'He ain't a real islander ... wouldn't be such a crank if he was. We have our peculiarities but we're *civilized*' (MONT-GOMERY, LUCY MAUD, *Anne of Windy Poplars*, 1936, 127). Nowhere on earth are there good folk who can compare with the Islanders for clannishness and an attitude in general that almost makes them a race apart. Don't mistake my meaning. You will not find a kindlier, more genial, more hospitable people anywhere. They are always ready to lend a hand, will go out of their way to get you information, but you sense that in their heart of hearts they feel sorry for your hard luck in not being born on the Island (BIRD, WILL, *These Are the Maritimes*, 1959, 192–93). Daddy's hand came free of the blankets. He seized Mr. Kendrick's hand and pumped it vigorously. 'For a newcomer,' Daddy said, with the ghost of a chuckle in his voice, 'you're not so bad. You might even make an Islander yet, Kendricks – in a generation or two (BARKER, H.T., *The Ice Road*, 1964, 49). Well this is one Islander thinking the main support for the anti-litton Bunch comes from 'OFF ISLAND.' ... The average Islander is cute like a fox, so you Peacenicks are not fooling anyone (*The Guardian*, February 12, 1986, 4). For most / of us here / being islanders / is a ter- / minal condition. / But those who / go away / aren't cured. / They simply die / of the same / ailment / on alien soil (LEDWELL, FRANK, *The North Shore of Home*, 1986, 167).
2. A person living on Prince Edward Island.
The Islanders having, in 1872, commenced railway construction, have done their work so thoroughly that but little more can be done in that way unless the locomotive is to be brought to every man's door (*The Gazetteer and Guide to the Lower Provinces, for 1876–77*, 1876, 147). 'That is my funniest story but the nicest is about old Mr. George McFadyen who died four

years ago and went to heaven. At first he couldn't find any Islanders but after awhile he found out there were lots of them, only they had to be kept locked up for fear they would try to get back to the Island' (MONTGOMERY, LUCY MAUD, *Pat of Silver Bush*, 1933, 195). It is estimated that over 100,000 Islanders and visitors attended the Community Day programs, and a further estimate is that the majority of those attending were Islanders (PRINCE EDWARD ISLAND 1973 CENTENNIAL COMMISSION, *Centennial '73*, 1973, 174). Ask any Islander that has reason to leave the ferry terminal frequently, and he'll tell you about waiting ... in ferry terminals, in air terminals, and in parking lots. In winter, the ice still blocks the ferries sometimes, and changes a one-hour crossing to anywhere from a four to twenty-four hour endurance test. In summer, vacationers' cars often are backed up for several crossings (EVANS, MILLIE, and ERIC MULLEN, *Our Maritimes*, 1979, 190). As a transplanted rather than a native Islander, I have often been struck by Prince Edward Island speech-ways (PRATT, T.K., *Island English: The Case of the Disappearing Dialect*, 1982, 231). 'I can't think of any award I would rather have,' said Roy Lambie upon being presented with *The Evening Patriot's* Islander of the year Award at Charlottetown Rotary Monday. ... Mr. Lambie, a B.C. native, came to the Island twenty years ago. ...' I have thought of myself as an Islander for some time but I never knew if that thought was shared by Island natives, this (award) will certainly help in my defence,' quipped Mr. Lambie (*The Guardian*, April 12, 1983).

J

Jack Blunt
Noun.
A plain-spoken or blunt person (O).

[From English] *OED; EDD*.

jag
Noun. Occasionally (sense 2) in phrase **to have a jag on**.
1. A small load in a truck, wagon, or boat.
A small load, drawn by horse or tractor, of wood or hay (P1-053). A small load on a wagon (P1-092).
2. A minor case of intoxication.
A drunk has a jag on (P1-033). Referring to the amount of liquor consumed (P1-049).

[From British and Irish] *OED* 1597–1893; *W3*; *EDD*; *DAE* 'Now dial' 1633–1892; *OEDS*; *SSPB2*; *GCD* 'Dialect'; *FW* 'Dial.'; *WNW* 'Dial.'; *COD* '16th c.'

jam
Noun. Compare **gimp**.
   Courage, bravery, daring.
   A man has to have lots of jam to work on an oil rig (P2-055). It's an expression of courage, 'That man sure has jam' (P2-066). 'Jam' means guts (P2-067).

jap
Transitive verb.
   To spill (a liquid) (O).

[From British and Irish] *SND* 1721–1946; *EDD. ESI* 'to splash with mud. (Ulster)'

jaunting sleigh
Noun. Archaic. Compare **pung**.
   A light, horse-drawn sleigh with a high build, a cutter.
   Thursday. A regular swinger of a cold day. Did not go to school. Papa went to Black-Smith shop to get the jaunting sleigh fixed (OLIVER, GERTRUDE, *Diaries of Gertrude Hazel Meggison Oliver*, January 10, 1907). A jaunting sleigh, with or without side doors, was a prized possession on almost every farm during the last thirty to thirty-five years before snow-ploughed roads (MACNEVIN, MRS. LORNE, *Past and Present: A History of Brae*, 1979, 63). Some families kept wood sleighs, with sides and ends, so passengers could be hauled when work was done. In addition to these, the jaunting sleigh, light 'box sleigh', and 'pung' sleigh was used by couples for travelling to rink, church and other distant places. One Island firm manufactured jaunting sleighs. Many of them were sold in the area (FREETOWN HISTORICAL SOCIETY, *Freetown Past and Present*, 1985, 18). They were the stylish ones. The 'pung' sleigh was for the middle class and the wood sleigh for the poor (P1-038). They had a rounded back and were higher and fancier than a 'pung' (P1-065).

*Possibly this term is derived from *jaunting car* 'a light cart having two seats back to back, formerly used in Ireland' (*GCD*).

jerker
See **kicker**.

jerks, the
Plural noun phrase. Historical. Compare **jumper, kicker², McDonaldite.**

   Synonym for 'the works': convulsive distortions of the body or face during religious excitement.
   Your great grandmother West was a Mac-Allister. Her brother Amos was a Mcdonaldite in religion. I am told he used to take the jerks something fearful (MONTGOMERY, LUCY MAUD, *Rilla of Ingleside*, [1920], 142).

*Reverend Donald MacDonald (1783–1867), a member of the Church of Scotland (unattached), founded thirteen McDonaldite churches on Prince Edward Island which had some 5,000 adherents.
[North American] *OED* 1805–1874; *DA* 'Now *hist.*'; *DAE.*

jick
Noun. Informal. Occasional in Cardigan, infrequent in Egmont, rare elsewhere; significantly rural.
   Word, utterance, peep.
   Not another jick out of you (O).

jiffey
Noun. Also **jiffey rig.** Archaic. Rare.
   A small, light, horse-drawn wagon.
   A light wagon old people used to run around in (II 058). A light wagon with a low back (II 100). It wasn't a farm wagon. A go-cart, road cart (II 112).

jigamirandee
Noun.
   Synonym for 'doings': a person or thing whose name cannot be recalled at the moment.
   A name for any gizmo, device or thing that you can't remember the name for. Like a little plastic sprue on a toy truck, or even a connecting arm or bolt on, say, a carburetor (O).

jiggamy: *EDD* 'A name given to an implement, tool, &c., the proper name of which cannot be recalled at the moment.'

jigaree
Noun, usually in plural. \jə-'gā-rē\.
   Synonym for 'flagarie': a fancy piece of trimming or ornamentation.
   Then she didn't like his fussy, lace-trimmed house. Too many jigarees on it (MONTGOMERY, LUCY MAUD, *A Tangled Web*, 1972 [1931], 236).

DSUE 'jig(g)aree is a C.20 variant – esp. Naval – of jiggamaree.' *jiggamaree*: *OED* 'A fanciful contrivance, which the speaker thinks worthless or worthless'; *W3* 'slang: something (as a device or contrivance) felt to be too fanciful, difficult, or small in value to designate accurately'; *DA* 'colloq.' 1824–1908; *DAE*; *DSUE* 'ob.; coll.'

jigger[1]
Noun.
A folk musician in pioneer days.
Sometimes an entertainer-musician, called a 'jigger,' chanted wavering folk songs and told funny stories to add to the celebration (SAGE, MARY, *The Lord Selkirk Settlers in Belfast, Prince Edward Island*, [1973], 27).

jigger[2]
Noun. Archaic. Infrequent in Charlotte-town and Cardigan, rare elsewhere; especially middle-aged and older, less educated.
Synonym for 'sloven': a long horse-drawn wagon with the platform slung lower than the axles, close to the ground, formerly used for hauling heavy or awkward loads.
A lime tree which had to be removed from a property on Euston Street was dug up and brought out to Inkerman on a jigger (a four wheel long, low, horse-drawn vehicle popular at that time) (LAWSON, HELEN, *Colonel John Hamilton Gray*, 1973, 9). From the distance in the quiet early evening I could hear the rattle of steel-rimmed jigger wheels on cement and the slap of leather on a horse's flank (HEN-NESSEY, MICHAEL, *Mister Currie's Protestant Shoes*, 1984, 12). Jigger is associated with trans-porting of goods within a town (I 016). They were used in cities for trucking. The oil man in Montague had a jigger but most in Montague had truck wagons (I 049). It was a four wheeled cart, used for hauling paper for *The Guardian* (I 057). Small wagon used in cities for peddling mail (I 071). A very low wagon used in town for deliveries or hauling from the rail station (O).

*Many informants associated *jigger* with town hauling and *sloven* with farm work. The word has been used elsewhere for a railway hand-car (*DC*; *OEDS*; *GCD* 'Cdn.'), a horse-drawn streetcar (*OED* 'U.S.'), and 'an open vehicle for carrying trees from the forest' (*SND*; *EDD* 1883).
[From British.]

jigging clothes
Noun. Also **jigging around clothes**. Rare.
Good clothes that are not as good as one's best.
Second best dress (II 017). Clothes for jigging around in (II 110). In between good and work clothes. Semi-dress-up clothes (O). Usually put on in the evening for visiting (O).

jillic
Also **jillick, jillock**. See **gillock**.

John Joy Token
Noun. Historical. Compare **holey dollar, leather dollar, tree cent**.
See quotation.
'The Holey Dollar,' 'The Island Cent,' 'The Sheaf of Wheat,' the 'John Joy Token' – these and many others refer to the currency of this part of Atlantic Canada now known as the Province of Prince Edward Island. … they remain great finds for collectors (P.E.I. NUMIS-MATIC SOCIETY, *Island Currency*, 1973, 24–25).

jollop
Noun. Informal.
1. A purgative.
We used to give them a big bottle of kerosene and baking soda, go right after them, trade them – Harry Coulson's medicine. I seen Harry Coulson coming here one night and the horse was, oh, just like a bellows. He had a 'teddy,' got some kerosene and baking soda from the wife here and made a big jollop for him and give it to him (HORNBY, SUSAN, *George Young: Horsing Around*, 1981, 32).
2. A dish made from leftovers (O).

*Sense 1 is a slang version of standard *jalap*. *OEDS* 1920–1966; *EDD* 'A semi-fluid mess of any-thing; a big mess of food, a "dollop."'

Jordan rig
Noun.
See quotation.
This is used in the Murray Harbour area to describe any make-shift or patched-up ap-paratus. Named after one of the Jordan men who was noted for fixing things up with wire, twine, etc. (O).

jouk
Transitive and intransitive verb, sometimes (sense 2) followed by *out of*. \jo͞ok\. Also spelled *juke*. Rare.
1. To dodge, duck; to avoid, hide.
Somebody who wanted to avoid someone would jouk around (II 020). Being of Irish-Scottish parentage I've often heard the word 'juking' used, it means: to hide among the bushes to avoid being seen at that particular

time or place (O). Juking through the trees would be one who approached the place stealthily and peered through the trees surrounding a place to get a glimpse of any goings on (O).

2. To trick, deceive, cheat.

For example, 'juked them in a land deal' means to trick or cheat someone (I 043). To jouk someone is to have a joke over their head. It runs by them (II 049). He jouked him out of it (II 058). I jouked that fellow (II 112).

[From Irish and Scottish and northern English] [sense 1]: *OED* 1513–1871; *W3*; *EDD*; *DOST*; *EDSL*. [sense 2]: *W3* 'dial.'; *DOST* 'fig.'; *EDD*; *EDSL*.

joust

Transitive verb. Rare. Compare **cod.**

1. To tease or kid roughly; to bully.

Jousting is more serious than teasing (I 021). Jousting would be more physical than teasing, more like bullying (I 039).

2. To bounce (a child) on the knee (I).

jullic

See **gillock.**

jumper

Noun. Historical. Derogatory. Compare **jerks, kicker², McDonaldite, works.**

One of the followers of Reverend Donald McDonald, with reference to the convulsive distortions of the body or face sometimes experienced by these followers during religious excitement.

[Reverend Donald] McDonald's followers were often referred to derisively as the 'kickers' or the 'jumpers,' and it is unfortunate that while these 'works' were only one aspect of the 'McDonaldite faith, they became, in the popular mind, the customary means of identifying the group (WEALE, DAVID, 'The Minister': The Reverend Donald McDonald, 1977, 3).

*Reverend Donald McDonald (1783–1867), a member of the Church of Scotland (unattached), founded thirteen McDonaldite churches on Prince Edward Island which had some 5,000 adherents.

junk

Noun. Common in Egmont, occasional in Malpeque and Cardigan, infrequent elsewhere; significantly rural; especially male. Compare **junk** (verb).

1. A piece, length, or lump of anything, a chunk.

A fine junk of a day (OLIVER, GERTRUDE, Diary of Gertrude Hazel Meggison Oliver, 1908, August 31). I had a nice horse out here and he was quiet as could be. I was putting the back chain on the cart one day with him and went to go under his chin and he grabbed me by the arm and took a junk right out (HORNBY, SUSAN, George Young: Horsing Around, 1981, 30). Another junk of wreckage came hurtlin' past on a crest of a wave, struck Angus and knocked him off (JOHNSTON, LORNE, Recollections of an 'Ole Salt, 1982, 5). This particular evening we were coming home. We had to go through at least one mile of woods. … My brother … had a roast of meat in his arms, for Sunday. All of a sudden there was a young bear came down the road and he ran right between the four of us, grabbed this junk of meat from my brother and jumped into the woods (CAMPBELL, FRANK, As the Fella Says …, 1983, 39). 'He's quite a junk' describes a big person (I 014). 'Stog' a junk of rag in the window (I 056). I had a junk of cake (I 095). You know when you break the leg off the lobster and inside there's a big junk of meat (T B22). I'll have to get a junk of [plumber's] pipe (O). I was just a junk of a girl when I went down to Boston (O).

2. A young pig.

Another farmer had some young pigs for sale. His ad read, 'For sale – six pigs – good junks (SELLICK, LESTER, My Island Home, 1973, 50). A junk of a pig – but bigger than little (I 077). 'Junks of pigs' are pigs past weaning, 40–50 lb. but not market yet (I 092).

[From British] [sense 1]: *OED* 1726–1876; *W3*; *DC* 'esp. East'; *DNE*; *SSPB2*; *ML*; *SND*; *EDD*; *DJE*; *DBE*.

junk

Transitive verb, often followed by *up*. Also verbal noun **junking.** Compare **junk** (noun).

To cut (felled trees) into workable lengths or 'junks.'

As the trees are cut the branches are to be lopped off, and the trunks cut into lengths of 12 or 14 feet. This operation they call junking them; if they are not junked before fire is applied, they are much worse to junk them afterwards (JOHNSTONE, WALTER, 'Letters' and 'Travels' Prince Edward Island, 1821, 1955, 108). All the underwood and small trees were first cut down and the large trees were afterwards felled and cut into lengths that two men could pile which was called junking them (ALLEY, JUDGE, Prince Edward Island 100 Years Ago, [1890?], 8). The first type of fertilizer used, albeit inadvertently, by Islanders was the ash which remained after the 'junking' and burning of the trees and branches when the land was being cleared (HOWATT, CORNELIUS, *The Farm Family*, 1973, 63–64).

*The more general sense implied by *junk* (noun), and in *OED*, has not been found in this study.
OED 'To cut or divide into junks or chunks' 1803–1847.

K

keep your temper
Verb phrase serving as noun.
A parlour game similar to charades.
Wouldn't it be splendid if I could pounce in on you some evening and we'd play dominoes and 'keep your temper' in the parlour (MONT-GOMERY, LUCY MAUD, *Letter to Penzie MacNeill*, 1891, February 10).

kellick
Noun. Also spelled **kellog**. Archaic.
An anchor consisting of a stone framed in pieces of wood.
To both ends of each trawl is attached a stone 'kellog' or anchor (*Running the Lines*, April 25, 1903, 2). One summer I went to the shore to help some men with the fishing. Two of the men I was helping, had a narrow escape from drowning; they were four miles off shore setting out lines. They were throwing a heavy stone – called a kellick – out for an anchor for the lines and they let it fall on the gunwhale of the dory which tipped and began to fill (MELLICK, HENRY, *Timothy's Boyhood: Or Pioneer Country Life on Prince Edward Island*, 1933, 58). Fish were caught closer to the shore than today. The anchor was a large stone sometimes fitted between three pieces of wood and called a kellick, a word you find in no dictionary (*East Point United Baptist Church*, 1983, 52). It was a rock you got out of the woods from seventy to one hundred pounds. You got an alder and bent it around the rock, and then used it as an anchor (S 4).

killick: DNE 'An anchor made up of an elongated stone encased in pliable sticks bound at the top and fixed in two curved cross-pieces, used in mooring nets and small boats' 1760–1969; OED 1630–1897; DC '[origin unknown] Esp. East Coast'. *killock*: DAE 1649–1870. *kelk*: EDD 'A large detached stone or rock.'

kennebecker
Noun. Historical.
A lumberjack's duffle-bag or carpet-bag.
And one day early in the decade, a lean, leisurely, amiable menace parked its heavy kennebecker at a Paddy Lane (Grant Street) boarding house and got a job at Cushman's mill. Larry Gorman had arrived (IVES, EDWARD, *Larry Gorman: The Man Who Made the Songs*, [1964], 81). A suit of new clothes is prepared for the journey, / A pair of long boots made by Sherwood or Clark, / A long Kennebecker all stuffed with good homespun, / Then this young Islander he does embark (DIBLEE, RANDALL, *Folksongs from Prince Edward Island*, 1973, 44). A kennebecker, by the way, was about the same as what would be called a carpet bag elsewhere (IVES, EDWARD, *The Boys of the Island: P.I.'s in the Maine Lumberwoods*, 1984, 31). It was a bag to put their clothes in when the men went to the woods (II 066).

Kennebec and *Kennebunk* are place-names in Maine, where Islanders went to work in the woods during the late ninteenth and early twentieth centuries.
[Probably from New England] ML. *kennebunker*: DA 1895, 1902; DAE.

kicker[1]
Noun.
A cog or roller shaped off-round, to make the 'digger apron' on a potato digger vibrate, and so shake soil off the potatoes.
Do not use kickers except under extremely wet or weedy conditions (KHATTAK, JAHAN, and WILLIAM LEWIS, *Growing Potatoes for Processing in Prince Edward Island*, 1971, 15). A kicker is an elongated cog which will cause the chain to vibrate and will loosen the soil, and the soil will fall down between the links and the rods (S 1). A kicker is like a roller. They are long and make the chain shake (S 2).

W3 'a mechanical part that gives a sharp push to some object (as for feeding or ejecting work from a machine).'

kicker[2]
Noun. Also **jerker**. Historical. Derogatory. Compare **jerks, jumper, McDonaldite, works**.
One of the followers of Reverend Donald McDonald, with reference to the convulsive distortions of the body or face sometimes experienced by these followers during religious excitement.
I have known many, who claimed to be very

religious, who would never speak of him [Reverend Donald McDonald] except in such contemptible epithets as, 'McDonald the jerker,' 'Kicker McDonald,' etc. Those rumors referred to, were as diversified as they were false (LAMONT, EWEN, *A Biographical Sketch of the Late Rev. Donald McDonald*, 1892, 9). While Mr. McDonald lived, his adherents were visibly united as one ecclesiastical body, guided by the same rules, professing the same belief, yearly sitting at the same Communion Table, no matter how far they might be apart as to their different localities. I think it is right for me here to mention their numerical strength and social importance at the time of Mr. McDonald's death. From their small number of eleven, as at their first Sacrament, they increased to the number of many thousands. From the insignificantly small sect slurringly called 'jerkers', 'kickers,' etc., they became a large, influential, and respected body of people, who could, by their united votes, either sustain or upset a Government. Moreover, they would be more than welcome to join any branch of the Presbyterian Church. But after his death changes came and divisions arose, as might be easily foreseen (*ibid*, 32). [Reverend Donald] McDonald's followers were often referred to derisively as the 'kickers' or the 'jumpers,' and it is unfortunate that while these 'works' were only one aspect of the 'McDonaldite' faith, they became, in the popular mind, the customary means of identifying the group (WEALE, DAVID, *'The Minister': The Reverend Donald McDonald*, 1977, 3).

*Reverend Donald McDonald (1783–1867), a member of the Church of Scotland (unattached), founded thirteen McDonaldite churches on Prince Edward Island which had some 5,000 adherents.

killkid mud
Noun. Rare. Compare **alder mud, mussel mud, oyster mud, shell mud**.
  Mud from swamps and ponds, used as fertilizer.
  You dig down two or three feet deep. No weeds will grow first season (II 039). Mud from swamps and dried-up lakes. You'd pay five dollars for it today. It has a peat moss base (O).

king hair
Noun. Also (collectively) **king fur**. Compare **bar**.
  A totally black, unsilvered 'guard hair' on a silver fox.

Interspersed among the silver banded hairs and all over the back and sides of a good pelt in a well furred fox are pure black hairs, black throughout their entire length and known as 'king hairs'. These hairs and the long black tips of the silver hairs veil the silver imparting a beautiful sheen to the pelt and making it of great value. These and the banded hairs constitute the 'guard fur' of the fox and in a healthy animal which keeps them well oiled, seal out the rain and keep the animal dry (FRANK, LEO, *Silver Fox Farming: The Industrial Marvel of the Twentieth Century*, 1925, 10). A king hair is a guard hair that doesn't have a silver bar (S 7).

*DC, DNE, and W3 all equate *king hair* with *guard hair*. The Prince Edward Island evidence makes *king hair* one kind of *guard hair*.
W3; DC; DNE.

kipher
Intransitive verb. \'kī-fur\. Also spelled **kifer**. Rare.
  To coast out of control downhill.
  Well, I got on the thing [a bicycle] and started downhill. He hadn't told me how to stop it and it kept going faster and faster. Boy, we were kiphering (GREEN, ALICE, *Footprints on the Sands of Time*, 1980, 263). This young fellow asked Uncle Joe if he would like to ride it. Sure he would; all you got to do is sit on it and pedal, that's all you got to do and go down this long sloping hill. So that was fine, Uncle Joe got on and he said, 'Mr. Man I was a-kiphering down that hill' (T I14).

kippy
Adjective. Also **kipper**. Informal. Rare. Compare **dilsey, trappy**.
  Usually of a woman, well-dressed or attractive.
  She's quite the lady, she's quite kippy (I 032). It means real dressy. Also used for men (I 051). It's an old word, because there's no pretty girls now (I 087). 'Oh real kippy' is used more in fun (I 090).

kist
Noun. Also spelled and pronounced **chist** \chist\.
  A chest, box, or trunk.
  We called it a chist – a wooden chest for blankets (I 020). A pipe organ is called a kist of whistles (I 058). A Scottish term for hope chest as well as any other chest (II 099).

[Scottish Gaelic via northern Irish and Scottish and

northern English] *W3*; *OED* 1300–1888; *SND* 1724–
1956; *DOST* 1472–1698; *EDSL*; *DGL*; *GED*; *PEDGL*;
EDD; *MED*; *OEDS*.

kitchen
Noun. Compare **fishing end, parlour**.
   **The first, baited chamber of a lobster
trap, where the lobsters enter.**
   The trap is usually divided into two compartments, the 'kitchen,' where the bait is fastened
to a cord or wooden spindle, and the 'parlour'
or 'bedroom.' Usually two but sometimes three
mesh funnels ending in 4 to 6 inch diameter
rings lead to the kitchen. A similar, single
funnel leads from the kitchen to the parlour
from which escape is more difficult (WILDER,
D.G., *Canada's Lobster Fishery*, 1957, 15). At the
turn of the century the introduction of the
gasoline-powered lobster boat and the parlour
trap (with a second compartment or 'parlour'
separate from the bait-holding compartment
or 'kitchen') greatly increased the fishermen's
capacity to catch lobsters (RUTHERFORD, J.B.,
D.G. WILDER, and H.C. FRICK, *An Economic Appraisal of the Canadian Lobster Fishery*, 1967, 3).
The kitchen end is the end with the 'bait spear'
in it (S 5).

kitchen dance
Noun. Also **kitchen party**.
   **A dance held at home, especially in the
kitchen.**
   Entertainment? Well, we used to have quite a
lot of what we called kitchen dances around
the settlement. That is, oh when you'd get up to
15 or 16 and start going to those kitchen
dances. That was entertainment (T M84). We
were at a party, kitchen dances they called
them, kitchen parties and they were putting a
new piece to the house or a new floor (T B13).
We had kitchen dances, you know, just in the
homes (T B13).

[North American] *DA* 1880.

kittardy
Noun; occasionally adjective. \ki-'tahr-dē\
Also spelled and pronounced **kithardy**
\ki-'thahr-dē\. Rare. Compare **gommie,
nosic, omadan, oshick, stouk**.
   A half-witted or simple-minded person.
   A silly, featherbrained type was labelled a
'kithardy.' I cannot vouch for the spelling
that I have given those words, but I am sure
that it is far wide of the letter arrangement a
Gaelic dictionary would show. I have yet to see

a Gaelic word that bears the slightest re-
semblance to its pronunciation (DEVEREUX,
JOSEPH, *Looking Backward*, n.d., 118). A person
who is simpleminded or useless. He could do
more things wrong than he could do right (I 031).
Just not quite with it. You might say, 'He's an
old kittardy' (I 055). Worrying foolishly. Stupid
(I 087). Used more as an adjective – a kittardy
person (I 090).

[From Irish] *EDD*.

kitten
Noun, usually in phrase **kitten of gin**.
Rare. Compare **cat**.
   A half-pint or pint container (O).

[From Cockney] *DSUE* 'a pint or half-pint pewter pot
... ob.'; *EDD* 'Lon. slang' 1851.

kitty
Noun.
   **In lobster fishing, a chemical preserva-
tive used to retard deterioration of lobster
traps.**
   We don't tan our traps. A kitty preserves
them from the worms. Otherwise the barnacles
would fill them (S 4). That is a south shore
term. We don't use a kitty or a chemical dip
(S 5). A kitty is what we used to call dying the
traps (S 6).

knit
Transitive verb.
   **To knot twine for (the mesh pieces or
'heads' on a lobster trap).**
   One or both ends of the trap are closed in
with laths or hand-knitted cotton or nylon
netting (WILDER, D.G., *Canada's Lobster Fishery*,
1957, 15). For a start we'd go in the woods
and cut our boughs ['bows'], you know, small
spruce sticks or trees to make boughs out of,
and we'd go to the lumber mill and buy our lath
and our strapping for the bottoms, and then
you'd go around the shore and gather up flat
rocks for ballast, then you'd buy twine and
you'd knit all your headings yourself (ANDER-
SON, ALLAN, *Salt Water, Fresh Water*, 1979, 77).
Dear old granny, she'll knit the heads / She's
still going strong as the kids sleep in their beds
(FLEMING, RICHARD, *Lobstering*, 1985, 1). Before
the season starts we get someone to knit us
some heads although many are now buying
webbing (S 5). I used to hire to get my heads
knit (S 6).

DNE 'To make or repair a net; to knot "twine" into
meshes to form a fish-net.' *SSPB* 'knittin': making,

by a macrame technique, the mesh funnel for lobster pothead, using two flat wooden or bone (now plastic) needles and twine.'

knuckle picker
Noun. Compare **cracker, shaker**[1].
A worker in a lobster factory who removes meat from the lobster's knuckles and arms.

He then passed the cracked shells to the 'shaker' whose job it was to shake the meat from the shells and then pass it along to the 'knuckle-picker' who had the unenviable task of picking the meat from all the knuckles while the legs were squeezed between rollers to extract the meat and the remaining bodies were discarded (MORRISON, CLINTON, *Along the North Shore: A Social History of Township 11, P.E.I. 1765–1982*, 1983, 73). By 1918 wages and prices hadn't improved significantly when Steven MacDonald, of Murray Road, worked for E.A. Hardy for $15.00 per month as a 'knuckle-picker' in his sandhills factory at Hardy's Channel. Lobsters sold then for $5.00 a hundred pounds (*ibid*, 70). A knuckle-picker is an arm-picker. He picks the meat out of the long piece of the two parts of the arm (S 4). A knuckle-picker has his little flat end device for picking meat out of joints (S 5).

krotle
Also **kronthal**. See **crottle**.

kye
Noun.
A cow (O).

[From Scottish] *W3* 'now dial'; *SND*; *DOST*.

L

large day
Noun. Infrequent generally, but rare in Egmont and Summerside; significantly male.
1. A day in which much is acomplished.
A large day is a day in which you get a lot done (I 009). When I come home and I'm exhausted I say its a large day. I've accomplished a lot (I 033). Its a large day because of the amount of happenings packed into the day, or chores acomplished because of the weather (I 043). A big day – you get it all done (I 047).
2. A fine, bright day.
It refers to a fine day when lots of work can

be done (I 105). My husband says, 'Its a large day for such a small island' (I 110). A nice, bright, sunny day (P1-002). A beautiful day (P1-049).

law
Transitive verb. Rare.
To take to court, to sue.
I'm going to have that fellow lawed (I 037). You might say, 'Are you going to law me?' (I 044). They're going to law that fellow (I 049). They lawed him. They took him to law (I 052). They're going to law each other (I 090).

[From Scottish and northern English] *OED* 1647–1870; *SND* 'rare or dial.'; *W3* 'chiefly dial.'; *EDD*; *EDSL*; *FW* 'Informal or Dial.'; *WNW* 'Colloq. or Dial.'

leafroll
Noun.
A virus disease of potato plants, characterized by an upward rolling of the leaves and a lattice-work pattern of dead tissue on the tuber.
The plant as a whole becomes chlorotic and stunted, the leaves roll upward becoming brittle and pale grey and appear to be thicker than normal (*Prince Edward Island Potato Handbook*, 1980, 47). PLRV [Potato Leafroll Virus] causes loss of chlorophyll, rolling of leaves – which take on a leathery texture – and often severe stunting of the plant. Yield can be significantly reduced. An aphid transmits PLRV – unlike the mosaic viruses – by ingesting virus into its stomach and later regurgitating it in saliva when it moves to a new feeding site on a healthy plant (ADVISORY COMMITTEE ON POTATOES, *Atlantic Canada Potato Guide*, 1984, 30). Leafroll is a potato virus. The aphids spread it. The leaves roll. You used to be able to see it on the Irish Cobbler, but new varieties are more difficult. They had it eradicated but a freak storm brought it back (S 2).

W3; *OEDS*.

leap
Noun. Also **alley-alley over, andy-over, anti-over, aunty-over, Charlie Over, haley-over, handy over, leapo, leap ball, leap frog**. Occasional in Malpeque and Cardigan, infrequent in Egmont and Summerside, rare in Charlottetown.
A children's game in which a ball is thrown over a low building to a team on the opposite side.

Another game was 'Leap' over the school-
house. There was a team of several youngsters
on each side. The ball was thrown over the roof
and caught by the opposing team (SELLICK,
LESTER, *My Island Home*, 1973, 48). The most
renowned of them all were probably checkers,
hide and seek and London Bridge. ... Leapo,
double dodge, and drop-the-handkerchief were
also favorites. The first of these [Leapo] meant
choosing two teams each of which stood on a
side of the school. A ball would be hurled over
the building. The team catching it would run
around to try and hit their opponents with it
(*Bedeque Area Multicultural Family Tree Report*,
1978, C). During recess and for those who
remained at noon, the following games were
played – baseball, hand ball, leap over the
school – a game of ball where there are two
teams on either side of the school. A member
of the team in possession of the ball, threw it
over the school for the other team to catch it.
The catcher, ball in hand, took off immediately
around the school to hit a member of the first
team who ran as fast as he could out of the way.
The catcher threw the ball and hit a runner
who now had to join the hitter's team, and so
on the game continued (*Morell: Its History*,
1980, 20). It is played around a one room school
(I 004). Not played since consolidation. They
played it around the old schools (I 013). A
person would shout out 'leap' and you wouldn't
know from what direction it was coming
(I 037). They throw the ball, and you yell
'over.' If you caught it you threw it back. If
you missed it, you ran around and tagged a
member of the other team who went to your
team (I 046). We said 'alley-alley over' when
they threw the ball. If others caught it they'd
run and tag you. Also called Charlie Over.
We'd say 'pig's feet' when the ball didn't go
over (I 047). When we went to elementary
school we called it leap frog. We couldn't play it
when we moved to a new building because it
was too big (I 038).

*DARE includes many other variants for this term in
the United States.

leather dollar
Noun. Historical. Compare **holey dollar**,
John Joy Token, **Sheaf of Wheat**, **tree
cent**.
    See quotations.
    Another odd piece of money in circulation in
early days in the colony, was the leather
dollar, issued by a Mr. Fitzpatrick a shoemaker
who deposited sterling to the full value of the

leather notes printed (PRINCE EDWARD ISLAND
HISTORICAL SOCIETY, *Pioneers on the Island, Part
I*, [1959], 45). It was in March of that year [1836]
when William Fitzpatrick, a thrifty shoe maker
in the town deposited specie in the official
treasury to the amount of several hundred
pounds. Back in his little shoe shop he then
laboriously cut and tooled out a large quantity
of leather notes of small value using tough sole
leather for the purpose. He made only the
equivalent of his deposit in the treasury. His
notes became 'good as Gold' and for many
months Fitzpatrick's leather money eased the
difficulty of local Charlottetown trading (P.E.I.
NUMISMATIC SOCIETY, *Island Currency*, 1973,
24–25).

lender
See **linder**.

lift¹
Noun. Common in Egmont, frequent in
Malpeque and Cardigan, infrequent in
Summerside and Charlottetown; signifi-
cantly rural, especially male.
    A trick won in a card game.
    We took that lift (I 079). That was my lift
(I 087). Pull that lift in (I 121). I got a lift with the
ace (I 118). Used in bridge or P.E.I. auction
(P1-013). Still used in 45's (P1-049).

[From Scottish and northern English] *OED* 'Obs. exc.
dial.'; *SND* 'orig. meant a cut in a pack of cards'
1787–1960; *EDD*; *EDSL*.

lift²
See **on the lift**.

lifter
Noun.
    See quotation.
    A shield or lifter goes in front of a piece of
machinery in order to lift the tops [of potato
plants] so the wheels won't run over the plants
(S 1).

lighthouse buoy
See **staff buoy**.

lights, the
Plural noun phrase.
    Electricity, electrical power.
    This is a common phrase used more often
than real electricity: 'Oh, we got the lights.'
'The lights are off' means there's no electricity
(P2-019). When the electricity was on we said,

'The lights are on.' 'We got the lights' was what we said too (P2-031). We got the lights when rural electrification needed four people per mile (P2-038). The lights came to West Devon in '38 (P2-076).

lilac run
Noun. Compare **strawberry run**.

A run of sea trout upstream in June, coinciding with the lilac season.

Already the smelt that have frequented the estuary during late winter are starting upstream. Later they will be followed by runs of gasperaux and of course by the 'lilac' run of sea trout (*Morell: Its History*, 1980, 114). First good amount of trout migrating up the stream (P2-068). A run of trout about the time when the lilacs start to bloom (R).

linder
Noun. Also spelled and pronounced **lender**. Frequent in Egmont and Malpeque, occasional in Cardigan, infrequent in Summerside and Charlottetown; significantly rural, older; especially male, less educated.

A man's undershirt.

On long dark evenings, the women knit or crocheted. They never sat with idle hands. There was much knitting to be done, as even the men's underdrawers and linders (as they called their undershirts) were knit by hand of fine one-ply yarn. All the socks and mitts that were used in the family, and even long stockings for the women were knit by the warmth of the kitchen stove (BAGNALL, MARGARET, *When I Was Very Young*, [1964], 3). He has drawers too and lenders, the best you ever saw (IVES, EDWARD, *Lawrence Doyle: The Farmer Poet of Prince Edward Island*, 1971, 118). Mud digging required lots of warm clothing as did breaking roads and most other work the farmers had to do. ... All men wore 2-piece underwear and the top part was called a linder. In the winter when work on the farms was slack many men and boys went to New Brunswick and Maine to work in the lumber woods. When one young man arrived at a lumber camp in Maine he was asked where he came from. His answer was 'New York State.' But the men didn't believe him because his speech was definitely like that of Prince Edward Island. They argued it not but one evening when he laid his clean underwear and went to take a bath they tricked him. When he came back wrapped in a towel his underwear was missing and excitedly he demanded: 'Where's my

linder?' 'Here's your linder, you darn P.E. Islander. Who else would call his undershirt, a linder?' (PENDERGAST, JAMES, and GERTRUDE PENDERGAST, *Folklore Prince Edward Island*, [1974], 19). It's the top of a man's winter underwear. The bottom is called drawers. Also some women called linders their one-piece knee-length underwear (I 003). My grandmother even made the linder from the loom (I 050). 'Linders and drawers' – the old ones were fleece lined, not like today's (I 118).

[From Scottish] *OED*; *SND* 1768–1961; *W3* 'dial.'; *EDD*; *EDSL*.

line
Intransitive verb. Compare **liner**.

To read out the lines of a hymn one by one, prompting singers in church.

At a time when each person in the audience did not possess a book, it was necessary, if all were to sing, for someone at the beginning of each line or two to intone the words in a voice heard by the whole audience. This was known as lining. Once done each person had the words, and was thereby enabled to raise his voice in song. ... On one of these occasions the Cardigan visitors were holding a service on Saturday evening at the home of one of their Brown's Creek friends. William Lamont was lining, and all present were entering with the greatest fervor into the song (MACQUEEN, MALCOLM, *Skye Pioneers and 'The Island,'* 1929, 87).

[From Scottish] *DAE* 1822–1875; *EDD*; *SND*.

liner
Noun. Compare **line**.

One who 'lines,' that is, reads out the lines of a hymn one by one, prompting singers in church.

Although not a gifted singer William Lamont was an expert 'liner.' This was an important part of the precentor's duty, and it was well performed by him (MACQUEEN, MALCOLM, *Skye Pioneers and 'The Island,'* 1929, 87).

[From Scottish.]

line storm
Noun. Rare. Compare **St. Patrick's Day storm**.

A snow-storm that roughly coincides with the sun's crossing the line of the equator, an equinoctial storm.

When the sun is crossing the line, they

expect a storm at the vernal and the autumn equinox (I 020). My father used to say, 'When the sun crosses the line ... [watch out]' (I 044).

[From New England] *OED* 'U.S.'; *W3* 'chiefly new Eng.'; *DAE* 'local'; *DA* 'chiefly N Eng.' 1850–1948; *ML*; *SSPB2*; *OEDS*.

line tree

Noun, usually in plural. Infrequent in Egmont and Malpeque, rare elsewhere; significantly rural; especially older. Compare **cat spruce**, **pasture spruce**.

A tree, usually of little value, that forms part of a boundary line between fields.

A hedge between one field and the next (II 028). Line trees are any kind of trees left after the clearing (II 063). Old scraggly spruce (II 110). They are twisted from the weather because they have no shelter (O).

[North American] *DAE* 'A tree located on the line or boundary of a survey.'

little Christmas
See **Old Christmas**.

living gale
Noun.
A violent wind storm.

It was on that same barn that I was shingling one day when it was blowing a living gale (GREEN, ALICE, *Footprints on the Sands of Time*, 1980, 261).

OED 1883; *SSPB2*. *living*: *DNE* 'Of the wind or weather, strong, stormy.'

loaf bread
Noun.
Ordinary bread in loaves, as opposed to rolls, bannock, and so on (O).

[From Scottish and northern English] *OED* 'Now dial.'; *SND*; *EDD*; *DAE* 'now dial.'; *WGUS* [southern, coastal U.S.]; *DNE*.

loafing barn
Noun. Also **pole barn**.
A barn in which cattle can range at will, instead of being penned in stanchions.

If we substitute or add loafing barns, bulging at the seams with breeds such as Herefords, Shorthorns, or Aberdeen Angus, we have a modern beef operation. These agricultural changes have dramatically altered the appearance of the countryside (BOLGER, FRANCIS,

Memories of the Old Home Place, 1984, 67). Loafing barns are good for beef because each animal doesn't have to be cared for individually (DUFFY, CHARLES, *Lexicon of Beef Farming*, 1986, 13). An open place with roof but no door. For cattle (P1-029).

*Pole barn is standard for a building 'having a foundation made of piles or poles stuck in the ground' (*W3*), but is used additionally on Prince Edward Island as a synonym for *loafing barn* (the meaning in *DAE*, *OEDS*), and as a synonym for *barrack*.
W3.

log drag
See **split-log drag**.

lolly

Noun. Also **lollies, lullies, lully**. Frequent in Egmont and Summerside, infrequent elsewhere; significantly senior, male. Compare **slobby**, **slob ice**, **slurry**.

Soft, semi-congealed ice or floating snow.

'Lolly' is the term applied to a conglomeration of minute particles of ice, which is found some four feet deep in extensive patches, and which is most difficult to push through; as the oars cannot be out, and the boat-hooks are useless: nothing but the paddle employed with great strength could move us along. Then the surface frequently freezes over, and the danger of being caught by a nip is carefully guarded against. The lolly, which now boils and bubbles, will before night become a congealed consistency, and form 'field-ice' (SLEIGH, B.W.A., *Pine Forests and Hacmatack Clearings*, 1853, 131). In a storm it [a hole for mud-digging] would collect a great deal of snow-drift, so that the men, on resuming their work, would find the holes which they had left, filled with lolly, which would, perhaps, take all their hands a whole day to remove (PRINCE EDWARD ISLAND, *Debates and Proceedings of the Legislative Council*, 1868, 63). Wednesday night and Thursday morning is considered the coldest that has been for several years so early in the season. It froze all the lully in seashore out as far as could be seen with naked eye – no appearance of ice evening before now the gulph appears as if frozen all over – it must have been full of lully (LARKIN, ALEXANDER, *Diary: April 3, 1886–April 3, 1890*, 1886, December 29). The passage [between Cape Traverse and Cape Tormentine] usually occupies three and a half hours, but when there is much 'lolly' – small particles of ice floating in the water, often to the depth of several feet – and when tide and wind are unfavourable, the trip requires sometimes from five to seven hours (CROSSKILL, W.H., *Handbook of Prince Edward Island*, 1906, 93–94). 'It was slow going when there were lullies, though.' – 'Lullies?' – 'Snow packed up on the water, perhaps two or three feet deep. No boat could go through. It would stick to the sides and bottom. We couldn't do anything unless the tide changed or it froze' (CHAMPION, HELEN, *Over on the Island*, 1939, 18). We pulled about six miles windward on the board ice before launching out on the floating ice or lolly (MORRISON, CLINTON, *Emigrant from the Highlands: Robert W. Morrison, Sr. and His Descendants*, 1978, 70). Fishermen use the word (P1-028). When there was lully we were not allowed to go skating on the river (O).

*The relatively high use of this term in Egmont and Summerside may be connected to the former use of 'ice boats' across the Northumberland Strait. [From Newfoundland] *DC* '[< Brit. dial. *lolly* < *loblolly* thick soup or porridge] orig. Nfld' 1771–1963; *OEDS*; *DNE*; *DSUE*. *loblolly*: *EDD* 'porridge or gruel'; *OED* 1597–1786.

longer
Noun. Largely historical. Frequent in Cardigan, occasional in Malpeque, infrequent or rare elsewhere; significantly rural, older; especially male, less educated. Compare **longer fence**, **longer snow**.
   A long, unfinished wooden pole used especially for fencing.
   The way of fencing their ground is done in the following manner; they prepare a great number of small poles, called longers, about fourteen feet in length; of these they lay down a row upon the ground in a zig-zag manner, where they intend the fence to be erected (JOHNSTONE, WALTER, *A Series of Letters, Descriptive of Prince Edward Island*, 1822, 15). Fences are made with poles, called longers, 14 to 15 feet long, eight in number, placed one above another in a diagonal form, and secured at the angles … by stakes driven into the ground … the topmost pole or longer, stouter than the others, rests in the crutch made by these stakes (LEWELLIN, J.L., *Emigration. Prince Edward Island*, 1832, 13). Not very cold – wind S.W. – Charles went to the mud. I went to Don Martin's (Uigg) woods and cut Mals' 16 longers and hauled them here – in the eve I went to Dan Red Johns woods for a load of hardwood longers that I cut there – called at

Mals' who promised to come and sharpen the scircalar [sic] saw for us since I cut and hauled 8 longers over my share (LAMONT, MURDOCK, *Diary 1885–1888*, 1886, 14). Though wire fences are becoming somewhat prevalent, the old rail fence, in different forms, is still in common use, the material for which is generally referred to as fence rails or poles. But in the Garden of the Gulf, if not universally yet quite generally, these poles are called 'longers' (WIGHTMAN, F.A., *Maritime Provincialisms and Contrasts*, 1912, 5). Beyond it all the dells and slopes and fields of the old farm, some of them fenced in with the barbed wire Pat hated, others still surrounded by the snake fences of silvery-grey 'longers,' with golden-rod and aster thick in their angles (MONTGOMERY, LUCY MAUD, *Pat of Silver Bush*, 1933, 9). This type of fence was easy to construct, cheap and quite strong. It consisted of several four to five meter lengths of spruce or fire poles, called 'longers,' laid on top of each other with butt ends overlapping, small ends to large ends. The poles were zigzagged to provide the necessary balance and increased durability. Where the 'longers' joined at the butt ends there were two upright poles driven into the ground on either side of the fence. These were then bound together by withers. Occasionally the upright poles were driven into the ground on a slant so their tops cross-crossed [sic] above the fence. Into this 'V' formation was then placed a top-most 'longer' which was generally the largest of all. This type of 'snake fence' was undoubtedly the sturdiest. A few early pole fences can still be seen in certain sections of P.E.I. today (MORRISON, CLINTON, *Emigrant from the Highlands: Robert W. Morrison, Sr. and His Descendants*, 1978, 62–64). You would put a longer across for a gate (I 034). We went to the woods and we cut our own stuff. We cut a lot of stuff. We used to cut sometimes twelve, fourteen hundred what we called 'longers' – fence poles (T B4).

[Atlantic Provinces] *OEDS* 1772–1973; *DC*; *DNE*; *SSPB2*.

longer fence
Noun. Largely historical. Compare **French fence**, **longer**.
   A fence made of 'longers.'
   Many votaries of the chase, of both sexes, (for Charlottetown had then some ladies who lent grace and glamour to the hunting field) might be seen on an autumn day, urging their steeds along the lanes, or leisurely

'taking' the longer fences, in the hope of being in at the death of Reynard, and perhaps securing as a trophy the coveted 'brush' (SWABEY, M., *Fox Hunting in Prince Edward Island – 1840–1845*, 1899, 234). As soon as she got to the Bay Silver side road, she turned down it and very soon was at the lane of her house – an old, old lane, grassy and deep – rutted, with bleached old grey 'longer' fences hemming it in (MONTGOMERY, LUCY MAUD, *A Tangled Web*, [1931], 91). It will be maintained in a late 19th century manner, with red clay roads, longer fences, and lilac bushes (HENNESSEY, CATH-ERINE, *Heritage Foundation*, [1973], 67).

[Atlantic Provinces] *DC* 1832–1925; *DNE* 1835–1981.

longer snow
Noun. Rare. Compare **longer**, **robin snow**.
   See quotation.
   Rails (or 'longers') of spruce were usually cut in early spring, as soon as the snow had melted sufficiently. Mrs. Leslie Campbell of Montague explains that 'the last snow of spring was called the longer snow' (KNOX, GEORGE, *Island Fences*, 1980, 22).

long-necker
Noun. Compare **teddy**.
   A bottle with a long neck, especially a large whiskey bottle.
   It's a whiskey bottle, I've often heard it used. They used to put liquor up in long-neckers with woven reed all over the bottle (P2-032). If you couldn't afford the 24 oz. long-necker you could buy a 7 oz. 'teddy' (P2-038). Any long-necked bottle. They have long-neckers for beer now (P2-060). Old whiskey used to have a long, thin neck on the bottle (P2-066). I need a prescription for a long-necker (P2-082).

long sill
Noun. Also **side sill**. Compare **short sill**, **sill**.
   One of the two longer pieces of heavy wood that form the bottom frame of a lobster trap.
   The long sills are the ones you nail the bows on to to make your frame (S 4).

*In square lobster traps, sills are also used for the top frame.

look and a half, a
Noun phrase. Also **half a look**. Infrequent in Egmont and Summerside, rare else-where; especially middle-aged and older, less educated.
   An indeterminate short distance.
   Same as 'a cat jump away' (II 009). Spit and a jump (II 026). It's a look and a half down the road (O).

lorsh
Interjection.
   A blend of 'Lord' and 'gosh' (O).

lot
Noun. Largely historical.
   One of sixty-seven townships into which Prince Edward Island was divided by Samuel Holland's survey of 1764–1766.
   In 1767, after numerous foolish and abortive plans had been proposed for its subdivision, disposal and settlement, one was ultimately determined on, which does not appear to have been much wiser in some of its provisions than these which were abandoned. About this time a division of the whole island was made into sixty seven townships of lots, of 20,000 acres each, comprising 1,360,000 acres (MONRO, ALEXANDER, *New Brunswick; with a Brief Outline of Nova Scotia, and Prince Edward Island*, 1855, 354). The remaining 64 Town-ships were disposed of by the ballot-box. When an individual was to receive a whole Lot, his name alone appeared on the slip of paper; in other cases, two and sometimes three names were inscribed on the one paper, as sharers in the one Lot. Upwards of 100 individuals participated in these grants. Many were officers of the army and navy, others were members of parliament and merchants (SUTHERLAND, GEORGE, *A Manual of the Geography and Natural and Civil History of Prince Edward Island – For the Use of Schools, Families and Emigrants*, 1861, 91). Fine day Papa and I started for Lot 11 about nine in the morning and reached Mr. Henderson's at eleven we had a 'glorious' drive (OLIVER, GERTRUDE, *Diaries of Gertrude Hazel Meggison Oliver*, 1906, March 7). The long struggle to free the land from the grip of the landlords went on for over one hundred years, and lasted until Prince Edward Island joined in the Confederation with the rest of Canada in 1873. Then the lands were freed for sale. The 'Lots' no longer belonged to the landlord. Yet today many an Islander uses a Lot Number when writing his address, – perhaps the only place in the world where this is done (WARREN, EVANGELINE, *Andy the Milkman*, 1957, 6).

*Lots and lot numbers remain as both official and unofficial place-names on Prince Edward Island. *DC*.

lully
See **lolly**.

lumberman's rubber
Noun. Archaic.
A short, insulated rubber boot usually worn for winter work in the woods.
They were rubber boots with soles that were heavy and good for working in the woods (P2-037). Boots that were all rubber and did up with seven or eight eyelets (P2-038). Short boots with laces (P2-049). These boots had a heavy sole in the toes (P2-059). I still use my lumberman's rubbers for gardening (P2-065). The children in most rural areas wore 'lumberman's rubbers' to school in the 20's and 30's – sometimes called 'gum boots' (O).

lumberman's overs: *W3* 'thick felt boots combined with heavy rubber arctics worn esp. by lumbermen.'

lumberman's sock
Noun. Also **lumber sock**. Archaic. Frequent in Egmont, occasional in Summerside, infrequent elsewhere. Compare **barn sock, hardwood sock, moccan, oversock**.
A long, heavy sock worn over the pant leg.
They went over your pant leg and had tassels on top (II 003). They came over the knees and had a string (II 067). Men's heavy woollen socks (II 112).

M

mackerel breeze
Noun.
A wind that ruffles the sea lightly and is said to favour the catching of mackerel.
In the bays and along the coasts of the island they are taken with the scarlet fly, from a boat under easy sail, with a 'mackerel breeze,' and sometimes a heavy 'ground swell' (SWEETSER, MOSES, *The Maritime Provinces: Handbook for Travellers*, 1875, 182).

[From English] *OED*; *W3*; *COD*.

maifram
Noun. \'mā-frəm\.
A bout of sickness or nausea (P2; O).

mailbox money
Noun.
1. Social assistance money from a government.
Children's allowance or baby bonus (P2-017). Also called pogey money (P2-026). Old age pensions (P2-032). Name for welfare money (P2-035). Certain people lived on mail-box money (P2-036). I heard a certain politician saying everybody in his riding got mail-box money (P2-037).
2. See quotations.
Mailbox money is money put in the mailbox that the postman would pick up and he would deliver the stamps the next day (P2-003). Many people never got to the post office to buy stamps so when they wanted to mail a letter they would wrap the two or three cents in a bit of paper and tie it to the letter and put it in the mailbox. The kind mailman would buy the stamp and affix it to the letter before sending it on. I often heard my mother say, 'Don't lose your mailbox money' (P2-084).

make
Transitive verb. Rare. Compare **flake**.
To cure (fish) by drying them in the open air (I).

*Make in this general sense is more commonly used with *hay* on Prince Edward Island and elsewhere. [North American] *OED* 'Obs.' 1555–1809; *W3* 'dial.'; *DC* 'esp. Nfld.'; *DNE* 1578–1977; *DAE*; *OEDS*; *SSPB*.

make-and-break engine
Noun phrase. Archaic. Compare **one-lunger, picky puck**.
A two-cycle engine, chiefly on a fishing boat, that employs contact points within the cylinder head to create sparks by making and breaking contact.
They were all double-cylinder and known as 'make and break' engines because of their improved firing system which replaced the less efficient 'jump-spark' models in use a little earlier (MORRISON, CLINTON, *Along the North Shore: A Social History of Township 11, P.E.I. 1765–1982*, 1983, 72). Generally this is a one-cylinder gasoline engine: as the wheel turns it makes a connection. Used for farming, sawing wood, fishing boats about twenty-five years ago (P2-019). Lobster boats used them (P2-038). They used a make-and-break engine for threshing (P2-073).

SSPB2. breaker: ML 'On the original one-lunger marine engines, such as the Smith and Langmaid and the Hartford, the firing of the cylinders was done by a *breaker*. Mechanically these were known as *make and break* engines.'

Malpeque disease
Noun.
See quotations.
Our oyster disease which has been called the Malpeque disease was first noticed in Malpeque Bay, P.E.I., near Curtain Island. This was in 1915 following the importation of large quantities of small oysters from the United States east coast. ... It is not known just how it spread. It may have been carried by water currents or by fishermen moving infected fishing gear, boats and oysters from one harbour to another. ... In many cases infected oysters become weak. They do not fatten normally in autumn and if they survive the winter, they fail to grow or spawn the next summer. They soon gape if stored in air. This gaping shows up both in storage experiments and in marketing of oysters from affected areas. Sometimes the dying oysters have small yellowish-green pustules on their bodies but not always. These seem to be only a secondary symptom. Furthermore, affected oysters are sometimes fat and grow and seem normal until near death. Indeed, there are no obvious and unmistakable symptoms of the disease (MEDCOF, J.C., *Oyster Farming in the Maritimes*, 1961, 93–95). But, by 1915 Malpeque Disease was discovered in Malpeque Bay and in the following year had spread to Cascumpeque Bay. By 1939 the waters of the entire province were contaminated and as a result the Island's oyster production for the province had dropped to 5,500 boxes! It was not until 1935 that Malpeque Bay oyster stocks had once more been re-established (MORRISON, CLINTON, *Along the North Shore: A Social History of Township 11, P.E.I. 1765–1982*, 1983, 79). A long time ago almost all the oysters died off. They don't really know what happened if it was an infection or a bacteria. They refer to it as the Malpeque disease (S 15).

Malpeque oyster
Noun.
An oyster of high quality first harvested in Malpeque Bay, Prince Edward Island; later any Island oyster.
Malpeque oysters from Malpeque bay are famous for their flavour and quality and have often been called 'the world's most perfect oysters' (SHAW, LLOYD, *The Province of Prince Edward Island: Geographical Aspects*, [1940s], 17). In the late 80's as many as 55,000 barrels had been shipped from the Island in one season (those were three-bushel barrels) and the Malpeque oyster had won the gold medal at the Paris Exposition, but over fishing and the coming of the star fish into Malpeque Bay had so depleted the natural beds that few oysters were being taken in that locality (ARSENAULT, AUBIN, *Memoirs of the Hon. A.E. Arsenault*, [1951?], 87). Prince Edward Island's Malpeque oysters have long been recognized as the finest available to the oyster connoisseur. ... The luscious Malpeque oyster is especially popular for the half-shell trade. ... For seafood lovers, Malpeque oysters are a delicacy and a synonym for succulence (BOLGER, FRANCIS, *Memories of the Old Home Place*, 1984, 6). A Malpeque oyster is just any oyster from P.E.I. The majority, say ninety-five percent of Malpeque oysters, don't come from Malpeque Bay (S 14). When you call an oyster a Malpeque oyster it doesn't mean it came from Malpeque Bay. It is just an old traditional name passed on. They are called Malpeque but only one percent of Malpeque oysters would be from Malpeque now. It is a name used for marketing (S 15).

[*Malpeque*: From Micmac 'large bay' via Canadian French] DC 1901-1964; GCD.

man drag
Noun. Compare **hand scoop**.
A scoop attached by straps to a shoulder harness, and dragged through shallow water to harvest 'storm-tossed Irish moss' at the shore.
That man drag would be the same as what the horses would drag only smaller (S 11). A man drag is a scoop that a man hauls behind him. They put it over their back and haul through the water (S 12).

marak
Noun. Also **mealy pudding**. Also spelled and pronounced **maracan, maracon, maragan, marakan, marick, mariken, marrican, marrigan**. Rare.
A home-made sausage.
The intestines were cleaned and processed and stuffed with the delicious mixtures that produced the finished 'maraks,' yards of which could be found hanging near the ceiling back and above the kitchen stove for drying and maturing purposes (SHAW, WALTER, *Tell Me the Tales*, 1975, 35). We called them 'maragans.'

My aunt called them 'maraks' (I 090). Marikens was the big part of the intestines stuffed (I 095). The same as sausages only grandmother's recipe for making them, you know. You cut them up in 'junks' about that long and you'd hang them over a pole in one of the upstairs rooms that wasn't heated and freeze them solid and have them for the whole winter (T M106). My mother made them when I was a child and teenager. They were a homemade sausage stuffed with meat of fine oatmeal, onion, and spices. They were very good. I believe they were the entrails of an animal and were soaked in salt water for days. I'm sure some of the Scottish settlers will remember them (O).

[From Scottish Gaelic] *SND. marag*: *DGL*; *GED*; *PEDGL. mealie-pudding*: *SND* 'a sausage-shaped pudding made of oatmeal and fat, a white pudding.'

market
Noun. Also **market lobster**. Compare **canner, michaud, short**.
   A lobster sold for fresh consumption.
   In some areas the legal-sized lobsters are divided into two categories – the 'canners' ... and the 'markets,' over nine inches long that are shipped to market alive. ... Market lobsters are often held alive at the point of landing for varying lengths of time (WILDER, D.G., *Canada's Lobster Fishery*, 1957, 16, 18). The Beach Point Co-op also operates a market lobster business. In the early years, the lobsters were kept in floats which were anchored at Machon's Point. Around 1950, another fish house was purchased from the Government and tanks were installed in order to keep market lobsters (DALY, WHITMAN, *Prince Edward Island – The Way It Was*, 1978, 13–14). A market lobster is the larger size lobster, the higher priced lobster (S 4). A market is the size above the canner and is usually sold fresh or cooked (S 5).

masheer
Adverb. \ma-'shēr\. Derogatory.
   Supposedly.
   My mother and her sisters used it among them, and we children did. Interestingly, my sister and brother and I use it among us still. It carried more of a meaning of pretense ...' She wore a masheer stylish dress' or 'Her dress was stylish, masheer.' Very expressive for an exact meaning among us (R 5). It's slang for 'for sure' (R 25).

[From Irish and Scottish Gaelic, literally *ma* 'if' + *fior* 'true'] *IED*.

maukin
See **moccan**.

May snow
Noun. Frequent in Egmont, infrequent elsewhere, but unattested in Charlottetown; especially rural, less educated.
   1. Synonym for 'poor man's fertilizer': a late spring snow-fall. Compare **farmer's blessing, million-dollar rain**.
   Also in April. It's like fertilizer (II 006).
   2. Synonym for 'blindman's snow': a late snow-fall thought to have curative properties, especially for the eyes.
   Older people felt melted May snow was a great healer of all ailments (II 017). It's good for sore eyes (II 072). My mother used to go out and collect it to melt it. It was supposed to be blessed. She even put it on her hurting eyes. She never drank it. It had a healing power, a cure in it (II 074). It could cure blindness (II 090). Water from a snow in May is a good healer. You could soak your feet in it (O).

McDonaldite
Noun. Historical. Compare **jerks, jumper, kicker, works**.
   A follower of Reverend Donald McDonald (1783–1867), who founded thirteen independent churches on Prince Edward Island.
   Under Mr. McDonald's instructions the inordinate terror which had seized this man's mind on the appearance of the 'work' soon gave way to the spirit of true repentance, and the vehement desire for godliness which had been previously working in his soul went on with renewed energy accompanied by the outward operation until his soul was set at liberty. This operation appearing as it did in connection with the inward work of the Spirit, was hardly ever separated or looked upon as being separate from that inward work, by the 'McDonaldites' (LAMONT, MURDOCK, *Rev. Donald McDonald: Glimpses of His Life and Times*, 1902, 49). While theoretically McDonald remained a Church of Scotland minister, the members of his congregation became known as 'McDonaldites.' One of the spiritual phenomena associated with the McDonald ministry was the manifestation on the part of many during his services of extraordinary excitement characterized by unusual distortions of body and limbs (BOLGER, FRANCIS, WAYNE BARRATT, and ANNE MACKAY, *Memories of the Old Home Place*, 1984, 48).

mealy pudding
See **marak**.

mean-price
Transitive verb.
To take advantage of (someone) in a business transaction.
A fellow buying my shed said, 'I don't want to mean-price you' (O).

merchants' forgery
Noun. Historical.
A forged coin that replaced the 'holey dollar' as accepted currency in 1814.
On the withdrawal of the official issue, the local merchants, grown accustomed to an adequate supply of silver, agreed among themselves to accept the forgeries in trade at the official values of 5/– the ring and 1/– the plug. Thus the forgeries were raised to the status of private tokens, and were used for about ten years. For this reason they are called merchants' forgeries (WILLEY, R.C., *Early Coinages of Prince Edward Island*, 1979, 353).

mesh board
Noun.
A wooden device for regulating the size of the holes in the mesh 'heads' of a lobster trap.
A mesh board is used to size your twine mesh. If you want an inch mesh you size it on your mesh board (S 4). A mesh board is what we refer to as a mold here in North Rustico (S 5). A mesh board is a little piece of wood about so long. It is just like a piece of lath. It has to be precise or your heads will be too large (S 6).

michaud
Noun. \mē-'shō\. Informal. Compare **blink**.
Synonym for 'short': an undersized lobster, one below the legal length for fishing.
Mr. Michaud said to measure them from the nose to the end of the tail. That's hard to do (O).

*Joseph Michaud was the federal minister of fisheries from 1935 to 1942, during which time he introduced an unpopular system for determining the legal size of lobsters.

mickeram
Noun. \'mi-kur-əm\. Also (for French speakers) spelled and pronounced **Mi-Carême** 'mid-Lent.' Frequent in Egmont, infrequent in Summerside, rare elsewhere; significantly Acadian.
In Acadian and some Irish communities at mid-Lent, either a disguised person who brings treats to children, or one of a group of mummers who require onlookers to guess their identities.
The Mi-carême is a French tradition once popular in all Island Acadian villages and still alive in a few of them. This custom marks the middle of Lent, hence its name, Mi-carême or 'mid-Lent'. … Traditionally, each family usually had its own Mi-Carême who appeared at the kitchen door early in the evening. The role was habitually played by an adult member of the home, either a parent, a grandparent or a grown-up brother or sister. Mrs. Anne-Marie Perry of Tignish vividly recalls how her grand-uncle acted the Mi-Carême in her family when she was a child. This was in the 1920's: 'At our place, Joe Nezime was always the one who did the Mi-Carême. He was my mother's 'old uncle' and he lived with us. He never married. Anyway, after supper he would put on his disguise and come in to act the Mi-Carême. He always wore a big blanket and carried a long cane, a long pole. And we were dead-scared of him! He'd come in with a sack which he laid on the floor. He spoke no word. Each of us kids had to go one at a time to pick up our treats. Generally it was an apple, taffy or something like that' (ARSENAULT, GEORGES, *La Mi-Carême*, 1981, 8). It's a common word around Miminegash. We wouldn't go 'handy' the table (which had candy on it) because the mickeram might get us. The mickeram would have brought the treat but they'd be scared of that person (O).

*The French word *Mi-Carême* has been anglicized here by some English-speaking Irish households in Egmont, who have borrowed this Acadian custom.
[From Acadian French.]

million-dollar rain
Noun. Also **million-dollar snow**, **million-dollar storm**. Infrequent generally, but rare in Charlottetown; especially male. Compare **farmer's blessing**, **May snow**, **poor man's fertilizer**.
See quotations.
Rain after a dry spell that brings back the crops (II 063). If we need rain bad and it comes, then we say it (II 105). Farmers say it's for the crops (O).

mind

Transitive and intransitive verb. Frequent in Egmont, occasional in Malpeque and Cardigan, rare elsewhere; especially rural.

To remember.

Don't you mind the fun we used to have picking gum in the woods back of your place (MONTGOMERY, LUCY MAUD, *Letter to Penzie MacNeill*, 1890, October 6). 'Judy, don't you remember that Hilary and I called the little hill by the Haunted Spring Happiness? We used to have such lovely times there.' – 'Oh, I'm minding' (MONTGOMERY, LUCY MAUD, *Mistress Pat*, 1935, 17). Y-e-e-s. I mind me of a house not far from me own when I was a boy (CAMPBELL, ALPHONSUS, *Local Color*, 1973, 59). 'Deary me, but I am minding your great-aunt, when I see you, though she has been dead and gone for many a year!' (DIXON, MARGARET, *Going Home: An Autobiography*, 1979, 166). 'I was with Kippy when he died – remember? I asked him about it. "D'you mind, Kip," I said, "the time I beat you up in school?"' (HENNESSEY, MICHAEL, *The Priest and the Pallbearer*, 1984, 81).

[From British and Irish] *OED* 'Now arch. and dial.' 1382–1896; *W3* 'chiefly dial'; *SND* 'Gen Sc. Arch. or dial. in Eng.'; *DNE* 1792–1977; *EDD*; *DOST*; *EDSL*; *MED*; *GCD* 'Archaic or dialect'; *FW* 'Dial.'; *WNW* 'Dial.'

Minegoo

Noun. \'min-ə-,goo\. Also spelled and pronounced **Minago, Minagoo, Minegor, Munegoo**. Compare **Abegweit, Island**.

Prince Edward Island (a Micmac Indian name).

Minegoo or *Munegoo*: an island (RAND, SILAS, *Micmac Dictionary: Transcribed and Alphabetically Arranged*, 1902, 101). But the people did not forget Minegoo and to this day in the Maritimes, and beyond, my birthplace is simply 'the Island' (KELLEY, FRANCIS, *The Bishop Jots It Down: An Autobiographical Strain on Memories*, 1939, 7). Little is known about the Micmac who seasonally migrated to 'Minago' by canoe from places like 'Shediak' in search of a winter food supply. We do know they camped along the shores of Bedeque Bay ..., dried the fish they caught and hunted wild fowl, then returned to winter camping grounds across the strait (RANKIN, ALLEN, *Down at the Shore: A History of Summerside, Prince Edward Island (1752–1945)*, 1980, 5). The natives gave the island the very poetic name of ABEGWEIT, meaning 'Cradled on the Wave', though they sometimes called it THE

ISLAND – Minegoo in their language – just as we do (HART, GEORGE, *The Story of Old Abegweit: A Sketch of Prince Edward Island History*, n.d., 5).

*A volume of poetry by Milton Acorn is titled *The Island Means Minago* (Toronto: NC Press, 1975). [From Micmac: Algonkian.]

misery

Noun, often plural in phrase **to have the miseries**.

Any pain, ache, or discomfort.

She would have you out of your hard-earned bed in the middle of the night, doctor, dear, if she took a spell of misery, that she would (MONTGOMERY, LUCY MAUD, *Anne's House of Dreams*, 1917, 271). 'Oh, I got the miseries.' You're not sick enough to die, but you've got the miseries (P2-004). Refers to flu-like symptoms, nothing specific (P2-029). That used to be when people weren't feeling well in the spring. Old people's disease used to be the miseries (P2-031). Lots of people have the miseries – menstrual pain (P2-053). 'She's got the miseries' means a rash or shingles (P2-054). A chronic illness. 'Old Aunt Bertha is down with the miseries again' (P2-055). In my old age, I occasionally suffer from the miseries (P2-056). The runs (P2-060). A headache (P2-061). Usually an older woman that complains: 'She's got the miseries' (P2-066). The feeling of a person after having drunk too much (P2-069). Usually women's troubles (P2-078). She could not come as the miseries were on her (P2-085).

[From English] *OED* 'dial.'; *W3* 'dial'; *EDD*; *DSUE*; *FW* 'Dial.'; *WNW* 'Dial.'

miss

Intransitive verb.

Of potatoes, to fail.

Our crop of potatoes missed badly (MCCARVILL, LISA, *A Potato Farming Lexicon from Kinkora, P.E.I.*, 1986, n. pag.). Too cold weather can cause a crop to miss (S 1). To miss is when the potatoes don't grow, the eye is dormant. An awful lot of things can do it (S 2). To miss is when some of the sets don't grow. There are large gaps between tops, caused by poor seed or poor growing conditions (S 3).

[From British] *OED* 1615–1852; *W3*; *EDD*; *SND*.

mitch

Transitive and intransitive verb. Rare. Compare **trump**.

To play truant, to miss (school).
He's mitching school (II 038).

[From English and Irish] *OED* 'Now dial.' 1580–1900; *W3* 'now dial.'; *EDD*; *ESI*.

mither
Transitive and intransitive verb. Rare.
   To pester, bother, fatigue, or confuse (someone).
   I was mithered by mosquito bites (O).

*In Britain and Ireland, this word is a variant of *moider*.
[From English and Irish] *OED* 'dial.' 1670–1880; *W3* 'dial. Eng.'; *EDD*.

moccan
Noun. Also spelled **maukin, moggan.** Rare. Compare **barn sock, hardwood sock, lumberman's sock, oversock.**
   A woollen stocking with a thickened sole, usually worn without a boot.
   I remember also that my mother would put double feet in woollen socks and call them 'moccans.' My father assured us that these were used as outdoor wear in the olden days, and he was right, for 'mogan' was a cloth of some kind wound round the foot (CAMPBELL, AL-PHONSUS, *The Heritage of the Highland Scots in P.E.I.*, 1975, 55). The old people would take the heads of stockings with home-made drugget. Perhaps four or five layers. Not worn in boots, but right outside (I 044). Heavy socks with extra layers around the feet sewn on. They were made of sacks and old socks and worn without boots in frosty dry weather. They were worn for cutting woods in the winter. More comfortable than rubber boots in the right circumstances (I 051). Foot wear, home-made (O). Big rough socks pulled on like slippers. Worn outdoors in dry weather (O).

Moccan is derived from the Gaelic *mogun* 'a stocking without a sole' (*PEDGL*); it is not related to *moccasin*, which comes from Algonkian.
[From Scottish Gaelic.]

monkey fur
Noun. Also **monkey hair.** Compare **dirt², shoe-string.**
   A seaweed (*Halopteris*) that grows with 'Irish moss,' considered an impurity when found in the moss harvest.
   Monkey fur: a type of impurity in Irish moss which resembles thick brown hair. [1] I hate cleaning that damn monkey fur out of the moss. That's why I get my wife to do it. [2] Some fishermen don't bother cleaning the [monkey] hair out of the moss. They just sell it like that (BERNARD, BLAINE, *Dictionary of Irish Moss*, 1986, n. pag.). Monkey hair is a brown fuzzy impurity in the moss. It pretty well can't be picked out. They (the processors) don't want this in the moss. It ruins it by matting around the moss making it harder to dry (S 10).

moss
Noun. Compare **black moss, bleach moss, moss bag, mosser, missing, rake moss, shore moss, spring moss.**
   A short form for 'Irish moss': either of two edible seaweeds (*Gigartina mamillosa* or, more usually, *Chondrus crispus*) harvested from the sea bed, or from the shore after being washed up by storms, and sold for their extract, carrageenin, a stabilizing or thickening agent in a variety of foods and pharmaceutical products including ice-cream and toothpaste.
   Most of the areas raked for moss are also fished for lobsters, at times intensively. For example, off Tignish, Cape Tryon, N. Rustico & Covehead, 'raking' could never begin until after the lobster season closed on June 30 each year because of the large numbers of lobster traps set on the moss beds (SCARRATT, D.J., *Investigations into the Effects on Lobsters of Raking Irish Moss, 1970–1971*, 1972, 1). There are basically two methods by which this species of sea weed is landed on P.E.I. One is to simply gather up the Moss, 'storm tossed' upon the shores. The second method involves the actual harvesting of the Moss, by cutting it from the sea floor (MORRIS, DONALD, *An Introduction to the Current State of the P.E.I. Fishing Industry, Focusing on the Years 1971–1975*, 1976, 33). There is considerable drama associated with the gathering of moss. Very often the harvesting is a family affair, with women and children flocking to the beaches with men after heavy weather has sent the waves rolling in with fronds torn from the bottom. While the moss on the shore is being gathered up by rakes and forks, horses with scoops harnessed behind them trot or canter ... along the ebb waters to salvage the moss floating out of reach (BOLGER, FRANCIS, *Memories of the Old Home Place*, 1984, 1). Some people in the Miminegash area used to make puddings with moss. If it weren't for the moss in this area, many people would be

in trouble. Irish moss was really a God-send (BERNARD, BLAINE, *Dictionary of Irish Moss*, 1986, n. pag.).

moss bag
Noun phrase. Compare **bagger, moss**.
A large burlap bag similar to a potato bag, used to carry 'Irish moss.'
Moss bags are usually two 75-lb potato bags sewn together (BERNARD, BLAINE, *Dictionary of Irish Moss*, 1986, n. pag.). They bag 'moss' up at the 'Lake' [North Lake]. Once it goes through the grinder and the dryer it then goes into the moss bags. They are just bags like potato bags made of cloth (S 10). Years ago, all the moss taken to market was taken by moss bags. Now anybody doing a small bit of mossing still bags it (S 11). Some people use moss bags if they don't have carts. As well, companies ship their 'Irish moss' out in burlap bags (S 12).

mosser
Noun. Compare **comber, dragger, horse mosser, moss, mossing, shore mosser**.
1. A person who harvests 'Irish moss.'
'The mossers deserve support in their struggle for a just price for 'moss,'' said a spokesman for the federation [of Labour] (*The Guardian*, July 4, 1984, 3). There [on the seashore] mossers, with the aid of a horse, tractor and truck, a fork and a lot of hard work, reap the harvest (*The Guardian*, April 25, 1986, 3). That is what they call a fellow doing it on the beach, a mosser. It is a little bit of a slur. You have to be a bit ugly and competitive to get the 'moss' first (S 11). Mosser is the term they use here to refer to a 'moss' fisherman. They didn't consider it part of the fishery and mossers weren't considered fishermen (S 12).
2. A strong wind that brings 'Irish moss' to shore.
In Miminegash, a mosser is a nor'wester; in Tignish, it's a nor'easter (BERNARD, BLAINE, *Dictionary of Irish Moss*, 1986, n. pag.). A high southeast or northeast wind brought in the 'moss.' It was always nasty but brought in money after (II 098). Yeah, a strong wind that holds moss on shore is a mosser. A good northeasterly is a good mosser here [in northeastern PEI] (S 10). A good easterly wind is a good mosser here [in western PEI] (S 11). People say 'She is blowing from the nor west. She is going to be a mosser.' They mean that the wind is blowing the right way to cast 'moss' on shore (S 12).

moss horse
Noun. Compare **horse mosser, horse rake**.
A horse used in the harvesting of 'storm-tossed Irish moss' at the shore.
A moss horse would be one of those big horses they use up west to rake 'moss' (S 10). A moss horse would have to be a horse that wouldn't be scared of the water or anything else. Some horses would be no good for 'mossing.' You need a horse that isn't bothered by anything because you have thirty or forty horses in one area (S 11). A moss horse is a horse that is used for collecting 'Irish moss.' It is usually a good size and has to be used to going into water up to its neck (S 12).

mossing
Verbal noun. Compare **moss, mosser**.
The act of harvesting 'Irish moss.'
Plants are best harvested when full grown. The fronds are then larger and heavier and yield a better harvest. The season when 'mossing' should begin depends on the region and the prevailing weather conditions (MACFARLANE, CONSTANCE, *Irish Moss in the Maritime Provinces*, 1956, 5). Soon mossing featured lobster boats trailing several tandem 'Nova Scotia' rakes either from trap-haulers or from overhead winches. ... These technical innovations raised the cost of gathering 'moss,' but they dramatically increased the harvest (ANDERSON, NANCY, et al., *Global Village? Global Pillage: Irish Moss from P.E.I. in the World Market*, [1977], 3). Before the 60's mossing was so uncommon, that you had to clear a path through the 'moss' that lay on the beach in order to launch your boat (BERNARD, BLAINE, *Dictionary of Irish Moss*, 1986, n. pag.). Yeah, the different ways of mossing, some would be good on 'shore moss' and some would be good from a boat (S 11).

moss money
Noun. Compare **fox money**.
Money received from selling 'Irish moss.'
Moss money would apply more to the olden days: the women would have the egg money, the man the moss money (S 11).

mud
Transitive verb. Archaic.
To apply 'mussel mud' to (a field) as fertilizer.
'Those fields were mudded.' The speaker would assume you knew it was mussel mud (I 012). We mudded our fields. We usually dug

for mussel mud on the oyster beds (I 080). They mudded that farm (I 087).

mud clopper
Noun. Humorous.

A heavy shoe or boot used especially for farm work; a clodhopper.

They were great big boots, all the farmers wore them. They stuck in the mud (P2-026). Boots made for slopping around in the spring (P2-031). Heavy shoes for going to school (P2-059). They were big heavy boots for slopping around in mud, made of rubber on leather (O).

mudder
Noun. Archaic.

A person who dug 'mussel mud' for farmers to use as fertilizer.

'I doubt,' said Mr. Best, 'you'll find another old-time 'mudder' on the Island. I don't know how I got into such work, for it was about the hardest, coldest, dirtiest job a man could tackle. But I did, and then I was always in demand. You see, we had to wait until there was ice thick enough to carry us as you couldn't hoist mud in a boat or from a raft. And when there was ice thick enough there was always cold weather, freezing winds, blustering snow, ten below days on end. We'd rig a capstan and use a horse to run it and hoist up the mud from oyster beds. It was a steady job sixty-five years ago when I was in my prime. Three neighbors would work together and we'd have a hot breakfast, all a man could eat, wrap ourselves as warm as we could, but not make one's self awkward with bundling, and out we would go at daylight. The ice would be one to three feet thick and we'd have to chop or saw out an opening large enough to hoist through. We used to chop a long cut, say twenty feet, then make an almost square hole and use the scoop. That's where the trick came in – to use that scoop properly. It was hard to set. You had to know the exact way to tilt it and hit the bed. If you didn't set it right you'd only get half a load and it was mighty hard work. And when we had a load up we had to keep it going or the stuff would freeze. We'd haul that out on the land and it was better than manure. Cold! We'd be so cold back in those days that it would take all noon hour to thaw out. We'd drink quarts of hot tea, hot as you could take it' (BIRD, WILL, *These Are the Maritimes*, 1959, 214–15).

mud digger
Noun. Archaic. Compare **pin digger**.

A horse-powered device for lifting 'mussel mud' from the bottoms of bays and rivers, through a hole in the ice.

About noon I set off up the Kildare River to visit the Western Road District. Pretty good on the ice. Rather dangerous on the ice on account of so many mud diggers, got up though. ... Returned home down the river. Rather dangerous from so many holes made by the mud diggers (DYER, ROBERT, *Diary 1859–1883*, 1878, March 14). Papa and Mr. Lockerbie down to the ice about the mud digger (OLIVER, GERTRUDE, *Diaries of Gertrude Hazel Meggison Oliver*, 1909, March 2). A hundred diggers could be seen at one time at work and people from within a radius of 20 miles would be on hand by daylight from mid-February to the end of March. ... The machines were operated by one man but each customer was required to use his own horse on the capstan. This industry began to taper off about 1922 with the coming of interest in the white potato industry. It was found that too much limestone caused scab on potatoes and so by 1938 the last mud digger had been seen on Bedeque Bay (AFFLECK, MRS. DOUGLAS, *A History of Lower Bedeque*, 1972, 6). Ingenious farmers invented and constructed mud-diggers of different types, but quite efficient for the lifting of these deposits. Some of the first ones were mounted on scows, but it soon became a general practice to lift mud through the ice in winter (LEARD, GEORGE, *The George Leard Files*, 1977, reel 7). We didn't dig ourselves, you see not many people owned a mud digger, so when we went to the mud digging grounds there would be someone there operating a mud digger, he'd charge us 15 cents for a single load and 25 cents for a double load (*Down Memory Lane: Stories and Poems as Told by Residents of Maplewood Manor, and Senior Citizens of the Area*, 1982, 5). The main features of a mud-digger were: a huge prong-tipped scoop at the end of a squared piece of timber, four or five inches on a side and thirty or more feet in length; a supporting frame of heavy timber, and a capstan that stood a few feet to the rear of the frame. A cable connected the scoop to the drum of the capstan. Power to rotate the drum and thereby raise the loaded scoop from the river bottom was supplied by a horse hitched to the capstan shaft. The load was dumped into the waiting sleigh by means of a trip rope. Guiding the horse was a job for a boy – a light chore so far as exertion was concerned, but deadly monotonous and blood-chillingly cold. Since I was the only boy in our family old enough to fill the post, the honor fell to me on Saturdays and on weekdays after school. When the scoop broke the surface on its upward journey, everyone within a ten-foot radius was liberally sprayed with icy water; when it plunged down again, the deluge was repeated. Within an hour after the start of the day's operations, the horse was sheathed in a coat of glistening crystal (DEVEREUX, JOSEPH, *Looking Backward*, n.d., 19).

mudding
Verbal noun.
The act of applying 'mussel mud' to a field as fertilizer.
They found great mussel beds and someone discovered that the beds and silt made excellent fertilizer. Crops improved as much as forty per cent under its influence and at once 'Mudding' became a regular winter chore. ... 'Everybody was after the mud and so there come a time when we had dug practically all the mud that was of any use and that was the end of "mudding"' (BIRD, WILL, *These Are the Maritimes*, 1959, 214–15). The shell mud was a very economical form of lime for sour land but it could not be depended upon for maintaining the fertility of the soil. Also, mudding was often not recommended if a farmer was growing seed potatoes for it was generally found that it produced scabbing on the potatoes (MORRISON, CLINTON, *Along the North Shore: A Social History of Township 11, P.E.I. 1765–1982*, 1983, 11).

mud hole
Noun. Archaic.
A hole in river or bay ice, for digging 'mussel mud.'
One day, in the middle of March when breaking up the ice, he let the crowbar slip out of his hand into the mud-hole in twenty feet of water. His master sent him for it. He took a rope rein off one of his horses, put it around his waist, and down he went to the bottom of the mud-hole. In half a minute's time, his master pulled him up half dead, without the bar (CRAPAUD WOMEN'S INSTITUTE, *History of Crapaud*, n.d., 25).

mud lark
Noun. Rare.
A high overshoe, a galosh (II; P1).

mudscow
Noun. Compare **mud clopper**.
A light, low-cut work boot.
Up stood Bruin on his hind legs, stripped

his teeth and sprang at 'Samager' who floundered out of the way, but not before Bruin, with one stroke of his paw, had mown half the heel off his old mudscow (PIGOT, FRANKLIN, *A History of Mount Stewart, Prince Edward Island*, 1975, 127).

[North American] *DA* 1863.

mud sleigh
Noun. Archaic.
A sleigh used for hauling 'mussel mud.'
We may now note a difference in the scope given to the word sleigh in Canada's most eastern province, as compared with the adjoining provinces. Here everything that has runners is a sleigh, irrespective of its build or use, with the possible exception of a hearse. It may be a 'jaunting sleigh,' a 'pung' sleigh, a wood sleigh, a bob-sleigh, a mud sleigh, a drag sleigh, or a hand sleigh; it is always a sleigh, the particular kind being determined by the prefix. In the adjoining provinces, however, the term 'sleigh' is used in a much more limited sense, generally being applied to what has here been referred to as a 'jaunting sleigh.' The word 'sled,' seldom heard on the island, in the other provinces always is applied to the heaviest forms of runnered vehicles (WIGHTMAN, F.A., *Maritime Provincialisms and Contrasts*, 1912, 5). They put him in a mud sleigh and sent him home to change his clothes (CRAPAUD WOMEN'S INSTITUTE, *History of Crapaud*, n.d., 25).

mull
Noun. Also **blunt cow**, **mull cow**. Compare **baldy**, **poley cow**.
A cow with no horns.
Most of the principal breeds of cattle which we have now were represented at that time, and there were some cows called 'Mulls' which did not seem to be noted for anything in particular. Hornless like the Angus, they have apparently disappeared altogether (MAC-FARLANE, J. HARRISON, *When I Was Very Young*, [1964], 2). They have a white spot and no horns (II 002).

*The standard form is *muley* (also *molly*, *molley*, *moolley*, and *mulley*).
[From Scottish Gaelic] *OED* 'Obs. exc. dial. A heifer, a cow'; *EDD* 'the name by which milkmaids call their cows'; *SND* 'in comb. *mull-cow*, a cow without horns.' *maol*: *GED* 'hornless.'

mussel mud
Noun. Also spelled, humorously, **muscle**

mud. Archaic. Common in Egmont and Cardigan, frequent elsewhere; significantly rural, male. Compare **alder mud, killkid mud, mud** (verb), **mud sleigh, oyster mud, shell mud**.

  Sea mud thick with the remains of mussels or other bivalves, formerly dug up for fertilizer because of its lime content.

  Hauling mussel mud in dory (*Meggison Family Diary*, 1815, April 6). If they were to repair the shores to collect the kelp and sea weed – to the mussel banks for what is called mussel mud, … in all these ways they might provide good manure for their land (JOHNSTONE, WALTER, *'Letters' and 'Travels' Prince Edward Island, 1821*, 1955, 157–58). Muscle mud is a most valuable fertilizer, an alluvium containing living and dead shells, the latter being in a state of decomposition. It contains a considerable quantity of phosphate and carbonate of lime, so necessary to wheat and other kinds of grain (BAGSTER, BIRCH, *The Progress and Prospects of Prince Edward Island*, 1861, xxiii). The Island possesses one advantage which is unique and very valuable. I refer now to its thick beds of mussel mud or 'oyster mud,' which are found in all bays and river mouths. The deposit, which is commonly many feet thick, consists of the organic remains of countless generations of oysters, mussels, clams and other bivalves of the ocean, and of crustaceous animals generally. The shells are generally more or less intact, embedded in a dense deposit of mud-like stuff which is found to be a fertilizer of singular value and potency. The supply of it is said to be almost inexhaustible, and it is indeed a mine of wealth to the Island (CROSSKILL, W.H., *Handbook of Prince Edward Island: The Garden Province of Canada*, 1906, 67). A story is told of John Beer sitting as a magistrate in Tryon, on a case involving the piling of mussel mud on the side of the road to the inconvenience of the public. In his judgment he found for the defendant and said he'd like to see mussel mud, destined for the fields, piled not only on one side of the road but on both, all the way from Tryon to Bedeque (LEARD, GEORGE, *Historic Bedeque: The Loyalists at Work and Worship in Prince Edward Island*, 1948, 92). Most of the surface deposits of mussel mud were quickly exhausted. Underneath these there were usually deep deposits of oyster shells, sometimes almost pure oyster shell-mud was located that extended to a depth of more than twenty feet. These muds were all referred to as 'mussel mud' the name carried from the surface deposits that were first used on the land (LEARD, GEORGE, *The George Leard Files*, 1977, reel 7). Many farms still show evidence of applications of mussel mud by the shells that turn up during tilling (HOWATT, BETTY, *History Begins at Home*, 1981, 25). My husband used to get mud from Richmond Bay in winter and haul it home or dump it to haul home later in the spring (I 064). I used to haul it for my fields from oyster beds (I 082). Oyster and mussel mud was dug in Malpeque Bay when I was a child to be used as fertilizer on farms (P1-016). You'd put that on a field and you'd have a good piece of land. I can pick out every piece of land on this place that I put mud on. The shells, see, is very, very high in lime content and it don't give it off all at once (T B4). He sent a sample [of mussel mud] to Ottawa, and the word he got back was if it was available and easy got, you needed no lime it was the next thing to mussel mud (T I22). My husband dug it from Tracadie Bay and covered our entire 100 acres of land (O).

[North American] *DC* 'Maritimes' [PEI citations only]; *OEDS* 1825–1973; *OED*; *DA*.

N

nazen
Noun. Also spelled **nasen**. Archaic.
  A hen's nest (O).

[From English] *EDD* [a plural form of *nest*].

never-slip
Noun. Compare **sharp-shod**.
  A horseshoe with sharp projections on the bottom, to prevent the horse slipping on ice.
  Fine day. I got Joe shod with never slips. Made a stall in the stable (MEGGISON, GEORGE, *Diaries of George Eden Meggison*, 1917, January 4). We kept the horses shod all the time in the winter. And if the snow was very deep we'd take the hind shoes off so they wouldn't cut themselves. Then we got a kind of shoe called 'never-slips' for the ice (STEWART, DEBORAH, and DAVID STEWART, *Winter Travel*, 1979, 20). They always used them: an iron shoe shaped to the hoof with eight or nine nails. It protected the horse's feet on the ice and snow (P2-020). An ordinary shoe that can be put on and taken off during the winter (P2-027). It was a horseshoe made with a sharp screw in the back (P2-032).

Newfoundland turkey
See **Frenchman's turkey**.

nigger-head
Noun. Largely archaic. Compare **gurdy**.
   A winch on commercial fishing boats used for hauling nets or lobster traps.
   The vessel was equipped with a trap hauler, consisting of a 'girdie' and a nigger-head powered by a 4 h.p. Briggs and Stratton gasoline motor. ... When the first trap was sighted, the rope was switched to the nigger-head to facilitate more individual manipulation of the speed of hauling (PRINCE EDWARD ISLAND, DEPARTMENT OF FISHERIES, *Offshore Lobster: Technical Report #175, 1975*, 1975, 3–4). He starts up the hauler, it runs like a charm / He hitches the niggerhead with a flick of his arm (FLEMING, RICHARD, *Lobstering*, 1985, n. pag). Because there is nothing on the cylinder to hold the rope in place, someone must keep a strain on the rope in order for it to stay wrapped around the niggerhead. Some fishermen use both a niggerhead and a 'gurdy' to haul the traps. The line is initially wrapped around the 'gurdy' which hauls the traps up from the bottom on its own power. Then, as the first trap approaches the surface the rope is switched on to the niggerhead which allows the fishermen to slow the uptake and guide the trap on to the traplander (MACMILLAN, JANET, *The Language of Lobster Fishing*, 1985, 20). A nigger-head is the old fashioned trap hauler. It is gear-driven off a p.t.o. of a truck transmission. When the trap comes handy you have to reach down and pull it up onto the washboard (S 4). The nigger-head is the piece of equipment for to haul your traps with. You make a couple of turns around the nigger-head with the rope and then keep pulling the line in (S 5). The nigger-head was the part that done the hauling (S 6).

OEDS 1927; *W3* 'a drum on a windlass.'

nigger toe
Noun.
   A variety of dark blue potato.
   The closest to the nigger toes in an old variety is the MacIntyre, blue potatoes (S 1). Nigger toes were a type of potatoes. They were right blue or black, and very susceptible to blight (S 2).

DAE.

night-digger
Noun.

See quotation.
   There was once, it would seem, an active pirate traffic along the shore; in consequence, belief in huge caches of buried treasure spread and brought into being a race called the 'night-diggers.' The officers of this happy profession would spend weeks digging vast holes at the least likely points around the village. The occupation was necessarily fitted out with an appropriate doctrine. It was, for example, an article of faith that when the objectives of the profession were in progress 'nobody could make any noise; so the word was given now – nobody is gonna talk – and then if anybody be surprised in striking a rock, if he'd say a word, well that thing would disappear: they never could strike it again' (LEDWELL, FRANK, and RESHARD GOOL, *Portraits and Gastroscopes*, 1972, 38).

North Side
Noun. Compare **Northsider**.
   The northern shore of Prince Edward Island from Malpeque Bay to East Point.
   Malone borrowed sleigh to go to Charlottetown and North side (MCEACHERON, JOHN, *A Diary or Memorandum of Weather, Work and Other Incidents Connected with the Farm and District*, 1874, 11). Men from the North Side used this road to haul their potatoes to the starch factory at East Baltic (MACDONALD, MARY, and MRS. CLINTON STEWART, *Historical Sketch of Eastern Kings*, 1972, 51). Some of the tales are quite humorous. For example, there was supposed to be a haunted house – somewhere on the North Side where several people claimed to have seen ghosts (ROSE, PAT, *Ghost Tales and Mysterious Lights*, 1976, 14). So the three MacDonalds from the North side boarded the evening train for Souris a couple of days later and stayed overnite with their friend in Souris West. Everything was in order and the next morning they boarded the boat and made ready for the long voyage around East Point and on up the North side ... If they can get around East Point before the tide turns to rise, the South West wind on the North side will be off the land, so no worry there (JOHNSON, LORNE, *Recollections of an 'Ole Salt*, 1982, 13). Well, I was born in East Baltic about the turn of the century, 1901. We moved to the North Side, to this house in 1904 (T M74). She also belonged to the North Side. She was a MacKinnon (T M95). In my parents home [in Souris] strong tea is called 'real north-side tea.' North-side tea is so strong you can walk on it (O).

*For some informants in the east, *North Side* applies only to the north-east area.

Northsider
Noun.
   Someone who lives on the 'North Side' of Prince Edward Island.
   'Northsiders' along the coast from Cable head to Priest Pond got little if any sleep the week of November 2 to November 6 in the year 1906. On Friday, the second, the *Turret Bell*, a 2210-ton iron steamer, was wrecked on a bar off Cable Head (TOWNSHEND, ADELE, *The Wreck of the Sovinto*, 1978, 36). I can remember in between that era, my Grandfather Sterns ran a store in Souris, and he had a large family but he always had some help in the kitchen. But people would drive in from the North Side to shop in Souris and he'd always be bringing home Northsiders for a meal (T M135).

nosey weather
Noun. Also **nosey day**.
   Cold and windy weather that makes the nose run.
   Nosey weather making and stacking salt hay and digging potatoes and digging potatoes. Wind in all quarters (*Meggison Family Account Book*, 1817, September 6). A day in which it is sufficiently cold and windy and miserable to make the nose run (O).

nosic
Noun. Compare **gommie, kittardy, omadan, oshick, stouk**.
   A foolish person.
   A backward person (P2-016). A believing person (P2-069).

[Probably from Gaelic.]

nozzie
Adjective. Rare.
   Sticky, dirty.
   She's a little on the nozzie side yet [of a padlock being oiled] (O).

O

oil up
Intransitive verb.
   To put on oil clothes for fishing in foul weather.
   When the weather is bad I usually say we are going to oil up and get going (S 5).

Old Christmas
Noun. Also **little Christmas**. Common in Egmont and Summerside, occasional elsewhere; especially older, female.
   The twelfth day of Christmas or Epiphany, January 6.
   Feast of Epiphany, January sixth, when the three wise men came from the east (II 006). At Christmas we leave the tree up until Old Christmas (II 044). If you went out at midnight on Old Christmas all the cows would be kneeling in the barn. The children were too scared to check (II 089).

[From British] *W3* 'chiefly Midland'; *OED* 1863; *OEDS* 1931–1969; *DNE* 1937–1982; *EDD; SSPB*.

old fiddle
Noun. Humorous. Occasional in Egmont and Summerside, rare or unattested elsewhere; significantly male; especially middle-aged and older, less educated.
   A woman who is sexually experienced.
   There's a few good tunes left on the old fiddle (II 050). She was quite an old fiddle in her day. She played around a lot (II 058).

*This term probably comes from the proverb *There's many a good tune played on an old fiddle* (*ODEP*). *fiddle*: *SND* 'the female pudendum (Sc. 18th cent.)'; *DSUE*.

omadan
Noun. \'ah-mə-dahn\. Also spelled **amadan, amaden, omadawn, omadhawn** \'ah-mə-,thahn\, **omidown, omigon**. Rare. Compare **gommie, kittardy, nosic, oshick, stouk**.
   A fool or simpleton.
   Mike having lain down among fallen leaves, was dozing asleep, and Jim being alone, set up a dismal wail. 'Stop your miserable canniven, you omadan of nature; shure it's a dog barkin I hear,' put in Mike (MACKINNON, JOHN, *A Sketch Book: Comprising Historical Incidents, Traditional Tales and Translations*, 1915, 171). Someone who is always lamenting (I 010). A pure omigon (I 012).

[From Irish and Scottish Gaelic] *omadhaun*: *W3* '[Ir Gael *amadan*] chiefly Irish'; *EDD. amadan*: *GED*; *PEDGL*; *IED*.

one-lunger
Noun. Informal. Rare. Compare **make-and-break engine, picky puck, two-lunger**.
   A single-cylinder engine chiefly used in fishing boats; the boat itself.

For we still keep our time to the turn of the tide / And this boat that I built with my father / Still lifts to the sky! The one-lunger and I / Still talk like old friends on the water (ROGERS, STAN, *Make and Break Harbour*, [1976], 15). A one-lunger is a one-cylinder stationary motor in fishing boats (I 012). A one-lunger is a small motor boat used for fishing. It has one cylinder (I 017).

[North American] W3 'slang'; *DAS*; *DNE*; *SSPB2*; *ML*.

on the lift

Prepositional phrase. Also **on the lifting**, **on the lifts**. Usually humorous when applied to persons. Occasional generally, but rare in Summerside and Charlottetown; significantly rural, middle-aged and older.
   Of animals and persons, so ill as to be unable to rise.
   This is from pioneer days when cattle were often poorly fed in preference to horses. If the cattle fell down, then the men would have to lift them up and put them on their feet (I 012). You had to lift animals up in the spring because they were weak after the winter (I 013). When the cows are weak and slack and can't get up. 'If you don't watch out, you'll be on the lifts,' meaning you'll be run down (I 045). When you're in bed and not able to be about. Sometimes used for alcoholics (I 050). Used for livestock. When the feed is gone in the spring and the animals are weak they are on the lift. Literally, they have to be helped around (I 063). Horses picked up by sling because they were sick (I 066). Straw was fed to the cattle too weak to stand. There was a Cattle Lifting Day every spring to take cattle to the fields (I 092). Just being sick and in the house would make one on the lift (I 094).

[North American] W3; *OED* 'to be at the point of death.' *at the lifting*: *OEDS* 'very weak' 1812–1901.

orkin

Noun. Rare.
   A suckling pig (O).

[From Irish and Scottish Gaelic] *DGL*; *GED*; *PEDGL*; *IED*.

oshick

Noun. \'ah-shik\. Rare. Compare **gommie**, **kittardy**, **nosic**, **omadan**, **stouk**.
   A fool or simpleton.
   Half-witted (II 028). Foolish. Telling lies

(II 041). Don't be such an oshick (II 094). Referring to a useless person (P1 046). A silly person, one who behaves superciliously (O).

[Probably from Gaelic.]

other side, the

Noun phrase. Common. Compare **across**, **away**, **puddle**.
   The mainland, usually Nova Scotia or New Brunswick.
   John had a good property in Wilmot Valley. Why he left for 'the other side' (to use the Island term) we do not know; it may have been at his first wife's urging, for she had relatives there. At any rate to River Philip [Cumberland County, Nova Scotia] he went (GRAVES, ROSS, *William Schurman, Loyalist of Bedeque*, 1973, 57). For our ancestors living on Prince Edward Island in the 19th century, mail delivery was always a difficult problem. The great obstacle was not postal holidays, unions, or impassable roads but that narrow band of water which separates the Island from the Mainland, the Northumberland Strait. In the time before air transportation and radio, surface travel was the only means of communication with the 'other side' (MACRAE, ALLAN, *From Our Past*, 1982, 21). Old William Palmer, you know, John W.'s father, and I don't know who else was with him, went across to Buctouche, on the other side some place, for rum, and they got a supply of it. And they had it pretty rough comin' back around the North Cape. But old William claimed 'If God hadn't of been with us we never would've got around.' And him with a load of rum! (MORRISON, CLINTON, *Along the North Shore: A Social History of Township 11, P.E.I. 1765–1982*, 1983, 97–98). Nor should I be piqued when he goes as far as calling the mainland 'the other side' as if the entire continent of North America and this fair province were of equal size and import (*Unpublished student essay*, UPEI, 1983). 'The twins are thinking about going away to work,' Ronnie said. 'Oh where? Halifax?' Jimmy put in. 'Oh somewhere on the other side, I'm not sure where,' said Ronnie (LEDWELL, FRANK, *The North Shore of Home*, 1986, 123). That bear's tracks came up out of the water and he must have swum over from the other side (T B13). And if you're on the other side, why don't you come on over? ([radio disc jockey] O).

*For a small minority, this phrase has the meaning of 'the British Isles.' For prisoners, *the other side* can mean specifically Dorchester Penitentiary in New Brunswick.

ouncles

Noun. Also **ouncelets**. Occasional in Egmont, infrequent or rare elsewhere; significantly older, less educated; especially rural.

A small spring-balance with a hook, used for weighing light articles.

It's like a scale with a hook on it. You would hang something on the hook and weigh it (II 020). There was a hook on bottom where the thing to be measured was hung. It had a long arm where the measurement showed (II 071). It weighed up to twenty pounds (O).

[From Scottish] *SND* 1964. *ounsel: EDD. ouncle-weights: EDD* 'Obs. Scot. … A general name for all the weights that are used about farm houses' 1824; *EDSL*.

out east

Adverb phrase. Compare **down west, up east, up west**.

Synonym for 'down east': 1. In or to any part of Prince Edward Island east of Charlottetown; 2. In or to any part of Prince Edward Island east of one's habitual location.

That the lion's share of photographs are set in Charlottetown and the National Park may suggest something about the tourist market and the book's target audience, but it will do little to satisfy those who rankle at the traditional neglect of Out East and 'Up West' (MACDONALD, EDWARD, *Review of 'Memories of the Old Home Place,'* 1985, 38).

out of grade

Adjective phrase.

Of potatoes, too small or too large to meet government grading standards (S).

outside

Adverb. Compare **inside**.

In commercial fishing, away from shore.

Do you think the eggs hatch out in the cold water at that season? – A. I could not tell you whether they hatch outside or not, but I know that in the first gear they set outside, the outside gear, they will catch spawn lobsters but the inside gear will catch the most (CANADA, HOUSE OF COMMONS, *Lobster Fishery Evidence Taken before Commander William Wakeham, M.D., Officer in Charge of the Gulf Fisheries Division, in Quebec and the Maritime Provinces*, 1910, 430). The best wind for lobsters here on the north side is a north west for outside (deeper than six fathoms) and south west for inside fishing (inside of six fathoms) (*The Guardian*, June 16, 1975, 3). Deep water; away from the shoreline. used in phrases such as 'fishing outside' and 'blowing outside' (MACMILLAN, JANET, *The Language of Lobster Fishing*, 1985, 21). Outside water is deeper water from six to ten fathoms. We go farther now. It is usually the most productive ground to fish on (S 4). It varies from one area to another. Where we fish seventy to eighty feet is referred to as outside fishing (S 5). Fishing outside means to fish farther out and means a different distance in each port (S 6).

*The boundary between *inside* and *outside* is variable from port to port.
SSPB 'in the open ocean.'

over across

See **across**.

oversock

Noun. Archaic. Common in Egmont, occasional elsewhere; significantly middle-aged and older. Compare **barn sock, hardwood sock, lumberman's sock, moccan**.

A heavy second sock worn over the first, and sometimes over the pant leg or the shoe.

One pair was worn right over the other, and sometimes right over the boot (II 016). Mother would knit them and put them on over the thinner ones in winter. They went over the knee (II 017). A heavy sock that went over the pant leg and had a string at the top (II 019). A sock over another sock inside a work boot. A loose, neat larger sock (II 020). They were worn over shoes, a real warm rig (II 066). They were worn by men or children, a sock you tucked your pants into (II 076). They were heavy socks. You wore two pairs in workboots (II 101).

owly

Adjective. Common.

Irritated, out of sorts, in bad humour.

A little while before the last election, the Charlottetown *Guardian* had a big spread all on the official opening of the new North Rustico Liquor Store. Claimed in the paper that that there store does the highest volume business per capita of any liquor store in Canada. When Cyrus MacKenzie seen that, he was some owly (BOYLES, ANN, *Living in Harmony*, 1983, 91).

'Boy, you were owly at the softball game'
(I 006). It means just at the moment a bit
uncommunicative and disagreeable (I 057).
Don't look at him, he's owly (I 117). It's used
of tired kids to mean cranky (I 118). It means in
bad humor. I only use it when talking about
my wife (I 120). If I can't find it, I'll be some
owly (O).

SSPB. *take the owl*: *DSUE* 'To become angry: coll.: late
C.18–mid-19.'

oxter
Noun. Also **hoikster, uxter**. Rare.
   The armpit or underarm.
   When I taught first year a grandmother
would take a twin boy under each arm and call
it 'under my hoikster' (I 050). She was carrying
it under her uxter (I 052). All this fuss about a
few louses under your oxter (I 064).

[From Irish and Scottish and northern English] *OED*
1500–1893; *W3*; *SND* dial. 1700–1949; *DOST*; *EDSL*;
EDD; *FW*; *WNW*; *COD*.

oyster knife
Noun. Compare **cleaning iron**.
   **In oyster fishing, a strong knife with a
hand guard, used for opening oyster
shells.**
   An oyster knife is a straight knife with a
guard to protect your hands (S 14). An oyster
knife has a wooden handle, a guard and a
sharpened blade. We use oyster knives as
'cleaning irons' now. They don't break the
shells as much (S 15).

OED 1694; *OEDS* 1841–1973; *W3*; *DAE*; *COD*.

oyster mud
Noun. Also **oyster shell mud**. Archaic.
Infrequent; significantly middle-aged and
older; especially male, less educated.
Compare **alder mud, killkid mud, mussel
mud, shell mud**.
   **Synonym for 'mussel mud': sea mud
thick with the remains of mussels or
other bivalves, formerly dug up for fertilizer because of its lime content.**
   The chief natural manures afforded by the
Island, and which may be used in addition to
the farm manures to increase the fertility of the
soil, or restore it when exhausted, are (1)
mussle mud, or oyster shell mud of the bays.
Experience has proved this to be of the greatest value (*Prince Edward Island: Information
Regarding Its Climate, Soil, Resources, Suitability*

for Summer Visitors and Tourists, 1888, 6–7).
When the early settlers cleared the land of
trees and stumps the first crops were poor
but they soon found out by adding lime or
oyster mud they could grow excellent crops.
Oyster shells were 85% lime (THE LONG RIVER
WOMEN'S INSTITUTE, *A History of Long River,
Prince Edward Island*, 1967, 7). Hay was scarce
in those days so Mrs. Frost sent for a vessel
load of oyster mud. This mud had to be rafted
from the vessel to the shore and then carted to
a field, a tremendous amount of work. The
mud was spread on a six acre field on the point
and they say that the hay that grew there was
as high as your head and the field continued
to grow good hay for years and years (TOWN-
SHEND, ADELE, *Looking Back*, 1979, I, 32). They
mixed kelp with it to make it last (I 056). Oyster
mud was full of lime and shells, you see ... and
they never got fertilizer yet to take the place of
that lime. It could stay in the ground for ten
and twenty years (T M123).

[Maritimes] *DC* [PEI citation only].

oyster pick
Noun.
   **In oyster fishing, a ladle or cup on a
long handle, used for fishing individual
oysters in shallow water.**
   Sometimes you use an oyster pick. It has a
metal cup-shaped end and a five foot wooden
handle. You can use an oyster pick in about
two feet of water (S 15).

oyster tongs
Plural noun. Also **tongs**. Compare **tonging
board**.
   **In oyster fishing, a pair of long-
handled, wooden rakes, joined like scis-
sors and with the teeth pointing inward,
used for harvesting oysters.**
   A set of tongs is like a pair of rakes with the
handles fastened together, scissor-fashion,
about one third of the way up from their
heads. The teeth of the two rakes point inward.
Handles may be any length from about 8 to 24
feet but they are seldom more than 18 feet.
Heads may be of iron or wood and 2 to 3 feet
wide. Teeth are usually curved and about 3
inches long and 1 1/2 to 2 inches apart. They
are usually set in the head so as to be almost
parallel to bottom when the tongs are closed.
But they may be pointed a little downward if
you wish to dig into the bottom. Tongs may or
may not have a basket of wire netting on the
back of one or both of the heads. In fishing,

the tongs are lowered and the heads opened. They are closed by a series of short lifting jerks which scrape up oysters from an area of 2 to 3 square feet depending on the depth of the water and the length of the tong handles. They are then lifted and the oysters taken into the boat. ... If there is no wire basket on the heads, the tongs must be rested on a narrow 'culling board' that is fastened horizontally to the inner side of the gunwale and the handles must be kept vertical to prevent spilling the catch during culling. If there is a basket on one of the heads, no culling board is needed and the tongs are laid crosswise on the gunwales for culling. Oyster tongs are satisfactory on small areas of level bottom in moderate depths. They have been used in depths as great as 18 feet but the work increases with depth and the long handles needed for deep-water fishing are cumbersome. Currents make deep-water fishing difficult even with iron heads which weight tongs better than wooden heads. If there is any breeze, tongs are hard to handle when they are hoisted. Tonging is essentially a fine-weather job and the greatest depths for efficient working are 12 to 15 feet (MEDCOF, J.C., *Oyster Farming in the Maritimes*, 1961, 107). Oyster tongs are what you get the oysters off the bottom with. They have iron heads and the handles are made out of hard or soft wood. They call them oyster rakes in New Brunswick and Nova Scotia (S 14).

OED 1716; *OEDS* 1835–1949; *W3*; *DAE*; *DA*.

P

parlour
Noun. Also **bedroom**. Compare **kitchen**.
   The second and inner chamber of a lobster trap.
   Q. Why did the parlour trap supersede the original double headed trap? – A. For the reason that if, on account of bad weather, a man happened to be two days from his traps and went out, he would find the lobsters there. You lost more when you were pulling up the trap with rings at both ends (CANADA, HOUSE OF COMMONS, *Lobster Fishery Evidence Taken before Commander William Wakeham, M.D., Officer in Charge of the Gulf Fisheries Division, in Quebec and the Maritime Provinces*, 1910, 294). There were three large lobsters among the seaweed in the parlour of the trap (STIRLING, LILLA, *Jockie: A Story of Prince Edward Island*, 1951, 67). At the turn of the century the introduction of the gasoline-powered lobster

boat and the parlour trap (with a second compartment or 'parlour' separate from the bait-holding compartment or 'kitchen') greatly increased the fisherman's capacity to catch lobsters RUTHERFORD, J.B., D.G. WILDER, and H.C. FRICK, *An Economic Appraisal of the Canadian Lobster Fishery*, 1967, 3). The trap is usually divided into two compartments, the 'kitchen', where the bait is fastened to a cord or wooden spindle, and the 'parlour' or 'bedroom.' ... A similar, single funnel leads from the kitchen to the parlour from which escape is more difficult (WILDER, D.G., *Canada's Lobster Fishery*, 1957, 15). Ninety-nine percent of your lobsters are found in your parlour end. When they get into the parlour they are there to stay (S 5). The parlour end is where the lobsters are when you haul your traps (S 6).

[Atlantic Provinces] *DNE* 1964.

parlour head
See **centre head**.

pass
Noun, usually in phrase **to take pass of**.
   Notice, regard.
   It's taking notice of anything extraordinary. Anything rare you take pass of (P2-028). 'Don't take pass of that' means don't mind it (P2-054). It means to pass your eyes over: 'Take pass of that girl.' It's usually said of pretty girls or fish or machinery (P2-066). 'I pay you no pass' (P2-076). Did you take pass of the beautiful flowers? (P2-082). Take no pass of what he says (P2-083).

pasture lot
Noun. Historical.
   A plot of land outside the bounds of a town, used for pasturing animals.
   I remember when there were pasture lots in Charlottetown where residents left their cattle, at the time when a family would have a pig, cow, etc. (O).

[North American] *DC* 'Esp. Maritimes, Obs. ... 1763–1861'; *DAE* 1693–1902; *DA*.

pasture spruce
Noun. Also **scrub spruce**. Infrequent in Egmont and Summerside, rare elsewhere; significantly male; especially rural. Compare **cat spruce, line tree**.
   A spruce tree of little value that forms part of a boundary line between fields.

They never get very big because the animals rub up against them to scratch themselves (II 009). I heard this at a meeting – 'That'd only be pasture spruce anyway' – indicating its worthlessness (O).

*Scrub, as such, is standard.
scrub spruce: SSPB.*

pea
Noun. Archaic.
A small lead ball used in weighing potatoes (S).

[From English] *OED* 'The sliding weight used on a steelyard, safety-valve, etc.' 1761–1878; *EDD.*

peddle wagon
Noun. Also **peddling wagon**. Archaic.
A peddler's wagon for delivering groceries.
Perhaps the oldest general store in the area was established in 1902 under the name Mossey and Muttart, later J.F. Mossey and Sons. From this store a sizeable business was carried on by a 'peddling wagon.' This vehicle was operated by the Mosseys from 1902 to 1929 as a special service to customers in the horse and buggy age. Its route extended from East Point to Greenvale. A different road was covered each day, six days a week May to December. When the wagon did not have required items, orders were taken for next week's delivery. Purchases were mostly paid for with the products of the farm: eggs, butter, wool, calf and sheep skins. Children often bought treats with the proceeds of their collections of old rubbers and horsehair. The wagon was a colourful sight – its box was red and the under-structure yellow. On its journey homeward the wagon was more colourful still, embellished by the accumulation of the wide variety of commodities, carried on the axles or any place they could be secured. Mossey would call it a good day when cash receipts totalled $20. By 1929, with the younger generation preferring to visit the store by bicycle or car, the wagon service was discontinued (AULD, WALTER, *Voices of the Island: History of the Telephone on Prince Edward Island,* 1985, 203). He kept a little store here; he ran what we called at that time a peddle wagon. It was common practice of people getting their groceries and what have you. ... The stores were so far away and the means of travelling was so poor it was recognized as being the better way, you know, for that time (T M8).

peddler's wagon: 'a wagon or cart in which a peddler carries his goods' *DA.*

peevish
Adjective. Rare. Compare **droghey, snotty**.
Of weather, windy, cold, and wet.
Something has happened to sour February's temper. Such a peevish month. The weather for the past few weeks has certainly been living up to the Murray traditions. A dreary snowstorm is raging and the wind is pursuing tormented wraiths over the hills. I know that out beyond the trees Blair Water is a sad, black thing in a desert of whiteness (MONTGOMERY, LUCY MAUD, *Emily's Quest,* 1927, 174). This is a month of changing skies and fretful storms (the Irish people might say 'peevish days') when sleet, rain and an east wind come wailing up our valley (JOHNSTONE, RENA, *Journal of the Months at Strathaven,* 1980, 10). It's full of poison (II 111).

[From northern English] *OED* 'In mod. dial. Of the wind: Piercing, "shrewd"'; *EDD.*

pelt cheque
Noun. Compare **fox money**.
In fox ranching, a cheque received from the sale of fox pelts.
You would get a pelt cheque from the cleaning house (S 9).

pelter
Noun.
In fox ranching, a fox that is to be killed for its pelt.
Pelter: a fur bearing animal destined to be pelted (*Fox-Tales,* May 1982, 10). A pelter would refer to a fox that is ready for pelting as opposed to an old fox kept for a pet or a fox kept for breeding. It is a little bit contemptuous. You keep your best and pelt the poorer quality (S 9).

W3 'an animal raised for pelting.'

pelting board
Noun. Compare **boarded**.
In fox ranching, a wooden board used for drying, shaping, and displaying fox pelts.
To my mind, there are two main causes for difficult birth problems: 1. Poor conformation in the young females added to the herd. The pretty, little narrow-hipped females belong on the pelting board. Instead, choose the big,

roomy, bold, almost masculine appearing females (*Fox-Tales*, March 1982, 7). A pelting board is the board that is used for boarding foxes. It is used for shaping the pelt and drying it. There are two standard sizes. The farmer is trying to get a uniform look when the pelts go to market (S 7). The pelting board is the board that is used for putting pelts on after it is fleshed. We mostly used tacks to fasten the pelt on with (S 8). Pelts were put on a pelting board of about forty-eight inches long. It was usually a pine board (S 9).

fox board: DNE 'wooden board on which a fox pelt is stretched to dry.'

pelting pen
Noun. Compare **furring shed**.
   In fox ranching, one of the individual pens for foxes.
   Our pelting pens had wire floors and partitions. For comfort of these young litters we placed a 2' by 6' plank on edge, two feet out from the back wall, and secured it at both ends to the partitions (*Fox Tales*, May, 1982, 7).

pelting room
Noun.
   In fox ranching, a room where foxes are killed and pelted.
   The observation tower in use is merely a narrow building located in the centre and sufficiently elevated to give a clear view of all parts of the ranch. The top room has windows in all sides. A room may be built underneath to serve either as a pelting room or sleeping quarters for a watchman (ALLEN, J.A., and ENNIS SMITH, *Fox Ranching in Canada*, 1929, 9). The pelting room is where the actual pelting process takes place. There are different areas for the different pelting processes such as a pelting room, a cleaning room, and a boarding room (S 7). The pelting room would be part of the 'furring shed' (S 9).

pelt out
Transitive and intransitive verb.
   In fox ranching, to kill and pelt all the foxes on a ranch, keeping no breeding stock; in effect, to go out of business.
   The silver fox industry, despite its promise depended on fashion tastes and in 1935 suffered from serious overproduction. The outbreak of a second world war, while relieving the economy generally, caused familiar problems on the fox ranch, and by 1948 pelt prices had skidded to record lows. Many Island ranches, realizing the industry was in a state of collapse, simply opened their pens and allowed hitherto valuable animals to escape into the woods. Others pelted out their foxes. Only a few companies attempted to change with the tide and develop herds of more profitable, short-haired mink (RANKIN, ROBERT, *Down at the Shore: A History of Summerside, Prince Edward Island (1752–1945)*, 1980, 154). As the quality of the fox fur went down women lost interest. The cost of the fur went down and it seemed to become a novelty item. By 1948 many of the fox farmers had pelted out their animals (*The Guardian*, November 30, 1984, 6). The tide, however, was about to turn. Fox farming flourished briefly in the early 1940's after crafty breeders used 'freaks,' or mutations, to develop Platinums, Pearl Platinums, Pearlatinas , Glacier Blues and White faces, but in the postwar era, the industry simply collapsed. The future looked so grim that hundreds of ranchers 'pelted out' their entire herds (BRUCE, HARRY, *Silver into Gold: Alchemy in Action on Prince Edward Island's Booming Fox Farms*, 1985, 65). A farmer was said to have pelted out when he had gotten the hell out of this horrible business. Most farmers pelted out when the fur price plummeted in the 1930s (S 9).

pet day
Noun. Also **pet of a day**. Common in Egmont, frequent in Cardigan, occasional in Summerside and Malpeque, infrequent in Charlottetown; significantly rural, older, less educated. Compare **borrowed day**, **freshet**, **weather breeder**.
   A day of exceptionally fine weather, especially out of season, thought to precede a storm.
   It was a rarely beautiful evening; too fine, indeed – what old weather-prophets, call a 'pet' day. The sun set amid clouds of crimson, tinging the dusky wavelets with fire and lingering on the beautiful vessel as she lay at rest on the shining sea, while the fresh evening breeze danced over the purple waters. Who would have thought that, before morning, that lovely tranquil scene would have given place to one of tempestuous fury! (MONTGOMERY, LUCY MAUD, *The Wreck of the Marco Polo*, [1891], 35). A pet day I reckon (OLIVER, GERTRUDE, *Diaries of Gertrude Hazel Meggison Oliver*, 1906, December 16). 'Such a lovely day ... made for us,' said Diana. 'I'm afraid it's a pet day though ... there'll be rain tomorrow (MONT-

GOMERY, LUCY MAUD, *Anne of Ingleside*, [1939], 10). We say it was the worst one yet / The odd fine day we call a 'pet.' / And then from out the sky, though blue, / Would fall about a yard or two (ROSE, LIVINGSTONE, *Poems and Prose*, [1956], 2). It's an old term. It almost means 'beware.' Enjoy it now but look out tomorrow (I 029). When it's a pet day, you always expect something worse the next day (I 070). No wind and warm (I 079). Almost too nice. Good beyond normal (I 087). An exceptionally good day. Different weather than expected (P1-018). A mild sunny day in winter (P1-031). It makes you uneasy, since a storm is coming. 'I'm afraid this is a pet day' (O).

Pet winter 'an easy winter' has also been attested. [From Irish and Scottish] *SND* 1823–1937; *OED* 1823–1882; *W3* 'chiefly Scot.'; *EDD*; *IED*; *EDSL*; *DNE* 1933.

pick
Noun. Frequent in Egmont and Cardigan, infrequent elsewhere; significantly rural; especially less educated.
A scrap or morsel of food or of human flesh.
There was not a pick of meat on him. He didn't leave a pick (II 081). A crow couldn't get a pick off him (II 089). Eat every pick on your plate (O).

[From Irish and Scottish] *OED* 'the taking of a bit or mouthful of food; a slender or sparing meal. Now dial.' 1688–1899; *W3* 'dial'; *SND*; *EDD*; *IED*; *EDSL*; *DNE* 1924–1977.

picking table
Noun. Compare **digger apron**.
A conveyor belt on a potato digger that allows workers to separate stones, damaged potatoes, and other debris from the crop.
The picking table is up over the 'bed,' where they pick the stones out. It has rubber covered rods (S 2). The picking table is the chain area where people pick off rocks and sods from potatoes (S 3).

pickle
See **puckle**.

picky puck
Noun. Archaic. Compare **one-lunger**.
A synonym for 'make-and-break engine': a two-cycle engine, chiefly on a fishing boat, that employs contact points within the cylinder head to create sparks by making and breaking contact; also a fishing boat powered by such an engine.
We used to go up and down the coast in our picky-puck, looking for moss (BERNARD, BLAINE, *Dictionary of Irish Moss*, 1986, n. pag.). A picky puck is the old fashioned one-cylinder marine engine. It had a different carburetor and an attachment for the propellor shaft unlike the stationary motors used on land (S 11). A picky puck is an old one-cylinder engine used in boats. I never had one but my uncle told me about them (S 12).

pie social
Noun. Archaic. Compare **basket social, box social, concert**.
A fund-raising entertainment, during which pies were auctioned off and then shared by donor and buyer.
Claude MacDonald asked to go with me to the pie social Tuesday night. ... Didn't Gerard Danny Pius bid higher for my pie than Claude did. Claude wasn't very happy and either [sic] was I. Sharing a pie as well as two dances was too much for me with that man (BUSHEY, SARAH, *Memoirs of Sarah Bushey*, 1892, October 4). Fine day got a load of wood from Livingston's. Pie Social at High Bank (*Unidentified Diary*, 1898, January 20). 'Oh, Judy, I hate to think I'm so ugly my family will be ashamed of me ... people will call me 'that plain Gardiner girl.' Last week at the pie social at Silverbridge nobody would buy Minnie Fraser's pie because she was so ugly' (MONTGOMERY, LUCY MAUD, *Pat of Silver Bush*, 1933, 167). The early settlers found time during their busy work schedule to hold quilting bees, hooking parties, pie socials, basket socials, concerts, dances, and card parties (*Morell: Its History*, 1980, 51).

[Canadian] *DC* 1925 [PEI quotation] –1963.

pin digger
Noun. Compare **mud digger**.
See quotation.
The earlier '[mussel] mud' diggers were called pin diggers. Many of these were owned and operated by the farmers of the area, sometimes two or more in partnership, digging the mud for their own use and for sale to their neighbors (ALEXANDRA WOMEN'S INSTITUTE, *A Short History of the District of Alexandra*, 1965, 15).

pinny
Noun.
**A sleeveless, apronlike garment, a
pinafore.**
The volume of mail was light but a letter was
a treasured link with relatives far across the
sea, and would be carried for days in the
'pinny' pocket of a homesick pioneer wife
(PAYNTER, RUTH, *From the Top of the Hill: The
History of an Island Community*, 1977, 31). I
went up by the wood pile and in the back
window so my mother wouldn't see my dress.
... I got upstairs and took off the dress and
hung it over the railing and put on a pinny. I
came down and made sure she was in the
kitchen to see me (*Down Memory Lane: Stories
and Poems as Told by Residents of Maplewood
Manor, and Senior Citizens of the Area*, 1982, 9).

[From British] *OED* 1859–1884; *W3*; *EDD*; *SND*;
DSUE; *COD*.

pismire
Noun. Informal.
A spoil-sport or meddler; a brat.
A person of little significance (I 036). It was
a rude word to call someone (I 083). It was not
said in polite company (I 112).

*The standard meaning, now increasingly archaic
and dialectal, is 'ant' (*OED* 1385–1903).
OED 'Applied contemptuously to a person' 1569–
1818; *W3* 'an insignificant or contemptible person.'

piss clam
Noun. Compare **bar clam**.
A small, soft-shelled clam (O).

pitch
Noun. Archaic. Frequent generally, but
occasional in Malpeque, infrequent in
Charlottetown; significantly middle-aged
and older; especially male, less educated.
Compare **slough**.
**A hollow in a snow-covered road that
causes a vehicle such as a horse-drawn
sleigh to pitch forward.**
Clear with little frost. Splendid traveling
except pitches (VICKERSON, LEMUEL, *Diary:
1868*, January 25). We had not got about 100
yards before we went into a pitch, broke both
traces and the horse went out of the sleigh. ...
And then, about 200 or 300 yards before we
got to Mr. Caie's, we got stuck into a snow
pitch and could not move the sleigh (DYER,

ROBERT, *Diary, 1859–1883*, 1872, February 26).
Went to Kensington afternoon with 4 loads of
Potatoes 80 bus. (seconds). Terrible roads with
pitches (MACLEOD, ANDREW, *Diary: January 1,
1928–November 17, 1932*, 1930, February 11). As
the poet travelled the snow-roads, he came
upon 'pitches,' like the gulf between two
billows. These were filled with young fir-trees
cut from the forest. In the spring, when the
snow disappeared, these young trees lay trod-
den in the mire, stripped of their bark by the
incessant trampling of iron feet (MACPHAIL, SIR
ANDREW, *The Master's Wife*, [1939], 96). The
road overseer was responsible for hiring men
from the community in winter and summer to
keep the roads passable at all times. In winter
this included getting out after a storm to break
roads in time for the mailman to make his
rounds; filling pitches (those neck-snapping
cut out hollows that formed on the sleigh
tracks in mild weather causing distracted
horses, broken harness and upset sleighs) and
marking a track across the river ice by placing
spruce bushes in the ice at intervals of one
hundred feet (*A Bridge to the Past: Wilmot
Valley, 1784–1979*, 1980, 63). Our winter roads
were often full of deep hollows gouged out by
the sleighs, called 'pitches' through which the
sleigh would rise and fall with a thud that
would shake one up considerably. ... The
doctor sat in the back of the sleigh while the
driver sat in the front guiding the horse as best
he could through the 'pitches.' When the
driver pulled up at the doctor's door he looked
around but there was no sign of his passenger
– he had fallen out in one of the deeper
pitches (PENDERGAST, JAMES, and GERTRUDE
PENDERGAST, *Folklore Prince Edward Island*, [1974],
41). A depression in the snow. Every sleigh
would make it deeper (II 063). There was a
by-law that everyone who lived on the road
had to fill in the pitches in front of his home
(II 066). A pitch would be in the snow, not the
road itself (II 099).

*This term is restricted to snow conditions. *Pitch* for
'uneven ground' or 'a short steep hill' is known in
many dialects of the British Isles and North America
(*EDD*; *DAE*). *Pitch-hole* is recognized by *DC* for both
snow-covered and bare roads (1902–1946), and by
OEDS for bare roads only: 'a pot-hole' (1874–1890).

pitcher and catcher
Noun phrase. Informal.
**A pitcher and bowl used for washing
in the bedroom.**
Bedroom set of dishes. A pitcher, big basin,
and soap dish (R 28).

plastic bread
See **fog**.

plug
Noun. Archaic.
 A small, wooden wedge used to keep lobster's claws from grasping.
 As soon as convenient, the claws of the markets are plugged with small wooden or plastic plugs to keep them from damaging each other (WILDER, D.G., *Canada's Lobster Fishery*, 1957, 16). We used to take the wooden plugs and shove them in the joints and that paralyzed their strength. But the meat would spoil and go dark (S 4). The wooden plugs or pegs seemed to be injuring the lobster. Those pegs had been used a long time. I used them back in the mid–1940s (S 5). Plugs were used to keep the lobster from biting. They used to make them in the winter out of wood (S 6).

pochan
Noun. \'pah-kən\. Also spelled **pocan**.
 A small boy.
 It was affectionate in our family: 'Oh you little pochan' (O).

pod
Transitive verb. Occasional in Egmont and Cardigan, infrequent elsewhere; significantly rural; especially male.
 To shell (peas).
 You pod the peas and beans before drying them (I 038).

OED 1902; *COD*.

poganger days
Noun.
 Bygone days, especially pre-industrial times (O).

*This phrase is probably a variant of *pod auger days* 'olden times' (as in *DNE*, *DA*).

pogey
Noun. Infrequent generally, but rare in Egmont and Malpeque. Compare **washbait**.
 In commercial fishing, ground up fish mixed with oatmeal and thrown over the side of a boat as a lure.
 It's ground up fish. Oatmeal with sardines or salt herring. You use oily fish or add oil. The fish come to the slick (I 047). In deep sea fishing, the pogey is thrown over the side (I 119).

*There appears to be no connection with the general Canadian slang sense of 'unemployment insurance.'

pointing
Verbal noun.
 In fox ranching, the act of improving the appearance of a silver fox pelt by artificially inserting white hairs, or by dyeing.
 Pointing: ... Process by which pelts are supplied artificially with silky hairs (*Fox-Tales*, May 1982, 10). Some unscrupulous people would take a second rate fox and color the tips of the fur to imitate the 'veiling' by dying the tips of the fur (S 9).

point: *W3* 'to insert white hairs into (furs) to improve the appearance'; *OEDS*.

poison wind
Noun.
 A north-east wind thought to bring sickness.
 A wind that's full of germs (P2-001). Get out of the poison wind (P2-052). There is not only a poison wind, but in the spring the old folks spoke of the poison coming out of the ground. The poisons were said to be responsible for all manner of illnesses in the spring, such as colds, flu, pneumonia (P2-055).

pole barn
See **barrack, loafing barn**.

pole rake
Noun. Archaic.
 A long-handled rake used in harvesting 'Irish moss' from a boat.
 A 20-ft rake used to collect moss. [1] Pole rakes were made of just any long pole attached to a rake. [2] When the pole rake got caught on something, one had to let go. Fortunately, they floated – they had all that wood – so we'd just turn the boat around and get it. [3] Mossers stopped using pole rakes about 20 years ago, when they started using mechanical rakes (BERNARD, BLAINE, *Dictionary of Irish Moss*, 1986, n. pag.). Fishermen, after experimentation and accidental discovery, abandoned the hand-operated pole rake and began tying rakes on lines and dragging at higher speeds (ANDERSON, NANCY, *Global Village? Global Pillage: Irish Moss from P.E.I. in the World Market*, [1977], 27). A pole rake would be the old fashioned rake. It would have to be fifteen feet long or so (S 11). A pole rake is something the fisher-

men used to use. It was a rake attached to a long pole. They would let the boat drift and the man would hold on to the rakes over the side. It was fairly hard on the arms (S 12).

poley cow
Noun. Also **poll**. Rare. Compare **mull**.
Synonym for 'baldy': a cow without horns.

They are polls or poley cows. It's a more recent word for bred-in short horns (I 063). They are bred without horns. My first cow was a poley cow (I 065).

*The verb *to poll* 'to trim wool, hair, horns, etc.' is standard, as is the adjective *polled* 'hornless.' [From English] *DSUE*.

pond, the
See **puddle**.

poor man's fertilizer
Noun. Also **farmer's fertilizer, farmer's manure, poor man's manure**. Frequent generally, but infrequent in Charlottetown; significantly male; especially less educated. Compare **farmer's blessing, May snow, million-dollar rain**.
A late spring snow-fall.

And even yet there are Islanders who shrewdly rationalize that a heavy snow – particularly one late in the Spring – serves at least as a 'poor man's manure.' It is a consolation denied to the urbanite (HOWATT, CORNE-LIUS, *The Farm Family*, 1973, 65). A light snow-fall in late spring (May). Good because it contains nitrogen (II 063). Snow that would immediately melt and soak into the land. An older term (II 071). It's good for the land and free (II 106). Once that snow disappears you get a rush of green (P1-120). Snow is the poor man's fertilizer (O).

[Maritimes and New England] *SSPB* 'Blanche name for a late winter snow. It is also called "poor man's top dressing" and "farmer's fertilizer"'; *ML* [under *robin snow*].

poor man's turkey
See **Frenchman's turkey**.

poor man's weather glass
Noun.
See quotation.

Commonly called 'kelp,' *Laminaria* is the most obvious of seaweeds wherever it occurs.

The long brown fronds followed by the dark stems often cover the upper beach after a heavy storm. This brown algae is also known as the 'poor man's weather glass' because it may be used to predict weather. At the approach of rain the dried fronds go rather sticky, but remain dry and brittle in fine weather (PRINCE EDWARD ISLAND, DEPARTMENT OF THE ENVIRONMENT AND TOURISM, *Birds, Bush and Barnacles, Prince Edward Island*, [1974], 35).

OED 'the pimpernel, *Anagallis arvensis*, from its closing its flowers before rain'; *COD* 'pimpernel.'

popple
Noun. Informal. Common in Egmont, infrequent elsewhere; especially rural, male.
A poplar tree.

The wind had fallen asleep among the silver birches. The tall firs among them quivered with some kind of dark laughter. ... The popples, as Judy called them, were whispering around the granary (MONTGOMERY, LUCY MAUD, *Pat of Silver Bush*, 1933, 39). A 'junk' of popple is the worst stuff to burn (I 012). Not a good word. Users were scoffed at (I 055).

OED 'dial and U.S.' 1000–1879; *W3* 'chiefly dial.'; *EDD*; *EDSL*; *DC* 'North' 1903–1956; *DAE* 'dial.' 1670–1922; *WNW* 'dial. var. of poplar.'

pork and jerk
Noun phrase. Also **potatoes and drag, potatoes and draw back**. Humorous. Compare **potatoes and point**.
A scanty meal, during which a piece of pork or other food is passed around on a string by which it can be jerked from the mouth of an over-eager eater.

Poor families would put fish on a string, so when they ate it they could draw it back with a string (II 103). Suppose there was only one small piece of meat for everyone. The next guy got it from you after it was in your mouth because the meat was tied to a string and jerked out (O).

posy
Noun.
An attractive young woman.

My friend's mother, who was well over 100, used to use this expression (R 12). 'Posy' may also be the name given to a girl with loose morals (R 23).

[Scottish] *SND* 'A term of endearment for a child or a woman, a darling, sweetheart; sometimes sarcastically of an ill-favoured woman' 1816–1966.

potatoes and drag
Also **potatoes and drawback**. See **pork and jerk**.

potatoes and point
Noun phrase. Also **bread and point, bread and think, taties and point**. Humorous. Occasional in Egmont, infrequent or rare elsewhere; unattested under thirty; especially Irish, less educated. Compare **pork and jerk**.

A scanty meal, during which scarce or costly food is only pointed at or imagined.
'And you got up and gave him that steak – *all* that steak,' said Mrs. Doctor Dave, with a kind of triumphant reproof. 'Well, there wasn't anything else *to* give him,' said Captain Jim depreciatingly. 'Nothing a dog'd care for, that is. I reckon he *was* hungry, for he made about two bites of it. I had a fine sleep the rest of the night but my dinner had to be sorter scanty – potatoes and point, as you might say' (MONT-GOMERY, LUCY MAUD, *Anne's House of Dreams*, 1917, 43–44). 'Why, I've known young 'uns, who, mind you, had little else but blue pota-toes and herring to eat! And they were great scholars!' 'And, as I used to hear it, in my boyhood' Dad would offer, with a twinkle, 'Some didn't have the fish! It was 'potatoes and point, meaning, nothing else' (DIXON, MARGARET, *Going Home: An Autobiography*, 1979, 44). He said that they had never had anything more than 'potatoes and point' at his house. On inquiry, he explained that they had pota-toes and they were only allowed to 'point' at choicer items of food (PENDERGAST, GERTRUDE, *A Good Time Was Had by All*, 1981, 39). The old man would hang the herring from the ceiling and you'd point your fork at it (II 003). It was potatoes and buttermilk or everyday food. If there was no buttermilk, they'd point to the spot where the buttermilk should sit (II 019). It meant a lack of food in the whole household (II 076).

*Informants named the missing or pointed-at food variously as bacon, butter, buttermilk, ham, herring, and meat in general. The phrase is also reported in Cape Breton.
[From Irish] *OED* [*point*] 1831–1897; *OED* [*potato*] 1825 'The potatoes and point of an Irish peasant' [citation]; *ESI* [*dip*] 'You will sometimes read of "potatoes and point," namely, that each person, before taking a bite, *pointed* the potato at a salt herring or a bit of bacon hanging in front of the chimney: but this is mere fun, and never occurred in real life'; *ODEP*; *COD. bread and skip*: *DARE* 'bread and molasses, and skip the molasses' [citation, 1981].

pot-walloper
Noun. Informal.
A person who washes his or her dishes very frequently (O).

*Other dictionaries apply this word to one who works in an establishment, such as a ship's kitchen, a lumber camp, or a restaurant, and not, as here, in his or her home.
[From English and Irish] *OED*; *EDD*; *DSUE*; *DAS*; *ML*.

pound party
Noun.
A party to which guests bring a pound of something, usually food.
At least once a month they used to put on what they called a pound party. (Now this was a money-making business they had going.) A pound party meant that the boys brought a pound of butter or sugar or something else – perhaps soap (CAMPBELL, FRANK, *As the Fella Says ...*, 1983, 81).

[North American] *OED* 'U.S.'; *W3*; *DAE*; *DA*.

probs, the
Noun phrase. Informal. Frequent in Char-lottetown and Cardigan, occasional or infrequent elsewhere; significantly older.
The weather forecast, an abbreviation for *the probabilities*.
If this don't make you realize how much colder you could be, think of Cap. Bernier, who cannot find enough cold around here to suit him, but must go hunting around the North Pole after more. Also think of the man who sends us the 'Probs.' Whew! (*Prince Edward Island Magazine*, 1903, 410). One old fella from down Wood Islands way come by and announced that the long range probs was holding for another three weeks of fine weather at least, and it was looking worse and worse for the farmers (BOYLES, ANN, *Living in Har-mony*, 1983, 139). 'Did you get the probs' means 'Did you hear the forecast?' (I 031). Were you listening to the probs? (I 064). What are the probs today? (I 099).

*This term is also reported in Ontario. In the form *the probabilities*, it appears to be American.
Probabilities: *OED* 'U.S.' 1875, 1886; *DAE* 'colloq' 1886.

processing potato
Noun. Also **processed potato**. Compare **tablestock**.

**A potato intended for processing, usu-
ally as potato chips or french fries.**

The current trend to lower consumption of
'tablestock' has been offset by the increased
utilization of processed potatoes. Predictions
are that this trend will continue. ... Their
convenience and dependable quality and quick
preparation time make a strong and effective
appeal to both housewives and restaurant
operators (KHATTAK, JAHAN, and WILLIAM LEWIS,
*Growing Potatoes for Processing in Prince Edward
Island*, 1971, 1). For early market 'tablestock'
and processing potatoes, low stem densities
are usually obtained by planting cut sets from
larger tubers (ADVISORY COMMITTEE ON POTA-
TOES, *Atlantic Canada Potato Guide*, 1984, 3). A
processing potato is particularly adapted for
processing, such as russet burbank in the
manufacture of french fries. It's a big potato,
with low specific gravity (S 1). They got to
qualify for what you are going to process them
in. A french fry has to retain its color, it can't
turn black. You need a potato with dry matter
that will stand up (S 2).

providence bridge
Noun. Historical. Informal.
    **Ice on a river or bay that could be used
by travellers.**
    There is now much travelling on the rivers,
which are called here 'Providence Bridges.'
Robert is much stronger than he used to be: he
walked down the river on the ice from Long
Creek today (HARRIS, SARAH, *Letter to Martha
Harris*, [1858], 65). Winter was the time for
socializing. There was less work to do, and
travel was easier because of what the people
called 'providence bridges' – the frozen surfaces of rivers and bays (SOURIS ANNIVERSARY
COMMITTEE, *Souris, P.E.I., 1910–1980: A Profile
of the Town*, 1980, 6).

puckle
Noun. Also **pickle**. Rare.
    A small quantity or amount.
    The homeward ride in late afternoon with
the several bags of freshly milled flour and the
smaller 'puckles' of bran and shorts was full of
anticipation (*A Bridge to the Past: Wilmot Valley,
1784–1979*, 1980, 33). The word refers to fruit
and vegetables: 'a puckle of peas in your hand'
(I 021). A puckle is five to ten pounds. It is
what is left after you bag potatoes or grain.
You have so many bags and a puckle (I 031).
It can apply to anything, like a puckle of coal
(I 049). When they put too much water in the
flour they 'drowned the miller' and then had

to add a puckle of flour (I 063). Mother gave
me a puckle of buckwheat flour (O).

Puckle is a Scottish variant of *pickle* (W3).
[From Scottish] *SND* 1718–1955; *OED* 1724–1893; *W3*;
EDD; *EDSL*; *FW*.

puddle, the
Noun, often in phrase **across the puddle**.
Also **the brook, the pond**. Humorous.
Frequent in Egmont and Summerside,
infrequent elsewhere; especially younger,
male. Compare **across, other side**.
    **The Northumberland Strait between
Prince Edward Island and the mainland.**
    A trip across the puddle means going to
Dorchester to jail (II 047). It's the nine mile
puddle (II 070). Going 'across the puddle'
means to move there or emigrate to New
Brunswick (II 083).

puff
See **fog**.

puff up
Intransitive phrasal verb.
    Of the wind, to blow hard suddenly.
    'It's starting to puff up.' It's breezing up for
a blow (R 17). This is a common expression
among Miminegash fishermen (R 20).

*This term was associated by several informants with
fishing.

pung
Noun. Common in Egmont, occasional in
Malpeque, infrequent elsewhere; significantly rural, middle-aged and older; especially male, less educated. Compare **box
sleigh, jaunting sleigh**.
    **A box-shaped sleigh of varying height
drawn by one horse.**
    Seymour went to the factory with a load of
sundries. Mack Lewis to the horse and pung
for George and Emily to come back (WOODMAN,
SUSAN, *Diary: January 1, 1895–December 31,
1896*, April 11, 1896). The silence was filled
with a faint, fairy-like melody from afar down
the road where a pungful of young folks from
White Sands were singing hymns on their way
to meeting (MONTGOMERY, LUCY MAUD, *Further
Chronicles of Avonlea*, [1920], 254). The first
driving sleighs made in the district were the
pung and the piano box. At one time the
horse-drawn covered pung, painted red, blue,
or black was a common sight on Brae roads

during winter months. This type of pung had
small front and side windows and a front
opening through which the reigns were drawn
(MACNEVIN, MRS. LORNE, *Past and Present: A
History of Brae*, 1979, 63). Pung-sleighs were
short sleighs with an attached wooden seat
about a third of the way back. Some people
built a wooden enclosure over these sleighs
but they upset easily on roads with 'slues' and
'pitches' (HUDSON, ARTHUR, and JEAN MEGGISON,
*Preserving the Past: A History of Cascumpec-
Fortune Cove, 1779–1979*, 1979, 161). Men who
train horses still use a pung in winter (I 015).
A pung was for the middle class. A wood sleigh
was for the poor and jaunting sleighs were the
stylish ones (I 038). A low sleigh, straight lined
and partly closed in. A hatched back-seat to put
things in. Light and small. Often on the farm,
when I was a child, they took the box off and
used it on the hill to coast. It held about
twelve kids (I 065). You might build the box on
the sleigh itself (I 080). The neighbors had an
old pung sleigh and a horse, and they would
come along and pick us up [to go to school].
There was her two older sisters, there was
two at our house, and there was three at
McClures' and two at their house. And there
was not room to sit down, so we would stand
up on the pung sleigh and, of course, when
there was 'sloughs' we went out as often as we
stayed in (T I54).

*The word is short for *tom pung*, ultimately from
Algonkian, and is related to standard *toboggan*.
[Maritimes and New England] *OED* 1798–1876; *W3;
DAE; DA; FW* 'U.S. Dial.'; *GCD* 'Historical'; *WNW.*

pup
Noun. Rare. Compare **teddy, dish**[1].
   1. A small bottle for alcohol.
   It was less than a pint. My parents would
look for the pup so they could empty some of
the liquor from a big bottle into it and take it to a
party. People coming home from Boston would
take pups as gifts (II 058).
   2. The alcohol itself, usually illicit.
   Used in reference to moonshine (II 046).
Only when old guys would drink is it referred
to as 'pup' (II 049).

put
Intransitive verb. Occasional in Egmont,
infrequent or rare elsewhere; especially
rural, older, male, less educated.
   To leave in a hurry, to flee.
   He put in a hurry. He put for the woods
(II 017). After several warnings, I finally say

'put!' (II 028). To get out of the way altogether.
To put is to go (II 096). Make yourself scarce (II
112). It means to take off. My grandfather used
this and my aunts still do. When my mother
caught me stealing apples, I put (O).

Q

quill boot
Noun.
   See quotation.
   I remember one time there lived in Crapaud a
young shoemaker. At that time, there were no
imported shoes or boots. He got all the custom
from the girls in fancy boots, and to make them
squeak, he put a quill in the bottom of their
shoes between their soles, and at every step
they took up the aisle in the church, the shoes
would squeak, and the boys would look to see
who the girl was and have a look at her, and
if she pleased one of them, he would see her
home, and have an hour or so counting [sic],
and very often it would end in marriage. When
the imported shoes came into Crapaud, the
quill boots were done away with (AUTUMN,
GENE, *My Life in Crapaud*, 1929, 14).

quite
Intensifier, in noun phrase **quite a** or **quite
the** plus Christian name. Derogatory.
Common in Egmont, occasional elsewhere
except infrequent in Charlottetown.
   Very much the worst characteristics of.
   'He is quite the Harry' (O). 'He is quite the
Danny' (O). 'She is quite the Bertha' (O). 'He's
quite the Stephen' was overheard being said
by a native of Alberton (O).

R

rabbits' candles
Plural noun.
   **Moonlight or starlight sparkling on
snow.**
   It was especially delightful to write poetry on
a winter evening when the storm winds
howled without and heaped the garden and
orchard with big ghostly drifts, starred over
with rabbits' candles (MONTGOMERY, LUCY
MAUD, *Emily of New Moon*, 1923, 312).

raft
Intransitive verb. Compare **raft ice.**

Of ice floes, to pile up, one on top of the other or on shore.

The watch was sent on the ice with ice saws and Boathooks to cut a passage into one of the leads and kept the Engine going ahead and astern on the ship the ice was rafted in many place and 12 or 15 feet thick we had a hard job of it (MACDONALD, EDWARD, *Diary 1911*, July 29, 1911). River ice is one level, flat like a board. With raft ice, tidal action rafts it (I 120).

[Canadian] *DC* 1883–1958; *DNE* 1843–1978; *OEDS*. *rafter* [verb]: *W3*.

raft ice
Noun. Also **rafted ice**. Occasional in Egmont and Summerside, infrequent elsewhere; significantly male. Compare **clumpet, drift ice, ice cake, raft** (verb), **running ice**.

Ice floes piled one on top of the other or on shore.

Their [the ice-boats'] lightness of weight made for easy handling, yet their ruggedness could withstand the mauling dealt them by lolly, drift-ice, pressure ridges and raft ice (CALLBECK, LORNE, *Sagas of the Strait*, 1959, 58). It's piled up on shore (II 055). It's floating and broken up into different pieces right in 'handy' the shore or on a millpond (II 096). It's piled on top. Definitely out at sea (II 096). When board ice pieces slide on top of each other, they can become quite high (P1-029).

*The relatively high use of this term in Egmont and Summerside may be connected to the former employment of 'ice boats' across the Northumberland Strait. [Canadian] *OED* 'chiefly U.S.' 1852; *DC* 1897–1959; *DNE*; *GCD*; *COD*.

rail bird
Noun. Informal. Occasional in Egmont, infrequent elsewhere; significantly male.

1. A spectator at a trial, legislative debate, or other public event.

A large gallery of rail birds always gathered for cases of this kind [adultery] and thoroughly enjoyed the evidence (SHAW, WALTER, *Tell Me the Tales*, 1975, 120). They are people who watch work on construction jobs in the city. Same as sidewalk superintendent (II 003). Standing on edges watching other people's business. I heard at the scene of an accident, 'All these rail birds with nothing better to do' (II 058). Even in the Legislative Chamber they were called rail birds (II 067).

2. A horse-racing enthusiast.

Used for avid horse racing fans, those who would watch the horses exercise to keep an eye on how each one was doing (II 012). People who would, on the sly, watch the horses go round a track (during practice) to find out what the horses' best time would be (II 019). There was a reporter in the *Guardian* who kept track of the horses. He was called the Rail Bird (II 071).

[North American] [sense 1]: *DAE*; *DA*. [sense 2]: *W3*; *DSUE*; *DAS*; *DA*.

rake
See **drag rake**.

rake moss
Noun. Also **raked moss**. Compare **moss, raking¹, shore moss**.

'Irish moss' harvested by rakes dragged behind fishing boats.

We also raked moss from boats a few years ago. You had rakes that you drug behind the boat. You got a better quality moss from the boat than from shore moss (S 10). Rake moss is what is mostly collected by towing rakes behind a boat (S 11). Raked moss is raked by using a tool called a rake with a boat (S 12).

rake off
Transitive phrasal verb. Compare **raking¹**.

To clear (an area of the sea bed) of 'Irish moss'; to harvest ('Irish moss') thoroughly.

The (mechanical) rakers have just about raked off the moss on the South Shore. (This was before licensing came into effect.) (BERNARD, BLAINE, *Dictionary of Irish Moss*, 1986, n. pag.). Yeah, when a bed is raked off it has been picked clean. There is none left. You have bared the floor (S 11). Yes, an area could be completely raked off. That is, the bottom is raked off usually by 'draggers' (S 12).

raking¹
Verbal noun. Compare **dragging, drag rake, rake moss, rake off, wet raked**.

The harvesting of 'Irish moss' by rakes dragged behind fishing boats.

Moss raking is a method by which a huge basket-like rake is dragged behind a boat. The rake skims along the sea-bed gathering moss. ... This method has been banned in most areas of P.E.I., with fishermen arguing that raking destroys the breeding ground for lobsters. Indeed, checks of the harvested area which showed that lobsters were being damaged gave cause to the fishermen's concerns. In other areas it is felt that raking would destroy the beds which produce fucellaria, one of the two types of mosses which are harvested on P.E.I. (*The Guardian*, April 25, 1986, 3).

raking²
Verbal noun. Frequent generally, but occasional in Malpeque, infrequent in Charlottetown. Compare **carding**, **reading**.
   A scolding, a dressing-down.
   It's more to sort of degrade someone, more hateful and hurtful (II 019). More for adults (II 019). You jaw a fellow right hard – a good carding or raking (P1-010).

[From American] *DAE* 1854–1907; *OEDS. raking-down*: *EDD*; *ML*.

rakings
See **second rakings**.

rally
Noun, often in phrase **to thresh a rally**. Frequent in Cardigan, occasional in Malpeque, rare elsewhere; significantly rural, male; unattested under thirty.
   A spell of work; any spurt of activity.
   At roughly ninety-minute intervals, work was halted to allow the horses to rest. For no reason that I was ever able to discover, the ninety-minute work period was called a 'rally' (DEVEREUX, JOSEPH, *Looking Backward*, n.d., 10). Rally is also used when chopping wood: 'One little rally and we'll be all done' (I 017). Rally could be used with any work that you do in cycles or with playing cards (I 021). Rally is used for strenuous activity of a short duration (I 028). I also use rally for booze. 'Have one more rally before the bar closes.' It means an extra shot or boost (I 039). We always did an extra rally on Saturday to finish work. A number of sheaves would take an hour. It was done in the barn (I 042). With my father a rally is so many bags, maybe thirty-five. The amount done at one time (I 053). 'I guess we'll thresh a little rally' (I 118).

*The sense of rally as 'a recouping or reuniting of forces' (*W3*) is standard.

ram-pasture
Noun. Archaic. Informal.
   A men's bunkhouse, especially at a lumber camp.
   Larry disliked the ram-pasture, and when he woke up one morning and saw someone he didn't know sleeping on the floor (all the bunks were full), he is supposed to have fired this one off extempore: [verse follows] (IVES, EDWARD, *Larry Gorman: The Man Who Made the Songs*, [1964], 40).

*This term may have been current only with those who left Prince Edward Island to work in the woods.
[From New England] *DC* 1912–1925; *ML*.

rapure
Noun. \'rah-po͞or\. Also **chiard** \shē-'ahr\, **rappé pie** \'rah-pā\, **rapie pie** \'rah-pē\, **rapure pie**. Also spelled **râpure**. Occasional in Summerside, rare elsewhere; especially Acadian.
   See quotations.
   The meals consisted of traditional Acadian dishes. One of these, known as *râpure* or *chiard*, was the most popular. Its basic ingredients are grated potatoes, onions, fat, and pork. The woman of the house spent part of the morning getting this ready. She would put the mixture in a very large pan and cook it in the oven for a few hours while the dancing went on. If they made *râpure* on Shrove Friday, they would have to leave out the pork since no meat could be eaten on Friday (ARSENAULT, CARMELLA, *Acadian Celebration of Mardi Gras*, 1978, 30). Rapure is potatoes, onions, and pork baked in the oven. The potatoes are rapped, which refers to being grated and having the juice squeezed out (I 081). Chiard is like rappé pie. It's used around Tignish a lot (O).

*In French *râpé* means 'grated.'
[From Acadian French] *DC* 'Maritimes' 1934–1951. *rapé*: *OED* 'Obs. A dish in Mediaevel cookery, composed of many ingredients grated, stamped, or pounded, and highly seasoned' 1381–1467.

read
Transitive verb. Also **read out**. Rare. Compare **card**, **reading**, **skivver**.
   To reprimand, to scold severely.
   'Did you see the way she'd read that child?' (I 110). Read them out (II 027). His mother reads him about that often (O).

W3. redd: *SND. red up*: *EDSL*.

reading
Verbal noun. Rare. Compare **carding,
raking²**, **read**.
    **A severe scolding, a tongue lashing; a
whipping.**
    Scolding in an advisory manner (II 038). A
reading is a licking or switching (P1-052).

*Three informants identify this word with the
Kinkora region of Prince Edward Island.
redding: *SND* [under *redd*].

receipt
Noun. Archaic. Rare. Compare **rule**.
    A recipe.
    Free Cure for Men: A new remedy which
quickly cures sexual weakness, varicocele,
night emissions, premature discharge, etc., and
restores the organs to strength and vigor.
Dr. I.W. Knapp 2032 Hull Building, Detroit,
Mich., gladly sends free the receipt of this
wonderful remedy in order that every weak
man may cure himself at home (*The Island
Farmer*, January 4, 1900, 1,3). Aunt Elizabeth
had toothache all yesterday and Aunt Laura
was away at Priest Pond visiting Great Aunt
Nancy, so no cake was made. I prayed about
it and then I went to work and made a cake by
Aunt Laura's receet [sic] and it turned out all
right (MONTGOMERY, LUCY MAUD, *Emily of New
Moon*, 1923, 183). There do be some mats in
the garret I put away for ye, Patsy, and the
crame cow is yours and me Book av Useful
Knowledge and all the liddle things in me glory
box. And the book wid all my resates [sic] in
it (MONTGOMERY, LUCY MAUD, *Mistress Pat*, 1935,
319–20). In the following pages I will write
various receipts for people to prepare non-
alcohol drinks (*Unpublished student essay*, UPEI,
1973). Receipt was the old word, always (I 038).

*The Montgomery quotations contain deliberate
mis-spellings, not spelling variations. In the
Common Word Survey, two older informants chose
receipt over *recipe*. This archaic form of *recipe* is also
reported in New Brunswick and rural Ontario.
[From English] *OED* 1386–1859; *W3*; *SND* 'obs in
Eng.'; *GCD* 'Archaic'; *FW*.

redberry
Noun.
    **The partridge berry (*Vaccinium vitis-
idaea*).**
    Freezers are very popular and wild berries
are picked in great quantities and stored in
them. A berry like our cranberry only smaller is
called 'red berry' or 'partridge berry' (PENDER-

GAST, GERTRUDE, *A Good Time Was Had by All*,
1981, 76).

[From Newfoundland] *DC* 'Lab'; *DNE*.

redd
Transitive verb, usually with **up** or **off**.
Rare.
    **To put (a household or household
object) in order, arrange, make tidy,
clear.**
    Redd up also means cleaning up the house
before visitors. Not many people use it (I 015).
'Redd off the table' is used especially in card
games when the women want you to get ready
for lunch (I 032). For a game of cards you have
to redd the table (I 087).

*This is a Scottish, northern English, and Ulster
Scottish term with scattered distribution in New
Brunswick, Ontario, Pennsylvania, the Ohio valley,
and elsewhere in the United States (Michael Dress-
man, 'Redd Up,' 1979, 141–45).
OED 'Sc. & north. dial.' 1718–1887; *W3* 'chiefly dial.';
EDD; *SND*; *OEDS* 'Also in U.S. and general use'
1842–1912; *EDSL*; *ESI*; *WNW* 'Colloq. or Dial.'; *FW*
'Dial.'; *COD* 'Sc.'

Redfoot
Noun. Historical.
    See quotation.
    Its [PEI's] soil is a rich, red loam, marvelously
productive, from the prevailing color of which
the islanders get their local nickname of 'Red-
feet,' to distinguish them from the 'Bluenoses'
of Nova Scotia and the 'Buckwheats' of New
Brunswick (ROBERTS, CHARLES, *The Canadian
Guide-Book: The Tourist's and Sportsman's Guide
to Eastern Canada and Newfoundland*, 1892, 193).

rigging lath
Noun. Also **heading lath, head stick**.
    **One of the small laths on a lobster trap
to which the 'heads' or mesh pieces are
attached.**
    A head stick is a wooden lath that heads are
knit on to. This is then nailed on to the trap
(MACMILLAN, JANET, *The Language of Lobster
Fishing*, 1985, 17). A rigging lath is what we
use to nail the twine to in order to put it
through the heads and then these rigging
laths are meshed into the head and nailed to
the bottom of the trap (S 4). A rigging lath is
what we refer to as a heading lath or little slats
(S 5). A head stick is the short lath that runs
the length of the head (S 6).

rightify
Transitive verb. Infrequent or rare.
To rectify, put right.
For something you did wrong (I 065). You'd
better rightify that (I 095). If you made a mis-
take, you'd have to set things straight (I 119).

[From Irish] *EDD* 1848; *DNE* 1924.

riveter
Noun. Compare **smile**.
A drink of rum or of moonshine.
This is a very common expression, a real
hefty drink: 'We had a couple of riveters'
(R 20).

riz
Adjective.
Of bread or biscuit dough, risen.
She does remember his being enthusiastic
about camp cooking, though: 'Those riz biscuits
– as big as *that*! Man size, they were!' (IVES,
EDWARD, *Larry Gorman: The Man Who Made the
Songs*, [1964], 84). The Grist Mill was a busy
place, … and soon worn smooth in the process
of grinding the wheat into flour to be made into
'riz' bread from the hops on the fence (CRAPAUD
WOMEN'S INSTITUTE, *History of Crapaud*, n.d.,
I, 30).

road-breaking
Verbal noun. Compare **snow-fighting**.
The act of clearing snow from a road.
S. mild, roadbreaking (MCEACHERON, JOHN,
*A Diary or Memorandum of Weather, Work and
Other Incidents*, 1874, December 28). They
would break the road instead of plough it (R 12).

roader
Noun.
**A horse adapted for driving or riding on
the road.**
'Do they buy horses over here?' we queried.
'Sure do,' snapped red tie. 'I own two, and
one's a good enough roader. Don't have to get
him licensed every year or new tires. And
another thing, the model doesn't change.
There's plenty got horses out my way' (BIRD,
WILL, *These Are the Maritimes*, 1959, 195).

*This word appears to be a variant of standard
roadster.
[North American] *DAE* 1825.

robin snow
Noun. Rare. Compare **longer snow**.

A spring snow-fall occurring after the
return of the robin (O).

[From New England] *OED* 'U.S.'; *OEDS* 1853; *W3*
'chiefly New Eng.'; *DC* 1947–1955; *DAE*; *DA*; *ML*.

robin's pincushion
Noun.
**A mossy swelling on a rosebush
produced by parasites; a bedeguar or
rose-gall.**
Sweet Briar. … Introduced from Europe;
naturalized. No longer planted. Thickets
and dry pastures. Characterized by the large
brown galls like tufts of hair, called 'Robin's
Pincushions' (CANADA, DEPARTMENT OF AGRI-
CULTURE, *The Plants of Prince Edward Island*,
1960, 178).

OED 1850–1862; *SND. robin's cushions*: *EDD*.

rocking-chair money
Noun. Also **armchair money**, **bed money**,
fun money. Infrequent generally, but
rare in Malpeque and Charlottetown;
unattested under forty; especially less
educated.
**Money from a government social
assistance plan, especially Unemployment
Insurance or Old Age Security.**
Some people think fishermen have it easy:
fish all summer and then get rocking-chair
money in the winter (BERNARD, BLAINE, *Dictionary of Irish Moss*, 1986, n. pag.). It's a retirement pension (II 046). The Old Age Pension
(II 069). Money you get for doing nothing, such
as Family Allowance. Also called bed money
and fun money (II 070).

[Maritimes] *DC* 'Slang' 1959.

romance
Intransitive verb.
**To talk in a delirium, to talk con-
fusedly.**
When the shades began to fall they prepared
to bivouac for the night, one keeping watch.
Mike having lain down among fallen leaves,
was dozing asleep, and Jim being alone, set
up a dismal wail. 'Stop your miserable canniven, you 'omadan' of nature; shure it's a dog
barkin I hear,' put in Mike. 'You're romancin,
Mike so you are; what'ud a dog be doin in this
haythenish land, to be kilt by mosquitoes?'
(MACKINNON, JOHN, *A Sketch Book: Comprising
Historical Incidents, Traditional Tales and Transla-*

tions, 1915, 171). When they repeat the same words over and over again (I 037). A condition not usually noted today because ill people are in the hospital (I 114). High temperature talking (I 117). Mum used to say 'You were romancing all night long' (I 119).

*The related standard meaning is 'exaggerate, tell tales.'
[From English] *EDD*.

rook
Noun. Infrequent generally, but rare in Malpeque and Charlottetown.
   A small stack of hay outdoors, a rick.
   A lot of coils together. It's the shape: three times as long as it is wide (II 106).

[From Scottish and northern English] *OED* 'dial.';
EDD 'Yks.' 1863; *PEDGL* 'Irish, Old Norse, AngloSaxon'; *EDSL. ruck*: *OED* 'Sc. and North dial.'
1546–1871; *SND*; *EDSL*.

roseine
Noun. Rare.
   A red dye.
   The writer remembers being much puzzled in her childhood over the peculiar bloom that used to appear every afternoon on the face of a neighbor, later to find that it was the result of a mixture of magenta and roseine dye applied in a mathematical circle to the summit of each of her high cheek-bones (MACLEOD, ADA, *Roads to Summerside: The Story of Early Summerside and the Surrounding Area*, 1980, 91).

*This word appears to be an archaic technical term that later found more general usage.
OED 'Chem.' 1862–1883.

rouack
Adjective, often used after a person's name as a distinguishing nickname.
\'ru-ə\.
   Red-haired.
   After lining them up in a rather slouching negligent manner he [an old Scotsman conducting a drill] would call the individual roll, and all being named Donald MacDonald, he would enroll them by some special peculiarity; such as Donald MacDonald rouack (red) (SHAW, WALTER, *Tell Me the Tales*, 1975, 44). It's a Scottish word for red hair, and is used of people whose names are the same, like Johnny Rouack (P2-066).

[From Irish and Scottish Gaelic via Irish and Scottish]
DGL; *GED*; *PEDGL*; *IED*.

round
See **in the round**.

round base
Noun. Rare.
   A children's ball game resembling baseball or rounders.
   But though I remember a score of games, ball – the round base variety – stands out without a rival. Boys and girls, old and young, even our teachers took part in it; and to this day, I believe the sight of a good game of 'round base' would lure me from the staid and respectable path of old-ladyhood (MACLEOD, ADA, *Roads to Summerside*, 1980, 99). Something like tag. If you could reach the base, they couldn't tag you. There were other rules also (II 018). The ball would be homemade from twine or yarn (II 106).

round ball: *DAE* 'Obs.' 1688–; *DA*.

round gale
Noun, usually preceded by **whole**.
   A violent gale, a wind storm.
   Blowing a 'whole round gale' terrible storm, no school (OLIVER, GERTRUDE, *Diary of Gertrude Hazel Meggison Oliver*, 1909, March 29). It started to rain in good shape so Russell didn't go any farther it is blowing a whole 'round gale' (*ibid*, October 15).

round white
Noun.
   Any roundish, white-fleshed variety of potato.
   Kennebecs and Sebagoes are both round whites (MCCARVILL, LISA, *A Potato Farming Lexicon from Kinkora, P.E.I.*, 1986, n. pag.). This is a type of potato used sometimes for processing, a utility type of potato (S 1). A round white is round as opposed to long, and white as opposed to red or yellow (S 2).

rubber bread
See **fog**.

rule
Noun. Rare. Compare **receipt**.
   A recipe.
   I've a good rule for that (I 048). Cook by the rule (I 084). Heard from older people (I 118).

*This word was preferred by one Common Word informant over *recipe* and *receipt*.
W3 'dial.'

run
Noun.
A narrow channel leading into a harbour.
The fishermen have other buyers willing to set up at Tignish but as Melansons owns the wharf property at the run these other buyers are prevented from setting up there (*The Guardian*, April 9, 1979, 1). Fishermen sailing into harbours with runs (like Alberton) are in particularly dangerous situations during bad weather due to the narrow channels. About six island ports must be entered and exited by runs (*The Guardian*, June 13, 1984, 3). When you are going out of North Lake to the open sea, you go through the run (S 4).

[From Newfoundland] *DNE* 'A narrow salt-water strait or extended navigable passage between the coast and an island or series of islands; a passage between islands' 1842–1979; *DC*.

run line
Noun. Archaic. Compare **backline, trapline**.
In lobster fishing, a long rope to which a large number of lobster traps are tied.
The former method of lobster fishing where, rather than having the traps in trawls of 8, 10, or 12, 50–100 traps were tied to one piece of rope. In this method, the rope would be set first, then the traps would be tied on afterwards (ROBERTSON, JANICE, *A Dictionary of Lobster Fishing in the Eastern Kings Area*, 1985, 12). Run lines is the old method of lobster fishing. You would run the rope before the traps. You would mark the rope where the trap would be (S 4). The first year I ever fished we might have had a run line out. They had a long, long backline of fifty traps and the backline would be stationary (S 5). Run lines was the old way of fishing where you would run your rope first and then fasten the traps on later (S 6).

running ice
Noun. Compare **clumpet, drift ice, ice cake, raft ice**.
Pans of sea-ice that are driven by current or wind.
They reached the edge of the moving ice, about a mile and a half from Carleton Point, at five o'clock. The land was clearly seen by them. But the 'lolly' between the running ice and the 'board ice' was so deep that they could not force the boat through it. Meantime the storm grew furious. After repeated attempts, all unavailing, they were compelled to draw the boat back upon the running ice (COTTON, W.L., *Chapters in Our Island Story*, 1927, 103). According to the report of one of the passengers the wind was blowing briskly from the Eastward when the boats left the 'board ice' and the running ice was floating Westward at the rate of from three to four miles an hour (*ibid*, 106). The teams came up to the door and drove us to the edge of the 'board ice' – 'board ice' solids, in other words, frozen to the shore. The tide running up and down the strait has no effect upon it. The ice we had to cross was the running ice (LEARD, GEORGE, *The George Leard Files*, 1977, Reel #5).

[From Newfoundland] *DNE* 1846–1982; *DC*.

run off
Transitive phrasal verb.
To reset (lobster traps) after fishing them.
We run off our traps, some bunches are now set / We still have some more on shore we must get (FLEMING, RICHARD, *Lobstering*, 1985, 1). If you have your 'trawl' on the 'washboard' you would say 'I'm going to swing around and run these off' (S 4). When you are re-setting your traps you haul your 'dog trawl' and then run them off (S 5). You run off your traps after you have fished them (S 6).

run outs and walk ins, the
Plural noun phrase. Occasional in Egmont and Cardigan, infrequent or rare elsewhere; significantly older. Compare **back door trots, blueberry run, flying axehandles, green apple quick-step, shorttaken, skithers**.
Diarrhea.
He has the run outs and walk ins (P1-032). Diarrhea. Comes from outhouses (P1-062).

run-out: *EDD* 'to be afflicted with diarrhoea' 1796. *running*: *DBE* 'n. diarrhea.'

russet
Noun. Also **russeted potato**.
A potato having a cross-hatched pattern on the skin.
You use the long variety for baking. They are long and slim and bake better (S 2). Russet applies to the long type of potato like a Netted Gem (S 3).

Rustico steak
See **Frenchman's turkey**.

rutting gauge
Noun.
   An instrument used in fox ranching to measure the sexual readiness of females.
   Rutting gauge: ... A meter that measures a female fox's sexual resistance. It decreases with the female's increasing fertility (CARR, MARGARET, *Terms of Fox Farming on P.E.I.*, 1986, 14). A rutting gauge is an instrument that is used to determine the stage of estrus. It is electronic and you insert it in the vagina. A rutting gauge is on the market now. It has only been used the last four or five years (S 8).

S

sacket
Noun.
   A small sack or bag.
   No gardener worth her salt would be caught without a slip or two in her purse or a package of seeds in her sackets, if she was about to take up residence in a new land (MATTHEW, MARGARET, *Garden in the Gulph*, 1973, 14).

[From Scottish and northern English] *OED*; *W3*; *EDD*; *SND*.

Saint Anthony's fire
Noun.
   A glow sometimes given off by swamps (II; P2).

*In standard English, the term is used for certain inflammations of the skin (*W3*).

Saint Patrick's Day storm
Noun. Also **Saint Patrick's Day snow-storm, Saint Patrick's snow-storm, Saint Patrick's storm, Saint Pat's storm.** Common generally, but occasional in Charlottetown. Compare **line storm**.
   A blizzard in the middle of March, close to Saint Patrick's Day, March 17.
   St. Patrick's Storm today – Blowing a gale and snowing thickly all day. Boys heading traps in cellar (WOODMAN, SUSAN, *Diary, January 1, 1895–December 31, 1896*, 1896, March 17). The snow in March makes grass turn white, / And ghostly fields are such a sight (WHEELER, DAVID, *The Saint Patrick's Day Snow Storm*, 1983, n.p.). We always look for our Saint Pat's storm (II 021). A Saint Patrick's Day storm was a sure

thing (II 091). A little before or a little after Saint Patrick's Day (II 098). Usually the worst storm of the winter (O).

sallywinder
Noun.
   A hard, swinging blow from the side, a sidewinder.
   I'll give you a sallywinder if you don't be quiet (P2).

*The first element of the compound could relate to standard *sally* 'sudden start into activity' (*COD*).

saloon
Noun. Archaic. Common in Egmont, infrequent elsewhere; especially rural, senior.
   A booth, often sheltered by fresh-cut boughs, for serving food and drink at outside, summer events such as horse-races, picnics, and 'tea parties'; also a temporary hall for dancing.
   I went to the 'tea party' at East Point today. ... It was fun getting ready putting boughs around the outside of the saloons and setting up the tables this morning. I helped the women bake some cakes, cookies, and apple pies which were on the long tables. ... Father tended the saloon dishing out apple cider which was so delicious I must have had at least four helpings (BUSHEY, SARAH, *Memoirs of Sarah Bushey*, 1892, August 9). 'Tea parties' were held outdoors during the summer as money-making activities. The tables, laden with food, were surrounded by trees and boughs were placed above the tables to shield them from the sun and wind. A saloon for dancing, complete with music, was an important part of the 'tea party' (ANDERSON, WILLIAM, and DORIS ANDERSON, *Reflections on Life on a Farm at St. Peter's at the Turn of the Century*, 1979, 7). There's the dancing saloon and one where they sold bananas, pop, and oranges (II 003). Under the grandstand; ice cream and drinks (II 041). At a 'tea party' they have poles in the ground covered with brush and branches (II 090). Ice cream saloon (II 105).

*The standard sense of 'large hall' is sometimes used concurrently.

Samson
Noun. Also spelled **Sampson**. Archaic. Compare **fur out**.
   In fox ranching, a fox lacking 'guard hair,' and so having a worthless pelt.

Sampson: woolly haired variety of fox which almost completely lacks guard hair (*Fox Tales*, May 1982, 10). You don't hear or see Samson used much today. A Samson is a fox of extremely poor quality. It can be a poor fox in a litter or you can get a whole litter of them. Nobody ever wanted a Samson (S 7). Well, you don't very often hear about Samsons anymore. They are an out-of-condition fox that never 'furs out,' a very poor quality fox (S 8). A Samson is a fox you would hide or kill out behind the barn (S 9).

*The biblical reference is to Judges 15:4–5, in which Samson ties torches to the tails of foxes in order to burn down the Philistines' grain.
OEDS 'Samson fox ... a fox belonging to a variety of the North American red fox, *Vulpes fulva*, in which the fur lacks guard hairs and so has a scorched appearance' 1910; *DC* (1929–1933).

scoff
Noun. Informal.
   A big meal, often of seafood or other seasonal food and in connection with a party.
   It has special connotations. In a good scoff, you clean it all up. It's seasonal, mostly corn, clams, or oysters (I 046). McDonald's can be a scoff (I 060). Both quality and quantity are needed in a scoff (I 079). Only for a special need or some special form like oysters or lobsters (O).

*No Prince Edward Island examples of the verbal sense, 'to eat greedily,' were found, but it is probable that this sense does exist in the province, as in other dialects.
[From British] *OED* 'S. African. ... Food; also a meal' 1879–1900; *W3* 'food, meal'; *DNE* 'A cooked meal at sea or seashore, esp. at night and often part of an impromptu party' 1894–1974; *DSUE* 'Food: South African coll' 1856; *DSAE*; *WNW* 'Chiefly Brit. slang'; *COD*.

score board
See **dog trawl board**.

scout
Noun. Compare **scout** (verb).
   A worker who follows a potato digger to pick up any potatoes left behind.
   This would be maybe a child who would work for free. Due to mechanization the profession of scout is on the decline (S 1).

scout
Intransitive verb. Also verbal noun **scouting**. Compare **scout** (noun).

To follow a potato digger in order to pick up any potatoes left behind.
   Scouting is following behind the digger and picking up any potatoes that were left behind the digger and placing them between two other, unharvested rows. For the amount of potatoes they pick up, it's not really worth it to pay someone to scout. (This is usually a job for younger people because there is little involvement with dangerous equipment.) (MCCARVILL, LISA, *A Potato Farming Lexicon from Kinkora, P.E.I.*, 1986, n. pag.).

scow
Noun, usually in plural. Humorous. Occasional generally, but infrequent in Charlottetown; significantly older; especially male. Compare **spach**, **sprog**.
   Big, often flat, foot, shoe, or boot.
   A joke for big feet: 'Get your scows out of my way' (II 001). A teasing name for having big feet or wearing big shoes (II 014). Big feet: 'What a pair of scows' (II 021). 'Your shoes are big as scows' (II 032). Boots that resembled an old boat, too big for a person (II 074). My brother used to say, 'They're not scows, they're barges' (O).

scra
Noun. \skra\. Also spelled **skra**. Rare. Compare **scut**, **skite**.
   A worthless person, a good-for-nothing.
   It means scum. Not very respectable people. Like if there are a bunch of guys around the road drunk and driving up and down really fast, Mom often said, 'That's scra down there; keep away from that scra.' I guess also people who come to a dance and are drunk and cause trouble. Usually it's young kids, like teenagers. Sometimes it's older guys who should know better too (O [tape]).

[From Scottish] *scrae, skrae*: *SND* 'A stunted, shrivelled, or under-developed person or animal' 1803–1927; *EDSL* 'applied to anything puny, scraggy, or shrivelled'; *EDD* 'an ill-natured, fault-finding person. Ayr.'; *W3* 'Scot.'; *OED* '(To a crying child), Lie still, ye skrae' 1803.

scrimshanking
Verbal noun. Rare.
   Living in poverty (II; O).

*The word is probably related to standard *scrimp*. *W3* 'scrim-shank. ... [origin unknown] Brit: to shirk one's work or obligations'; *OED* 'To shirk duty' 1890–1903; *COD*. *scrimption*: *EDD* 'Irel. Nhp. e.An. Ken. Amer. ... A very small piece; a miserable pittance.'

scringe
Intransitive verb. Infrequent in Cardigan, rare elsewhere; significantly rural.

Of a sleigh's metal runners on a hard, snow-packed road, to creak or crackle.

The sleigh was scringeing after a frost (I 095). You hear it scringe especially on cold, star-filled winter nights (O).

[From British and northern Irish] *EDD. screenge: SND* 'A rubbing, scrubbing, scouring ...; the sound of this.'

script
Noun. Also spelled **scrip**. Archaic. Occasional in Cardigan, infrequent elsewhere; significantly older. Compare **book**.

In Prohibition days, a doctor's prescription for alcohol.

Liquor certainly played a big role in Island elections. ... A well-known Newfoundlander, arriving in Summerside to take up a position, was told he had to be sick to make a purchase. 'After I had paid a taxi driver $5.00 for a 'scrip' and $7.50 for a bottle of rum,' he moaned, 'then I *was* sick' (SELLICK, LESTER, *My Island Home*, 1973, 56–57). One had now to obtain a prescription or 'script' from a medical doctor in order to buy a bottle of liquor. ... the scripts were issued in large numbers, and this, together with the prevalence of rum-running and bootlegging, indicated a curiously ambivalent attitude among Islanders on the question of liquor control (PIGOT, FRANKLIN, *A History of Mount Stewart, Prince Edward Island*, 1975, 101). Physicians could prescribe alcohol to bolster their patients' health by providing them with a voucher, called 'script,' which patients could redeem for rum, brandy, whisky and so on from a local government vendor. Many foresaw the Prohibition Act as a positive step toward the eradication of alcohol from society. Others, it seems, took 'ill' at the news. In fact, the health of large segments of the population deteriorated. The waiting rooms outside doctors' offices filled with patients who believed that their health would be regained if only they had some 'script.' Some doctors profited by the scheme of selling script at exorbitant rates. Others found it a hindrance to their legitimate practice of medicine. But almost every doctor readily handed out the vouchers. Even doctors who believed in total abstinence found themselves in no-win positions. Although opposed to any alcohol consumption, they were doubly opposed to the consumption of moonshine because of the health risk from poor distillation techniques and unsanitary conditions. So, choosing the lesser of two evils, most pro-temperance doctors joined other physicians and provided alcohol prescriptions to patients who asked for them (MARTIN, FINLEY, *A View from the Bridge: Montague, P.E.I.*, 1984, 113). 'Must have been a lot of people going to the doctor in those days' – 'Yes, just for the script' (T B5).

*The word appears to be independent of standard *scrip* 'certificate of the bearer's right to something,' which derives from *subscription*.
[North American] *DNE* 1917–1964. *DAS* 'A prescription, almost always a forged or stolen prescription for narcotics.'

scriss
Noun. Sometimes humorous. Rare.
1. An omen of bad luck.
At that moment mother shook / A dash of salt over her left shoulder. / ... And Pat circled his chair and sat down again / To shake off any possible scriss (LEDWELL, FRANK, *The North Shore of Home*, 1986, 135). It's an Irishman's belief (I 117).
2. A curse.
Putting a scriss on somebody could be putting a curse on them (I 025). Put a scriss on that lad (II 112).
3. An unwelcome crowd.
A scriss of visitors (O). A scriss of kids (O).

[From Irish and Scottish Gaelic] *sgrios, scris: DGL, PEDGL, GED* 'destroy, ruin, annihilate.'

scrub spruce
See **pasture spruce**.

scuffle
Transitive and intransitive verb. Compare **bottom up**, **scuffler**, **scuffling**.

To cultivate (plants, particularly potato plants) by loosening the soil and removing weeds.

W. cool and dry, scuffling some potatoes, p.m. some thunder, got near a barrel herrings in 2 nets (MCEACHERON, JOHN, *A Diary of Weather, Work and Other Incidents Connected with the Farm and District*, 1874, July 14). Fine Papa and I scuffling potatoes in the morning (MEGGISON, GEORGE, *Diaries of George Eden Meggison*, 1908, July 15). We put Paris green on early potatoes and scuffled the late ones (*Foley Family Diary*, n.d.).

[From British] *OED* 1766–1807; *EDD*.

scuffler
Noun. Largely archaic. Compare **scuffle**, **scuffling**.

An old-fashioned cultivator for potatoes, usually horse-drawn.

In the early days, the hoe was the only implement used in cultivation and caring for the potato crop. When at length the potato patch became large enough to be called a field, a kind of horse (or ox)-drawn scuffler was made by the farmer to supplement the hoe which was still used to build up drills around the plants (MACNEVIN, MRS. LORNE, *Past and Present: A History of Brae*, 1979, 27). Between the rows was kept clean with a scuffler. Later as the tops enlarged mold boards were placed on the scuffler in place of the two back teeth which were removed and the potatoes were thus hilled up (MOASE, LOUISE, *The History of New Annan, Prince Edward Island, Canada, 1800–1971*, 1971, 30). A scuffler was a cultivator, a horse-drawn instrument with two handles. It removed weeds, couch grass, and loosened up the soil between the two rows. They are now called cultivators (S 1). A scuffler is not something we use anymore (S 3).

[From British] *OED* 1797–1891; *OEDS*; *W3*; *EDD*. *DAE* 'A gardener's hoe designed for thrusting.'

scuffling
Verbal noun. Compare **scuffle**, **scuffler**.

The act of cultivating plants, particularly potato plants by loosening soil and removing weeds.

Some scuffling is required for maximum yields. This operation keeps the soil from packing and provides sufficient soil for a good hill. Keep scuffling shallow to avoid damaging the plants, particularly the root system. It has been found that scuffling more than two to three times reduces yields (KHATTAK, JAHAN, and WILLIAM LEWIS, *Growing Potatoes for Processing in Prince Edward Island*, 1971, 14).

[From British] *OED* 1802–1847.

scut
Noun. Impolite, sometimes humorous. Infrequent generally, but rare in Summerside and Charlottetown; significantly older.
See **scra, skite, snollygoster, spleach**.

1. A low, mean, or unreliable person.

There was Gordon Rhodes back a bit ... but I niver belaved she'd take a scut like him. Too crooked to lie straight in bed like all the Rhodeses ...' (MONTGOMERY, LUCY MAUD, *Pat of Silver Bush*, 1933, 44). 'I was going out of London one day on a train that passed Gladstone's house,' remarked a traveled islander to me. 'I asked the man in the compartment with me when I could catch a glimpse of Haywarden Castle, the home of the Grand Old Man. What d'ye think he answered, the scut?' I shook my head despairingly as if I knew it must be something outrageously unlike what he ought to have said (KELLEY, FRANCIS, *The Bishop Jots It Down: An Autobiographical Strain on Memories*, 1939, 12). Originally the word had been 'scut,' which Doyle had meant as an insulting reference to John P. Sullivan, but Father Gillis did not feel that was quite right and Doyle changed it to 'Scott' at his request, just as he is supposed to have made a change in 'Fogan MacAleer' (IVES, EDWARD, *Lawrence Doyle: The Farmer Poet of Prince Edward Island*, 1971, 111). I was only ten when my father died and was sent to live with my Uncle John. He was a mean old scut. He used to beat me regularly, specially when he was drinking (HENNESSEY, MICHAEL, *The Trial of Minnie McGee*, 1983, 12). 'You miserable scut' (I 014). 'You dirty scut' – used when playing cards (I 038). He's nothing but a Fort Augustus scut, the bla'guard (O).

2. An immoral young woman (I; P1).

3. A mischievous child (I).

*Harold Thompson's *Body, Boots and Britches*, 1940, 500, records 'God speed scut! (When you are glad to see something or someone go. – Irish.),' for New York State. One PEI observer attests *scut-work* 'tedious paperwork,' also reported from the United States for any drudge-work.
[From English] *ESI* 'the tail of a hare or rabbit: often applied in scorn to a contemptible fellow'; *OEDS* 'colloq. or dial.' 1895 1929; *DSUE*; *DAS*; *W3*; *WNW*. *scout: OED* 'a term of contempt applied to both men and women' 1380–1869.

sea foam soap
Noun. Archaic. Infrequent in Egmont and Summerside, rare elsewhere; especially senior.

1. A (former) brand of toilet soap.

It's a brand name toilet soap, like any other white soap that you washed your face with (II 019). Just regular soap but they called it sea foam; used to buy little bars of it (II 057). Around during World War I; made nice suds. Marked 'Sea Foam' with a line in the middle where you could cut it (II 068). We used it for washing hands, etc.; you would cut it in two with string (O).

2. Home-made laundry soap.

Grandmother referred to the soap they made themselves by this term (II 018). Homemade soap that made suds like sea foam (II 063). Homemade washing soap (II 096).

3. See quotation.

They're sea sponges used for scrubbing floors. They were sudsy because of air in them but they really didn't contain any soap, even though they were thought to contain soap (II 006).

*This term is a trade name which became general.

sea manure
Noun. Historical.

A species of seaweed formerly gathered for fertilizer.

Leading out sea manure and – potato seed (*Meggison Family Account Book*, 1811, May 20). The rivers – rather, arms of the sea – creeks, and inlets, which almost everywhere indent the land, have deposited vast stores of sea-manure, which, when spread over the exhausted soil, has the most beneficial effect in fertilizing it (HIND, H.Y., *Eighty Years' Progress of British North America*, 1864, 735). 'Sea manure' was also applied to the land. The kelp or seaweed was gathered and spread on the land. For some farmers, gathering seaweed for fertilizer was an ongoing job. They would travel to the shore at low tide to get a load of seaweed (MACDONALD, ROSE MARIE, *Those Were the Days: A History of the North Side of the Boughton River*, [1980?], 10).

SSPB 'red, feathery seaweed put on gardens to rot and enrich them, also known as rockweed.'

sea moss pudding
Noun. Also **Irish moss pudding**. Archaic. Infrequent; significantly female; especially older.

Blancmange made by boiling Irish moss with milk.

The Irish moss industry is attracting attention and government money at the present. Our ancestors used the moss to make 'seamoss pudding.' Preparation was simple. The moss was brought home, washed, dried, and stored until needed. The old recipe is as follows: '1/2 cup Irish moss. Wash in tepid water, pick over and put into a double boiler with 1 quart milk. Boil until it thickens, when dropped on a cold plate. Add salt and strain, not allowing any moss to pass. Add flavour and turn into a

mould.' I have eaten pudding made this way by my mother-in-law, and it tasted just like cornstarch puddings of today (HOWATT, BETTY, *History Begins at Home*, 1981, 25). It's Irish moss pudding; the people up west would take this home and put it in some milk on the back of the stove. They called it blancmange, turn of the century (II 006). My aunt in High Bank collected moss to make blancmange or sea-moss pudding. It's good for you because of the iodine (II 107).

sea thistle
Noun. Compare **Aristotle's lantern**.

Synonym for 'whore's egg': a small, roundish shell fish with sharp spines, a sea urchin.

Sea thistle is used by the more modest [instead of *whore's egg*] to describe a sea urchin (I 012). We call them sea urchins or sea thistles if there are women around and 'whore's eggs' if they aren't (S 5).

OED.

sea turkey
See **Frenchman's turkey**.

second rakings
Plural noun. Also **rakings**. Archaic. Common in Egmont, occasional in Cardigan, infrequent elsewhere; significantly male; especially rural, older.

Hay that is missed in the first gathering.

Bits dropped out of sheaves as they were collected. They were dry and didn't pack well. Father drove around forking them into a wagon, and kids stomped them down (I 064). The workers would have to go back for the bits of hay that were dropped during the gathering (II 001). This second part of crop perhaps paid for hired help. That's what you figured paid for your workers (II 039). After the hay was taken, they would rake where the hay coils were (II 041).

[From British] *raking*: EDD 'Gen. in pl.'; OED 1851; SND.

seed out
Transitive phrasal verb.

To sow (grain, grass, or hay) in a field to restore the soil (S).

set
Noun.

1. A portion of a potato used as seed.

Many experiments have been tried to determine the best kind of sets to plant, and, on the whole, it has been found that good marketable tubers cut into pieces so as to have, at least, three good eyes to a piece, and a liberal amount of flesh, are the best. A medium sized potato should make three to four sets (MACOUN, W.T., *The Potato in Canada: Its Cultivation and Varieties*, 1918, 6). Cutting sets is one of the necessary jobs that takes a lot of time, but with the help of set cutters the work is done more easily (*Journal-Pioneer Annual Farm Issue*, 1977, 3). When ploughs came into use, potato sets were planted in rows every second or third round behind the single-furrow plough and covered on the next round (MACNEVIN, MRS. LORNE, *Past and Present: A History of Brae*, 1979, 21).

2. The number of potatoes obtained from a single potato plant.

After you plant a seed piece in the ground, the first thing that emerges is the stem, and then the root system also develops. The set is the number of tubers derived from one single seed piece. It's a relatively new term, and is used late in the potato season. A small set means the tubers will grow too large (S 1).

[From British] [sense 1]: *OED* 1767–1908; *W3*; *EDD*; *GCD*; *FW*; *WNW*; *COD*.

setting
Noun. Frequent in Egmont and Summerside, occasional in Malpeque and Cardigan, infrequent in Charlottetown; significantly older, less educated; especially rural.

1. In baking bread, an amount made at one time, a batch.

A setting of bread is eight or nine loaves (II 002). In the process of making bread mother would say she had enough flour for a setting (II 019).

2. An amount of flour sufficient for a batch or setting of bread.

Four or five large sifters of flour, twelve to fifteen cups (II 001). A small setting is enough to make three loaves; a big setting makes six to nine loaves (II 039). A setting of flour is enough for three loaves of bread, nine or ten cups. You would ask to borrow 'a setting of flour' (O).

setting day
Noun.
The day before the opening of the lobster fishing season, on which fishermen set their traps.

Setting day is the day the fishermen first set their traps. This is the only day that traps are set. After that they may be 'moved' or 'shifted' to another area or 'run off' after they've been fished, but they are not 'set' again (MACMILLAN, JANET, *The Language of Lobster Fishing*, 1985, 23).

shaker¹
Noun. Compare **cracker, knuckle picker**.
A worker in a lobster factory who shakes the meat out of lobster claws.

He then passed the cracked shells to the 'shaker' whose job it was to shake the meat from the shells and then pass it along to the knuckle-picker who had the unenviable task of picking the meat from all the knuckles while the legs were squeezed between rollers to extract the meat and the remaining bodies were discarded (MORRISON, CLINTON, *Along the North Shore: A Social History of Township 11, P.E.I. 1765–1982*, 1983, 73).

W3 'a worker who shakes things by hand or by machine to clean, separate, size, settle, loosen, or dry them.'

shaker²
Noun. Compare **cleaning drum**.
In fox ranching, a perforated cylinder that shakes sawdust from fox pelts after they have been cleaned (S).

shako
Noun. Informal.
An alcoholic, especially one who drinks alcohol in unusual forms.

The shaving lotion came out afterwards; shakos they called them fellows that were drinking that. Meet them in town and you could smell them coming (T B5). There are a lot of shakos hanging around downtown looking for a handout (P2-055). They shake from drinking too much (P2-057). Shakos are men who are addicted to alcohol in any form: for instance, vanilla, lysol, shaving lotion, rubbing alcohol. The name comes probably from these men shaking so bad after drinking these concoctions (O).

shank
Noun, usually in plural. Archaic.
See quotation.

The shoes in use were either wooden clogs such as were worn by the French and called by them Sabots or moccasins some of which were made of sealskin some of tanned leather and others of green hide with the hair outside which were taken from the lower legs of an ox and were called 'Shanks' (ALLEY, JUDGE, *Prince Edward Island 100 Years Ago*, [1890?], 9).

[North American] *DC 'Esp. Maritimes* leggings made from the hide, peeled off and cured, from the hind legs of a moose, caribou, etc.' 1943–1952; *W3*; *OED* 'a stocking. ... Also U.S. pl. leggings' 1546–1888.

sharp-shod
Verbal adjective. Compare **never-slip**.
  Of a horse, shod with shoes having sharpened projections to prevent slipping on ice.
  It is possible that more horse shoes were made and sharpened by Patrick McCourt than by any other blacksmith of Brae. All through the days when horses of the district were 'sharp-shod' for mussel-mud digging, his shop ... was the horse-shoeing centre of the community (MACNEVIN, MRS. LORNE, *Past and Present: A History of Brae*, 1979, 51). Winter shoes with spikes on them for winter: 'sharp-shod' is what they said (P2-002).

OEDS 'Chiefly N. Amer.'; *EDD* Cum. Wm.; *W3*; *COD*.

Sheaf of Wheat, the
Noun phrase. Historical. Compare **holey dollar, John Joy Token, leather dollar, tree cent**.
  See quotation.
  'The Holy Dollar,' 'The Island Cent,' 'The Sheaf of Wheat,' the 'John Joy Token' – these and many others refer to the currency of this part of Atlantic Canada now known as the Province of Prince Edward Island. ... they remain great finds for collectors (P.E.I. NUMISMATIC SOCIETY, *Island Currency*, 1973, 24–25).

sheep dung tea
Noun.
  A medicinal tea made from sheep's dung.
  They use sheep dung tea for sick people ... and sheep dung is not a euphemism (II 024).

sheep's dung: *EDD* 'an ointment applied to broken chillblains.'

sheep poison
Noun.
  Sheep laurel, a dwarf shrub (*Kalmia angustifolia*), poisonous to sheep and other animals (O).

[North American] *OED*; *W3*; *DAE*; *DA*.

sheep-snout apple
Noun.
  See quotations.
  Further along lay the orchard where a gnarled old tree produced fruit with the intriguing name of 'Sheep-snout apple.' The name was certainly not one easily forgotten and neither was the apple itself. The flesh was very sweet and almost banana colored (STEWART, MARION, *Marion Stewart's Journal*, 1976, 8). Odd-shaped apple (P2-049).

[From English] *EDD* ' "Sheep-snout tree," an apple tree bearing a rather small favourite eating apple'; *OED*. *sheep nose*: *DAE* 'any of several varieties of apple'; *sheep apple*: *DA* 'a sheep nose apple.'

sheep storm
Noun. Frequent generally, but infrequent in Charlottetown; significantly middle-aged and older.
  1. A storm of cold wind and heavy rain, usually in early June.
  Still wet and windy. They say this is the sheep storm (*Unidentified Diary, 1941–1942*, 1941, June 11). First the sheep were shorn in the spring, about the first week in June. A cold driving rain in early June was then and is still called 'the sheep storm.' It had nothing to do with sheep, but it was a June storm, invariably coming soon after the sheep were shorn. The wind would set in from the north-east, bitterly cold and blow hard from that direction two and sometimes three days with driving, stinging rain. The unlucky sheep, their warm coats reft away, would feel it bitterly and sometimes die from exposure. Hence, the name (SPRINGFIELD WOMEN'S INSTITUTE, *Springfield 1828–1953*, 1954, 43). I remember Grandapa talking about the June 'sheep storms' as those raw, miserable days that came after the shearing, when the sheep were naked and defenceless (HOWATT, BETTY, *History Begins at Home*, 1981, 24). A cold rain storm in June or July. We get it nearly every year (I 013). It comes around the first of June when sheep are shorn so they have to put them in the barn so they won't freeze (I 063). The sheep storm comes only in June. Called 'sheep storm' because you're not supposed to shear sheep before it comes, about June 10th. Lasts about three days (C 146).
  2. The last big snow-storm of the year,

in April or May. Compare **black snow**, **smelt storm**.

Sometimes there is a surprise snowstorm as late as May; the local people call them 'sheep storms' because the farmers must quickly bring in their freshly sheared sheep and newborn lambs before they freeze (CLIMO, LINDEE, *Chester's Barn*, 1982, 21). Snow in May (I 077). May snow (C 182).

*In the Common Word Survey, 21% preferred *sheep storm* over other variants for a late spring snow-fall.

sheep weather
Noun.
A period of mild weather in autumn, Indian summer (C; R).

she-lad
Noun.
A tomboy.
Just recently I heard an elderly man say 'I was hoping they would have a boy to carry on the name but they had another she-lad' (P2-084).

shell ice
Noun. Common generally, but occasional in Summerside and Malpeque; significantly rural, older, male. Compare **black ice**, **cat ice**, **double ice**, **shelly**, **top ice**.
1. A patch or layer of thin ice over thicker ice, with an air space in between, caused by refreezing or by freezing rain.
The Bay was cold smooth glass. Thud! Mary Ann was down on a little shell-ice. She was up again dashing on just out of Jockie's reach (STIRLING, LILLA, *Jockie: A Story of Prince Edward Island*, 1951, 15–16). On the return journey, a wild snowstorm arose, changing to frozen rain, which caused a hard shell of ice through which their feet broke at every step until their footgear was torn to ribbons (MACLEOD, ADA, *Roads to Summerside: The Story of Early Summerside and the Surrounding Area*, 1980, 14). You could have thicker ice underneath with shell ice on top like a blister, which ruins the skating (I 029). It comes after a thaw and water on top of ice freezes and is crumbly (I 049).
2. A thin layer of ice, under which the water has retreated.
Roads better this morning as there was frost in the night. … Seymour started for Hernwood

but found shell-ice so turned back going to factory after dinner with rope (WOODMAN, SUSAN, *Diary: January 1, 1895–December 31, 1896*, 1895, March 21). When water evaporates from under thin ice (I 053). Ice not supported by water is dangerous because it looks O.K. but isn't (O).
3. Ice that is pocked like a honeycomb.
Small patches of shell ice, resembling appliques of silver lace were reflected on the magic carpet (JOHNSTONE, RENA, *Journal of the Months at Strathaven*, 1980, 2). Shell ice is unsafe ice. Either the water goes from underneath it, or it is honeycombed in spring (I 002). The Gaelic word for *shell ice* also means 'spider's web' (I 051).

*After standard *skim*, *shell ice* was the most popular response in the Common Word Survey for 'The first thin layer of ice on a pond.'
[Canadian] *DC* 'North' 1924–1963; *GCD* 'Cdn; in the north'; *W3*; *OEDS*.

shell mud
Noun. Archaic. Compare **aldermud**, **killkid mud**, **mussel mud**, **oyster mud**.
Mud thick with mussel or oyster shells, formerly dug from bays and river mouths and used as fertilizer.
This 'mussel-mud,' as it is called, is a very valuable fertilizer and, up to two years ago, the immense shell-mud deposits of St. Peter bay were practically untouched, as the only means of obtaining the mud was by horse-power dredges which can only operate on ice in winter time, and, as this bay does not freeze over, the dredges cannot operate on it (CANADA, COMMISSION OF CONSERVATION, *Conservation of Fish, Birds and Game*, 1916, 71). The digging of shell mud from the large deposits in the river by large horse-operated power, supplied the lime requirements to the soil. Early efforts in this respect were with small scows and boats anchored at the channel's edge at low tide and filled by small mud forks made by the blacksmith, a really back-breaking task (SHAW, WALTER, *Tell Me the Tales*, 1975, 24). Farmers studied the potential of Island soils. It was realized that most Island soils needed lime. Farmers made use of the source of lime that was at hand and spent a good part of each winter digging the shell mud from the rivers and bays (BLOOMFIELD HISTORICAL SOCIETY, *History of Saint Anthony Parish, 1803–1980*, 1980, 38). I don't know, it kind of seems hard that the people worked so hard to get the land in good

heart as they called it, hauling shell mud all the cold days, you know, going twelve and fifteen miles. There was no fertilizer them days (T M37).

shell worm
Noun.
See quotations.
Down in Orwell Cove, some kind of a shell worm is killing the oysters. The shell worm drills a hole in the oyster's shell (S 14). A shell worm or boring worm bores into the shell and makes it brittle and this makes the oyster soft (S 15).

shelly
Adjective. Compare **shell ice**.
Of ice, thin or honeycombed.
Don't go there, the ice is shelly (I 118). We can't skate, the ice is too shelly (R 13). It is often a term of caution. 'Watch out, that ice is shelly!' It can give you a nasty fall or, even worse, a bad cut on a bare hand (R 20).

shin of heat, a
Noun phrase. Also **a shinny of heat**. Rare.
Heat found close to the stove or fire; a small degree of heat.
Just put a shin of heat on (O).

[From Irish] *shin-heat*: EDD 1899.

shoe-string
Noun. Compare **dirt²**, **monkey fur**.
A seaweed (genus *Chorda*) often gathered with 'Irish Moss,' and considered an impurity.
Monkey fur and shoe-string are the worst things to get out of the moss (BERNARD, BLAINE, *Dictionary of Irish Moss*, 1986, n. pag.). I'm not sure where shoe-string comes from. It looks like the tentacles of a lobster, except longer and usually a greenish color (S 10). Shoestring looks something like eel grass (S 11).

shook
Noun. Compare **snool**.
A nosy person (II; R; o).

shore dance
Noun. Archaic.
A dance held on the sea-shore.
'Miss Oliver, shall I wear my white dress tonight or my green one? The green one is by far the prettier, of course, but I'm almost afraid to wear it to a shore dance for fear something will happen to it' (MONTGOMERY, LUCY MAUD, *Rilla of Ingleside*, 1973 [1920], 17). By moonrise everything was ready for the shore dance. The boys had a huge bonfire of driftwood ablaze on the point, and the waters of the harbor were creaming and shimmering in the moonlight (MONTGOMERY, LUCY MAUD, *Anne of Windy Poplars*, 1936, 108).

DC 'Esp. Maritimes' [citing *Rilla of Ingleside* only].

shore ice
Noun. Compare **board ice**, **field ice**.
Synonym for 'board ice': solid, flat, sea ice attached to a shore and extending out to broken ice or open water.
We had proceeded about a mile on the shore-ice, when we halted for a few moments to enable us to remove our outer garments, which had become unbearable from the warmth the rapid exercise had created. ... We had soon reached the extent of the shore-ice, and now commenced our labours (SLEIGH, B.W.A., *Pine Forests and Hacmatack Clearings*, 1853, 122). To my extreme satisfaction he reported the Straits as favourable for a passage. The previous tempest had pretty well cleared the Gulf of ice, and nought but shore-ice leading to open water was to be found on this side (*ibid*, 130). It was now four in the afternoon. We had been out eleven hours, and only two remained of daylight. We had approached to within three miles of Cape Tormentine. The distance made by us in our direct course was but seven miles in the space of time I have mentioned, although we had probably gone over above twenty during our circuitous navigation. The shore ice, which is safe, appeared to stretch about a mile and a half out, consequently not more than the same distance had to be traversed to place us beyond the danger by which we were now imminently surrounded (*ibid*, 138). Stayed at Mr. Yeo's till 2 o'clock ... [and] then started up Kildare River. Went all the way on the ice to Haywood's, shore ice pretty good (DYER, ROBERT, *Diary, 1859–1883*, 1881, April 7). During the winter, the various bays and channels, which lay along the north shore from St. Peter's to Cascumpeque, with stretches of land travel and sometime [sic] parts of shore ice, this formed his [Bishop MacEachern's] route (PRINCE EDWARD ISLAND HISTORICAL SOCIETY, *Pioneers on the Island, Part 1*, [1959], 91). At seven in the morning they were down at the boat, where all the men put on leather harnesses and grasped the gunwale of the boat. After four hours' pulling over the shore ice, they reached

open water (BLAKELEY, PHYLLIS, and MYRA VERNON, *The Story of Prince Edward Island*, 1963, 162).

[Canadian] *DC* 'Esp. North' 1752–1953; *DNE* 1887–1969; *OEDS*.

shore moss
Noun. Compare **moss, rake moss, shore mosser, storm-tossed moss**.
   'Irish moss' as harvested at the seashore after it has been washed up by a storm or as dropped from a 'drag rake.'
   Shore moss is moss gathered on the shore. That is the difference between the rake moss on boats and shore moss. Shore moss is ground up and harder to pick (S 10). Shore moss is moss that has been dropped from the boat rake and comes ashore (S 12).

shore mosser
Noun. Compare **horse mosser, mosser, shore moss**.
   A person who collects 'Irish moss' on shore.
   A shore mosser is someone who just gathers moss on shore. We are all shore mossers here. We are not allowed to rake because we would damage the lobster ground (S 10).

shorewatching
Verbal noun.
   The act of watching for the best time to harvest 'Irish moss' that has been washed ashore.
   It's a great way to spend a Sunday afternoon: sitting in a truck, shorewatching, and drinking beer (BERNARD, BLAINE, *Dictionary of Irish Moss*, 1986, n.pag.). Shorewatching can be a vigil at night or anytime where you are watching the shore for moss. A good north east wind holds the moss on shore here (S 10). Shorewatching is going on here all the time. They (mossers) watch it all hours of the day and night, especially if there is a breeze. It is pretty near one fellow's job to shorewatch (S 11). Shore-watching is the practice of people who watch the shore for 'storm-tossed moss' twenty-four hours a day (S 12).

short
Noun. Compare **blink, canner, market, michaud**.
   An undersized lobster, below the legal length for fishing.

To obtain the greatest benefit from a size limit the short lobsters should be left undisturbed on their feeding grounds. Even though short lobsters are released they may be injured or killed by rough handling or exposure to wind, rain, or sunlight. As the released 'shorts' sink to the bottom some are undoubtedly eaten by cod and other fish. These deaths and injuries are largely unnecessary and are a direct loss to the fishermen. This unnecessary loss can be greatly reduced by spacing trap laths far enough apart to allow most of the 'shorts' to escape alive and uninjured (WILDER, D.G., *The Lobster Fishery of the Southern Gulf of St. Lawrence*, 1954, 16). The second item of adjustment is the addition of a value for the lobster consumed in the fisherman's household. These are likely to have been culls or 'shorts', to which regular prices do not apply (RUTHERFORD, J.B., D.G. WILDER, and H.C. FRICK, *An Economic Appraisal of the Canadian Lobster Fishery*, 1967, 64). Those Fisheries boys are pretty good sports / As long as you don't take the 'berried' and shorts (FLEMING, RICHARD, *Lobstering*, 1985, 1). There is a carapace measurement from the eye to the back of the body. A short is one below the size of a saleable lobster (S 4). A short is a lobster that is undersized as between the eye sockets and the back of the body, and which has to be put back in the water (S 5).

W3; WNW.

short sill
Noun. Also **cross sill**. Compare **long sill, sill**.
   One of the two shorter, cross pieces of heavy wood that form the bottom frame of a lobster trap.
   The sill which runs across the width of the trap. Holes are drilled in the short sills and the ends of the 'bow' are inserted (ROBERTSON, JANICE, *A Dictionary of Lobster Fishing in the Eastern Kings Area*, 1985, 12). The short sill or cross sill runs the width of the trap and is what you set your 'bow' into (S 6).

*In square lobster traps, sills are also used for the top frame.

short-taken
Verbal adjective. Common; rare under thirty. Compare **back door trots, blueberry run, flying axehandles, green apple quick-step, run outs and walk ins, skithers**.

Needing urgently to empty the bowels or bladder.

All down the ages, as decreed by fate, / Time, tide, and diarrhea never wait. / How oft, short-taken in green apple time, / the frantic swains upon yon counter climb (DOCKERTY, MALCOLM, *Rhymed Reminiscences of a Pathologist: His Life's Story*, 1980, 93). If a person were outdoors, then he could be short-taken (I 093). An emergency trip to the bathroom (P1-002).

*The reverse, *taken short*, is informal standard. *taken short, be*: *DSUE* 'To be pressed with the need of evacuation of faeces: coll (−1890)'; *OEDS* 1890−1977.

showhall
Noun.
A building where movies are shown; an informal movie theatre.

Before the days of cinemas or theatres the smaller halls were used. A man would come each week on a regular basis and show a movie. The term 'showhall' is quite reasonable (R 8). Occasionally the Ellerslie movie hall (R 12). The 'term' showhall I would say is used by approximately 95% of the people in the Souris area. An example in context would be 'Did you see that on T.V. or at the showhall?' (R 22).

*Several informants associated this term with eastern Prince Edward Island. It derives from the time when movies were shown regularly in community halls.

side head
See **fishing head**.

sill
Noun. Compare **bottom sill, long sill, short sill, top sill**.
One of the heavy pieces of wood that form the frame of a lobster trap.

Set up the saw and cut the sills / Get the laths and palings from the mills (FLEMING, RICHARD, *Lobstering*, 1985, 1). Thick wooden laths that form the shell of the lobster trap. The average trap (square) consists of two top sills, two bottom sills and six cross sills (MACMILLAN, JANET, *The Language of Lobster Fishing*, 1985, 23). A sill is what you frame the trap on the bows with (S 4). A sill is the heavy piece on the bottom of the traps to keep the traps together (S 5).

*In 'bow traps' (with curved tops), sills are used only for the bottom; in square traps, sills frame both the bottom and the top.

silver freeze
Noun. Infrequent generally, but un-attested in Charlottetown.
Synonym for 'silver frost': a glitter of ice on exposed surfaces, usually seen in the morning after a freezing rain over-night.

Warm day, silver freeze at night (CAIRNS, SCOTT, *Diary: January 1, 1909−May 31, 1920*, 1912, March 7). Very windy with silver freeze (CAIRNS, SCOTT, *Diary: January 1, 1932 − March 31, 1939*, 1932, April 5). Two of this couple's grandchildren, Stephen's twins, Ronnie and Reggie, caused quite a flurry when they de-cided to arrive in January, 1957, during a very heavy 'Silver Freeze,' which knocked out all power in Prince County, leaving complete darkness everywhere including the hospital. ... The trees at the homestead still show the scars from that icy weight, some so bent they straightened toward the sun again from that bent position, others broken off, grew a new top which looks quite unnatural. It was months before all telephone and light wires were com-pletely restored again (INDIAN RIVER WOMEN'S INSTITUTE, *History of Indian River*, 1973, 54). *Silver freeze* is more common than *silver thaw* (I 072).

*Some informants in the fieldwork may have conflated this term with *silver frost*, which was not itself tested; thus the frequency of *silver freeze* may not be as high as indicated. The standard term is *silver thaw*.

silver frost
Noun. Compare **silver freeze**.
A glitter of ice on exposed surfaces, usually seen in the morning after a freezing rain overnight.

A phenomenon appears frequently during winter known here by the appellation of Silver Frost. When a fine misty rain takes place, with the wind at the east or north east, the frost not being sufficiently keen to congeal the rain until it falls, but, at the moment it rests on any substance, it adheres and freezes, incrusting every tree, shrub, and whatever else is exposed to the weather, with ice. The forest assumes in consequence, the most magnificant splendour, and continues in this state until it thaws, or until the *icy shell* is shaken off by the winds. The woods, while in this state, especially if the sun shine [sic], exhibit the most brilliant appearance. Every tree is loaded as with a natural production of silver spangles, and there is not, probably, anything in the appearance of nature, that would more adequately baffle the powers of a landscape painter (*Prince Edward Island Register*, October 14, 1828, 4). Silver frost at night (*Meggison Family Diary*, 1832, September 15).

*An informal student survey of usage in Egmont, 1983, found that *silver frost* and the standard *silver thaw* were approximately equal in popularity. [Canadian] *DC* 1828–1889; *DNE* 1832; *WNW* [under *silver thaw*:] 'also *silver frost.*'

silvering
Noun. Compare **bar, veiling**.
The distribution of the silver-white coloring on a silver fox pelt.

Some of the fox ranchers … are endeavoring to establish a standard type of silver black fox. This is now being done without any inbreeding, and the result of systematic and scientific management may be seen in many cases amongst this year's pups, perhaps very noticeably at James C. Tuplin's ranch, where 30 well developed pups show an evenness in silvering that is remarkable (*The Black Fox Industry in P.E.I.*, September, 1913, 6–8). Silvering: … The amount of silver pigment in the fox fur (CARR, MARGARET, *Terms of Fox Farming on P.E.I.*, 1986, 11). The silvering of a fox is a matter of degree. If a fox has a large amount of silvering it is determined by the length of the silver bar and the density of the guard hair (S 7). Silvering is the standard by which foxes are graded. You would have the quarter silver, the half silver, the three quarter and the full. A garment maker requires uniform silvering when making good coats with luminescent quality (S 9).

W3 'a sprinkling of white or light hairs in the coat of a mammal.'

singing sand
Noun. Also **barking sand, squeaking sand**.
Sand that makes a squeaking noise when walked on.

Those who like to squeak as they walk can try the 'singing sand' of the northeast corner of the island, so called because the texture of the silica underfoot causes a sharp crunching sound when the foot is lifted (*The Globe and Mail*, April 23, 1983, ET9). Sand so fine it squeaks when you walk on it (O).

*Observers have associated the term particularly with Basin Head, PEI.
OEDS 'desert or beach sand that emits a singing, whistling hummming or other continuous sound

when disturbed' 1884–1970. *squeaking sand*: *OEDS* 1966–1976.

single ice
Noun phrase.
Ice formed in a single layer, as opposed to 'double ice' or 'shell ice.'

In the spring of the year it was bad because you had times of double ice and there were times of single ice (STEWART, DEBORAH, and DAVID STEWART, *Winter Travel*, 1979, 24).

skag
Noun. Derogatory. Infrequent generally, but unattested in Malpeque.
A homely woman (O).

*This word is possibly related to standard *scrag* 'a scrawny person or animal.'
DAS.

skeil
Noun.
See quotation.

I had an interesting trip to Cleveland, Ohio, last fall, to speak to a Woman's Club there. One evening we danced at a 'cabaret,' listened to 'jazz' music and watched the modern dances concerning which there are such skeils of wrath in the journals of the period (MONTGOMERY, LUCY MAUD, *My Dear Mr. M: Letters to G.B. MacMillan from L.M. Montgomery*, 1980 [1922], 107).

skiff
Noun. Also **skit** and adjective **skifting**. Frequent generally, but infrequent in Malpeque and Charlottetown; significantly older, male; especially rural. Compare **skim**.
A light, even fall of snow or, occasionally, of rain.

But to return to the history of the winter. January passed over with clear dry frost, with now and then a skifting snow shower (JOHNSTONE, WALTER, 'Letters' and 'Travels' *Prince Edward Island, 1821*, 1955, 137). The wind had changed at sunset and the evening was cold and edged. What Jimmy called a 'skiff' of snow had fallen suddenly whitening the world and the withered, unlovely garden (MONTGOMERY, LUCY MAUD, *Emily's Quest*, 1927, 234). Enough to make a sleigh road, no wind (II 100). A skit of snow fell last night (P2-082). A skiff of snow – just a covering on the ice (O). Skit – rather a light sprinkle of snow (O).

[From Scottish] *OED; EDD; OEDS; SND* [verb]. *skit*: *OED; W3* 'dial *Eng*: a sudden sharp shower or gust of rain.' *skift*: *W3* 'a light fall of snow or rain.'

skillick
Noun, used after a negative. Also spelled **skellick**. Frequent in Egmont, infrequent in Summerside and Malpeque, rare elsewhere; especially older, less educated.
   A small, almost worthless amount of something.
   I haven't got a skillick of tobacco left (II 019). I didn't get a skillick of moss (O). Referring to something very small; e.g. 'There wasn't a skillick left' (O).

OED 'rare' 1835.

skim
Noun. Compare **skiff**.
   A light, even fall of snow.
   It's a cold frosty night out with a skim of snow on the ground and a silvery new moon floating over the orchard in a sea of saffron yellow sky (MONTGOMERY, LUCY MAUD, *My Dear Mr. M.: Letters to G.B. MacMillan from L.M. Montgomery*, 1980 [1904], 5).

*This variant was also volunteered in the Common Word Survey. The standard sense is 'a thin layer of ice' (see *shell ice*).
W3 'a thin layer, coating or film.' *skimmin*: *SND* 'a sprinkling, a light surface covering.'

skin
Intransitive verb. Informal.
   Of men, to cruise for women.
   It's chasing girls, as in 'I'm going skinning tonight' (O). This is used by younger men (O).

Getting your skin: *SSPB* 'used by a male to describe sexual intercourse.'

skinflint
Noun. Humorous. Compare **skooligan**.
   A mischievous child.
   Referring to a bad child: 'You skinflint' (O). My mother used to use it – still uses it on the cat – when we did something a little bit naughty that we should have known better about. It was almost an endearment (O).

skit
See **skiff**.

skite
Noun. Sometimes humorous. Occasional in Egmont, infrequent elsewhere; signi-ficantly middle-aged and older; especially male.
   1. A quick, glancing blow, especially on the ear or rump; a nudge in the ribs.
   Heard from my father: 'Stop your whinging or I'll give you another skite' (I 010). Get a skite on the rear-end (I 094). You'll get a skite on the ear if you don't behave yourself (I 095). A skite on the bum (I 116).
   2. A contemptible young person. Compare **scra, scut**.
   I've heard skite used to mean a young scoundrel or a bad kid (I 030). He's nothing but a skite (I 052). Used by my father, as in 'You little skite, you' (O).

[From northern Irish and Scottish and northern English] *OED* [sense 1] 1785–1895, [sense 2] 1808–1850; *W3; EDD; SND; EDSL; FW; DSUE*.

skithers, the
Plural noun phrase. Also **skitters**. Frequent in Egmont, occasional in Cardigan, infrequent elsewhere; especially rural, older, male. Compare **back door trots, blueberry run, flying axehandles, green apple quick-step, run outs and walk ins, short-taken**.
   Diarrhea, especially in animals.
   It was serious when calves got the skitters (II 001).

[From Scottish and northern English] *OED* 1595–1823; *OEDS* 1939-1948; *EDD; SND; EDSL; DSUE. scutters* 'diarrhea': *DNE, EDD*.

skithry
Adjective. Occasional in Egmont and Summerside, infrequent in Cardigan, rare elsewhere.
   Of persons and, occasionally, of horses, unreliable, flighty.
   Not reliable, wandering-minded (II 003). Wishy-washy (II 103).

skiver
Noun. \'ski-vur\. Compare **splinterkin, split, swift-stick**.
   A thin shaving of wood used in place of a match.
   They're used to light pipes and such (P2-015). We used a shaving of wood peeled with a knife and lit with a flint (P2-033). Pine skivers were used when matches were scarce (P2-034).

[From British and northern Irish] *EDD; SND*.

skivver
Transitive verb. Especially to a child.
Compare **card**, **read**.
To scold or to punish physically.
I'll skivver you if you don't look out. Turn
you upside down and give you a whack
(P2-054). I'll skivver you for pulling up all my
flowers (O).

[From Scottish and northern English] *EDD* 'To cut up;
to disperse by force; to punish'; *SND* 'To pierce or
stab as with a skewer, to transfix, often in jocular
contexts' 1819–1947.

skooligan
Noun. Humorous. Rare. Compare **skin-flint**.
A mischievous child.
A half-teasing expression to a naughty child
(II 101).

skra
See **scra**.

skuzzle
Intransitive verb.
Of youngsters, to wrestle playfully, to scuffle.
Boys like skuzzling in the fields (P2-017).

slat rack
Noun.
A rack for grading potatoes.
A slat rack is a device of wooden construction of about 24' wide by 3 1/2 feet high, where
you could put on a bag of potatoes to inspect
quality (S 1). A slat rack is the old hand grader.
You put the bag at one end and shovel the
potatoes on to the other. The inspectors still
use them (S 2).

sleeper
Noun. Rare.
A partially buried or hidden obstruc-tion in a field, especially a root (I).

[From English] *DC* 'Maritimes' 1954; *OED* 'the dead
stub of a tree' (Suffolk, 1823); *EDD* 'The stump of a
tree left in the ground. e.An. Nrf. ... Suf.'

slew
See **slough**.

slippy
Adjective. Informal. Frequent; especially
younger.

1. Of a surface, slippery, slick.
Started this morning about 11 o'clock to go
and see Mr. and Mrs. McCabe at the lighthouse. I walked over the ice from the shore and
oh, it was very slippy; I could hardly start.
However, I got there without falling, thank
God (DYER, ROBERT, *Diary, 1859–1883*, 1875,
December 28). We could hardly get the cows
out to water with how slippy it is (LAMONT,
MURDOCK, *Diary, 1885–1888*, 1886, 5). It rains
every day this time of year. Not a steady down-
pour but enough to keep the ground slippy and
everything damp all the time (CROCKETT,
VERNON, *Diary from York, 1915–1917*, 28). To
Abijah's morn, threshing afternoon Raining,
roads very slippy (CAIRNS, SCOTT, *Diary: January
1, 1932–March 31, 1939*, 1932, December 5). The
roads are terrible slippy (I 082). Gosh, it's a
slippy day (I 099).
2. Of a person, dishonest, sly.
Watch for him because he's a bit slippy
(I 015). A slippy guy, that (I 087). A slippy
person is one who is hard to get along with
(I 101). One who can trick a person into a big
deal with a slippy tongue (P1-044).

*Many informants regarded this word as substandard.
In the Common Word Survey, 25% chose *slippy* over
slippery to complete the sentence 'Watch out, the
road is ————.'
[From British and Irish] *OED* 1548–1891; *W3*; *EDD* 'In
gen. dial. and colloq. use in Sc. Irel. Eng. and Aus.';
SND 'Gen. Sc.'; *WGE* 'widespread [chiefly *Midlands*].
Probably Low German in origin'; *WNW* 'Colloq. or
Dial.'; *COD* 'colloq.'

slippy axehandles
See **flying axehandles**.

slobby
Adjective. Compare **lolly**, **slob ice**, **slurry**.
Of the sea, covered with a dense, slushy mass of ice fragments, snow and freezing water.
The whole ice is slobby. You'd go right
through it (I 097).

*The definition is quoted from *DNE*.
[From Irish via Newfoundland] *DNE* 1973; *OED*
'muddy' 1854–1897; *EDD* 'muddy, sloppy'; *W3* '1.
muddy 2. slobbery.'

slob ice
Noun. Rare. Compare **lolly**, **slobby**,
slurry.
A sludgy mass of densely packed pieces of sea ice.

Slob ice is 'lolly' that is frozen (I 010). Slob ice is a less common term than 'lolly' (I 014). Holey ice in spring. Ready to disintegrate (I 099).

[From Irish via Newfoundland] *DNE* 1836–1981; *DC*; *OEDS*; *COD*; *GCD* 'Cdn.'; *FW* 'Canadian'; *W3*; *WNW*. *slob*: *OED* 'Chiefly in Irish use or with reference to Ireland. ... Mud, esp. soft mud on the sea-shore; ooze'; *EDD*.

slocum

Noun. Also spelled **slowcome**. Infrequent in Egmont, rare elsewhere; significantly rural.

A slow-moving or slow-thinking person; also a lazy person (II; O).

[From English] *EDD*.

slough

Noun. \slōō\. Also spelled **slew, sloo, slue**. Archaic. Compare **pitch**.

A hollow in an uneven or snow-covered road that causes a vehicle such as a horse-drawn sleigh to lurch sideways.

The mountain road in Maine, where our Gray Dort broke down on our trip east in 1921 was terrible. But it was a boulevard compared to that awful Kentucky detour of hills and sloughs, bumps and rocks (MONTGOMERY, LUCY MAUD, *My Dear Mr. M.: Letters to G.B. MacMillan from L.M. Montgomery*, [1924], 121–22). The younger people went to church twice on Sunday, driving four miles over sandy bumpy roads in the summer, and thro' a snow clogged road in the winter time. They had to contend with 'pitches' and 'slews' and gullies of slush which delighted the children but which must have been nigh to unbearable to both adults and horses (BAGNALL, MARGARET, *When I Was Very Young*, [1964], 1). If the sleigh slipped off the beaten track in soft snow the next sleigh would do the same and the sleighs would all slip sideways until they hit something solid, harder snow for example. The slue is created by the successive passing of sleighs in this manner (II 009). The neighbors had an old 'pung' sleigh and a horse, and they would come along and pick us up [to go to school]. There was her two older sisters, there was two at our house, and there was three at McClure's and two at their house. And there was not room to sit down, so we would stand up on the 'pung' sleigh, and, of course, when there was sloughs we went out as often as we stayed in (T I54).

OED 'A piece of soft, miry, or muddy ground; esp. a place or hole in a road or way filled with wet mud or mire and impassable by heavy vehicles, horses, etc.' 900–1891.

sloven

Noun. Archaic. Occasional in Egmont, infrequent elsewhere; significantly senior. Compare **devil, jigger**.

A long, horse-drawn wagon with the platform slung lower than the axles, close to the ground, formerly used for hauling heavy or awkward loads.

Dug 6 acres potatoes, potatoes are scarce very light crop 38 sloven loads from 17 acres (CAIRNS, SCOTT, *Diary: January 1, 1932–March 31, 1939*, 1938, October 14). The 'sloven,' a low-slung wagon, transported freight to and from the wharves and railway station (RANKIN, ALLAN, *Down at the Shore: A History of Summerside, Prince Edward Island (1752–1945)*, 1980, 57). If you wanted something transported you could go to the area of the corner of Water and Spring streets and there would find another kind of horse-drawn vehicle. These were sluvans, (unsure of spelling) a very low-slung wagon for easy loading (MURPHY, J. ELMER, *A Newspaperman Remembers*, [1980?], 105). Kinked axle and platform near ground. Easier to load spuds on (I 063). Used to use sloven for loading potatoes as one man could walk on quite easily by himself (I 080). I remember seeing local policemen taking a drunkard to jail on one (O).

[Atlantic Provinces] *DC* 1895–1964; *DNE* 1896–1973; *OEDS*.

slump

Noun. Also **slumpy snow**.
   Saggy snow in old drifts.

Mrs. Theodora ... saw two sleighs approaching, the horses of which were going at a gallop. One was trundling down the main road, headlong through old drifts and slumpy snow, where a false step might send the horse floundering to the bottom (MONTGOMERY, LUCY MAUD, *The Doctor's Sweetheart*, [1908], 55). It has been pouring rain all day and this coming on a lot of recent March snow has made fearful slush, slump and mud. The world hereabouts is so ugly that it hurts me to look on it (MONTGOMERY, LUCY MAUD, *Letter to Ephraim Weber*, [1909], 84). Snow after a rain (P2-017). Compressed snow; gone down (P2-031).

slurry

Noun. Also **slur ice**. Rare. Compare **lolly**, **slobby**, **slob ice**.

   Mushy, watery ice; slush.
   Slurry – not quite frozen (I 056). Slush on the streets (II 109). Thin soupy ice (O).

[From English] *OED* '[related to *slur*] … Thin sloppy mud or cement' 1440–1901; *EDD* 'any thin and watery matter'; *GCD* 'a thin mixture of powdered coal, ore, cement, etc. and water'; *COD. Slur: OED*: '[Of obscure origin …] Thin or fluid mud' 1440–1878; *EDD* 'Thin, watery mud; dirt'; *W3; FW. Slur ice: DC* 'Maritimes a thin mixture of mushy ice and water, found especially near shore' 1965.

slut rock

Noun.

   In lobster fishing, a rock used to sink a line of traps.
   We use one rock in each end of the trawl to sink the traps when they are dry and light in the spring. You can pick up any rocks around shore. These are slut rocks (S 4). Slut rocks were two stones tied together and then thrown over the run line to make the line sink at the first of the season (S 6). A rock or block of cement weighing around twenty pounds which is placed at both ends of a dog trawl to cause the sinking in the first day of the season (O).

smelt storm

Noun. Infrequent in Cardigan, rare elsewhere; especially rural, older, male, less educated. Compare **black storm**, **sheep storm**[2].

   A spring snow-storm or wind storm, coinciding with the spawning of smelts.
   I see by all the gulls the smelts are starting to come up the river. We should soon get our smelt storm. It's not spring yet until we've had it (DUFFY, CHARLES, *Lexicon of Beef Farming*, 1986, 17). A smelt storm is just before the smelts come into the harbour the end of April (I 030). In May when the ice has just left the rivers a wind storm takes the ice out and the smelts go to spawn (I 070). In early spring there is often a wind storm that causes the smelts to go up or down stream (O).

*This term scored only 1% in the Common Word Survey against such variants as *spring storm* and *sheep storm*.
[Maritimes] *DC* 1955 'Hants Jnl [Nova Scotia] 9 Mar. 1/5: Last Tuesday we had what some old-timers call the "Smelt Storm," a mixture of snow and rain with the thermometer hovering around the freezing

point … presumably on the theory that the smelt sneak up the rivers … under cover of the snow'; *SSPB2.*

smile

Noun. Informal. Compare **riveter**.
   1. A drink of liquor, especially rum (O).
   2. A slight dint in a car (O).

[North American] *DAE; DA; OED* 'esp. of whiskey'; *DAS* 'To drink, esp. to drink whiskey. Some use C 1850; obs.'; *ML*; 'Do you smile?'

smitch

Noun. Rare.
   The smell or smoke from something burning unexpectedly.
   My father would come home and say, 'What's making the smitch?' (O).

[From English] *OED* 'now dial.'; 893–1880; *EDD.*

snag

Noun, usually in plural. Also **snag rubber**. Rare.
   A short, laced, rubber boot.
   These are gum rubbers, ankle high, with laces and a bellows tongue. Children wore them to school all winter. They had felt insoles (II 009). Between high and low boots. Work-boots for going to the woods. Flat soled; not lined (II 112).

[Maritimes] *DC* 1934.

snap

Noun. Also **snapper**. Informal. Infrequent generally, but unattested in Charlotte-town; significantly male; especially rural, less educated.
   A mouthful of liquor; a drink taken in one draft.
   Have a snap, a quick drink: 'He had a few snaps before I got home' (II 058). We'll go for a snapper (II 061). Whatever you can get out of the bottle in one try (II 065).

EDD 'a slight or hasty meal.'

snap lath

Noun.
   A flexible lath that acts as a catch for the door of a lobster trap.
   A snap lath is what we use to keep the door shut on the trap (S 4). We don't use snap lathes ourselves. I use a piece of a car tire to keep the trap shut (S 5). The snap lath goes

on the top to hold the door closed. We used a 'button' before the snap lath. The snap lath works great after it gets good and wet (S 6).

sneak boat
See **goose boat**.

snib
Noun. Rare. Compare **snib** (verb).
   The hull of a strawberry.
   We're just taking the snibs off them (II 096).

snib
Transitive verb. Infrequent generally, but rare in Summerside and Charlottetown; less educated. Compare **snib** (noun).
   To remove the ends from (strawberries or beans), to hull.
   We're all day snibbing damn berries (II 058).

[From Scottish and northern Irish] EDD 'To cut ... to separate. ... Ant. To cut off small slices from the top ends of potatoes' 1892; SND 'To cut, cut short of or off, curtail, to slice, cut into' 1788–1873.

snig
Transitive and intransitive verb. Archaic.
   Synonym for 'twitch': to drag (logs) out of the woods by horse.
   They'd take a horse into the woods, hitch a chain or rope to it and snig them out to the field (P2-020). We would snig them out in the winter where we could get them in the field. Not used much now because of tractors (P2-021). My husband used to go snigging (P2-030).

[Scottish and northern English] EDD; SND; W3 'chiefly dial.'; DNE 'To haul logs out of woods by hand'; OEDS 'north dial., Austral., N.Z., and Canad. local [origin obscure].'

snollygoster
Noun. Rare. Compare **scut, spleach**.
   An unreliable or unethical person.
   'He's quite an old snollygoster,' my father used to say (I 042).

*This word may be based on *snallygaster*, a mythical creature, part reptile and part bird (W3), though the latter is of more recent appearance in writing (OEDS).
[North American] DA and DAE 1862, 1895; W3 'an unprincipled but shrewd person'; OEDS 'U.S. dial. and slang. A shrewd, unprincipled person, esp. a politician. Also in other more or less fanciful uses' 1846–1972; DAS '1. A politician who relies on oratory

rather than knowledge or ability; a politician who speaks much and does little. 2. An inept, talkative, or unethical lawyer; a shyster. Both uses since C 1860. Mainly dial.'; COD.

snood
Noun. \snood\. Compare **bridle, haul-up**.
   In lobster fishing, the rope that connects a lobster trap to the 'backline,' or main fishing line.
   The snood is the piece of rope that attaches the bridle on the lobster trap to the backline. It is usually not that long (O).

OED 'In sea fishing: one of a number of short lines each carrying a baited hook, attached at regular distances along the main line'; EDD; COD.

snood end
Noun.
   The end of a lobster trap to which the 'snood' is attached.
   The snood end is the end where the 'bridle' is attached to the trap (S 5). The snood end is where the trap is bridled (S 6).

snool
Noun. Rare.
   1. A cringing or subservient person (O).
   2. A sneaking or nosy person (I; O).
Compare **shook**.

*Constance Cullen, in 'Dialect Research on Prince Edward Island,' 1971, found that 20% of her informants in Kinkora (Irish-settled) knew this word; no one knew it in her three other non-Irish communities. Though rare among informants for the Fieldwork Surveys, *snool* was well attested by observers. [From northern Irish and Scottish and northern English] OED 1718–1882; EDD; SND; W3; EDSL; FW.

snotty
Adjective. Informal. Compare **droghey, peevish**.
   Of weather, damp or drizzly.
   After three days of snotty weather, it was good to get out of the house (GOJMERAC, ANNA, *Prince Edward Island Expressions*, 1986, 19).

snow-fighting
Verbal noun. Archaic. Frequent in Egmont, occasional elsewhere; significantly older, male, less educated. Compare **road-breaking**.
   The act of clearing railway tracks of snow after a storm.

In 1926 ... the coal tender was part water. In snowfighting steam from the boiler onto the tender would melt the snow, then more snow would be added to get more water (MAC-DONALD, MARY, and MRS. CLINTON STEWART, *Historical Sketch of Eastern Kings*, 1972, 60). I was 19 days on a train to Tignish and back, snow-fighting all the way. It was wringing wet all the time around the engines and down around the wheels. It was slavish work. The engine took a run at the drifts and then we'd have to get down and dig the old train out, dig the wheels out. And she'd get backed out of that and take another shunt and hit her again and go about half a length of herself and we'd dig her out again. We'd chuck the snow up. One fellow'd chuck it up to another fellow and that fellow'd chuck it farther to another fella. We went as high as five throws before we got it off the track and out of the cut (STEWART, DEBORAH, and DAVID STEWART, *Winter Travel*, 1979, 21). Another activity which involved the men of the community from January to April each winter was snow fighting for the trains. The train engines were not powerful enough to break through the high cuttings following storms and men spent many days each winter shovelling out the trains. Wages paid were $1.00 per day (ANDERSON, WILLIAM, and DORIS ANDERSON, *Reflections on Life on a Farm at St. Peter's at the Turn of the Century*, 1979, 5).

*This term has occasionally been used for clearing roads as well.

sod-soaker
Noun. Compare **gullywasher**.
   See quotation.
   This can happen any time. A 'sod-soaker' is a steady rain that sinks into the soil, whereas a 'gullywasher' runs off into the gullies (I 009).

[North American] *DA* 'That part of the state [Missouri] known as the short grass country needs a sod-soaker' 1923; *OEDS* 1903–1953.

solomon gundy
Noun. Rare.
   A dish of salted herring marinated in vinegar, pickling spices, and onions.
   My husband makes it all the time (I 099). My grandmother used to have it; my brother-in-law made some last year (I 119).

*This word is chiefly associated with Nova Scotia. It is folk etymology for *salmagundi* 'a dish composed of

chopped meat, anchovies, eggs, onions with oil and condiments' (*OED*). *DC* speculates that the nursery rhyme about Solomon Gundy aided the change.
SSPB; *DC* 'N.S.' 1959–1964; *DSUE*; *OED* 1764–1892. *Salmagundi*: *OED* 'of obscure origin' 1674–1892; *DAS* 'Any stewlike concoction, esp. a watery meat and vegetable stew, the vegetables usu. being potatoes.'

sonsy
Adjective. \'sahn-sē\. Also spelled **soncy**.
   Of a woman, buxom and comfortable-looking, pleasant, or jolly.
   In the exigencies of the life they found themselves in ... outside help was required. ... This necessitated outside help in the kitchen as well. On one occasion Mrs. Millar hired a big soncy girl from Grand River ... (MOLLISON, JOHN, *Reminiscent*, 1900, 231). David, as he trudged sorrowfully homeward across the fields, carried with him the mental picture of a plump, sonsy woman, in a trim dress of plum-coloured homespun and ruffled blue-checked apron, haloed by candlelight (MONTGOMERY, LUCY MAUD, *The Doctor's Sweetheart*, [1908], 94). Mrs. Lynde was behind her, sonsy, kindly, matronly, as of yore (MONTGOMERY, LUCY MAUD, *Anne of the Island*, 1915, 69). She was a big, sonsy woman, with full-blown peony cheeks and large, dreamy, brown eyes. When she had been a slim, pink-and-white girl those eyes had been very romantic. Now they were so out of keeping with the rest of her appearance as to be ludicrous (MONTGOMERY, LUCY MAUD, *Further Chronicles of Avonlea*, 1953 [1920], 146). A woman who is fat, jolly, and full of spirit, as in 'The young woman was fat and sonsy' (P2-066).

[From Scottish] *OED*; *EDD*; *SND* 'sometimes also of young children: chubby, sturdy, thriving' 1725–1964; *ESI* 'Irish *sonas*, luck'; *W3*; *COD*; *WNW*; *FW*.

sook
Noun. \sook\. Also **sooky**.
   A person who is acting childishly, or who clings to another.
   He [a retarded boy] was mother's little sooky (O). So I went, like, 'Be a little sooky, and see if I care' (O).

[From Scottish] *SND* 'a child at the breast, a suckling; also extended to unfledged birds and hence fig. applied to persons, feeble in body or mind, silly, foolish' 1832–1920; *OEDS* 'Austral and N.Z. slang.'

... A stupid or timid person; a coward; a softy'; *DAC*; *SSPB* 'crybaby. – Lunenberg. "A sooky baby."'

sour apple quick-step
See **green apple quick-step**.

spach
Noun, usually in plural. \spahk\ Derogatory. Rare. Compare **scow**, **sprog**.
    A big foot or boot.
    Look at the big spachs there (I 020).

[From Irish and Scottish Gaelic] *spag*: *GED* 'Long flat foot. ... Clumsy foot'; *PEDGL*; *IED*. *spaug*: *ESI* 'a big clumsy foot. ... Irish *spag*, same sound and sense.'

spar buoy
See **ice pole**.

spawn
Noun. Also **spawn lobster**. Compare **berried**.
    An egg-bearing lobster.
    The Dept. of Fisheries operated an incubator spawn hatchery in Georgetown. Each fisherman separated the spawn lobsters and placed them in a special container (after he received credit) for them (*The Guardian*, June 2, 1979, 5). In standard definitions, spawn usually refers to the eggs laid by a species. However in lobster fishing, the female lobster carrying the eggs is a spawn or a spawn lobster (ROBERTSON, JANICE, *A Dictionary of Lobster Fishing in the Eastern Kings Area*, 1985, 14). A spawn is the one that got the berries that lays the eggs that become the lobsters (S 4). A spawn is a female lobster ready to lay her eggs. The eggs are usually darkish brown or on some they are green (S 5). A spawn, they call them a 'berried' lobster, a female with eggs on it, you know (S 6).

spider bread
Noun. Archaic.
    Pancake-like bread fried in a spider or frying-pan.
    Spider bread was made early on the Island when the people had only flour and water to cook with (P2-032). Fried dough, eaten in the morning when the supply of baked bread was gone, was known as 'spider bread.' Spider was an old term for frying pan. The fresh dough which had been set the night before was sliced and the pieces fried in the spider. It was eaten with molasses generally (O).

*The word *spider*, as such, 'frying pan with three legs' is common in many North American dialects but has not been attested in this study.
spider-cake: *OED* 'A cake cooked in a spider pan' 1869; *ML*.

spindle tuber
Noun. Compare **blackleg**, **hollow heart**.
    A virus disease of potatoes causing upright tops and thin, spindle-shaped tubers.
    Infected plants have an upright appearance. Acute angles are formed at the junction of the main vine with its branches. The leaves become narrow and the plant may take on an overall grey or slate-colored appearance. Tubers are spindle-shaped and growth cracks are numerous (*Prince Edward Island Potato Handbook*, 1980, 46). While never very common, it was once troublesome in our seed growing areas. It has become much less common in recent years due to movement of healthy stocks from the seed farms (ADVISORY COMMITTEE ON POTATOES, *Atlantic Canada Potato Guide*, 1984, 31). A potato that is long, thin and abnormally shaped . Also called Potato Mosaic (MCCARVILL, LISA, *A Potato Farming Lexicon from Kinkora, P.E.I.*, 1986, n. pag.). Because of the insistence of the Europeans, it has been eliminated from P.E.I. (S 1).

W3.

spleach
Noun. Rare. Compare **scut**, **snollygoster**.
    A disorganized or unreliable person.
    A spleach is impulsive, disorganized, untidy, undependable, and lacking in judgement (O).

*The pronunciation is uncertain.
[Probably from Gaelic.]

spleet-new
Adjective. Rare.
    Perfectly new, brand new.
    Well, *Anne* was accepted; but I had to wait another year before the book was published. Then on June 20th, 1908, I wrote in my journal: 'Today has been, as Anne herself would say, 'an epoch in my life.' My book came to-day, 'spleet-new' from the publishers. I candidly confess that it was to me a proud and wonderful and thrilling moment' (MONTGOMERY, LUCY MAUD, *The Alpine Path: The Story of My Career*, 1917, 77). There lay her book. *Her* book spleet-

new from the publishers. It was a proud, wonderful, thrilling moment (MONTGOMERY, LUCY MAUD, *Emily's Quest*, 1927, 232).

[From Scottish and northern English] *OED*; *EDD*; *SND* 1768–1929; *EDSL*.

splinterkin
Noun, usually in plural. Compare **skiver**, **split**, **swift-stick**.
 A small chip of kindling for starting a fire (P2; O).

splinter: *DAE* 'A thin strip of wood used as a light.'

split
Noun, usually in plural. Archaic. Occasional in Egmont, infrequent elsewhere; significantly older; especially less educated. Compare **skiver**, **splinterkin**, **swift-stick**.
 1. A thin piece of kindling.
 A split is a piece of wood that you cut into strips about half the length of the stick. It catches fire more quickly this way (II 095).
 2. A long shaving of wood used either for a match to light candles, pipes, etc., or for a candle.
 Pitch pine was also carefully gathered to burn at nights for light; the pitch pine blocks were split into long splits to burn instead of tallow candles; the hearth-stone usually had a receptacle for these pine splits; the women did sewing, knitting, and reading by this light (PRINCE EDWARD ISLAND HISTORICAL SOCIETY, *Pioneers on the Island, Part 1*, [1959], 43). Thin pieces of wood, very fine. Used to light candles, pipes. Could be one foot long but very thin (II 016). Years ago they made splits to save matches (II 078).

OED 'a piece of wood separated or formed by splitting' 1617–1875; *DAE*; *W3*; *WNW*; *DNE* 'a thin piece of wood, about 12 to 14 inches long, used chiefly as kindling' 1858–1973; *EDD* 'long, thin pieces of bogwood used as lights. Ant.' 1892.

split-log drag
Noun. Also **log drag**. Archaic.
 A heavy, wooden sledge dragged by two horses, used formerly to scrape and smooth dirt roads.
 It was April, the frost had left our lane rutted and bumpy and we saw the horses had been hitched to the 'Split-Log Drag,' a crude but practical affair of logs separated by several inches and bolted to runners. This meant very

precarious footing for the driver, especially if he had placed two or three heavy stones on board for added weight (the load had to be heavy) (STEWART, MARION, *Marion Stewart's Journal*, 1976, 10). As the settlement grew more men were available to help level the trail and make it wide enough for the two-wheeled carts. The split-log drag was brought into use and later the horse-drawn steel bladed road machines (*A Bridge to the Past: Wilmot Valley, 1784–1979*, 1980, 59). Older residents can remember when road work was done with horse-drawn machines, horse and cart, and split-log drag (GREEN, ALICE, *Footprints on the Sands of Time*, 1980, 63). In later years, of course, they had graders and the machinery, dozers, etc. You know, this was just before the paving. They had some machinery around 1930, but prior to that they just had to use, years ago in the twenties and away back before that, they used a split-log drag (T 182).

*The term *drag*, as such, is standard in this sense.

spouty
Adjective. Rare.
 Of land or ground, so wet as to spout water when walked on, marshy.
 There is no spouty ground here, and if any of it is swampy and wet [where a road is needed], they cut down small soft wood trees, and lay across the bottom as close as one can lie at the side of another, and by casting earth from the sides of the road upon these, make it both firm and durable (JOHNSTONE, WALTER, 'Letters' and 'Travels' Prince Edward Island, 1821, 1955, 122–23).

[From Scottish] *OED*; *EDD*; *SND* 1715–1892; *EDSL*; *W3*.

sprayhouse
Also **sprayshield**. See **doghouse**.

spreckled
Verbal adjective. Occasional in Egmont, infrequent in Cardigan, rare elsewhere; significantly male; especially senior, less educated.
 Speckled, dotted; freckled.
 Spreckled trout have little spots on them (II 107). A spreckled cow has lots of little spots. L.M. Montgomery's brother-in-law was called Roddy Spreck because his father had freckles (O).

[From Scottish and northern English] *OED* 1535–1867; *W3* 'of Scand. origin ... dial. Brit.'; *EDD* [also *spreckle*, verb and noun]; *SND*; *EDSL*; *DJE*.

spring herring
Noun. Compare **fall herring**.
   The alewife or gaspereau.
   We are inclined to believe that what are
called fall herring, is as much a different
species of herring from the Spring herring, as
Winter wheat differs from Summer wheat. It
is in all respects a better article, and we do not
see why merely because it is apparently more
grown, it should be considered the same as the
Spring herring, when there are more marked
differences, not to be so easily accounted for
and reconciled (BAGSTER, BIRCH, *The Progress
and Prospects of Prince Edward Island*, 1861, 96).

[North American] *DC* 'Maritimes' 1861–1924; *DNE*;
OED; *W3*; *DAE* 1839–1911; *DA*.

spring-hole
Noun.
   See quotations.
   The bushes were to guide people [on ice] in
case of a storm or at night, as there were
many spring holes, that a man or horse could
drop into (MACDOUGALL, ARLENE, and VIOLET
MACEACHERN, *The Banks of the Elliott*, 1973, 52).
Then there was pretty Mrs. Morrison who
described with dramatic gestures and soulful
expressions the time her husband, Jim, lost his
way on the ice, and his horse fell into a
spring-hole. The spring-hole is a familiar danger in ice-travel and greatly feared (MACLEOD,
MARGARET, *Four Scripts Inspired by Childhood
Memories in Prince Edward Island*, n.d., [13]).

[North American] *DAE*; *DA* 'an air hole in ice.'

spring moss
Noun. Compare **moss**.
   'Irish moss' harvested in the spring.
   Spring moss is just that, moss gathered in the
spring of the year. Spring moss is lying there
in the water all winter and it gets limp. Spring
moss is poorer quality than moss harvested
in early fall, or late summer (S 10). Spring moss
is moss harvested before mid June. The sea
ice takes it off the rocks and then it comes
ashore. It is not as high in carrageenin content
as moss later in the year (S 11). Spring moss
comes in as soon as the ice leaves. The ice
loosens it by scraping on the bottom. There is a
bit more foreign material in it (S 12).

spring skate
Noun, usually in plural. Archaic. Frequent
in Egmont, occasional elsewhere, but

rare in Charlottetown; significantly older.
Compare **double runner**[1], **stock skate**.
   **A metal ice-skate that clamps on to the
sole of one's boot by means of a spring
and a lever or key.**
   'Spring' skates came next which had a blade
on a metal platform frame that tightened to
the skater's boot by winding a key as on some
present day roller skates. These proved less
awkward than the old 'stocks' (BURT, RONA,
From Roots and Ashes the Gardens Grow, 1979,
13). At first I had spring skates which fastened
on one's boots with clamps and had straps
around the ankles, but I used them only a short
time (GREEN, ALICE, *Footprints on the Sands of
Time*, 1980, 234). In winter we skated there with
our Acme spring skates and scooped smelts
out of the water after the ice melted in April
(INCE, C.C., *Old DeSable*, 1982, 23). Most of us
had what were known as 'spring' skates, which
clamped onto the heels and soles of our
everyday boots. The slightly concave contours
of the blade edges were scarcely conducive
to any degree of speed – which was probably a
good feature. The ponds in our neighborhood
were limited in size, which meant numerous
collisions that could have resulted in injuries,
had we been moving at any speed. Those skates
had a major defect; a tendency to part company
with the boot when the skater made anything
resembling a sharp turn (DEVEREUX, JOSEPH,
Looking Backward, n.d., 44). And across the way
on a large Mill Pond dozens of skaters were
enjoying the shimmering sheet of ice in speed
contests, and some form of hockey on skates
invented by the village blacksmith, made with
files inserted in blocks of wood, straps and
buckles, and known as wood-stocks; they were
preferred over the somewhat useless spring
skate, the only skate that could be bought in
those years (COULSON, MRS. JOHN, *A Phantom
Train*, n.d., 42–43). He skated with his old
fashioned skates with wooden stocks – his
competitors wearing their 'new spring skates'
(CRAPAUD WOMEN'S INSTITUTE, *History of Crapaud*, n.d., 119). They were hard on the heels
of your boots (II 009). Spring on to boots – pretty
near spring the sole off (II 074). Usually a
child's first skates (II 099).

springtime splash
Noun.
   Springtime diarrhea in cows.
   There is also a fall version, caused by eating
mushrooms. I don't know if they are magic
ones or not. However they did cause the cows
to go rather strange (R 23).

sprog

Noun, usually in plural. Also **sproggin**.
Occasional in Egmont, infrequent in Mal-
peque and Cardigan, but unattested in
Summerside and Charlottetown; signifi-
cantly rural; especially older, Irish. See
scow, **spach**.
   An oversized or clumsy foot or boot.
   Get those sprogs out of the kitchen (I 043).
Big old boots: 'Get your sprogs out of here'
(I 053). My mother used this to make the boys
wash their feet: 'Put your sprogs in the water'
(P1-033). Get your sproggins off the table (O).

*R.E. McConnell, in *Our Own Voice: Canadian English
and How It Is Studied*, 1979, 172, reports that this
word is recognized in Irish-settled Kinkora, though
no longer widely used. In British dialects it can mean
'small child' or, in the Services, 'recruit' (*DSUE*).
[From Irish and Scottish Gaelic via Irish and Scottish]
EDD; *SND*; *EDSL*; *DNE*; *DSUE*. spaug: *ESI* 'a big
clumsy foot. ... Irish *spag*, same sound and sense.'
spag: *GED*; *PEDGL*; *IED*.

sprouter

Noun.
   **A machine used to remove premature
sprouts from potatoes.**
   About 200 pieces of equipment are produced;
conveyors, graders, sprouters, dumpers,
and most anything a potato farmer requires
(*Journal-Pioneer Annual Farm Issue*, 1975, 15).
An attachment on a potato-grader consisting
of a series of rollers with projecting rubber
prongs to remove sprouts from potatoes
(MCCARVILL, LISA, *A Potato Farming Lexicon from
Kinkora, P.E.I.*, 1986, n. pag.). It pulls them off
by a series of rollers about an inch apart (S 2).

sprout: *GCD* 'Informal. remove sprouts from'; *FW*.

spruce barrens

Noun. Compare **blueberry barrens**,
cranberry barrens, **fire barrens**.
   **A tract of untillable or burnt-over land
on which scrub spruce trees grow.**
   This afternoon after school Teddy rowed Ilse
and me across the harbour to pick May-flowers
in the spruce barrens up the Green River
(MONTGOMERY, LUCY MAUD, *Emily Climbs*, 1925,
151). The road to the Bay Shore was mostly
down hill, running for part of the way through
spruce 'barrens,' its banks edged with ferns,
sweetsmelling bay bushes, and clusters of scarlet
pigeon-berries (MONTGOMERY, LUCY MAUD, *Pat
of Silver Bush*, 1933, 71).

Barrens, as such, is standard in North America for
any tract of wasteland supporting only low vegetation, 'sometimes with defining terms prefixed, as *pine-
barrens*' (*DAE*).
barrens: *DC* 'in the Atlantic Provinces, an elevated
tract of exposed land that nourishes only scrubby
trees, shrubs, berries, etc. and resembles a moor';
SSPB 'usually a northern word for "tundra," this
word is used in Nova Scotia to describe bogs in which
blueberries, cloudberries, low stunted spruce, and
mosses grow'; *OED* 'In Nova Scotia and New
Brunswick ... an open marshy space in the forest,
sometimes so soft as to be almost impassable, at other
times composed of good solid hard peat.'

spurtle

Noun.
   **A wooden stick for stirring porridge,
berries, etc.; now often a spoon with a
hole** (P2; O).

[From northern Irish and Scottish and northern
English] *OED* 1572–1894; *W3*; *SND*; *FW*; *EDD*.

squamish

Adjective.
   Squeamish, uneasy in the stomach (O).

ML 'the word suggests spleeny [timid about pain] ...
but also carries the sense of stomach uneasiness. It
is reserved for that god-awful moment that precedes
mal de mer.' squalm: *EDD* 'Obs. A dial. form of
"qualm"' Yks, Lin 1896.

squeaking sand

See **singing sand**.

squinteyed head

Noun. Compare **head** (noun).
   **In lobster fishing, one of two 'fishing
heads,' or funnels of twine mesh by
which lobsters enter a trap, offset from
each other instead of directly opposite.**
   Squinteyed heads are two fishing heads.
One is looking one way and one is looking
the other way. They are squinteyed from one
another (S 4).

staff buoy

Noun. Also **lighthouse buoy**.
   **A buoy with a pole standing up from it,
used to mark the end of a line of lobster
traps.**
   Second man gets his gaff as the staff buoy
comes into sight / He hauls it aboard as he
gaffs it just right (FLEMING, RICHARD, *Lobster-*

ing, 1985, 1). A styrofoam buoy that has a wooden staff protruding out of it that has a flag on the top. These usually have some cement on the bottom of them to give them some weight (MACMILLAN, JANET, *The Language of Lobster Fishing*, 1985, 24). A staff buoy is the same as a lighthouse buoy. Usually the staff is still showing in a heavy tide (S 4). The staff buoy is what we use right now. It is a poly buoy with a hole through the centre, with a stick through it (S 5). A staff buoy is just one of these plastic buoys with a staff driven in to make it easier to catch when you are hauling your traps (S 6).

stage
Noun. Archaic.
A wooden platform supported by poles, used for unloading, drying, and processing fish.
It's like a small wharf. Not a permanent structure (II 058). It's not as permanent as a dock. A fisherman built his own on piles. Temporary. Not used today (II 099). Stages were used a lot before cement came into use for wharves. They had them down at Beach Point. They were just poles in the water with a platform to land the fish (S 6). There is a difference between a wharf and a stage. A stage consisted of stakes and posts and a platform to land and do up the fish on (S 13).

[From Newfoundland] *OED*; *OEDS*; *GCD*; *DNE* 1589–1980.*W3* 'an elevated structure used for drying fish'; *DC* 'Esp. Nfld'; *DAE*.

staggy
Adjective.
Of an improperly castrated steer, having the appearance of a mature bull.
If you leave any part of the testes in the scrotum the animal will be staggy (DUFFY, CHARLES, *Lexicon of Beef Farming*, 1986, 17).

W3; *EDD*.

stamp collector
Noun. Informal. Compare **government man**.
One who works only long enough to qualify for Unemployment Insurance (P2; O).

staving
Adjective. Also intensifier in phrase **staving drunk**. Informal. Infrequent in Charlottetown and Cardigan, rare or

unattested elsewhere; significantly younger; especially male.
Very drunk, dead drunk (I; O).

[From Irish] *OED* 1850–1882; *EDD*; *DAE* 1902; *DA* 1862–1902.

stenchel
Noun. Archaic.
A mixture of molasses and water, used especially on porridge.
I heard of this in my younger days, and it was also used as a drink, chiefly in haying time: 1 cup of molasses, 1 cup of vinegar, 2 tbls ginger, 1 gal. water (R 29).

switchel: *W3* '(origin unknown): a drink made of molasses or sometimes honey or maple syrup, water, and sometimes rum and usu. flavoured with ginger and vinegar.'

stepmother's breath
Noun.
A cold draught of wind indoors (O).

[From Irish] *EDD* 'Of weather: coldness, frostiness'; *ESI* p.139 'A chilly day: – "There's a stepmother's breath in the air"'; *DNE*.

stirk
Noun. Infrequent generally, but unattested in Charlottetown; especially middle-aged and older.
A big, clumsy person, a lout.
Look at that big stirk (I 009). A big stirk of a girl (I 042). My mother always called me 'a lazy stirk' (I 052). You overgrown stirk (I 116).

*The standard meaning is 'a heifer between one and two years old.'
[From Scottish] *OED* 1590–1894; *SND*; *EDSL*; *EDD*; *FW*.

stob
Noun. Infrequent in Malpeque and Cardigan, rare elsewhere; significantly male; especially older, less educated.
A splinter in the finger (II; O).

[From Scottish Gaelic via Scottish] *OED*; *EDD*; *SND* 1716–1965; *EDSL*; *DGL*; *GED*; *PEDGL*.

stock skate
Noun, usually in plural. Also **stock, wood-stock, wood-stock skate, wooden-stocked skate**. Archaic. Frequent in

Egmont, infrequent in Cardigan, rare elsewhere; significantly rural, older, male. Compare **double runner**[1], **spring skate**.

A home-made ice-skate consisting of a metal blade inserted into a wooden block or stock, fastened to the shoe with straps and a screw.

The writer still has a pair of 'stock skates' made for him by his father. They consisted of a blade, curled at the front, made by the blacksmith, attached to a wooden 'stock' which was fastened to the shoe by a screw into the heel and by straps (SIMPSON, HAROLD, *Cavendish: Its History, Its People*, 1973, 139). James Pendergast, co-author of this story, relates that his first skates were made by his father in his blacksmith shop. They were called stocks and were made like a sleigh runner with steel shoeing. … In 1900 he bought a pair of stocks, 18 inches long, in Boston (PENDERGAST, JAMES, and GERTRUDE PENDERGAST, *Folklore Prince Edward Island*, [1974], 4). As for ice-skating it existed long before indoor rinks were dreamed of. Just eighty years ago, two sturdy chaps, Robert McStavert and William Small, strapped on their wooden-stocked skates and set forth to have a spin up Wilmot river (MACLEOD, ADA, *Roads to Summerside: The Story of Early Summerside and the Surrounding Area*, 1980, 122). And across the way on a large Mill Pond dozens of skaters were enjoying the shimmering sheet of ice in speed contests, and some form of hockey on skates invented by the village blacksmith, made with files inserted in blocks of wood, straps and buckles, and known as wood-stocks; they were preferred over the somewhat useless spring skate, the only skate that could be bought in those years (COULSON, MRS. JOHN, *A Phantom Train*, n.d., 42–43). Stock skates have wood and straps. You can't do anything with them (II 003). They were a piece of wood with a blade put in them, and they were strapped on your boots; wood-stock skates is what we called them (P2-031).

stog
Transitive verb. Often in expression **to stog one's face or mouth**. Common; especially under thirty. Compare **stoggings**.
  1. To stuff completely with food.
  There she goes, stogging her mouth again (I 001). He's great for stogging his face (I 049). [Of animals:] Stog them with grain before you sell them (I 058). Don't stog your mouth so full when you're trying to talk (I 076).

  2. To stuff or dress (a fowl) (I).
  3. To stuff (a crack, a drain, or other opening).
  Stog a junk of rag in the window (I 056).

[From English] *DC* [sense 3] 'Esp. Nfld.' 1835, 1937; *DNE*; *SSPB*; *EDD*; *OEDS*.

stoggings
Noun. Compare **stog**.
  Stuffing or dressing for a fowl (I; P1).

stone bucket
Noun.
  A container on a potato digger for collecting debris to be dumped.
  A bucket attached to the digger which collects stones and other unwanted heavy objects from the potatoes. This is emptied at the end of each row (MCCARVILL, LISA, *A Potato Farming Lexicon from Kinkora, P.E.I.*, 1986, n. pag.).

stormstayed
Verbal adjective, usually in phrase **to be or get stormstayed**. Also spelled **stormstaid**, **storm-stayed**. Common.
  Unable to leave a place because of bad weather, especially a heavy snow-storm or drifting snow.
  Snowing fast. We shall get but very few at Ch. [church] today. About dozen came. Had service. Preached from Heb. I, 1,2. When we came out of Ch. it was blowing and snowing and drifting. … Very bad after dinner. No going to Alberton. I am storm-stayed. Roads filled up. Stayed all night (DYER, ROBERT, *Diary 1859–1883*, 1877, March 18). Albert Miller here to dinner and started home, having been stormstayed since Thursday night (WOODMAN, SUSAN, *Diary: January 1, 1895–December 31, 1896*, 1895, December 7). 'I haven't been turned out,' grinned Mary, as she stepped in and shut her door. 'I came up to Carter Flagg's two days ago and I've been stormstayed there ever since. But old Abbie Flagg got on my nerves at last, and tonight I just made up my mind to come up here. I thought I could wade this far but I can tell you it was as much as a bargain. Once I thought I was stuck for keeps. Ain't it an awful night?' (MONTGOMERY, LUCY MAUD, *Rilla of Ingleside*, [1920], 207). Didn't make any difference to him, snow or anything else, no, didn't bother him any. [He didn't get stormstayed], not when he could move at all (HORNBY, SUSAN, *George Young: Horsing Around*, 1981, 32 [brackets

in original]). We were bothered a lot, you
know, with people coming in in the evening
and getting stormstayed when they'd arrive
at the station and we'd have to keep them and
bed them down, you know, until they got a
way out after the storm (T M61). You are
'stormstayed' when you are at a place and
can't leave because of a snowstorm and are
supposed to be some place else. You are
'stormstayed at home' if there is a party in
Charlottetown that you can't get to. Negative
feelings. Or you can be stormstayed at the party
and unable to return home. If it's a thriving
party, this can have positive feelings (O).

*The Common Word Survey offered a choice among
stormstayed, snowed in, and *snowbound*; 77% of the
informants chose *stormstayed.* However some
speakers prefer to reserve the word for being kept
away from home, using one of the alternatives, or
stormed in, for being kept *at* home.
[From Scottish and northern English] *OED* 1491–1880;
EDD; SND; EDSL; SSPB.

storm-tossed moss
Noun.
    **A synonym for 'shore moss': 'Irish
moss' as harvested at the sea-shore after
it has been washed up by a storm.**
    Stormtossed moss is gathered from the surf.
Horses are still used for this operation, but
will probably disappear with increasing mechanization (FFRENCH, A., *A Current Appraisal
of the Irish Moss Industry,* 1970, 13). In certain
areas, ... where harvesting is primarily of
storm-tossed moss, the method has not changed
over the years. ... The moss is gathered by
ordinary rakes from the shore or the surf closely
adjoining the shoreline. The major problem
underlying consideration of any sort of mechanization is the lack of a symmetrical pattern
when moss may be harvested. Under this
method, harvesting becomes a function of the
weather elements (*ibid,* 77). Storm-tossed moss
is the moss tossed on shore after a storm. It is
moss that has been loosened up and blown
ashore (S 10). Storm-tossed moss is cast on
shore by storm and wave action (S 12).

stouk
Noun. \stōōk\. Compare **gommie, kittardy,
nosic, omadan, oshick.**
    A stupid person (O).

[From Irish and Scottish and northern English] *EDD.*

strap
Noun. Archaic.
    **A job on the amphibious 'ice-boats' that
plied across the Northumberland Strait
in winter before the establishment of
powered ferries.**
    About his 'first strap' – the men hauled the
boats across the 'board' ice, with straps like
harnesses, around their bodies – the captain is
drily ironical. A liberal [sic] government was
enthroned in Charlottetown. 'I was twenty,' he
relates, 'and there was an election that year,
and our neighbor here, he had the contract of
haulin' the boats out. He was a Liberal, and
he got at me to go up and vote. Well, father
always voted Conservative. But I thought to
please this neighbor I'll go up an' vote. I was
two days from bein' of age and I thought
they'd turn me down. It was an open vote then.
I went in, and they asked me who I was goin' to
vote for, and I told them, and they never said yes
or no, so that winter my neighbor asked me if I
wanted a regular strap' (LEDWELL, FRANK, and
RESHARD GOOL, *Portraits and Gastroscopes,* 1972,
29).

strawberry run
Noun. Rare. Compare **lilac run.**
    **A run of sea trout or mackerel upstream
early in July, coinciding with the strawberry season.**
    What foods there were! Oysters for the pick-
ing, and clams. Spring brought the Alewives,
the boney Gaspereaux, in from the reaches, pink
sea trout too, in the 'strawberry run,' and come
Autumn as well, lads with wisdom not learned
of school, angled happily, and 'Somewhere'
speared the big ones (DIXON, MARGARET, *Going
Home: An Autobiography,* 1979, 176). He's using
streamers, red Ibis and shrimp, to lure what
he expects to be the tail end of the 'strawberry
run' below the old West River Bridge at St.
Catherine's (*The Guardian,* August 5, 1980, 1).

[North American] *DA* 'local' 1891.

streaky
Adjective.
    Of weather, changeable, uncertain.
    It was what Susan called a streaky winter ... all
thaws and freezes that kept Ingleside decorated
with fantastic fringes of icicles (MONTGOMERY,
LUCY MAUD, *Anne of Ingleside,* [1939], 68).

OED; EDD.

streel
Noun. Also **sthreel, streal, streeler** and adjectives **streely, strooly**. Impolite. Infrequent in all groups; significantly Irish; especially senior.
1. A slovenly or untidy woman.
Come on, you big streel (I 010). 'Streely' applies to hair more than anything else (I 017). She is a real strooly person, not a bit tidy (P2-095).
2. A woman of low character.
And when you all get together [in hell] you'll have glorious fun, / There'll be Monaghans, streals, yourself and Old Dunn. / Each one with a club smashing brimstone ... (IVES, EDWARD, *Larry Gorman: The Man Who Made the Songs*, 1977 [1964], 45). A streel has moral connotations, like a loose woman (I 013). Nothing but a streel, running the roads and not doing too much work (I 041). 'That one's a pure streel' – worst thing you could be called (I 099).

[From Irish Gaelic via Irish] *OED* 1839–1892; *OEDS* 'chiefly Anglo-Ir.'; *W3*; *EDD*; *ESI*; *DNE* 1937–1968; *IED*.

striking party
Noun. Historical. Compare **cooligan**.
See quotation.
The early settlers had few holidays.·... New Year's Day was the great day of the year. On the Eve of that day 'striking parties,' composed of young folk of the district, armed with sticks, marched through the settlement. When they arrived at a house they surrounded it, and to the accompaniment of music from the sticks beating the log walls, vigorously sang a Gaelic refrain. ... 'Get up an gie us oor hogmanay.' If, as happened but rarely, there was no 'Scotch' on hand, they were given cakes. ... When log houses were replaced by shingled ones, these parties were discouraged and finally abandoned (MACQUEEN, MALCOLM, *Skye Pioneers and 'The Island,'* 1929, 71).

DC 'Maritimes' [citing MacQueen only].

string
Noun.
In lobster fishing, several 'dog trawls,' or settings of lobster traps, placed in a straight line, one behind the other.
Each area surveyed was fished at least 2 to 3 days before moving on. As each string was fished it was loaded aboard and all were reset in the same general area or on different ground depending on that day's catch (PRINCE EDWARD ISLAND, DEPARTMENT OF FISHERIES,

Offshore Lobster: Technical Report #175, 1975, 1975, 4). A set of trawls which have been placed in a straight line. Often a fisherman will refer to his 'inside' string or his 'outside' string (ROBERTSON, JANICE, *A Dictionary of Lobster Fishing in the Eastern Kings Area*, 1985, 15). A string is a line of 'dog trawls' one 'dump' right after another. It makes it easier to find your 'dump' if you fish an 'inside' and 'outside' string instead of scattering them (S 4). Half a dozen or so 'dog trawls' in a straight line is a string of traps (S 5). A string is a bunch of 'dumps' placed in a straight line. You always put them out in strings but they soon get scattered around (S 6).

stripper
Noun. Frequent in Cardigan, infrequent elsewhere; significantly rural, older; especially male.
A cow that is giving little or no milk.
A lady bought a milk separator and then wanted to take it back. This went to court. Her reason was 'We have nothing but a bunch of strippers' (I 064).

*To strip (a cow) 'to milk dry' is standard.
[From English and Irish] *OED* 1856; *OEDS*; *EDD*; *W3*.

strunt
Noun. Often in expressions **get, have, pull, or take a strunt (on)**. Also adjective **strunty**. Occasional in Egmont, infrequent elsewhere, but unattested in Charlottetown. Compare **strunt** (verb).
A fit of ill humour or sulkiness.
Boy, you've got a strunt on today (I 061). A stubborn child would take a strunt (I 121).

[From northern Irish and Scottish and northern English] *OED* 1721–1895; *EDD*; *SND*; *ESI*; *W3*; *FW*.

strunt
Intransitive verb. Also verbal adjective **strunted**. Compare **strunt** (noun).
To sulk, take offence, be in ill humour.
He's mad; he's strunting along (I 110).

[From northern Irish and Scottish and northern English.]

strupac
Noun. Also spelled **strupak**. Archaic. Rare.
A cup of tea and something to eat; tea-time, either at mid-afternoon or at the end of the evening.

The latter part of the evening, old and young took part in singing the old songs, expressive of the character of the people and the conditions of the times. Then the 'strupac,' or tea hour would come along with the scones, molasses and other condiments. The departure for home, and the warm friendly handshakes and affectionate hearty goodbyes and 'God bless you' terms followed (SHAW, WALTER, *Tell Me the Tales*, 1975, 43). On this particular occasion, a friendly neighbor had called and was having a tasty 'strupac' in mid-afternoon (*ibid*, 83).

[From Scottish Gaelic] *SND. strupag: GED* 'Little drop of spirits.'

stump

Transitive verb. Usually applied to children. Frequent in Charlottetown, rare elsewhere; significantly urban.

To play on (broken ice), especially to jump from cake to cake.

We used to go stumping 'cakes.' Hopped or poled around on them like a raft (P1-046).

stump fence

Noun. Sometimes in phrase **as homely (or ugly) as a stump fence**. Archaic.

A fence consisting of a line of the stumps pulled up when the land was cleared.

Warm, burning bush, fire got in stump fence (CAIRNS, SCOTT, *Diary: January 1, 1932–March 31, 1939*, 1932, December 30). 'Ugly as a stump fence' is a well-known phrase, fraught with meaning for any Canadian. For, truly, stump fences are most delightfully and decidedly ugly – like the English bulldog. Now they are scarce in this land. We cycled for miles, almost in despair, before we saw a stump fence. True, it was not beautiful. The stumps were thrown together in rows, their roots piteously pawing the empty air. Tangled and uneven, they lay there like giant molars extracted from the bleeding earth (CHAMPION, HELEN, *Over on the Island*, 1939, 181). Skating parties were held on the swamp ... or Clark's millpond. Huge bonfires were made using pine stumps and the gaps in the stump fences were not noticed until the cattle broke out the following summer (*A Bridge to the Past: Wilmot Valley, 1784–1979*, 1980, 121). This picture [*A Wilderness Farm, P.E.I., 1832*, by A.L. Morrison] depicts a primitive farm in Prince Edward Island. It illustrates an early method of fencing with large stumps which have been dug out of the ground three or four years after the felling of the trees. There was an old saying on the island in bygone days, that 'so and so was as homely as a stump fence' (MORRISON, A.L., *My Island Pictures: The Story of Prince Edward Island*, 1980, 17).

[North American] *OED* 1897; *DC* 1932–1963; *DA*; *DAE*; *SSPB2* [see *homely*].

stumping

Verbal noun.

See quotation.

In that year [1905], Mortimer Jordan, of Guernsey Cove rented the fish house building and converted it into a lobster processing plant. ... James Mackenzie remembers working in this factory for 50 cents per day during two seasons. His job was known as 'stumping' breaking off lobster tails and claws (DALY, WHITMAN, *Prince Edward Island – The Way It Was*, 1978, 7).

sugan

Noun. \'sōo-gən\.

See quotation.

As there are no natural resources on the Island, except the forest and soil, there is no manufacturing. As a result, the level of material prosperity has been low and people have had to do without many things considered necessary elsewhere. For instance, the farmer, lacking wire and hemp, made rope of grass or straw, called 'sugan,' for use in protecting his stacks from the gales that lash the coast. A handful of material was hooked over the end teeth of a hand rake, which was then twirled by a man retreating from the person feeding the material to the lengthening cord. Two or three lengths of this rope were thrown across the stack with pieces of fence rail attached to the ends to weigh them down (MACQUEEN, MALCOLM, *Hebridean Pioneers*, 1957, 25).

[From Irish and Scottish Gaelic] *OED*; *OEDS*; *W3*; *ESI*; *DA*; *PEDGL*; *DGL*; *IED*.

sugar string

Noun. Archaic. Compare **tea twine**.

Ordinary twine used initally to wrap sugar but then saved for general purposes.

The storekeepers in the old days used to weigh out the sugar and then tie it with a string; we saved it (P2-038).

summer complaint

Noun.

Diarrhea, especially in children in hot weather.

For upset stomach and diarrhea (called summer complaint) the remedies were simple and effective (MACDONALD, BERTHA, *Through All the Days Gone By*, [1983?], 55).

[North American] *DA* 'colloq.' 1847–1944; *DAE*; *W3*.

summer kitchen
See **back kitchen**.

sunburn
Noun.
A green discoloration of potatoes caused by exposure to sunlight.
The processor does have lower size limits and he usually has certain tolerances for smalls as well as for certain defects such as off-type, sunburn, bruises and rot (KHATTAK, JAHAN, and WILLIAM LEWIS, *Growing Potatoes for Processing on Prince Edward Island*, 1971, 18–19). Sunburn can take place in the field if a potato is growing too close to the ground or wind or erosion causes soil loss and tubers turn green. It can happen in a warehouse if light enters (S 1). We never had a lot of trouble with sunburn after we learned how to store potatoes properly. Sunburn is something that your cultivating practice can have a lot to do with (S 2).

OED; *W3*.

swift-stick
Noun. Compare **skiver, splinterkin, split**.
A thin sliver of kindling that makes a ready fire.
Wet forenoon, thinning turnips afternoon, made swift-sticks for Mamma (CAIRNS, SCOTT, *Diary: January 1, 1909–May 31, 1920*, 1909, July 21).

swinge
Transitive verb. Infrequent in Egmont and Cardigan, rare elsewhere; significantly less educated; especially older.
To scald or scorch the feathers off (a chicken) (I).

[From British and Irish] *OED*; *W3*; *EDD*; *DNE* 'To singe, scorch; to burn the down off sea-birds after plucking the feathers' 1896–1976; *DBE* 'to singe or scorch'; *DJE* 'phon var. of *singe*.'

T

tablestock Noun. Also spelled **table stock**. Compare **processing potato**.

A grade of potatoes sold for home consumption.
Tablestock potatoes are stored separate from seed potatoes. ... Prince Edward Island ships a much higher portion of its total crop to the tablestock market than most other potato growing regions (MCCABE, WAYNE, *Potato Wash and Wax Test*, 1974, 5). Home gardeners often plant table stocks obtained at a supermarket (CANADA DEPARTMENT OF AGRICULTURE, *Growing Garden Potatoes*, 1976, 7). Very dry potatoes are good tablestock (S 2). Tablestock potatoes are sold to the consumer in raw unprocessed form (S 3).

tail-shaker
Noun. Archaic. Compare **thrash chain**.
A vibrating extension on an old-fashioned 'elevator' potato digger that separated tops and debris from the potatoes.
The set of rollers at the top of the digger that pulls off potatoes. Applies more so to horse-drawn diggers (MCCARVILL, LISA, *A Potato Farming Lexicon from Kinkora, P.E.I.*, 1986, n. pag.). The rear section of an elevated digger served as an additional chain and the soil would drop through and the tubers would end up on top of the ground (S 1). On the first diggers, the back vibrated and let a lot of the clay out and brought the tops out (S 2).

take up
Intransitive phrasal verb.
To take another serving of food.
To put a little more on your plate (P2-031). 'Take up now,' my Aunt Margaret used to say (O).

tallyboard
See **dog trawl board**.

targer
Noun. \'tahr-jur\. Rare.
A person, especially a woman, who scolds or quarrels.
She's a real old targer (I 003). A targer is someone who is always giving someone else a dressing down (I 019). Always cranky and finding fault (I 095). They figure I'm a targer because I'm strict. I want things done my way (I 117).

[From northern Irish and Scottish and northern English] *OED*; *EDD*. *targe* [noun]: *SND* 'A violent scolding woman, a shrew, a virago.' *targe* [verb]: *W3* 'chiefly Scot: beat, scold'; *OED*; *EDD*; *SND*.

taties and point
See **potatoes and point**.

taxi-driver
Noun.
 The sculpin, a bony and usually scaleless fish with a spiny head (family Cottidae).
 A small fish with sharp prongs sticking out of the head as protection. This originated in the Souris area from the small groundfish draggers. If walked on they stick to your boot, hence 'taxi-driver' (O).

*This term is reported from Cape Breton as applying to the pollock, a food fish of the cod family.

team boat
Noun. Historical.
 A paddle ferry propelled by two horses.
 Ie a faint recollection of when I was a child of crossing [the Hillsborough River between Charlottetown and Southport] on a side-wheel paddle boat, the motive power of which came from a pair of horses going round and round on a kind of treadmill (BREMNER, BENJAMIN, *Memories of Long Ago: Being a Series of Sketches Pertaining to Charlottetown in the Past*, 1930, 21). There was also, in the 1860s, a steam service at frequent intervals during the day from Charlottetown southeast across the harbour to Southport (the connection of Charlottetown with eastern and southeastern Queens County), replacing a variety of experimental craft including an interesting tread-mill paddle-wheel craft, of about 1850, powered by horses, which was somewhat humorously, but accurately, described as a 'team-boat' (CLARK, ANDREW, *Three Centuries and the Island: A Historical Geography of Settlement and Agriculture in Prince Edward Island, Canada*, 1959, 144).

[North American] *DC* 1825–1835; *OED*; *W3*; *DAE*; *DA*.

tea party
Noun. Also **tea**. Archaic. Compare **saloon**.
 A large, all-day picnic, usually church-sponsored to raise money, at which food was sold or auctioned, and games, music, and dancing were featured.
 The Drill and Tea Party of the Scotia Volunteers ... came off on Thursday last, at Rustico. ... Under a double line of arbors formed of young trees, bent over and covered with green boughs, were spread tables plenti-

fully covered with viands suitable to the taste of the company (*The Islander*, July 31, 1860). The Tea Party held on the beautiful Chapel grounds at the head of St. Peter's Bay on Wednesday last, was a very successful affair in every respect. The concourse present was not much, if at all, under three thousand. ... The party was given for the purpose of realizing funds to be applied towards the building of a new Chapel. ... Nearly every Protestant of any influence or standing – not merely residents of St. Peter's, but residents of other localities for twenty miles around – aided by their presence and their purse the interesting affair – several of the large and splendid collection of Cakes having been contributed by Protestant ladies (*The Examiner*, July 10, 1865). I went to the tea party at East Point today. ... It was fun getting ready putting boughs around the outside of the 'saloons' and setting up the tables this morning. I helped the women bake some cakes, cookies, and apple pies which were on the long tables. ... Father tended the 'saloon' dishing out apple cider which was so delicious I must have had at least four helpings (BUSHEY, SARAH, *Memoirs of Sarah Bushey*, 1892, August 9). 'Tea parties' were held outdoors during the summer as money-making activities. The tables, laden with food, were surrounded by trees and boughs were placed above the tables to shield them from the sun and wind. A 'saloon' for dancing, complete with music, was an important part of the tea party (ANDERSON, WILLIAM, and DORIS ANDERSON, *Reflections on Life on a Farm at St. Peter's at the Turn of the Century*, 1979, 7).

tea twine
Noun. Archaic. Compare **sugar string**.
 Ordinary twine used initially to wrap tea but saved for general purposes (O).

[From Scottish] *SND* 1901.

teddy
Noun, often in phrase **a teddy of shine**. Archaic. Frequent in Cardigan, occasional in Charlottetown and Malpeque, infrequent elsewhere; significantly male. Compare **dish**[1], **long necker**, **pup**.
 1. A long-necked, twelve to sixteen ounce bottle, commonly a beer bottle, usually as used for illicit alcohol.
 I seen Harry Coulson coming here one night and the horse was, oh, just like a bellows. He had a teddy, got some kerosene and baking

soda from the wife here and made a big 'jollop' for him and give it to him (HORNBY, SUSAN, *George Young: Horsing Around*, 1981, 32). In my dearth, I doubtless appreciated her donations as much as my father welcomed visits from friends with a 'teddy' in their pockets and hospitality in their hearts. For both generations, it was a dry, dry time in those prohibition years (MACQUARRIE, HEATH, *Recollections of His Early Childhood and Society on Prince Edward Island*, 1985, 4). Offered him a nip to raise his droopin' spirits. / ... I left the teddy in the toilet (LEDWELL, FRANK, *The North Shore of Home*, 1986, 140–41). They still go to the bootleggers for a teddy (I 011). Teddy was the old name for beer bottles. They were made of green glass and had sloping sides (I 031). A small bottle from bootlegging days. Guys used to stand on the street in Summerside calling 'teddies and quarts,' meaning they had them for sale (I 063). They'd brew it and bottle it, put it in teddies or a gallon, whatever you wanted. You'd get a gallon for six dollars, you'd get a teddy for a dollar and a half, a thirteen ounce bottle. ... I remember when you'd get a teddy for seventy-five cents (T B14). A fellow wanted a teddy of rum or a bottle of rum or whatever he wanted (O). In some areas it was identified with the old green beer bottles, but it was a teddy when filled with shine (O).

2. A rough measure of liquid, equal to the amount held by a teddy.

My husband uses teddy as a measure, especially with older farmers. 'Give that cow about a teddy of water' (I 017). A teddy of shine. Any hard liquor you got in a gallon, you poured into twelve ounce bottles. Twelve teddies and a half in a gallon (I 056). A half quart or a pint (I 059).

*This term was associated by some informants both with bootlegging and with bribery during elections.

teeth sweep
Noun.
   In scallop fishing, iron prongs or teeth attached to the front of a 'chain sweep' or drag net.
   The same as a 'chain sweep' only there are long spikes or teeth in the front of the bag, used for muddy or mucky bottoms (KENNEDY, LIBBY, *A Visitor's Guide to the Language of the Wharf*, 1985, 8). A teeth sweep is the spikes in a scallop drag which pick up the shells off the bottom (S 6).

ten-gallon
Adjective phrase. Humorous. Compare **five-gallon.**
   Of a social occasion, especially a wake or funeral, lavish or well-attended.
   You'd come in and get your drink, there'd be five-gallon and ten-gallon funerals. The ten-gallon funeral'd be the big one. You wouldn't want to miss that one. But you had to get an invitation (T B14). Referring to the size of booze container at said wake or funeral (R 13). This is a common term for size and could be applied to many things, such as a ten-gallon celebration (R 20).

thin
Adjective.
   Of the wind: cold, sharp, piercing (O).

[From English and Irish] *EDD.*

thirty-day cake
See **friendship cake.**

thorncod
Noun.
   The tomcod (genus *Microgadus*).
   They [the people of St. Peter's Harbour] have also a vast quantity of plaice, thorncods, carbels, mackerels and herrings (WARBURTON, A.B., *A History of Prince Edward Island from Its Discovery in 1534 until the Departure of Lieutenant-Governor Ready in A.D. 1831*, 1923, 57). Tommy cod, you catch them in the smelt nets. The Indians used to eat them (P2-032).

thra
Noun, often in phrase **old thra.** \tra\. Also spelled **thrae, thragh, trah, treagh.** Rare. Compare **thra** (verb).
   1. A complainer; a bore, a waster of time.
   In Irish-oriented communities, such as Kelly's Cross and Emyvale, there was a variety of Gaelic words in daily use. A boring, tiresome, or argumentative person was described as a 'thragh' (DEVEREUX, JOSEPH, *Looking Backward*, n.d., 117–18). My mother would use it for someone who is kind of a bore (I 015). Thra is an Irish word. Not complaining but being a nuisance by monopolizing your time (I 019). They talked a lot. Tiresome. An old thra (I 055). My husband says, 'She's just an old thra' (I 112). Sort of referring to a person whose conversation was not very interesting, a gossiper (O). A no-account fellow (O).

2. An untidy or dirty person, a sloven (O).

*Constance Cullen, in 'Dialect Research on Prince
Edward Island,' found this word known by 20%
of her (Irish) Kinkora sample, but unknown to her
other three (non-Irish) communities.
[From Irish and Scottish Gaelic] *traill: IED* 'a thrall, a
wretch, a time-server, a dirty old woman'; *PEDGL.*

thra
Intransitive verb. Compare **thra** (noun).
   To complain.
   All they did was thra all the time (I 110).

[From Irish and Scottish Gaelic.]

thrash chain
Noun. Compare **tail shaker**.
   **A chain on a potato digger that removes
the tops from the potatoes.**
   A chain made of long rods on the back of the
digger which pulls stalks off the 'apron' and
deposits them on the ground (MCCARVILL, LISA,
A Potato Farming Lexicon from Kinkora, P.E.I.,
1986, n. pag.) The thrash chain, when it goes
over the bed, lets the tops, couch, and weeds
out of the potatoes (S 2).

threap
Intransitive verb. Rare.
   To nag; to bicker or dispute.
   I've always threaped at your father to send
you to school – learning at home ain't the
same thing – but he wouldn't listen to me, of
course (MONTGOMERY, LUCY MAUD, *Emily of
New Moon*, 1923, 22). To 'threap right down'
means to try to get a point across (II 046).

[From British and Irish] *OED* 1200–1873; *W3*; *EDD*;
EDSL; *ESI*; *FW*; *WNW*.

three-bow trap
See **bow trap**.

three-prong drag
Noun. Archaic. Compare **graip** (noun).
   **An old-fashioned hand digger for
harvesting potatoes.**
   In the fall, potatoes were ploughed out,
scratched by hand from the furrow, picked
into buckets or baskets, hauled from the field in
a cart, and dumped into the cellar. Sometimes,
a three-prong drag was used by one person to
remove the potatoes from the ground while
another followed behind to do the picking up
(MACNEVIN, MRS. LORNE, *Past and Present: A
History of Brae*, 1979, 27). A three-prong drag is

an old-fashioned harvester, an old top beater,
shaped like a hoe with prongs used for digging
(S 3).

three-stack marsh
Noun.
   See quotation.
   The importance of the marsh is reflected in
the many old deeds that designated parts of
it as belonging to certain farms. Dykes were still
in existence when my mother-in-law helped
her father make marsh hay. She recalls that the
marshes were named by the number of stacks
they were expected to produce, such as a 'three
stack marsh' or a 'five stack marsh' (HOWATT,
BETTY, *History Begins at Home*, 1981, 24–25).

throughother
Noun. Compare **throughother** (adjective).
   A disorganized, untidy housekeeper.
   A throughother is someone who is sloppy,
who doesn't do things right, and really
doesn't care (I 030). Topsy-turvy, or having
trouble keeping work done on schedule (O).

*R.E. McConnell, in *Our Own Voice: Canadian English
and How It Is Studied*, 1979, 172, reports that this
word is known in Irish areas of Prince Edward Island
but is no longer widely used.
[From northern Irish and Scottish and northern
English.]

throughother
Adjective. Also **throughotherish**. Rare.
Compare **throughother** (noun).
   Of a house, untidy, in disorder.
   'Things all throughother' was used to
describe the mess and confusion (I 063). 'The
house was very throughother.' 'Everything
looked very throughother' (I 084). No order
to anything (P1-034).

[From northern Irish and Scottish and northern
English] *OED* 1596–1880; *OEDS*; *W3* 'chiefly Scot.';
EDD; *SND*; *EDSL. throughother* [verb] *DAE* 'To con-
fuse' 1862.

throwing axehandles, the
See **flying axehandles**.

thunderjug
Noun. Also **thunderbowl**. Humorous.
Occasional in Charlottetown, infrequent
elsewhere, but unattested in Summerside;
significantly older. Compare **chamberdish,
charlie, dish², thundermug**.
   1. A jug for alcohol.

A thunderjug was a crock for booze (I 017). The term thunderjug is used if you are telling a story or joke (I 100).

2. A 'thundermug' or chamber-pot.

At that time there was no bathrooms or washrooms or anything in those farmhouses; there wasn't even a sink. What they usually had was a washbasin on a small cupboard or something in the kitchen, and a thunderjug under the bed! (CAMPBELL, FRANK, *As the Fella Says ...* , 1983, 97). The boys used to call it a thunderjug (I 070).

thundermug

Noun. Also **thunderbowl**. Humorous. Compare **chamberdish, charlie, dish², thunderjug**.

A chamber-pot.

Hallowe'en was a great event. We'd plan for weeks. One year stands out in my imagination. We threw a turnip through a neighbour's up-stairs window. The window was open, and the turnip hit the 'thunder mug' dead centre. First we heard a splash. Then a crash! (FREETOWN HISTORICAL SOCIETY, *Freetown Past and Present*, 1985, 176).

DSUE 'low: C18–mid-19. Ex noise therein caused'; *OEDS*.

tickle fish

Noun. Humorous. Infrequent in Egmont and Charlottetown, rare elsewhere.

A tiny fish close to shore; a minnow.

They're mostly at the south shore (II 110). Small fish along beach in warm shore water. Look like shrimp (O). They tickle you when you're swimming (O).

*The word may come from the Newfoundland *tickle* 'a narrow saltwater strait' (*DNE*), but more prob-ably it describes the sensation from such fish for swimmers.

tidewash ice

Noun. Infrequent in Egmont and Summer-side, rare elsewhere.

Lolly or soft ice deposited on shore by the tide.

Tidewash ice is found where the tide comes in and out on the beach. It isn't very solid (II 019). The ice changes every six hours. So there are four changes in appearance on one day. Changes pattern of shoreline (II 039).

tight

Adjective. Rare.

Of the sky, overcast, cloudy.

An overcast, humid, muggy day (II 011). In Rustico, it means cloudy. Used by fishermen (O).

DNE 'Of the air, close, stuffy.'

Tignish hush puppy

Noun. Humorous.

A rubber boot (O).

*For Tignish, see map, p. xviii.

tilt

Noun. Also **tilting board, tilter**. Common in Egmont and Malpeque, frequent else-where; significantly less educated; infre-quent under thirty. Compare **tilt** (verb).

A board used for a home-made seesaw or teeter-totter.

It was a board and a block of wood, as opposed to a new kind of teeter-totter (I 011). A board on a block (I 051).

GCD, 1973, labels *tilt* as 'Maritimes.' The 1983 edition does not include this word. *WGUS* says '*Tilt*, *tilting board* ... is the regular term for the seesaw in Southeastern New England (from the islands in Narraganset Bay eastward). This term occurs also in Essex County. In the coast towns of New Hampshire and Maine the variant *tilter, tilter board* is current, which is probably a blend of the Cape Cod term *tilt* and the Massachusetts Bay term *teeter*.' *tilter*: *OEDS* 'A see-saw' U.S.; *DAE* 1727–1891; *DA*.

tilt

Intransitive verb. Compare **tilt** (noun).

To play on a seesaw or teeter-totter.

I've seen men and boys tilting at picnics. Not a planned thing. They'd just grab a board and do it (I 030). Would you like to tilt? (I 120).

time

Noun. Common generally, but frequent in Summerside, infrequent in Charlottetown; especially rural.

A party or community gathering, es-pecially in celebration of some occasion, such as a marriage, anniversary, or grad-uation.

No invitation was for him. He really knew not why. / It made him so infernal mad, he swore to match his foes / To get up a ten-dollar time (*The Opposition Break-down*, [1898–1901], 25). We should expect, then, that Lawrence Doyle's songs and the satirical and local pieces of others would be more likely to be sung in the informal context of the '*ceilidh*,' the 'time,' the spree, the 'frolic,' than in the concert with its suggestions of 'culture' (IVES, EDWARD, *Lawrence Doyle: The Farmer Poet of Prince Edward Island*, 1971, 235). When Catherine LaBrie an' Jim Liddy got married, dey all wanted to go to de time dat night (GALLANT, ANTOINETTE, '*Little Jack an' de Tax-man' and Other Acadian Stories from Prince Edward Island*, 1979, 56). Bill had been attending Kinkora High School and I had promised him that if he made the grade he could invite his friends and classmates for a 'Time.' We used to dance on the hardwood floor of the big farm kitchen (PENDERGAST, GERTRUDE, *A Good Time Was Had by All*, 1981, 55). 'How was the time last night?' (I 002). Donny played for the time (I 117). There's a big time in the hall here tonight (I 038). Then there was the Irishmen. They generally had a time once a year and some of them always asked me to that (T M130). To my generation, any social function was a 'time.' I heard it lately in referring to a gathering after a ball game. The person who used the word was not young (O).

*Constance Cullen in 'Dialect Research on Prince Edward Island,' 1971, p. 53, finds this word to be widely used to mean 'any kind of party.' [Atlantic Provinces and New England] *DC*; *DNE* 1878–1981; *OEDS* 'N. Amer.'

tonging board

Noun. \'tahng-ing\. Also **culling board**.

   A shelf or ledge in the bows of an oyster-fishing boat, used for sorting and cleaning oysters brought up by 'oyster tongs.'

   Although 'dredging' and handpicking are popular methods of harvesting, the dory, the oyster tongs, and the tonging board are the hallmarks of the typical public oyster fisherman (BOLGER, FRANCIS, *Memories of the Old Home Place*, 1984, 6). Tonging boards are boards built onto the bow of the boat. You bring the tongs up when they are full and dump the oysters on the tonging board (S 14). Tonging boards are attached to the front part of the boat. You put your shells on them. They are about twelve inches wide and three feet long and they act as a platform (S 15).

tonging: *OED* 'the taking of oysters with tongs.'

ton timber

Noun.

   See third quotation.

   Infectious distempers, fish barrels, statistical information, and education, were the primary subjects of the year 1841. Coroners in King's and Prince Counties were appointed, burial grounds established outside Georgetown, and ton timber, fisheries, and offenders ended the parliamentary doings (BAGSTER, BIRCH, *The Progress and Prospects of Prince Edward Island*, 1861, 27). In ship-building, carriage-building, mill-work, machinery, the construction of bridges and houses where strength is required, in cabinet and many other trades, it [yellow birch] is the timber most valued and used. Large quantities are exported as ton-timber (BAIN, FRANCIS, *The Natural History of Prince Edward Island*, 1890, 61). 'Ton Timber' … was hardwood, cut and hewed at least twelve inches square and so many lineal feet as estimated to make a ton. The ton timber was shipped principally to England (MACDOUGALL, ARLENE, and VIOLET MACEACHERN, *The Banks of the Elliott*, 1973, 27).

[Atlantic Provinces and New England] *DNE* 'a tree of large size, shipped in hewn or 'squatted' form' 1876–1952; *ML* 'A squared log laid by after slabbing and meant to be sawn into boards at another time. … they were paid for by weight instead of board feet.'

top ice

Noun. Compare **cat ice**, **double ice**.

   Synonym for 'shell ice': a patch or layer of thin ice over thicker ice, with an air space in between, caused by refreezing or by freezing rain.

   Then [I] called at Mr. Patterson's, … had prayers with them and then started for home and oh, what a journey I had over the ice! I never, I think, saw the ice in such a state, with ice and water on top of the old ice. The horse had to break the top ice, an inch and a quarter thick, from McIntyre's to Yeo's, and cut the ice all the way with the sleigh. I think that I never had such a journey before (DYER, ROBERT, *Diary, 1859–1883*, 1876, April 3). It had frozen some and we got into what they call top ice. About two inches thick. We had the wood-sleigh. And we got in a little deeper. And we stopped the horse. Didn't know what to do. Couldn't turn around on account of the ice binding the sleigh. So we kept going on and going on and finally the horse stopped and wouldn't go any farther. And he pranced up

and down and went right through the ice
(STEWART, DAVID, and DEBORAH STEWART, *Winter
Travel*, 1979, 23).

top sill
Noun. Compare **bottom sill, sill**.
**One of the thick pieces of wood that
form the top frame of a square lobster
trap.**
The long thick lath found on the top of each
side of a square lobster trap (MACMILLAN, JANET,
The Language of Lobster Fishing, 1985, 25). That'd
have to be part of a square trap. We don't have
a top sill on a bow trap (S 4).

trailer buoy
Noun.
**In lobster fishing, an additional buoy
for marking a line of traps.**
You get one buoy on and then another
fathom up you put another buoy on. In a
heavy tide if one buoy goes down the other is
still up. The other buoy is the trailer buoy
(S 4). A trailer buoy is a buoy tied on behind
another one. We used them in places where
the tide is running strong (S 6).

trap bow
See **bow**.

trap knot
Noun.
**A knot that attaches the 'haul-up' line
on a lobster trap to the 'backline,' or
main fishing line.**
A trap knot is a proper knot that comes off
easy and doesn't usually get tight. A baby
could open the knot (S 4). I usually use a
bowline on a bight. It is a fairly simple trap
knot to make and to undo. Sometimes though
you have to cut your 'snood' off if the knot
gets too tight (S 5). There are several trap knots.
I use a roll and hitch myself. For the most
part they don't tighten up (S 6).

trap lander
Noun.
**A device on a lobster boat for lifting
traps from the water.**
A Marlin trap lander was used with the
hauler to board the traps, some of which
were quite heavy and awkward to handle.
When the first trap was sighted, the rope
was switched to the 'nigger-head' to facilitate
more individual manipulation of the speed of
hauling. As the trap was hauled up the side of

the boat, it tripped the trap lander which
placed it on the 'washboard.' From there it was
fished (PRINCE EDWARD ISLAND, DEPARTMENT
OF FISHERIES, *Offshore Lobster: Technical Report
#175*, 1975, 3–4). A metal framework which
hangs over the side of the boat. When a trap
comes to the surface of the water, it is pulled
up against the trap lander which is then tripped
to bring the trap up on to the boat (MACMILLAN,
JANET, *The Language of Lobster Fishing*, 1985, 26).
I don't use a trap lander but one of the guys
uses it. When the trap comes up it trips a finger
and the trap flips it (S 5). I put a trap lander on
one time but I didn't have much success with it.
They are a good rig for fishing alone (S 6).

trapline
Noun. Compare **run line**.
**Synonym for 'backline': a long rope,
buoyed at both ends, to which a set
number of lobster traps are attached by
means of shorter ropes or 'snoods.'**
Each fisherman fished in the vicinity of three
hundred and fifty traps at that time and there
were traplines as we called it, and that line was
set out on the 26th of April and was never taken
in until the 26th of June. Each one of those lines
contained one hundred traps, and those lines
were pulled by hand, the hard way (ANDERSON,
ALLAN, *Salt Water, Fresh Water*, 1979, 77). Jim
Reggie MacDonald and son Art Reggie Mac-
Donald were pulling in their traps approximately 1 1/2 kilometres east of the Souris
lighthouse when the trapline became entangled
in the Master Art's propeller, stalling the boat's
engine. The vessel was left dead in the water
and a strong on-shore wind and rising tide
carried it toward shore and it struck a rock (*The
Guardian*, June 20, 1985, 1).

DAE 'A line used in trap fishing.'

trappy
Adjective. Common in Malpeque, frequent
elsewhere. Informal. Compare **dilsey,
kippy**.
**1. Usually of a woman or her clothes,
well turned out, stylish.**
The news would go about, – 'New patient
in.' 'Have you seen her?' 'Yah pretty trappy
too!' And then in the corridor you see a vision
in pink, – rose velvet bath robe, pink mules
and pajamas and a gorgeous apple blossom
complexion. 'Why, hully gee!' Hike back to
the room – put a little more slickum on your hair
and then off to make a call (LEARD, GEORGE,
What a Life, 1929, 14). Neat in appearance. Used

for a woman of any age (I 003). You could
say 'She's a trappy-looking woman,' to a lively
woman at a dance (I 009). 'A trappy rig you
have on' (I 052). For an elderly person who is
smart looking: 'Trappy for her age' (I 076).
One who dresses according to the present
fashion (O).

2. Of a horse, smartly rigged.
'Isn't that trappy looking?' Referring to a
horse and sleigh (I 030). A trappy horse has
polished harness (I 058). Isn't that trappy-
looking horse? (I 118).

DAE 'of a horse: Having a quick, short, high gait'
1872–1902.

trap smasher
Noun. Frequent in Egmont, infrequent or
rare elsewhere; significantly rural; especially less educated.
   **In lobster fishing, a severe wind storm
during the fishing season.**
   North Lake fishermen will readily admit they
may have been dubious about the senior
seaman's predictions at one time. But they are
quick to tell about the storm of 1974, when
Mr. Bruce literally begged them to put their
traps out in deeper water because a 'trap
smasher' was coming. ... Next morning the
wreckage of the traps littered the shoreline.
'At Black Point (just east of North Lake) the
traps of four fleets were piled up like a
haystack. It was about the worst surf I have
ever seen that night. I saved most of my 400
traps but some fishermen lost all their traps'
(*The Guardian*, April 24, 1984, 5). The traps
are smashed on shore, and you get lobsters free
(II 099). When the wind blows from the same
direction it will work up a big sea, and this
could result in a big storm or a trap smasher (S 6).

trawl
See **dog trawl**.

tree
Noun. Abbreviation of *Christmas tree*.
Archaic.
   A school party at Christmas time.
   They'll have the tree on Dec. 23rd (P2-029).
'Are you going to the tree tonight?' Same as
Christmas party (P2-043). There was a small
school every mile or two, so there was great
care taken to make sure the tree was not held in
one school the same night as a neighboring
one P2-084). At Christmas, the schools had a
tree and concert. Everyone would say 'going
to the tree' (O).

[Canadian] *Christmas tree*: *GCD* '*Cdn.* a party held at
Christmastime for entertaining children and presenting gifts to them, usually sponsored by a church,
school, or other organization'; *DC* 1882–1965.

tree cent
Noun. Also **Island cent**. Compare **holey
dollar, John Joy Token, leather dollar,
Sheaf of Wheat**.
   See quotations.
   The Island certainly had a variety of coins in
its day. None of the pre-Confederation coins,
however, except the 'tree' cents, had govern-
ment sanction (CHAMPION, HELEN, *Over on the
Island*, 1939, 122). In that year [1871] the
Government introduced the well-known 'tree
cent,' so called because it bore the great oak and
the three small oaks on one face (CALLBECK,
LORNE, *The Cradle of Confederation*, 1964, 133–34).
Readers will note that the Island tree cent came
into circulation when the change was made to
Decimal Currency from the previous Sterling,
and the accounts presented to the Executive
Council on February 2, 1872 were shown in
Dollars and Cents for the first time (KENNEDY,
EARLE, *The Prince Edward Island Tree Cent*, 1976,
n.p.).

*The Arms of Prince Edward Island feature three
small oak trees beside a larger one.

truck wagon
Noun.
   **A four-wheeled wooden wagon used
primarily for hauling potatoes.**
   The farm implements used at that time [1861]
for potatoes were: harrows, horse-hoes, iron
ploughs, carts, truck wagons, cultivators, wood
ploughs and 'mussel mud' diggers (FREETOWN
HISTORICAL SOCIETY, *Freetown Past and Present*,
1985, 43). A wagon used for carrying potatoes;
higher off the ground than a 'sloven' (MCCAR-
VILL, LISA, *A Potato Farming Lexicon from Kinkora,
P.E.I.*, 1986, n. pag.). A truck wagon is a
four-wheeled (usually wooden wheels with
steel rims) wagon used for hauling potatoes or
lumber. You could put 120 bushels on a truck
wagon, an enormous load. The platform was
2 1/2 feet off ground (S 1).

[North American] *OED* 'U.S'; *DA* 1805–1913; *DAE*.

trump
Intransitive verb. Compare **mitch**.
   To play truant (II).

tuber unit
Noun, often in phrase **tuber unit planting**.
The 'sets' from a single potato tuber.
The most accurate way to carry on hill selection is by the individual tuber or tuber-unit method by which the yield from each individual tuber is kept separate (MACOUN, W.T., *The Potato in Canada: Its Cultivation and Varieties*, 1918, 6). Their entire acreage is hand-planted by the tuber-unit method, which they have followed almost without interruption since the thirties, when they pioneered this method of planting in this area (*Journal-Pioneer Annual Farm Issue*, 1976, 12). Another method for improving the standards was tuber unit planting. This method required the farmer to plant all sets from each tuber together. If one set from a tuber was diseased all plants from that tuber could be eradicated. Tuber unit planting was mainly done by hand and is more costly and laborious than other methods (FREETOWN HISTORICAL SOCIETY, *Freetown Past and Present*, 1985, 50). Tuber unit planting is the process of taking one tuber and cutting it with a knife into four pieces and planting them one after another and then leaving a small space between them and the next seed. This is a way of identifying seed disease and purifying the crop (S 1). The whole tuber is planted as a unit. Elite seed is planted this way (S 3).

tucker party
Noun.
See quotation.
For many years the farm house in Brae was the social centre of the community and amusements and entertainment were the 'homespun' kind which included 'frolics,' chivarees, dances in homes, tucker parties where musical games were played, taffy or fudge parties, and, in later years, sing songs around the parlour organ. Musical instruments used at the early parties were violin, mouth organ, and jews' harp. One occasion is remembered when music for a tucker party was furnished by a mother and son who used combs covered with tissue paper for mouth organs (MACNEVIN, MRS. LORNE, *Past and Present: A History of Brae*, 1979, 69).

tucker: W3 'a square dance in which there is a dancer without a partner.'

turn
Noun, usually in plural. Occasional generally, but infrequent in Egmont and Charlottetown.
A household or farm chore, a piece of work, a job.
When children came home from school they would have their turns to do (I 019). This word is used for household tidying up, sweeping, etc. (I 024). Father did the chores and coaxed the kids to help him, to do turns as a favor. The kids doing turns would give the older folks a chance to talk (I 056). Do up the turns (I 073). A few turns to do around the barn (I 077). I've been doing a few turns around the house (I 101).

[Probably from Scottish] *OED* 'A stroke or spell of work; a piece of work; a task, a job. ... Obs. except in *hand's turn*' 1375–1791; W3; *SND* 1709–1949; *EDSL*; *WNW*.

turn, the
Noun.
Any slight illness going around (R; O).

*The meaning is different from the standard 'fainting spell' or 'sudden change for the worse.'

turtot
Noun. \tur-'tō\.
Bannock (P2; R).

[From Acadian French.]

tweeker
Noun.
A small child (R; O).

twine needle
See **heading needle**.

twitch
Transitive verb. Compare **snig**.
To drag (logs) out of the woods by horse.
'Snig' is rarely heard; twitching logs is more common (P2-028).

[Atlantic Provinces and New England] *OED* 1835–1848; W3; *DA* 17731942; *DAE*; *FW*.

two-boater
Noun. Historical. Rare. Also **Irish two-boater, two-boat people** [plural].
An immigrant who came to Prince Edward Island after an interim period elsewhere, usually in Newfoundland.
Many Irishmen were employed in the Newfoundland fishery which had begun to

show signs of decline after 1800. They therefore sought other opportunities and commenced to migrate to neighbouring Atlantic colonies. Patrick Murphy (and perhaps also John Callaghan) was very likely one of those. Since they reached Prince Edward Island via Newfoundland, hence requiring two vessels to complete the emigration journey from 'the old country,' they have been referred to as 'Irish two-boaters' (MORRISON, CLINTON, *Along the North Shore: A Social History of Township 11, P.E.I. 1765–1982*, 1983, 10). Other vessels from Nova Scotia, New Brunswick, and Newfoundland brought settlers, too, and it appears quite probable that some of these may have been immigrants who landed in those colonies first, later coming to Prince Edward Island as the second stage of their journey; hence the term 'two-boaters' (JONES, ORLO, and DOUGLAS FRASER, *Those Elusive Immigrants*, 1984, 37). People who left Ireland often had free passage on the ship in return for their labour elsewhere, such as Newfoundland, before they came here [Iona]. Better off people financially got off at Charlottetown directly before they came here (II 038). This refers to Irish people who went to Newfoundland first and then over to P.E.I. (P1-039).

two-eyed beefsteak
Noun. Infrequent generally, but rare in Malpeque and Charlottetown; unattested under forty; significantly male; especially less educated.

A pickled herring (P1).

[From Northern Irish and Scottish] *EDD* 'a slang expression for a herring' N. Ireland; *SND* 'a jocular name for a herring or kipper.' *two-eyed steak*: *OED* 'a Yarmouth bloater' 1864; *DSUE*.

two-headed trap
Noun. Archaic. Compare **bow trap**.

A lobster trap with only one chamber, and so bounded by two heads, as opposed to traps with both a 'kitchen' and a 'parlour.'

Q. Is there any difference between the trap you use now and the one you first fished? – A. There is a difference. There is the four headed trap now. We used to use the two headed trap. Q. Where do the fishermen consider the advantage lies in the present trap? – A. It holds the lobsters longer (CANADA, HOUSE OF COMMONS, *Lobster Fishery Evidence Taken before Commander William Wakeham, M.D., Officer in Charge of the Gulf Fisheries Division, in Quebec and the Maritime Provinces*, 1910, 274).

two-lunger
Noun. Informal. Compare **one-lunger**.

A two-cylinder engine.

There's Fords, Chevs and Plymouths, and even two-lungers, / Are getting tuned up for the lobstering ground (ROSE, LIVINGSTONE, *Poems and Prose*, [1956], 12). Two-cylinder gasoline engine for boats. It could be used for other things too (P2-019). We used it on the farm for the thrashers and to run implements (P2-032).

two-step
See **green apple quick-step**.

U

up east
Adverb phrase. Common in Cardigan, occasional in Charlottetown, rare or unattested elsewhere; significantly male. Compare **down east, down west, out east, up west.**

In or to the most easterly part of Prince Edward Island, especially east of St. Peter's or Souris.

And I know fellas who come in all the way from Souris and Tignish just to see them play a game. Too bad they don't run special trains in from up east and down west any more, like they used to when the Junior Royals were playing. That'd fill the old Forum like it used to then (LEDWELL, FRANK, and RESHARD GOOL, *Portraits and Gastroscopes*, 1972, 74). What if they [the people of St. Peter's] object to my binges and my heavy smoking? Will they take it in stride like the people up east? (LEDWELL, FRANK, *The North Shore of Home*, 1986, 39). Were you ever east to Munns Road or anywhere like that? … It's up east there, east of our place (T M133). I was listening to the news there today. I guess with that wind last night they thought they lost a boat that left up east here (T M124). If you are from east of Charlottetown and you leave the city you go 'up east' but if you are from Charlottetown and west you go 'down east' (O).

*This term was used primarily by informants who themselves lived 'down east,' that is, east of Charlottetown.

upstreet
Adverb. Common in Egmont, frequent elsewhere, but infrequent in Charlottetown.

Synonym for 'downstreet': in or to the centre of a town; the shopping district, or main street.

Beautiful day for Wintertime. 'Normie' up Street this afternoon – did Bank and other business and made a call. I did not feel well enough to go (OLIVER, GERTRUDE, *Diaries of Gertrude Hazel Meggison Oliver, 1964,* January 3). I 'mind' when I'd git on-shore after three months at sea the only woman yu'd see would be in yu'r dreams then I'd be headin' up street, feelin' like an animal jis cummin'edda th' jungle (JOHNSTON, LORNE, *More Recollections of an Ole Salt,* [1983?], 16). I would use it when in my cottage in Lower Montague to refer to Montague, but not when living in Montague and referring to the centre of town (II 097). People use 'upstreet' when they live on the side of town (P1-011). Yes. I live on the south side of Tignish; the road is lower too (P1-037).

*This term was used particularly by informants who lived on the outskirts of towns, rather than close to the centres.
OEDS 'colloq. and dial.' 1828–1933.

up west
Adverb phrase. Common. Compare **down east, down west, out east, up east.**
In or to any part of Prince Edward Island west of Summerside, especially the most western area.

I remember one time, when I was teaching school up west I went home to dinner one day and found a 'preacher' there (MONTGOMERY, LUCY MAUD, *Letter to Ephraim Weber,* [1908], 67). Her daughter Elizabeth moved with husband and children 'up west,' as Islanders put it, to Enmore, in the western part of Prince Edward Island, a section of the province economically depressed for generations (GRAVES, ROSS, *William Schurman, Loyalist of Bedeque, Prince Edward Island; and His Descendants,* 1973, I, 54). Tignish is no longer 'away up west' but within driving distance some evening after tea (SELLICK, LESTER, *My Island Home,* 1973, 85). I would have been interested also in an account of our sense of direction. For example, we go 'up West' or 'our [sic] West,' the difference being about two thousand miles (GREEN, JOHN, *Review of 'The Garden Transformed,'* 1982, 31). She went up west and she died up there (T M121).

*Generally, the further east the speaker, the wider the area covered by this term.

uxter
See **oxter.**

V

var
Noun. Common in Cardigan, frequent in Egmont and Malpeque, occasional in Summerside and Charlottetown.
A pronunciation variant of *fir*, especially used for the balsam fir.

After the land here has been cleared and under cultivation many years, and afterwards left to itself, it is immediately covered anew with some kind of wood, generally of spruce, var (silver fir) white birch (JOHNSTONE, WALTER, *'Letters' and 'Travels' Prince Edward Island, 1821,* 1955, 94). The woodman's axe, forest fires and the fore-time prosperous ship-building industry have swept away 'the forest primeval,' leaving but insignificant growths of the cone-bearing, softwood species, the commonest being the balsam fir or var, and spruce; and still less of pine, larch, maple, poplar, beech, birch and cedar (CROSSKILL, W.H., *Handbook of Prince Edward Island: The Garden Province of Canada,* 1906, 82–83). A common variety of wood from which these 'longers' are made introduces us to another provincialism common in this region. This is the general use of the term 'var,' as applied to the fir tree, so called elsewhere. There is, of course, good authority for the use of the word 'var,' but it is quite safe to say that it is practically obsolete in Canada, except in isolated communities (WIGHTMAN, F.A., *Maritime Provincialisms and Contrasts,* 1912, 5). One of the earliest memories of the farm was the hauling of 'var longers' from the woods to repair and build an endless number of fences. 'Var' and 'longer' are colloquial names formerly used quite generally on the Island. 'Var' is the rapidly growing balsam fir, whose wood is generally considered of little value, except for light lumber and fir sheathing (LEARD, GEORGE, *The George Leard Files,* 1977, 006892).

[Atlantic Provinces] *DC; DNE; OEDS* 'Canad.' 1793–1982.

veiling
Verbal noun. Also **veil.** Compare **bar, guard hair, silvering.**
The black-on-white overlay of hairs on a silver fox pelt.

Look for a dense cushion of underfur with good veiling of strong, silky 'guard hair' which covers the underfur smoothly and completely. … The veiling should be lustrous blue-black and the silver 'bar' should be long and sharply defined (CANADA, AGRICULTURE CANADA, LIVE-STOCK DIVISION and ANIMAL PATHOLOGY DIVISION, *Fox Farming in Canada*, 1979, 15). Its silvery sheen is produced by three separate bands of color: starting at the base with the main color which is jet black, bluish black or slate black, followed by a band of clear white, varying in width from 1/2" to 3/4" and tipped by a short section of black at the end of the shaft of the hair providing the 'veiling' so important to lend contrast and sparkle to the overall silvery colouration (FORESTER, JOSEPH, and ANNE FORESTER, *Silver Fox Odyssey: History of the Canadian Silver Fox Industry*, 1980, 89). The veil is created by the amount of black tip of the 'guard hair' (density) and the length of the black tip (S 7). The veil is the effect of the black tip that comes over the finished pelt (S 8).

veneer ring
Noun.
   See quotation.
   A veneer ring is a five-inch circle of thin wood coated with cement. It is used for catching oyster spat. They hang veneer rings on lines in the water (S 15).

vent-view
Noun.
   A potato bag with a netted section that allows the customer to see the product.
   A paper bag with a mesh-screened section for viewing the potatoes inside. This type of potato bag is usually seen in food stores in order that the customer can see what he or she is buying (MCCARVILL, LISA, *A Potato Farming Lexicon from Kinkora, P.E.I.*, 1986, n. pag.). A vent-view is a ten-pound bag with a netted vent maybe about 3' by 5' which gives a customer a chance to look at the quality (S 1). The vent-view is an area of the bag which has an open weave which allows the customer to see the potatoes (S 3).

vito
See **bito**.

W

wakehouse
Noun.

A funeral parlour, or a house where a corpse is laid out for a wake (O).

OED 1814; *DNE*.

warpy
Adjective.
   1. Of wood, gnarled, twisted, warped.
   Wood that sticks is warpy (P2-059). Warpy wood is twisted out of shape (P2-083).
   2. Of food, shrivelled, stale, sour.
   This cake is warpy (P2-082).

washbait
Noun.
   Synonym for 'pogey': ground-up fish mixed with oatmeal and thrown over the side of a boat as a lure (I).

washboard
Noun.
   A ledge running inboard along the sides and stern of a lobster boat, where traps may be placed for fishing.
   When the first trap was sighted, the rope was switched to the 'nigger-head' to facilitate more individual manipulation. As the trap was hauled up the side of the boat, it tripped the 'trap lander' which placed it on the washboard. From there it was fished (PRINCE EDWARD ISLAND, DEPARTMENT OF FISHERIES, *Offshore Lobster: Technical Report 175, 1975*, 1975, 3–4).

washstand soap
Noun. Archaic. Rare.
   Mild home-made soap.
   'Washstand soap' refers to where the soap was kept (I 014). Homemade soap would be put into a cup and made fancy (I 038). Where you'd first wash up when coming in from the barn, out in the porch (I 058). Distinguished from the homemade lye soap which would burn your eyes if used on your face (I 063). Used for the body rather than clothes (I 116).

watchtower
Noun.
   A small, centrally located building on a fox ranch used for observation of the foxes, especially during the breeding season.
   Some of the [ranches] have installed watch-towers, elevated houses something like a look-out or 'crow's nest,' where the keeper can watch

the foxes, especially during mating season, without disturbing them in any way (BARR, J.R., *The Golden Pelt*, 1913, 18). The watch tower is not an essential part of the equipment of a fox ranch, but some ranchers find it invaluable in keeping their animals under surveillance during the breeding season, so that accurate mating charts may be kept and the expected date of whelping recorded. Other ranchers obtain this information by allowing the males into the breeding pens only in the day time. The observation tower in use is merely a narrow building located in the centre and sufficiently elevated to give a clear view of all parts of the ranch. The top room has windows on all sides. A room may be built underneath to serve either as a 'pelting room' or sleeping quarters for a watchman (ALLEN, J.A., and G. ENNIS SMITH, *Fox Ranching in Canada*, 1929, 9). The other crucial building on the ranch, besides the 'feedhouse,' was the 'watchtower.' It resembled a miniature lighthouse and was the important vantage point from where the fox farmer observed his animals during the breeding season (RANKIN, ROBERT, *Down at the Shore: A History of Summerside, Prince Edward Island (1752–1945)*, 1980, 136). A watchtower would be a building you put up on top of another building so you could see your ranch. In the breeding season this would be used more (S 8). There are not too many watchtowers left. They were more or less a lighthouse-shaped object. You would peer over the edge at all the fox kennels. A watchtower would be a surreptitious elevated platform where a fox farmer would watch the various foxes (S 9).

waterhaul
Noun.
   In fishing, a haul of a net or lobster trap that yields no catch.
   If you haul traps and don't get any lobsters you would say it was kind of a waterhaul today (S 4). You say that more in seining, a waterhaul, than in lobster fishing (S 5).

DNE.

waulking
Verbal noun. \'wah-king\. Also verb **waulk**. Also spelled **wauking**. Archaic. Rare.
   The act of thickening new cloth by kneading it when wet.
   The 'Wauking' or 'thickening Frolic' was the happiest day of the year. These 'frolics' were common in the winter time. When the web of cloth containing generally 20 or 30 yards, according to the needs of the family, was ready for thickening, word was sent through the settlement. When those who wished to do so had assembled, the web which had been soaking for some time in soap and water, was wrung out by hand, was then placed on a long table, the young women lining each side of the table, then grasped the cloth in their hands, at the same time giving a kneading movement as they advanced along and around it. This was accompanied by a Gaelic song, the rhythm of which lent itself to the movement (MACDONALD, HUBERT, *The Lords of the Isles and Their Descendants*, 1944, 93).
Their pleasures and recreations were few, but quilting parties, stumping 'frolics,' waulkings, and weddings were all events for merriment. 'Waulking' is stretching of newly woven cloth when wet into a proper shape, The settlers waulked, worked and pulled the bolts of wet cloth (BREHAUT, MARY, *Historic Highlights of Prince Edward Island*, [1959], 37). When making wool blankets you had to do this waulking (II 021). Heard old people speak of this. There were waulking songs to go with it (II 055). My mother would accidently shrink a sweater and try to 'wauk it out' (II 110).

[From Scottish and northern English] *waulk*: *SND* 'The process was performed by hand in the Hebrides until fairly recently to the accompaniment of rhythmic Gaelic songs to coordinate the movements of the waulking team' 1703–1873; *W3* 'Scot. var. of *walk* [to thicken cloth]'; *OED* 'Now only dial. and Hist.' 1437–1814; *EDD*; *EDSL*.

weak
Adjective, often modifying *time*. Informal. Occasional in Egmont, rare or unattested elsewhere.
   Good, enjoyable; strong.
   Kids use 'weak' more than older people (I 010). A serious word in Tignish (I 036). 'A weak time' means a very good time had at a party, etc. (O). If you have a student from Tignish you'll notice right away, he doesn't pronounce his *th*'s – weak, eh? (O [letter]). That's a weak car, eh? (O). A weak [i.e. strong] headache (O). One Sister who was not from the area but was teaching school up there used to write 'weak ending' on many compositions, until she discovered that the students regarded it as a compliment (O).

*Phrases in which *weak* means *very*, like *weak ugly*, have also been reported.

weather-breeder

Noun. Compare **pet day**.

A calm and sunny day supposed to bring on a storm.

Tuesday was disagreeable and stormy as Monday was mild, and the landsmen were thrown on their beam ends at short notice. Instead of Monday being an omen of success, it was a mere 'weatherbreeder,' the first three or four days being about the meanest part of the voyage (MACKINNON, JOHN, *A Sketch Book: Comprising Historical Incidents, Traditional Tales and Translations*, 1915, 78). Peace and tranquillity brooded over the Glen; the sky was fleeced over with silvery, shining clouds. Rainbow Valley lay in a soft, autumnal haze of fairy purple. ... Even Cousin Sophia looked less melancholy than usual and admitted that there was not much fault to be found in the day, although there was no doubt it was a weather-breeder and there would be an awful storm on its heels (MONTGOMERY, LUCY MAUD, *Rilla of Ingleside*, [1920], 81). This is a common Souris expression (O).

OED 1655–1903; *W3*; *GCD*. *DSUE* 'A fine bright day: nautical.'

wet-raked

Verbal adjective. Compare **raking**[1].

Of 'Irish moss,' collected by boat.

Yeah, wet-raked moss is moss that comes off the boat drags before it is dried. Once they dry it they call it 'ground dried' or sun-dried moss (S 11). Wet-raked moss is moss that has not been dried and has been raked by boat (S 12).

whelping den

Noun. Also **whelping pen**. Compare **denning box**.

In fox ranching, a box sometimes placed inside a fox kennel as a shelter for the female to whelp in.

A nest box or whelping den is necessary to provide a comfortable place for the vixen to whelp her pups. ... Fill the box with hay. The vixen will make a nest here to whelp her pups. In districts where severe weather may occur after the pups arrive, the inner nest can be a separate box about 60 cm square. Place this box at one end of the larger structure and pack shavings or other insulating material around and below it (CANADA, AGRICULTURE CANADA, LIVESTOCK DIVISION and ANIMAL PATHOLOGY DIVISION, *Fox Farming in Canada*, 1979, 8). A whelping pen is where you put your female

before she has her pups, to let her be by herself (S 8). A whelping pen is a place where a fox farmer has prepared a pen for a fox to give birth in. This would leave the female fox free from the male (S 9).

whiff

Transitive verb, usually with *out*. Infrequent generally, but rare in Egmont.

To throw.

To pitch a ball at someone (II 027). Pitch it out (II 032). Whiff that out to the hens (II 068). Just with broom, no dust pan. Just whiff it out the back door (II 096). 'What'll I do with this?' 'Oh, just whiff it out' (O).

whinge

Intransitive verb. Also verbal noun **whingeing**. Often used of children or pets. Common in Egmont, occasional in Malpeque and Cardigan, infrequent in Summerside and Charlottetown; significantly rural; especially older, male.

To whine, whimper, complain fretfully.

Stop your whingeing or I'll give you another 'skite' (I 010). Dogs whinge – sort of an annoying sound, more like intermittent whimpering (I 019). Sounds of an unwell child complaining (I 045). Complaining incessantly without real meaning (I 050). Trying to get your attention for something. Pulling at you, interrupting. Whingeing at you (I 099). Often used with whining: whingeing and whining (I 116). Used for a bellyacher, a whiner, often in combination: a whingeing bastard (O).

*This word is standard usage in Australia and New Zealand.
[From Scottish and northern English] *OED* 1150–1867; *W3*; *SND*; *EDSL*; *OEDS*; *COD* 'dial or Austral.'

whisht

Exclamation. Also spelled **hist, whist**. Frequent in Egmont and Malpeque, occasional in Summerside and Cardigan, rare in Charlottetown; especially rural; unattested under thirty.

Be quiet, hush!

The father looking daggers at his son said with upraised hand, 'whist! you'll waken him up!' nodding to the loft (LAWSON, JAMES, *The Wreck of the Laurentian – Concluded*, 1902, 15). Whisht, child ... don't be talking av witches in the open daylight like this. Little ye know what might happen (MONTGOMERY, LUCY MAUD, *Pat of Silver Bush*, 1933, 97). Women say it (II 019). It's used around a horse also (II 055). It's a polite way of saying 'Shut up' (II 096). When they wanted someone to be quiet, my parents would say 'wisht' for 'shhh' (O).

[From Irish and Scottish] *EDD*; *SND* 1718–1967; *DNE* 1937–1968.

white one
Noun. Compare **hitchhiker**.
In lobster fishing, a white crab often found in lobster traps.
I would say we had a lot of white ones to tell the other fellows we had crabs in the trap (S 05).

whitewashed American
Noun. Humorous. Rare. Compare
whitewashed Islander.
See quotation.
This means a Canadian who has gone to the U.S.A. and puts on American airs (O).

[Canadian] *DC* '*Slang*. … a native of Canada who had been naturalized in the United States and then secured repatriation in his own country'; *OEDS* 'whitewashed American, Yank, or Yankee, a person who affects American manners or who has spent a short time in America' 1855–1970.

whitewashed Islander
Noun. Humorous. Rare. Compare
whitewashed American.
A Prince Edward Islander who has picked up affected 'foreign' manners, especially in the 'Boston States.'
In the early 1900s, people would go to the 'Boston States' and then spend the rest of their life talking with a made-up Boston accent, especially women (I 016). 'Yankified' (I 070). They went away in a car and came back in a *cah* (I 082). They go away and come back as 'tourists' and eat every damn thing in the garden (I 096). Girls going to the States for housework would come home to visit with a phony accent that they would sometimes forget to use (II 001).

*Frank Ledwell, in *The North Shore of Home*, 1986, 23, illustrates the type: 'Mary M_____, for one, had been to Boston for just a year / and came back with too quick a personality transplant. / Her broad Island accent was too camouflaged / by exaggerated long "a's" and sliding "r's", and / Good God, she even had to be introduced to the very people / whose midst she had departed so recently.'

white whiskey
Noun.
A drinkable dilution of ethyl alcohol, distilled from cereals.
Hardy's Harbour, Goose Harbour and 'Little' Harbour, all on Lot 11 sandhills, off the north shore, saw the passage of many a keg of rum or can of alcohol ('white whiskey') during the prohibition years (MORRISON, CLINTON, *Along the North Shore: A Social History of Township 11, P.E.I. 1765–1982*, 1983, 97).

*The definition is quoted from the *Dictionary of Canadianisms*.
[From Canadian French *whiskey blanc*] *DC* 'Esp. Que.' 1897–1965.

whore's egg
Noun. Also **devil's egg**. Informal. Occasional in Egmont, rare elsewhere; significantly rural, male. Compare **Aristotle's lantern, sea-thistle**.
A small, roundish shellfish with sharp spines, a sea urchin.
A trap's coming up, we see the 'haulup' real clear / We 'washboard' the trap, the first one this year / A crab, a starfish and a lousey whore's egg / Two 'canners' and a 'market' whose claws we must peg (FLEMING, RICHARD, *Lobstering*, 1985, n. pag.). 'Sea thistle' is used by 'the more modest' to describe a sea urchin (I 012). Also called 'devil's eggs.' They kill the fisherman's catch (I 063). We call them sea urchins or 'sea thistles' if there are women around and whore's eggs if they aren't (S 5). A fisherman's name for sea urchins (O).

*A possible derivation is French *oursin* 'sea urchin' combined with *sea egg* (see *DNE ose egg*).
[Atlantic Provinces and New England] *DNE*; *ML*; *OEDS* 'N. Amer. (chiefly Newfoundland).'

widow maker
Noun.
A rake with teeth curved outward, used at the shore for collecting Irish moss.
A widow maker is a big fork, and they are just that if you aren't careful with them, a widow maker. They were probably a silage fork if I am not mistaken. As long as you took your time with them and had a strong back you were safe. Sometimes you could scoop the moss out of the water with this (S 10).

W3 'something dangerous to a worker's health; specif: a loose limb hanging in or falling from a tree in logging'; *FW*.

widow man
Noun. Compare **widow woman**.
  A widower (I 020).

[From British and Irish] *SND* 1860–1956; *W3* 'chiefly dial.'; *EDD*; *ESI*; *DNE*; *OEDS* 'dial.'

widow woman
Noun. Also **widow lady**, **widow person**. Archaic. Sometimes humorous. Occasional in Egmont and Cardigan, infrequent elsewhere. Compare **widow man**.
  A widow.
  'Widow woman' is an older term used as a joke now (I 020). Bachelors in Flat River talk about the widow woman down the road (I 050).

*R.E. McConnell, *Our Own Voice: Canadian English and How It Is Studied*, 1979, 172, reports that this term 'is slowly disappearing [in Prince Edward Island] in favour of *widow*.' In the Common Word Survey, *widow woman* was chosen by only one informant in preference to *widow*.
[From British] *W3*; *SND*; *EDD*; *DNE* 1846–1900.

wild axehandles, the
See **flying axehandles**.

wild pear
Noun. Frequent in Cardigan, infrequent elsewhere.
  A small, early-blooming tree (genus *Pyrus*) that produces large, edible berries of a deep purple colour.
  These are the first trees to come to bloom in the West Prince area in the spring: 'The wild pear is in bloom' (II 032). A very good edible fruit, the first of the season (II 039). They are shaped a bit like a pear. But they're not good to eat until they are almost black (II 067). They range in colour from blackish to purple. Very sweet tasting when ripe, and twice the size of blueberries. An old saying in the York area is 'You should not plant corn before the wild pears come in bloom' (II 076).

[From New England] *W3*; *EDD*; *DAE*; *DA*; *DNE*.

wind
Transitive verb. \wind\. Archaic.
  To winnow.
  A bucket of berries was poured slowly onto a blanket or similar device on a windy day thus 'winding' leaves and chaff out of berries (O).

[From British] *OED* 'dial.' 1500–1919; *W3* 'dial chiefly Brit'; *EDD*; *SND*.

windrower
Noun.
  A machine that digs potatoes and deposits them in the path of a potato harvester.
  The windrower moves ahead of the harvester digging two rows and places them between the two rows to be dug by the harvester providing four row digging (*Journal-Pioneer Annual Farm Issue*, 1975, 15). The use of windrowers is becoming common and has been effective for opening fields and reducing harvester travel. However, in order to maintain good forward speed when using a windrower, a harvester must have wider cross and side conveyors. Some of the newer harvesters have 80–90 cm conveyors to handle windrowers (ADVISORY COMMITTEE ON POTATOES, *Atlantic Canada Potato Guide*, 1984, 31). It doesn't take long to do a field when you have two diggers and a windrower going (MCCARVILL, LISA, *A Potato Farming Lexicon from Kinkora, P.E.I.*, 1986, n. pag.). When you use a two-row digger, a windrower enables you to do four rows at once. A windrower has a bed and a thrash chain and throws the potatoes into the next rows over (S 2).

windy
Adjective. Rare.
  1. Of butter or cheese, rancid or spoiled.
  'The butter is going windy.' Cheese can be windy (I 060). Windy butter (I 068). 'Windy' was used when the farm wife made bad-tasting butter (O).
  2. Of some foods, especially beans and cabbage, liable to cause wind or gas in the stomach or intestines.
  Cabbages and beans and food like them are windy because the person eating them breaks wind after (I 003). Beans are windy food (I 053).

[From British] [sense 2]: *OED*; *W3*; *EDD. windy milk*: *EDD* 'milk that has turned sour.' *wind*: *EDD* 'To taint; to become tainted or sour; esp. used of butter, milk, and bacon.'

wood-stock skate
Also **wooden-stocked skate**. See **stock skate**.

work down
Transitive phrasal verb.
  To reduce gradually the temperature of (potatoes in storage).

To gradually decrease in temperature after having begun to rise in temperature due to being kept in storage. This process is carried on to prevent potatoes from spoiling from too high temperatures in the warehouse (MCCARVILL, LISA, *A Potato Farming Lexicon from Kinkora, P.E.I.*, 1986, n.p.). You work down the temperature of the potatoes to reduce the damage of a frost (S 1).

works, the
Plural noun phrase, infrequently singular. Occasionally in phrase **under the work(s)**. Historical. Compare **jerks, jumper, kicker², McDonaldite**.
   Convulsive distortions of the body or face during religious excitement.
   A girl who was awakened at this meeting went home to her parents 'under the work.' They concluded at once that she had been bewitched. They ordered her to bed, but there the work increased. They now remembered of a 'charm' of which they had heard in Scotland by which she could be cured. She was to be taken to the sea and towed after a boat, etc., but before this was attempted they were made aware of the real nature of the trouble and were induced to leave her to herself. This girl was relieved soon afterwards and led a life consistent with her profession and is yet living to testify to the above (LAMONT, MURDOCH, *Rev. Donald McDonald: Glimpses of His Life and Times*, 1902, 51–52). The other clipping is not intended for a literary gem but I merely send it as giving an account of a very interesting religious sect of which P.E. Island boasts a monopoly. They are known as 'McDonaldites' after their founder and are principally noted for 'the works,' a very strange manifestation of psychic excitement that comes over them in preaching. They will go through the wildest contortions, some of them impossible in a normal state, yet no injury ever results. They cannot resist the impulses of this strange power and the scenes at a McDonaldite sacrament are wild in the extreme. Outsiders are often affected, even the most skeptical – and frequently take 'the jerks' as bad as the sect themselves (MONTGOMERY, LUCY MAUD, *My Dear Mr. M: Letters to G.B. MacMillan from L.M. Montgomery*, 1980 [1906], 22–23). A feature of his service with which they were unaquainted was the 'works' or trancelike ecstasy, accompanied by gesticulation and shouts, which overcame many of the audience (MACQUEEN, MALCOLM, *Skye Pioneers and 'The Island,'* 1929, 83). McDonald's followers were often referred to derisively

as the 'kickers' or the 'jumpers,' and it is unfortunate that while these 'works' were only one aspect of the 'McDonaldite' faith, they became, in the popular mind, the customary means of identifying the group. ... By 1830 approximately 300 persons had experienced 'the works,' and it is likely that several hundred more might have been affected in this way before the revival ended (WEALE, DAVID, *'The Minister': The Reverend Donald McDonald*, 1977, 3).

*Reverend Donald McDonald (1783–1867), a member of the Church of Scotland (unattached), founded thirteen McDonaldite churches on Prince Edward Island which had some 5,000 adherents. The phenomenon of 'the works' continued in some Church of Scotland services even after McDonald's death. [From Scottish and northern English] *work*: EDD 11. 'A religious revival' 1887; EDD 22. 'To struggle convulsively; to twitch as in pain or in a fit' 1849–1900; SND.

wrap-jacket
Noun. Also **hot-jacket**.
   See quotation.
   Fighting boys were made to play wrap-jacket or hot-jacket before all the school, i.e., each armed with a switch was forced to scourge the other. Play hours were generally spent in fighting: for in those days the young man's fancy, instead of turning to thoughts of love on the approach of Spring, usually turned to thoughts of blood (*Prince Edward Island Magazine*, 4.11, January 1903, 406).

wrister
Noun.
   A close-fitting, knitted band worn on the wrist for warmth.
   Aunt Mary Maria had knitted 'wristers' for all the children out of a dreadful shade of magenta yarn (MONTGOMERY, LUCY MAUD, *Anne of Ingleside*, [1939], 67).

*This word is a variation on the standard *wristlet*. [North American] OED; DA 1879–1945; W3; DAE. *wristikin*: SND.

Y

yarr
Noun. Also spelled **yar**. Infrequent generally, but unattested in Charlottetown.
   A persistent reddish weed growing on poor land, spurry.

There is a small weed which they call yar, (spirie) which greatly damages the crops; on some lands, when once it gets into the ground, there is no method yet discovered of clearing it away. When the seed ripens, it will lie under ground, I have heard, for twenty years. ... I have seen wheat damaged so much by it, as not to be more than a fourth of an average crop. But if they were to plough, instead of harrowing their seed wheat into old potatoe land, with a very light harrowing ... this ... would destroy the first growth of yar (JOHNSTONE, WALTER, *A Series of Letters, Descriptive of Prince Edward Island*, 1822, 42). It's a small weed that grows in the grain, approximately three and a half inches high. Hard to kill (II 075). It looks like a carrot. Comes from lack of lime in soil. Red and brown (II 077).

[From Scottish and northern English] *OED* 1775–1829; *EDD*; *W3*; *SND*; *EDSL*.

yellowberry
See **bakeapple**.

Z

zed cold
Adjective phrase. Rare.
   As cold as it can be (O).

The Dictionary in Profile

I

A literate but unlearned Scotsman, who had never seen a dictionary before, encountered one in a public library. He read with mounting interest, but finally threw it down. 'It's got guid incidents,' he said to the librarian, 'but the plot is verra disconnected!'

It is not difficult to sympathize with this fictitious reader about the disconnectedness of dictionaries. But perhaps it *is* possible to make some connections for this dictionary, by presenting a kind of statistical plot, or profile, of what has been given piecemeal. In a second section, the vocabulary so outlined will be shown in relief against other aspects of Prince Edward Island dialect.

Many people are naturally curious about where words come from. Such information has been presented in the present volume, where possible, in the dictionary notes. If these notes are collected together, we find that 471 of the 873 main-entry words are assigned a definite source, and can be put into broad categories as follows:

English (incl. 7.9% northern)	25.9%
Scottish	24.8%
North American	23.4%
Irish	15.9%
Gaelic	7.2%
French and Micmac	2.7%

Assuming that these words may be treated as representative of the total, this breakdown is very much what one would expect from the settlement history of Prince Edward Island. Andrew Hill Clark's *Three Centuries and the Island: A Historical Geography of Settlement and Agriculture in Prince Edward Island, Canada*, 1959, pp. 207–8, gives the major ethnic groups as Scottish (32%), English (30%), Irish (19%), and Acadian (16%). Of course, the lack of borrowing from Acadian and other French only reflects the relatively low status accorded to French speakers in the region before recent times.

If we now move, still within ethnicity, from word origin to word use, we find an interesting discrepancy. It will be recalled that the head notes hold open the possibility of words from Fieldwork Surveys I and II being labelled 'especially' or 'significantly' English, Scottish, Irish, or Acadian, according to which speakers particularly favour them. As it turns out, the ethnic labels are almost never applied, for the returns do not justify them; whatever their origin, most words are diffused in the general population. The lack of correlation between the ethnic backgrounds of word and user may be seen, for example, in a variety of Scottish words under the letter *S*. The numbers indicate the percentage of users within each of the identified ethnic groups:

	Scottish	Irish	English	Acadian
scra	2	6	4	17
skithers	28	39	36	0
spouty	2	18	4	17
stirk	18	10	29	0
stob	9	15	12	0

The fieldwork sample of Island citizens could always be skewed; yet it does meet expectations in other ways, as we shall see. Moreover the first postal survey, which involved seventy-two older informants not in the groups above, found a similar absence of pattern between word background and user background. The conclusion must be that, although ethnic connections on Prince Edward Island are vital to many people, such connections are not particularly strong in vocabulary. This statement runs counter to the assumptions of Constance Cullen's 'Dialect Research on Prince Edward Island,' 1971.

After word origin, another popular interest in language concerns dialects, in this case internal divisions within the general Island speech. It appears that there are no sharp geographical boundaries in the vocabulary taken as a whole. Nevertheless, by totalling the frequency labels in the head notes, it is possible to show that the Egmont area is stronger in dialect than the other designated regions, and that Charlottetown is relatively weak. The figures following indicate the number of words given one of the five frequency labels in each region, from the data collected in Fieldwork Surveys I and II:

	Common	Fre-quent	Occa-sional	Infre-quent	Rare
Egmont	46	41	45	46	19
Cardigan	32	29	29	85	24
Summerside	25	26	27	81	37
Malpeque	24	20	32	80	40
Charlotte-town	18	13	16	87	56

It should be remembered that some additional words used by fewer than 10% of all informants are simply labelled 'Rare,' with no region given; their number is 126, over one-quarter of the total words in these two surveys.

Another way to illustrate this point is to establish what might be called a 'recognition rate' for each of the five regions. A hypothetical informant with a rating of 100% has recognized (and claimed to use) every one of the 442 words put to him or her in the two fieldwork surveys. The higher the score the greater percentage of dialect (in terms of vocabulary) that a person speaks. After we average all the scores in each region, we find that the recognition rates are as follows:

Egmont	62.8%
Cardigan	49.2%
Summerside	43.8%
Malpeque	39.4%
Charlottetown	28.6%

Thus, Charlottetown, the most urban area, is the least dialectal, while Egmont, the area most remote from the capital, is the most. That Summerside, an urban area, should surpass the chiefly rural Malpeque in these figures is only a slight anomaly, possibly explained by the strong influence of neighbouring Egmont.

The rural-urban distinction is a very important one overall, because the greater conservatism of rural life encourages the retention of traditional dialect. (We might note in passing that eighty-six of the words, close to one-tenth of the total, could be called traditional in that they are labelled 'archaic.') The point can be further illustrated here by considering the head note labels 'rural' and 'urban,' which were defined according to the Census of 1976. This definition enlarges the scope of 'urban' beyond the two concentrations of Charlottetown and Summerside. Even by this more difficult test, Island words are labelled as 'especially' or 'significantly' rural 63 times and urban only 3 times. Similarly, the recognition rates for the rural and urban populations thus defined are

48.7% and 38.8% respectively. These figures do not apply to the Special Lexicon words, which, along with the informants called upon, are rural by design, but rather to the wide range of general words in Fieldwork Surveys I and II. Clearly, if one wants to hear Islanders using Island words, it is better to stay away from town.

Another important dimension in dialect studies generally is age. As mentioned in 'The Making of the Dictionary,' this consideration affected the choice of fieldwork informants in advance: half of the total were over sixty years old. Nevertheless, enough people of all ages were selected to allow adequate groupings of other kinds. These fit the expected pattern that older speakers are the more likely ones to use dialect words. Again the collected head note labels from the fieldwork surveys tell the story. As before, the numbers below combine the categories 'especially' and 'significantly':

senior (over 60)	7
older (over 50)	72
middle-aged (40–59)	17
younger (under 40)	3
under 30	1

Note that the label 'older,' applied in many entries, can include informants that are elsewhere isolated as 'senior,' as well as some that are elsewhere in the 'middle-aged' category.

Individual words can often show a quite dramatic falling off through the age ranks in percentage of use. The recognition rates by age show such percentages averaged for the entire dictionary:

over 60	50.8%
50–59	50.5%
40–49	39.8%
30–39	38.2%
under 30	20.5%

The strong showing of the two groups

over fifty might very well be explained by the fact that all of these informants grew up before a period of major urbanization in Prince Edward Island began in the 1950s. The sharp downward break of the under 30s can, in turn, be attributed to the recent intensification of this trend, in particular to the establishment of consolidated schools.

Perhaps the single most consistent finding to emerge in recent years from studies in dialect and other kinds of language variation is that the speech of the two sexes can differ appreciably. In some languages, the differences are quite marked. In English and its dialects they are more subtle, but nonetheless present. This study is a confirmation. For example, words labelled in the head note especially or significantly 'male' outnumber 'female' words 63 to 5. Similarly, the recognition rates for the two groups are 50.0% and 39.1% respectively. These striking figures are partly, but not greatly, biased by the fact that some of the labelled words are associated with rural occupations that are traditionally male in our culture, and so invite that designation. But it should be remembered that the bulk of such words came to the Dictionary through the Special Lexicon study, which did not allow for social labels of any kind. Hence these words are not even counted in this analysis.

Why then *should* men use ordinary, nonstandard English more than women? The arguments that generally hold are that women are more conscious users of the standard because they are more conscious of its status, having had little access until recently to status in other areas. At the same time, non-standard language can have a kind of unadmitted prestige with men, because of its occasional associations with toughness and group solidarity.

It is interesting to consider whether the sex of a speaker counts as much in Island speech as the previous two factors, rural locality and age. If we combine the three factors in all possible combinations (but with 'age' divided into only 'older' and 'younger,' over and under 60), we get eight groups with their recognition rates in order as follows:

older rural men	60.0%
older urban men	54.1%
older rural women	48.5%
younger rural men	47.6%
younger rural women	38.6%
older urban women	37.5%
younger urban men	34.0%
younger urban women	30.7%

Since 'rural' comes in four of the first five combinations, we could argue that it is the most important determiner, after which comes 'older' (four of six) and lastly 'men' (four of seven).

To conclude this profile of the Dictionary's word list, we may leave the head note, and its resultant statistics, to consider the definitions. Do the meanings of the words, taken together, fit into any pattern? In at least two ways they do so by design. Since technical, scientific, and learned words were excluded from the collection, what has been included has the general feel of being homey, familiar, and down to earth. At the same time, since certain rural occupations have been highlighted in the research, we cannot escape their strong influence on the text. The categories established for convenience in the fieldwork questionnaires seem to cover equally well the other three-fifths of the words garnered, from whatever source: weather, nature, fishing, farming, house, food and drink, special occasions, people, clothing, the body, and places. The categories are similar to those listed by Hans Kurath in *WGUS* (*Word Geography of the Eastern United States*), 1949, pp. 9–10, as central to regional speech everywhere.

There is also the darker side of any rural, island way of life. A category like 'distrust of things different' could take in a surprisingly large number of words, from the numerous put-downs of people who resist their community norms (*breachy*), to words for strangers, like the universal *from away*, which puts into one indiscriminate group the entire non-Island, or at least non-Maritimes, world. On the other hand, the vocabulary can be seen as presenting a face of great courage (*pork and jerk* as an answer to poverty for example) and of good humour. One sub-field of the latter that might be established could be called 'Egmont opposites.' It would take in tongue-in-cheek words like *chocolates, fudge*, and *weak*, all of which are used in the western end of the province, especially around Tignish, to mean roughly the opposite of what they seem to mean. The practice extends to words not in this dictionary (for various reasons), like *handsome, hateful, intelligent, like* (verb), *sad, stupid*, and *ugly*.

II

It is perhaps fitting to reflect at the end of this volume that Island words are not the only aspect of Island speech. It is true that, to some extent, features of grammar and pronunciation are touched upon in the Dictionary entries, but, like the words, they too need to be given fuller connections. Few of these features are unique to the province; it is their amalgam, and the relative frequency of each, that make the dialect. In any case, since little formal work has been done in such areas, what follows must be more a program for future action than a final report. Nevertheless, the conclusion is very strong that the general points made above about the vocabulary apply equally to the whole dialect. All the levels of language work in a natural way together.

To begin with grammar, one noteworthy area is that of intensifiers, that is, words like *very* that intensify the force of following words. Examples like *some* and *right* (*some nice, right fine*) are found regionally in

Britain and the United States, but are particularly common in the Maritime provinces of Canada. Most dictionaries label them as 'dialectal' or 'archaic,' yet they are used at almost all levels of Prince Edward Island society. Lucy Maud Montgomery has an otherwise standard narrator in *The Doctor's Sweetheart and Other Stories*, [1908], say 'She and I were right good friends from the beginning' (p. 73). A less common but still well-attested type of intensifier is exemplified by *desperate* and *dreadful*, which, despite their negative associations in standard speech, can be used to modify either unpleasant adjectives or pleasant ones (*I'm desperate glad to see you*). All of these examples fit into a larger pattern, common in North American folk speech, of making adverbs from adjectives (as in *love me tender*); *real* used this way ('Isaac … turned his back, real considerately,' in Montgomery's *The Doctor's Sweetheart and Other Stories*, p. 88) is all but standard. This point is well exemplified in Frederic G. Cassidy's 'Language Changes Especially Common in American Folk Speech,' *DARE*, p. xxxviii.

Non-standard verbs in Island speech are also worthy of attention. One category would be the replacement of the past participle by the past tense, as in the common non-standard *How much have you drank?* (instead of *drunk*). An example in Prince Edward Island English that has actually been subject to survey is *wore* for *worn*: 'I'm wore out.' 'The Survey of Canadian English,' a country-wide investigation of various usages among grade nine students and their parents in 1972, discovered that Newfoundland and Prince Edward Island led the nation in this usage, though the majority preference in both provinces is still *I'm worn out*. (The complete survey results are in M.H. Scargill's *Modern Canadian English Usage*, 1974.) The reverse phenomenon, that is, past participle for past tense (like *I seen it, I done it*), is part of non-standard English everywhere, and is very widespread on

Prince Edward Island. Also noticeable in verbs are irregular past tenses, such as *drug* for *drag* (*They drug the road*), *wed* for *weeded* (*I wed the garden*), the pronunciation of *beat* as *bet* (*We bet their team 6–0*, and similarly *heated* as *het*). The most popular of these, found even in relatively formal contexts, is *come* for *came*, as in one of Frank Ledwell's poems in his *The North Shore of Home*, 1986, p. 107:

Winter came romping like a hare up the bay
And blew the scrunched sconce back into its
   shell.
On course, the turtle made the bridge at a snail's
   pace
And come to my store.

All of these verb examples can be recognized as simply another front in the longstanding conflict between so-called strong and weak English verbs, a conflict in which standard and folk speech have often taken opposing sides.

Other, more occasional characteristics of grammar that would bear investigation are intrusive prepositions (*Where are you at?*, *I'll come where you're to* – also well attested in Newfoundland), zero plurals (*forty bushel of wheat*), the use of *how* for *why* (Jack: 'I think we should go up the hill tomorrow.' Jill: 'How?'), the use of *never* as a stronger version of *not* ('I never went to work this morning'), and the use of archaic *ye* and *be*. Some people in Egmont are known unkindly by their neighbours as the 'Do-Bees,' because of sentences like 'I do be tired at the end of the day.' The Dictionary entries on *after* and *handy* should also be added to this list.

The total *DPEIE* file on non-standard grammar as used on Prince Edward Island, consisting of informal observations by the editor, examples in writing, and many contributions from observers, suggests that this kind of language matches the vocabulary: it is especially used by older, rural men.

From grammar we turn to pronunciation.

It is convenient to consider first individual words with distinctive pronunciations, and then the general features of accent that run through many words. Individual words whose pronunciations on Prince Edward Island might catch a visitor's ear include:

1 *Aunt* rhyming with *font*. This is a general Maritime usage, especially favoured in New Brunswick, reflecting British heritage.

2 *Calm* rhyming with *Sam*. This pronunciation is also found in Newfoundland. There is some evidence that it applies more to weather than to mood, and that force of analogy can affect *balm*, *palm*, and *psalm*. In *The Bishop Jots It Down: An Autobiographical Strain on Memories*, 1939, p. 12, Francis Kelley writes:

The islander is a mortal enemy of 'putting on,' which means affectation. The way he speaks the English tongue shows it, for his slight brogue is only a protest against softness. He does not pronounce *psalm*, for example, as if the 'a' were an 'ah.' The word is 'sam.' 'Calm' and 'palm' are 'cam' and 'pam,' since in them the 'a' is single and not double. To pronounce otherwise was, in my day, 'Bostonian,' a form of 'putting on.' The islander of today has had to reconcile himself to Boston English on account of his many American relatives.

3 *Creek* rhyming with *rick*. The *Dictionary of Canadianisms* enters this pronunciation as 'long established in Canada at the popular, especially rural, level; the variant exists in many British dialects and goes back several centuries.' The first Canadian citation on record involves Prince Edward Island, as it comes from Thomas Curtis's *A Narrative of the Voyage of Thos. Curtis to the Island of St. John's in the Gulf of St. Lawrence in North America, in the Year 1775* (St. John's being an earlier name for the Island).

4 *Deaf* rhyming with *leaf*. As an older Scottish form, this is another example of the conservatism of rural and colonial speech. Henry Alexander, in the first linguistic fieldwork ever done in the Maritimes, found it frequently used in Nova Scotia in 1940 ('Linguistic Geography,' 1940, p.8).

5 *Film* sounding like *fill'em*, with two syllables. Less frequently, the same intruding vowel can be heard before the *m* in *elm*, and before the *n* in *eastern*, *northern*, *pattern*, and *Tignish*, in other words, before nasals. Inserted sounds of this kind, usually making the word easier to pronounce, are part of the normal process of the evolving language, and have affected the standard as much as dialects. One such insertion – *wash* as *warsh* – currently receives strong condemnation on Prince Edward Island, but remains undefeated, along with the analogous but rarer *swath* as *swarth*.

6 *Greasy* rhyming with *easy*. This pronunciation is more usually associated with British English and southern American English.

7 *Route* rhyming with *out*. This is a common American pronunciation, while the British and usual Canadian variant sounds like *root*. Both are part of a general sound change in progress since the Middle Ages, with different dialects moving slower or faster on different words.

8 *Vase* rhyming with *face*. Several other pronunciations are found in Canada. This one, though now low in prestige, has its roots in older British English.

For all of these pronunciations, the 1972 'Survey of Canadian English' found Prince Edward Islanders either the highest users in the country or close to highest. This finding certainly strengthens their legitimacy in the amalgam that is Island dialect. However, a further study in 1978, Claire Nantes's 'Regional Pronunciation Variants on Prince Edward Island,' set out to test the hypothesis that there are significant rural-urban differences in the pronunciation of these and other words. Her sample, chosen to match that of the 'Survey of Canadian English,' was grade nine students in Charlottetown, Tignish, and Souris. It can be argued that Charlottetown is the only truly urban community of the three, while Tignish and Souris are 'rural towns,' representing west (Egmont) and east (Cardigan) respectively. Nantes gives such figures as *vase* rhyming with *face* used by 84% of the Tignish students and 73% of those in Souris, but by only 28% of the Charlottetonians. Similarly the figures for *calm* rhyming with *Sam* are Tignish 38%, Souris 25%, and Charlottetown 2%; for *film* said as two syllables, they are Tignish 56%, Souris 40%, Charlottetown 24%; for *greasy* sounding like *easy*, they are Tignish 13%, Souris 25%, and Charlottetown 0%. In case after case, Charlottetown, the urban community, uses the 'Island' pronunciation less. Thus, to look at Island usage as a totality, as the 'Survey of Canadian English' did, is to gloss over the important rural-urban distinction, and to average figures that should be kept separate. Prince Edward Island as a *whole* may stand out in Canada in the use of certain pronunciations, but one may find these pronunciations most easily in the countryside. It is obvious that this conclusion supports section I above, in its contention that the rural factor is vital in Island dialect.

A few other noteworthy pronunciations can be listed to complete this point. Although they have not featured in any study they appear to fit into the generalization of the last paragraph. They include: *buoy* rhyming with *chewy* (common in the Maritimes), the proper name *Gaudet* said like *goody*, the letter *H* pronounced *haitch*, *potato* said as *bodado*, the prefix *un-* said as *on*, and the word *yes* indicated by forming the *y* consonant with the mouth and sucking in the breath rather than expelling it. The last two pronunciations can also be observed in New Brunswick speech.

The other main element of pronunciation to be considered is accent. Here, with the help of the Pronunciation Key at the beginning of the entries, and using standard Canadian English as the vantage-point, we might note that some Islanders partake of some of the following:

1 The substitution of \t\ and \d\ for \th\ and \th\. Native English speakers in certain pockets like Tignish and North Rustico have been affected by the local French accent in a few words such as *think*, *three*, *them*, and *these*.

2 The effect of \r\ on certain preceding vowels. By this process, words like *courage*, *thorough*, and *tourist* can change their initial syllable to something like \ōr\; *poor* can do the same, though from a different starting vowel.

3 The substitution of \s\ for \z\. The *spelling*, whether *s* or *z*, is irrelevant. The word *result* is really \rəzult\ in standard Canadian English, whereas on Prince Edward Island it is often \rəsult\. Media coverage on election nights invariably brings out many such utterances of this word. Others noted include *Eliza*, *husband*, *position*, *present*, *represented*, and *resume*. One observer writes that she misheard an acquaintance's hobby as 'racing cats'; what was actually said was 'raising cats.' This characteristic, technically known as 'devoicing,' is probably a legacy from Scottish Gaelic.

4 The 'glottal stop' substituting for \t\. The glottal stop is a consonant that is really a moment of silence, created by the abrupt closing of the vocal cords so that none of the pent-up lung air can get through, followed by a sudden release of that air into the next syllable. (The release is also the sound of the small grunt one makes when lifting a heavy object.) This kind of substitution is a well-known feature of Scottish English, where it involves several consonants. Recorded examples on Prince Edward Island include *bottle*, *mattress*, and *vital*, as well as the second \t\ in *departmental* and *totally*.

5 The substitution of \oo\ for other vowels. This tendency is most noticeable for \u\, and involves words of different spelling all having this vowel in sound: *budget, does, lovely, mud, once, run, was.* Isolated words with other nearby vowels can be part of this phenomenon, especially *won't* \woont\. This feature is probably derived from the north of England.

6 'Dropping the *g*' in verbs like *coming* and *going*. This international marker of informal speech is, strictly, not a case in *sound* of dropping any \g\, for there is none to drop; it is a substitution of one nasal, \n\, for another, \ng\, both of them single sounds. It is listed here only on the grounds that it appears to be accepted in relatively formal contexts in Prince Edward Island English. One observer writes, 'If you hear someone say a distinct *-ing*, you can assume they are either from the University staff or Confederation Centre (the arts centre in Charlottetown; both institutions hire many people "from away").'

7 The substitution of \i\ for \oi\. This feature, definitely a ruralism, affects words like *boil, boy, coil, joint, oil, oyster, point,* and *poison.* In *Folklore Prince Edward Island,* 1974, p. 44, by James and Gertrude Pendergast, a speaker shows his ability to manipulate both the dialect pronunciation and the standard:

One merchant had not learned the slogan 'the customer is always right.' A local resident came into his store and asked 'Have you any biled ile?'

'No,' said the proprietor, 'but we have some boiled oil.'

The deeply offended customer reacted violently shouting, 'Well boil it some more and boil your bloody red head in it;' and out he stalked to buy his 'biled ile' at another store.

8 The substitution of \oi\ for \i\. In the reverse of 7, we have the most wide-spread of all the accentual features in Prince Edward Island English. It is not as strongly articulated as the pronunciation symbols would indicate, being essentially a simple rounding of the lips in words like *ice, ripe, right,* and *wife.* As a rule, the following consonants in these words are 'unvoiced,' spoken without vocal cord vibration. Thus one observer submitted in writing to *DPEIE* an unconscious but revealing mis-spelling: 'shoister – a crook or dishonest fellow.' Noted exceptions to the voicing rule, however, are *fine, pint, violent,* and *violets,* where the vowel is rounded before \n\ and \l\. Antoinette Gallant's 1979 collection of Island Acadian stories, *Little Jack an' de Tax-Man,* has one called 'Little Jack an' de Big Joint' (giant). Almost certainly Ireland is the source of this variant, having given it also to Newfoundland and certain other North American dialects. Generally, the vowel \i\, along with several others, has a centuries-old history of shifting positions, often depending on the following consonant. Even in standard Canadian English, there is a regular alternation between this sound and a neighbouring one, so that *bide* does not have the same vowel as *bite.*

A partial study of the last feature has been done at the University of Prince Edward Island by four linguistics students, and published in T.K. Pratt, 'I Dwell in Possibility: Variable (ay) in Prince Edward Island,' 1982. Recognizing that the pronunciation, though prevalent, was far from universal, this study attempted to correlate \i\ rounding with social factors such as age and sex. While the results were mixed, they appeared to indicate that the feature decreases with education, urban orientation, and negative attitudes towards living on the Island. One very strong finding was that \i\ rounding is not ethnic-predictable: persons of Irish descent are no more likely to say \ois\ for *ice*

than anyone else. As with Irish words
and other words in the Dictionary, the
accent has spread beyond, and partially
abandoned, its point of entry.

Having reviewed accent, and pronunciation generally, we may now glance at a
final aspect of Island dialect, namely folk
sayings. As noted in 'The Scope of the
Dictionary' these have been deliberately
excluded from the present work, even
though they are a kind of vocabulary item.
Nevertheless some indication of their
flavour can be given here. They range from
model proverbs (*I see shells, I can guess
eggs* 'Don't try to fool me'), to proverbial
sayings (*The sun is splitting the trees* 'It's
very hot'), to similes (*as straight as a sleigh
track on the Western Road*), to catch phrases
(*half fun, full earnest*) and sheer nonsense
(*There were thousands and thousands from
Tyne Valley alone* – a jocular estimate of a
not very big crowd).

Such utterances support and amplify the
categories of meaning suggested for the
word list. For example, rural sayings, like
Crooked furrows grow straight grain and
It's down cellar behind the axe (a flippant
reply), are in great abundance. A single
Island proverb can call up a whole farming

scene. *You'll soon see the rabbit* ('The job
is almost done') derives from the cutting of
a hayfield in which the rabbit keeps retreating to the centre, until finally, with no
cover left, it has to bolt. *As ugly as a
stump fence*, which occurs also in the Dictionary entry for *stump fence*, gives a
keen look at the appearance of pioneer
farms: 'The stumps were thrown together
in rows, their roots piteously pawing the
air. Tangled and uneven, they lay there
like giant molars extracted from the bleeding earth' (Helen Champion, *Over on the
Island*, 1939, p. 181). Understatement trivi-
alizes a howling blizzard in *It's a poor day to
set a hen*, while exaggeration defies poverty
in *He hasn't got a pot to pee in or a window to
throw it out of*. Such examples of humour
and courage exist alongside the numerous
squelches (*If your brass were gold you'd be
a millionaire*), the distrust of things different
(*There's one room in his attic not plastered*),
and the vulgarity (*He knows as much about
that as my arse-hole knows about soap-
blowing*).

Folk sayings, like dialect words, can be a
powerful social and psychic probe. They
deserve, in fact, a separate volume on
Prince Edward Island.

Bibliography

Acorn, Milton. *The Island Means Minago*. Toronto: NC Press, 1975
– *I've Tasted My Blood*. Toronto: Ryerson Press, 1969
Advisory Committee on Potatoes. *Atlantic Canada Potato Guide*. N.p.: Published by the authority of the Atlantic Provinces Agricultural Services Co-ordinating Committee, 1984
Affleck, Mrs. Douglas. 'A History of Lower Bedeque.' Unpublished ms. PEI Collection. UPEI, Charlottetown, 1972
Alexander, Henry. 'Linguistic Geography.' 1940. *Journal of the Atlantic Provinces Linguistic Association* 4 (1982): 3–8
Alexandra Women's Institute. *A Short History of the District of Alexandra, Prince Edward Island*. 1965
Allen, J.A., and G. Ennis Smith. *Fox Ranching in Canada*. Ottawa: Department of Agriculture, 1929
Allen, J.A., and W. Chester S. McLure. *Theory and Practice of Fox Ranching*. Charlottetown: Irwin Printing Company, 1926
Alley, Judge. *Prince Edward Island 100 Years Ago*. Lecture transcript. PAPEI, Charlottetown, [1890?]
Andersen, Maude Lane. 'Under Our Own Roof Tree: A Saga of the Lane Family.' Unpublished manuscript. PAPEI, Charlottetown, n.d.
Anderson, Allan. *Salt Water, Fresh Water*. Toronto: Macmillan Canada, 1979
Anderson, Nancy, et al. *Global Village? Global Pillage: Irish Moss from P.E.I. in the World Market*. Charlottetown: Social Action Committee of the Roman Catholic Diocese of Charlottetown, [1977]
Anderson, William W., and Doris Anderson. *Reflections on Life on a Farm at St. Peter's at the Turn of the Century*. Tape recording, UPEI, 1979.
The Anglo-American Magazine 7.1 (July 1855)
Arsenault, Aubin Edmond, ed. *Memoirs of The Hon. A.E. Arsenault*. N.p: n.p., [1951?]
Arsenault, Carmella. 'Acadian Celebration of Mardi Gras.' *The Island Magazine* 4 (Spring-Summer 1978): 29–32
Arsenault, Georges. 'La Mi-Carême.' *The Island Magazine* 9 (Spring-Summer 1981): 8–11
Atlantic Post Calls, 17 November 1982: 11
Auld, Walter C. *Voices of the Island: History of the Telephone on Prince Edward Island*. Halifax: Nimbus Publishing Limited, 1985
Autumn, Gene [George Fall]. 'My Life in Crapaud.' *The Guardian* [Charlottetown] 9 November 1929: 2, 14, 16
Baglole, Harry, comp. *Readings in Prince Edward Island History*. [Charlottetown]: Curriculum Division Staff, Department of Education, Province of Prince Edward Island, 1976
Bagnall, Margaret Ruth. 'The Red Fox.' *Historic Sidelights*. [Charlottetown]: Historical Society of Prince Edward Island, 1956
– 'When I Was Very Young.' Unpublished essay. PAPEI, Charlottetown, [1964]
Bagster, C. Birch. *The Progress and Prospects of Prince Edward Island, Written during the Leisure of a Visit in 1861*. Charlottetown: Queen's Printer, 1861
Bain, Francis. *The Natural History of Prince Edward Island*. Charlottetown: Herbert Haszard, 1890

- 'Notes in Natural History – Prince Edward Island 1868–1877.' Unpublished diary. PAPEI, Charlottetown

Baltic Lot 18 Women's Institute. *History of Baltic Lot 18*. n.d.

Barker, H.T. 'The Ice Road.' *The Atlantic Advocate* 54.6 (February 1964): 49–54

Barr, J.R. *The Golden Pelt*. Ottawa: n.p., 1913

'Beaches Bless P.E.I. Shores.' *The Globe and Mail*, 23 April 1983: ET 9

Bedeque Area Multicultural Family Tree Report. Bedeque Days Committee, 1978

Bernard, J. Blaine. 'Dictionary of Irish Moss.' Unpublished student essay. UPEI, Charlottetown, 1986

Bird, Will R. *These Are the Maritimes*. Toronto: The Ryerson Press, 1959

'The Black Fox Industry in P.E.I.' *The Busy East of Canada* 3.12 (September 1913): 6–8

Blakely, Phyllis Ruth, and Myra C. Vernon. *The Story of Prince Edward Island*. Toronto: J.M. Dent and Sons (Canada) Limited, 1963

Bloomfield Historical Society. *History of Saint Anthony Parish, 1803–1980*. The Research Committee of the Bloomfield Historical Society, 1980

Blue, Alex, et al., comps. *History of Hopefield*. Young Canada Works project, 1978

Bolger, Francis W.P., Wayne Barrett, and Anne Mackay. *Memories of the Old Home Place*. [Toronto]: Oxford University Press, 1984

Bouchette, Joseph. *The British Dominions in North America; or a Topographical and Statistical Description of the Provinces of Lower and Upper Canada*. 2 vols. London, 1832

Boyles, Anne. 'Living in Harmony.' MA Diss. University of New Brunswick, 1983

Brehaut, Mary, ed. *Historic Highlights of Prince Edward Island*. Charlottetown: Historical Society of Prince Edward Island, [1959]

Bremner, Benjamin. *An Island Scrap Book: Historical and Traditional*. Charlottetown: Irwin Printing Company, 1932

- *Memories of Long Ago: Being a Series of Sketches Pertaining to Charlottetown in the Past*. Charlottetown: Irwin Printing Company, 1930

A Bridge to the Past: Wilmot Valley, 1784–1979. Wilmot Valley Historical Society, 1980

Brookes, Alan A. 'Islanders in the Boston States 1850–1900.' *The Island Magazine* 2 (Spring-Summer 1977): 11–15

Brown, Ira M. *Sketches of the First Settlers of Little York*. York Women's Institute, 1967

Bruce, Harry. 'Silver into Gold: Alchemy in Action on Prince Edward Island's Booming Fox Farms.' *Equinox* 4.4 (July/August 1985): 56–69

Burnett, Mary. 'Handwoven and Homespun.' *Canadian Antiques Collector: A Journal of Antiques and Fine Arts* 8.1 (1973): 20–23

Burpee, Lawrence J. 'Prince Edward Island.' *Canadian Geographical Journal* 33 (November 1946): 193–213

Burt, Rona. *From Roots and Ashes the Gardens Grow*. Kensington, PEI: Senior Citizens Happy Group of Kensington, 1979

Bushey, Sarah. 'Memoirs of Sarah Bushey.' Unpublished diary. April 21, 1891–April 14, 1894

Cairns, Scott. 'Diary: January 1, 1909–May 31, 1920.' Unpublished diary. David Weale Collection. UPEI, Charlottetown

- 'Diary: January 1, 1932–March 31, 1939.' Unpublished diary. David Weale Collection. UPEI, Charlottetown

Callbeck, Lorne C. *The Cradle of Confederation: A Brief History of Prince Edward Island from Its Discovery in 1534 to the Present Time*. Fredericton, NB: Brunswick Press, 1964

- *My Island, My People*. Charlottetown: The Prince Edward Island Heritage Foundation, 1979

- 'Sagas of the Strait.' *The Atlantic Advocate* 49.6 (February 1959): 58–61

Campbell, Alphonsus P. 'The Heritage of the Highland Scot in Prince Edward Island.' *The Island Magazine* 15 (Spring-Summer 1984): 3–8

- 'The Heritage of the Highland Scots in P.E.I.' *Revue de l'Université d'Ottawa*, 51–55. Ottawa: Editions de l'Université d'Ottawa, 1975

- 'Local Color.' *Variations on a Gulf Breeze*. Ed. Florence Roper. The Literary Committee, Prince Edward Island 1973 Centennial Commission, 1973

Campbell, Frank. *As the Fella Says …* Charlottetown: Kay Cee Publications, 1983

Canada. Agriculture Canada. Livestock Division and Animal Pathology Division. *Fox Farming in Canada.* Ottawa, 1979

Canada. Commission of Conservation. Committee on Fisheries, Game and Fur-bearing Animals. *Conservation of Fish, Birds and Game: Proceedings at a Meeting of the Committee, November 1 and 2, 1915.* Toronto: The Methodist Book and Publishing House, 1916

Canada. Department of Agriculture. *Growing Garden Potatoes* Ottawa, 1976

– *The Plants of Prince Edward Island.* By David S. Erskine. Ottawa, 1960

Canada. Department of Marine and Fisheries. *Report of the Commissioners ... to Enquire into and Report upon the Lobster and Oyster Fisheries of Canada.* Ottawa, 1887

Canada. Fisheries Research Board of Canada. Atlantic Biological Station, St. Andrews, N.B. *Irish Moss Industry in the Maritime Provinces.* St. Andrews, NB, 1947

Canada. House of Commons. Select Standing Committee on Marine and Fisheries. *Lobster Fishery Evidence Taken before Commander William Wakeham, M.D., Officer in Charge of the Gulf Fisheries Division, in Quebec and the Maritime Provinces.* Ottawa, 1910

Carleton Women's Institute. *A History of Carleton, Prince Edward Island.* n.d.

Carr, Margaret. 'Terms of Fox Farming on P.E.I.' Unpublished student essay. UPEI, Charlottetown, 1986

Cavendish, Maud [Lucy Maud Montgomery]. 'Our Charivari.' *The Years before 'Anne.'* By Francis W.P. Bolger. [Charlottetown]: The Prince Edward Island Heritage Foundation, 1974

Champion, Helen Jean. *Over on the Island.* Toronto: The Ryerson Press, 1939

Cheverie, Leo. 'Johnson's Lobster Factory 1935–1945.' Unpublished essay. PEI Collection. UPEI, Charlottetown, 1982

Clark, Andrew Hill. *Three Centuries and the Island: A Historical Geography of Settlement and Agriculture in Prince Edward Island, Canada.* Toronto: University of Toronto Press; London: Oxford University Press, 1959

Climo, Lindee. *Chester's Barn.* Montreal: Tundra Books, 1982

'Come Listen My Friends.' Unpublished poem. David Weale Collection. UPEI, Charlottetown, n.d.

Connors, Tom. 'Song of the Irish Moss.' 1967

Cotton, W.L. *Chapters in Our Island Story.* Charlottetown: Irwin Printing Company, 1927

Coulson, Mrs. John. 'A Phantom Train.' *Folklore of Prince Edward Island,* 42–4. [Charlottetown]: Historical Society of P.E.I., n.d.

Crapaud Women's Institute. *History of Crapaud, Prince Edward Island.* 2 vols. n.d

Crockett, Vernon. 'Diary from York: First World War, 1915–1917.' Unpublished diary. David Weale Collection. UPEI, Charlottetown

Crosskill, W.H. *Handbook of Prince Edward Island; The Garden Province of Canada.* Charlottetown: Published by the Provincial Government, 1906

Cullen, Constance. 'Dialect Research on Prince Edward Island.' *The English Quarterly* 4.3 (1971): 51–3

Cullen, Timothy Peter. 'Some Pages from a Diary of T.P. Cullen, 1888–1889.' Unpublished diary. PEI Collection. UPEI, Charlottetown

Curtis, Thomas. 'A Narrative of the Voyage of Thos. Curtis to the Island of St. John's in the Gulf of the St. Lawrence in North America, in the Year 1775.' *Journeys to the Island of St. John or Prince Edward Island, 1775–1832.* Ed. D.C. Harvey. Toronto: Macmillan, 1955

Daley, Hartwell. *Volunteers in Action – The Prince Edward Island Division, Canadian Red Cross, 1907–1979.* Charlottetown: PEI Red Cross Society, 1981

Daly, Whitman C. 'Daly: The Saga of a Family 1820–1926 and My Boyhood on Prince Edward, Island.' PEI Collection. UPEI, Charlottetown, [1969]

– *Prince Edward Island – The Way It Was.* N.p.: Privately published, 1978

A Description of Prince Edward Island in the Gulf of St. Laurence, North America; with a Map of the Island and a Few Cursory Observations. ... London: Robert Ashby and Co., 1805

Devereux, Joseph. *Looking Backward.* N.p.: n.p., [post 1979]

Dewar, Lloyd George. *A History of My Family and the Family Farm at New Perth, Prince*

Edward Island. [Summerside]: Williams and Crue, 1975

Diblee, Randall. *Folksongs from Prince Edward Island*. Summerside: Williams and Crue, 1973

Dixon, Margaret. *Going Home: An Autobiography*. Privately published, 1979

Dockerty, Malcolm B. *Rhymed Reminiscences of a Pathologist: His Life's Story*. Privately published, 1980

– *Streamside Reminiscences: Selected Instant Replays*. Privately published, [1981]

Dominion Fox Illustration Station P.E.I., N.S. and N.B. *Progress Report, 1943–1947*. Ottawa: Queen's Printer, 1949

Down Memory Lane: Stories and Poems as Told by Residents of Maplewood Manor, and Senior Citizens of the Area. Privately published with the assistance of a Summer Canada: Community Project and with the assistance of Holland College, West Prince and Summerside Center, 1982

Dressman, Michael R. 'Redd Up.' *American Speech* 54 (1979): 141–5

Duffy, Charles. 'Lexicon of Beef Farming.' Unpublished student essay. UPEI, Charlottetown, 1986

Dyer, Rev. Robert. 'Diary, 1859–1883.' Unpublished diary. PAPEI, Charlottetown

East Point United Baptist Church 1833–1983 Historical Record. Charlottetown: Island Offset, 1983

Evans, Millie, and Eric Mullen. *Our Maritimes*. Tantallon, NS: Four East Publications, 1979

The Examiner – Weekly Edition, 11 February 1881, n. pag.

Ferguson, Donald. *Agricultural Education: A Lecture, Delivered before the Young Men's Christian Association, Charlottetown, P.E. Island, on Thursday Evening, January 17th, 1884*. Charlottetown: J.W. Mitchell, 1884

Ffrench, A. *A Current Appraisal of the Irish Moss Industry*. N.p.: Departments of Fisheries, Nova Scotia, New Brunswick, Prince Edward Island; and the Industrial Branch, Fisheries Service, Department of Fisheries and Forestry of Canada, 1970

Fischer, Lewis R. 'The Shipping Industry of Nineteenth-Century Prince Edward Island: A Brief History.' *The Island Magazine* 4 (Spring-Summer 1978): 15–21

Fleming, Richard. 'Lobstering.' Unpublished poem, 1985

Flood, Shannon. 'Fox Farming.' Unpublished student essay. UPEI, Charlottetown, 1986

'Foley Family Diary 1876–1971.' Unpublished diary. PAPEI, Charlottetown

Forester, Joseph E., and Anne D. Forester. *Silver Fox Odyssey: History of the Canadian Silver Fox Industry*. Charlottetown: The Canadian Silver Fox Breeders Association with the P.E.I. Department of Agriculture and Forestry, 1980

Fox-Tales. Summerside: Greater Summerside Chamber of Commerce, 1.1–12 (November 1981–October 1982)

Frank, Leo. *Silver Fox Farming: The Industrial Marvel of the Twentieth Century*. Southport, PEI: Rosebank Fur Farms Ltd., 1925

Freetown Historical Society. *Freetown Past and Present*, 1985

Gallant, Antoinette. *'Little Jack an' de Tax Man' and Other Acadian Stories from Prince Edward Island*. Fernwood, PEI: Elaine Harrison and Associates, 1979

The Gazetteer and Guide to the Lower Provinces, for 1876–77: Containing Routes for Summer Travel. Halifax: Charles D. McAlpine, 1876

Gojmerac, Anna. 'Prince Edward Island Expressions.' Unpublished student essay. UPEI, Charlottetown, 1986

Graves, Ross. *William Schurman, Loyalist of Bedeque, Prince Edward Island; and His Descendants*. 2 vols. Summerside: Harold B. Schurman, 1973

Green, Alice. *Footprints on the Sands of Time*. Summerside: Williams and Crue, 1980

Green, John Eldon. Rev. of *The Garden Transformed*, ed. Verner Smitheram, David Milne, and Sadatal Dasgupta. *The Island Magazine* 12 (Fall-Winter 1982): 30–31

Greenhill, Basil, and Ann Giffard. *Westcountrymen in Prince Edward's Isle*. Newton Abbot, Devon: David and Charles (Publishers); Toronto: University of Toronto Press, 1967

Griffin, Diane. *Atlantic Wildflowers*. Toronto: Oxford University Press, 1984

The Guardian, Charlottetown

Gunn, Paul. 'The Silver Fox Industry on Prince

Edward Island.' M.A. Diss. Mount Allison University, 1973

Hammond, Elaine. 'The Sinking of the "Thisisit".' *Atlantic Insight* 6.5 (May 1984): 31–3

Hansuld, E.J. *Effie's Rock: A Tale of Prince Edward Island*. Mississauga, Ontario: Self Publisher's Press, 1980

Harris, Elmer. *Johnny Belinda: A Play*. London: Samuel French, 1956

Harris, Robert. *Some Pages From An Artist's Life*. Charlottetown: n.p., n.d.

Harris, Sarah. 'Letter to Martha Harris' [1858]. *The Island Family Harris*. By Robert Critchlow Tuck. Charlottetown: Ragweed Press, 1983

Hart, George Edward. *The Story of Old Abegweit: A Sketch of Prince Edward Island History*. N.p.: n.p., n.d.

Haslam, Doris Muncey. *The Wrights of Bedeque, Prince Edward Island: A Loyalist Family*. 2 vols. Summerside: Williams and Crue, 1978

Hemphill, John. 'Some of My Experiences at Sea, Part One.' *The Island Magazine* 11 (Spring-Summer 1982): 29–33

Hennessey, Catherine G. 'Heritage Foundation.' *Canadian Antiques Collector: A Journal of Antiques and Fine Arts* 8.1 [1973]: 66–7

Hennessey, Michael. 'Mister Currie's Protestant Shoes.' *An Arch for the King and Other Stories*, 11–19. Charlottetown: Ragweed Press, 1984

– 'The Priest and the Pallbearer.' *An Arch for the King and Other Stories*, 75–82. Charlottetown: Ragweed Press, 1984

– 'Sainthood and the CCM Bicycle.' *An Arch for the King and Other Stories*, 33–9. Charlottetown: Ragweed Press, 1984

– 'The Trial of Minnie McGee.' Unpublished play. 1983

Hickman, W. Albert. *The Sacrifice of the Shannon*. New York: Frederick A. Stokes Company, 1903

Hill, S.S. *A Short Account of Prince Edward Island, Designed Chiefly for the Information of Agriculturist and Other Emigrants of Small Capital*. London: Madden and Co., 1839

Hind, H.Y. *Eighty Years' Progress of British North America*. Toronto: L. Stebbins, 1864

History of North Tryon, Prince Edward Island, 1663–1973. North Tryon Women's Institute, [1973]

Hocking, Anthony. *Prince Edward Island*. Toronto: McGraw-Hill Ryerson, 1978

Hornby, Susan J. 'George Young: Horsing Around.' *The Island Magazine* 10 (Fall-Winter 1981): 27–32

Howatt, Betty. 'History Begins at Home.' *The Island Magazine* 9 (Spring-Summer 1981): 23–7

Howatt, Cornelius. 'The Farm Family.' *Canadian Antiques Collector: A Journal of Antiques and Fine Arts* 8.1 (1973): 61–5

Hudson, J. Arthur, and S. Jean Meggison. *Preserving the Past: A History of Cascumpec – Fortune Cove, 1779–1979*. Cascumpec – Fortune Cove Heritage Society, 1979

Ince, C.C. *Old DeSable*. DeSable Women's Institute, 1982

Indian River Women's Institute. *History of Indian River*. 1973

The Island Farmer. Summerside: The Pioneer Publishing Co., 1900–7

Ives, Edward D. 'The Boys of the Island: P.I.'s in the Maine Lumberwoods.' *The Island Magazine* 16 (Fall-Winter 1984): 28–35

– *Larry Gorman: The Man Who Made the Songs*. Bloomington: Indiana University Press, 1977 [1964]

– *Lawrence Doyle: The Farmer Poet of Prince Edward Island. A Study in Local Songmaking*. Orono: University of Maine Press, 1971

Jeffery, Mary, and Eva Jeffery. *The Diary of Mary and Eva Jeffery* [1926].Ed. Carter W. Jeffery. Privately published, 1984

Jenkins, J.B. 'Lobstering in the Maritimes.' *The P.E.I. Environeer* 6.3 (Summer 1978): 7

Johnson, Georgina May. *Life in the Parsonage*. N.p.: n.p., n.d.

Johnston, Lorne. *More Recollections of an Ole Salt*. Charlottetown: Prince Edward Island Heritage Foundation, [1983?]

– *Recollections of an 'Ole Salt*. Privately published, 1982

Johnstone, Mrs. Andrew. 'Making Cloth.' Unpublished essay. PAPEI, Charlottetown, [1964]

Johnstone, Rena Wood. *Journal of the Months at Strathaven. Observations, Thoughts and Sounds Experienced in Retirement Years at New Haven, Prince Edward Island*. [Summerside]: Williams and Crue, 1980

Johnstone, Walter. ' "Letters" and "Travels" Prince Edward Island, 1821.' *Journeys to the Island of St. John or Prince Edward Island*. Ed. D.C. Harvey. Toronto: Macmillan Canada, 1955

– *A Series of Letters, Descriptive of Prince Edward Island ... To the Rev. John Wightman, Minister of Kirkmahoe, Dumfries-Shire*. Dumfries, 1822

Jones, J. Walter. *Fur-Farming in Canada*. 2nd ed. Ottawa: The Mortimer Company, 1914

Jones, Orlo, and Douglas Fraser. 'Those Elusive Immigrants.' *The Island Magazine* 16 (Fall-Winter 1984): 36–41

The Journal-Pioneer, Summerside

Journal-Pioneer Annual Farm Issue. Summerside: Journal Pioneer, 1972–78

Kelley, Francis Clement. *The Bishop Jots It Down: An Autobiographical Strain on Memories*. New York: Harper and Brothers, 1939

Kennedy, Earle K. *The Prince Edward Island Tree Cent*. Privately published, 1976

Kennedy, Libby. 'A Visitor's Guide to the Language of the Wharf.' Unpublished student essay. UPEI, Charlottetown, 1985

Khattak, Jahan N., and William Lewis. *Growing Potatoes for Processing in Prince Edward Island*. Charlottetown: n.p., 1971

Knox, George. 'Island Fences.' *The Island Magazine* 8 (1980): 21–6

Lamont, Ewen. *A Biographical Sketch of the Late Rev. Donald McDonald*. Charlottetown: John Coombs, 1892

Lamont, Murdoch. 'Diary, 1885–1888.' Unpublished diary. PEI Collection. UPEI, Charlottetown

– *Rev. Donald McDonald: Glimpses of His Life and Times*. Charlottetown: Murley and Garnhum, 1902

Larkin, Alexander. 'Diary: April 3, 1886–April 3, 1890.' Unpublished diary. David Weale Collection. UPEI, Charlottetown

Laviolette, Emily A. *The Oyster and the Mermaid and Other Island Stories*. Fernwood, PEI: Elaine Harrison and Associates, 1975

Lawson, Helen A. *Colonel John Hamilton Gray (Father of Confederation) and Inkerman House*. Charlottetown: n.p., 1973

Lawson, James D. 'The Wreck of the Laurentian – Concluded.' *The Prince Edward Island Magazine* 4.1 (March 1902): 13–17

Leard, George Artemas. 'The George Leard Files.' PAPEI, Charlottetown, 1977

– *Historic Bedeque: The Loyalists at Work and Worship in Prince Edward Island. A History of Bedeque United Church*. Bedeque, PEI: Bedeque United Church, 1948

– 'What a Life.' *Health Rays* 2.3 (April 1929): 13–17

Ledwell, Frank J. *The North Shore of Home*. Halifax: Nimbus Publishing Limited, 1986

Ledwell, Frank, and Reshard Gool. *Portraits and Gastroscopes*. Charlottetown: Square Deal Publications, 1972

Lewellin, J.L. *Emigration. Prince Edward Island, a Brief Account of This Fine Colony*. Charlottetown, 1832

Linkletter, Graeme. 'Potato Storage Important.' *The Corner Post* 2.9 (October 1982): 6–7

The Long River Women's Institute. *A History of Long River, Prince Edward Island, Canada, 1787–1967*. 1967

MacArthur, F.H. 'The Ghost of Barlow Road.' *Folklore of Prince Edward Island*. [Charlottetown]: Historical Society of Prince Edward Island, n.d.

MacDonald, Austin C. 'Diary 1881–1916.' Unpublished diary. PAPEI, Charlottetown

MacDonald, Bertha Mae MacIntyre. *Through All the Days Gone By*. Privately published, [1983?]

MacDonald, Edward. 'Diaries of Edward MacDonald, Vol. 1, June 30, 1910–Dec. 31, 1910.' Unpublished diary. PAPEI, Charlottetown

– 'Diary 1911.' Unpublished diary. David Weale Collection. UPEI, Charlottetown

MacDonald, Edward. 'The Great Adventure: Travel Letters of William MacDonald.' *The Island Magazine* 17 (Summer 1985): 24–31

– Rev. of *Memories of the Old Home Place: Prince Edward Island*. *The Island Magazine* 17 (Summer 1985): 38–9

MacDonald, Hubert T. *The Lords of the Isles and Their Descendants*. Winnipeg: n.p., 1944

MacDonald, Mary, and Mrs. Clinton Stewart. *Historical Sketch of Eastern Kings*. N.p.: n.p., 1972

MacDonald, Rose Marie, et al. *Those Were the Days: A History of the North Side of the Boughton River*. [1980?]

MacDougall, Arlene, and Violet MacEachern. *The Banks of the Elliott*. [Charlottetown]: Irwin Printing Company, 1973

McEacheron, John. 'A Diary or Memorandum of Weather, Work and Other Incidents Connected with the Farm and District Being a Continuation of Such since 1839.' Ed. David Weale. David Weale Collection. UPEI, Charlottetown

MacFadyen, Jean. *For the Sake of the Record*. Summerside: Williams and Crue, n.d.

MacFarlane, Constance I. *Irish Moss in the Maritime Provinces*. Halifax: Nova Scotia Research Foundation, 1956

MacFarlane, J. Harrison. 'When I Was Very Young.' Unpublished essay. PAPEI, Charlottetown, [1964]

McGaucen, Mrs. John. 'Diary of Mrs. John McGaucen (1914–1916).' Unpublished diary. PAPEI, Charlottetown

MacGregor, John. *British America*. 2nd ed. London, 1833

MacKinnon, John. *A Sketch Book: Comprising Historical Incidents, Traditional Tales and Translations*. Privately published, 1915

MacKinnon, Wayne E. 'A Short History of Prince Edward Island.' *Readings in Prince Edward Island History*, 115–22. Comp. Harry Baglole. [Charlottetown]: Curriculum Division Staff, Department of Education, Province of Prince Edward Island, 1976

MacLeod, Ada. *Roads to Summerside: The Story of Early Summerside and the Surrounding Area*. N.p.: n.p., 1980

MacLeod, Andrew. 'Diary: January 1, 1928–November 17, 1932.' Unpublished diary. David Weale Collection. UPEI, Charlottetown

MacLeod, Margaret Furness. 'Four Scripts Inspired by Childhood Memories in Prince Edward Island.' Unpublished CBC script, n.d.

MacLeod, Salome. *Memories of Beach Point and Cape Bear*. N.p.: n.p., n.d.

MacMillan, Janet. 'The Language of Lobster Fishing.' Unpublished student essay. UPEI, Charlottetown, 1985

MacNevin, Mrs. Lorne. *Past and Present: A History of Brae*. Summerside: Brae Heritage Group, 1979

Macoun, W.T. *The Potato in Canada: Its Cultiva-*

tion and Varieties. Ottawa: Department of Agriculture, 1918

MacPhail, Sir Andrew. *The Master's Wife*. Toronto: McClelland and Stewart, 1977 [1939]

MacQuarrie, Heath. 'Recollections of His Early Childhood and Society on Prince Edward Island.' Unpublished compilation. PEI Collection. UPEI, Charlottetown, 1985

Macqueen, Malcolm. *Hebridean Pioneers*. Winnipeg: Printed by Henderson Directories, 1957

– *Skye Pioneers and 'The Island.'* Winnipeg: Stovel, 1929

MacRae, Allan. 'From Our Past.' Column, Oct. 14, 1981–Dec. 15, 1982. Compiled from issues of *The Eastern Graphic* (Montague) and *The West Prince Graphic* (Alberton). 1983

Martin, Finley. *A View from the Bridge: Montague, P.E.I.* Montague, 1984

Matthew, Margaret. 'Garden in the Gulph.' *Canadian Antiques Collector. A Journal of Antiques and Fine Arts* 8.1 (1973): 13–14

McCabe, Wayne. *Potato Wash and Wax Test*. Charlottetown: Market Development Centre, 1974

McCarvill, Lisa. 'A Potato Farming Lexicon from Kinkora, P.E.I.' Unpublished student essay. UPEI, Charlottetown, 1986

McConnell, R.E. *Our Own Voice: Canadian English and How It Is Studied*. Toronto: Gage Educational Publishing, 1979

McCready, J.E.B. 'Traditions of Prince Edward Island.' *Dalhousie Review* 3 (July 1923): 204–11

McLeod, Neil. *Prince Edward Island*. N.p.: n.p., [1900?]

M'Cormac, G.J. 'The Kingdom of Fish.' *Prince Edward Island Magazine* 3 (July 1901): 176–80

McSwain, John. 'Our Feathered Friends – No. 5. Second Series.' *Prince Edward Island Magazine* 7.1 (January 1905): 4–7

Medcof, J.C. *Oyster Farming in the Maritimes*. Ottawa: Fisheries Research Board of Canada, 1961

Meggison, Eleanor Carr. 'Diaries of Eleanor Carr Meggison.' Unpublished diary, [1923–1939]. PAPEI, Charlottetown

'Meggison Family Account Book.' Unpublished ms., [1811–1874]. PAPEI, Charlottetown

'Meggison Family Diary, 1809–1950.' Unpublished diary. PAPEI, Charlottetown

Meggison, George Eden. 'Diaries of George Eden Meggison.' Unpublished diary, [1906–1918]. PAPEI, Charlottetown.

Mellick, Henry George. *Timothy's Boyhood: or Pioneer Country Life on Prince Edward Island.* Kentville, NS: The Kentville Publishing Co., 1933

Miller, Lloyd J. *Our Forefathers Builded Wisely.* N.p.: n.p., [post-1979]

Milligan, Doris. *Shipwreck: A Novelette.* N.p.: West Prince Arts Council, 1983

Moar, George. 'Diary: February 1, 1881–July 31, 1881.' David Weale Collection. UPEI, Charlottetown

Moase, M. Louise. *The History of New Annan, Prince Edward Island, Canada, 1800–1971.* N.p.: New Annan Women's Institute, 1971

Mollison, John. 'Reminiscent.' *The Prince Edward Island Magazine* 2.7 (September 1900): 231–2

Monro, Alexander. *New Brunswick; with a Brief Outline of Nova Scotia, and Prince Edward Island.* Halifax: Printed by Richard Nugent, 1855

Montgomery, Lucy Maud. *The Alpine Path: The Story of My Career.* Don Mills, Ont: Fitzhenry and Whiteside, 1917

– *Anne of Green Gables.* Boston: L.C. Page Company, 1908

– *Anne of Ingleside.* London: George G. Harrap and Co., 1978 [1939]

– *Anne of the Island.* Boston: The Page Company, 1915

– *Anne of Windy Poplars.* Toronto: McClelland and Stewart, 1936

– *Anne's House of Dreams.* New York: Frederick A. Stokes Company, 1917

– *The Blue Castle: A Novel.* Toronto: McClelland and Stewart, 1926

– 'The Doctor's Sweetheart.' *The Doctor's Sweetheart and Other Stories,* 72–80. Toronto: McGraw-Hill Ryerson, 1979 [1908]

– *Emily Climbs.* Toronto: McClelland and Stewart, 1925

– *Emily of New Moon.* Toronto: McClelland and Stewart, 1923

– *Emily's Quest.* New York: Frederick A. Stokes Company, 1927

– *From Prince Albert to P.E. Island. The Daily Patriot,* 31 October 1891: 1–2

– *Further Chronicles of Avonlea.* Toronto: McGraw-Hill Ryerson, 1953 [1920]

– *The Golden Road.* Toronto: McGraw-Hill Ryerson, 1944 [1910]

– *Jane of Lantern Hill.* Toronto: McClelland and Stewart, 1936

– 'Letter to Penzie MacNeill.' [1890]. *The Years before 'Anne,'* 91–3. By Francis W.P. Bolger. [Charlottetown]: Prince Edward Island Heritage Foundation, 1974

– 'Letter to Ephraim Weber.' *The Green Gables Letters: From L.M. Montgomery to Ephraim Weber, 1905–1909.* Toronto: The Ryerson Press, 1960

– *Mistress Pat.* Toronto: McClelland and Stewart, 1935

– *My Dear Mr. M: Letters to G.B. MacMillan from L.M. Montgomery.* Ed. Francis W.P. Bolger and Elizabeth R. Epperly. Toronto: McGraw-Hill Ryerson, 1980

– *Pat of Silver Bush.* Toronto: McClelland and Stewart, 1933

– 'Prince Edward Island.' *The Spirit of Canada: A Souvenir of Welcome to H.M. George VI and H.M. Queen Elizabeth.* N.p.: Canadian Pacific Railway, 1939

– *Rainbow Valley.* Toronto: McClelland and Stewart, 1923

– *Rilla of Ingleside.* Toronto: McClelland and Stewart, 1973 [1920]

– *The Road to Yesterday.* Toronto: McGraw-Hill Ryerson, 1974 [pre-1940]

– *Spirit of Place: Lucy Maud Montgomery and Prince Edward Island.* Ed. Francis W.P. Bolger, Wayne Barrett, and Anne MacKay. Toronto: Oxford University Press, 1982

– *A Tangled Web.* Toronto: McClelland and Stewart, 1972 [1931]

– 'The Wreck of the Marco Polo.' 1891. *The Years before 'Anne,'* 33–6. By Francis W.P. Bolger. [Charlottetown]: Prince Edward Island Heritage Foundation, 1974

Morell: Its History. Morell: Jubilee Senior Citizens Club, 1980

Morris, Donald W. *An Introduction to the Current State of the P.E.I. Fishing Industry, Focusing on the Years 1971–1975.* Charlottetown: Department of Regional and Economic Expansion, 1976

Morris, Mary Elizabeth. *The Way It Was: A Brief Social History of the Boughton River Area 1890–1930*. St. George's, PEI: n.p., 1981

Morrison, A.L. *My Island Pictures: The Story of Prince Edward Island*. Charlottetown: Ragweed Press, 1980

– *A History of Grand Tracadie*. N.p.: n.p., 1963

Morrison, Allan. *A Giant among Friends*. Cornerbrook, Newfoundland: MacKenzie Books, 1980

Morrison, J. Clinton Jr. *Along the North Shore: A Social History of Township 11, P.E.I. 1765–1982*. St. Eleanor's, PEI: Privately published, 1983

– *Emigrant from the Highlands: Robert W. Morrison, Sr. and His Descendants; the Genealogy of a P.E.I Family 1831–1978*. N.p.: n.p., 1978

Murphy, J. Elmer. *A Newspaperman Remembers*. Summerside: Williams and Crue, [1980?]

Nantes, Claire. 'Regional Pronunciation Variants on Prince Edward Island.' Unpublished student essay. UPEI, Charlottetown, 1978

Nicholson, Mrs. Angus A. 'A Story of Early Days in Belfast.' *Folklore of Prince Edward Island*. [Charlottetown]: Historical Society of Prince Edward Island, n.d.

O'Connor, Maurice. 'Diary: January 1–December 31, 1895.' David Weale Collection. UPEI, Charlottetown

'The Opposition Break-down' [ballad, 1898–1901]. 'Looking Back.' Unpublished compilation from issues of *The Eastern Graphic*, 1978–1980. 2 vols. Comp. Adele Townshend. PEI Collection. UPEI, Charlottetown, 1979

Oliver, Gertrude Hazel Meggison. 'Diaries of Gertrude Hazel Meggison Oliver.' Unpublished diary, [1905–1970]. PAPEI, Charlottetown

Orton, Harold, and Eugen Dieth. *Survey of English Dialects*. Leeds: E.J. Arnold, 1962

Paynter, Ruth L. *From the Top of the Hill: The History of an Island Community – Irishtown-Burlington*. The Heritage Group of Irishtown-Burlington, 1977

P.E.I. Mutual Fire Insurance Company. *Annual Report, 1983*

P.E.I. Numismatic Society. 'Island Currency.' *Canadian Antiques Collector* 8.1 (1973): 24–5

Pendergast, Gertrude. *A Good Time Was Had by All*. Summerside: Williams and Crue, 1981

Pendergast, James, and Gertrude Pendergast. *Folklore Prince Edward Island*. N.p.: n.p., [1974]

Pigot, Franklin L. *A History of Mount Stewart, Prince Edward Island*. Charlottetown: n.p., 1975

Pratt, T[erry] K[enneth]. 'I Dwell in Possibility: Variable (ay) in Prince Edward Island.' *Journal of the Atlantic Provinces Linguistic Association* 4 (1982): 27–35

– 'Island English: The Case of the Disappearing Dialect.' *The Garden Transformed: Prince Edward Island, 1945–1980*, 231–43. Ed. Verner Smitheram, David Milne, and Sadatal Dasgupta. Charlottetown: Ragweed Press, 1982

Prince Edward Island. *Debates and Proceedings of the Legislative Council*. PAPEI, Charlottetown, [1868]

Prince Edward Island. *P.E.I. Legislative Assembly Journal*. Appendix H. 1864–65

Prince Edward Island. Department of the Environment and Tourism. *Birds, Bush and Barnacles, Prince Edward Island*. [1974]

Prince Edward Island. Department of Fisheries. *Lobster Bait Net: 1975*. PEI Collection. UPEI, Charlottetown

– *Offshore Lobster: Technical Report #175, 1975*. PEI Collection. UPEI, Charlottetown

Prince Edward Island Historical Society. *Folklore of Prince Edward Island*. [Charlottetown], n.d.

– *Pioneers on the Island, part 1*. N.p., [1959]

– *Pioneers on the Island, part 2*. N.p., n.d.

Prince Edward Island: information regarding its climate, soil, resources suitability for summer visitors and tourists, etc., etc. Ottawa: Maclean Roger and Co., 1888

Prince Edward Island Magazine. Charlottetown: The Examiner Publishing Company, March 1899–January 1905

Prince Edward Island Multicultural Council of Charlottetown. *An Exploratory Survey of First-Generation Immigrants Living on Prince Edward Island*. Charlottetown: n.p., 1980

Prince Edward Island. Natural History Society. *Winds of Sea and Wood*. N.p., 1975

Prince Edward Island 1973 Centennial Commission. *Centennial '73*. Charlottetown: n.p., 1973

Prince Edward Island Potato Handbook. Charlotte-town: The Prince Edward Island Potato Marketing Board, 1980

Prince Edward Island. Roads Correspondence. 'Letters. 1913.' Unpublished letters. PAPEI, Charlottetown

'Prince Edward Island: The Garden of the Gulf; its men of action and its resources.' Supplement to *The Charlottetown Guardian*, July 1915

Prince Edward Island Register. [Charlottetown, 1828]. UPEI, Charlottetown

Ramsay, Sterling. *Folklore Prince Edward Island*. Charlottetown: Square Deal Publications, 1973

Rand, Rev. Silas T. *Micmac Dictionary*. Charlottetown: Published by direction of the Canadian Government, 1902

Rankin, Robert Allan. *Down at the Shore: A History of Summerside, Prince Edward Island (1752–1945)*. Charlottetown: Prince Edward Island Heritage Foundation, 1980

Ready, J.A. 'Lot Twenty: From Forest to Farm, II.' *Prince Edward Island Magazine* 1.5 (July 1899): 192–5

Roberts, Charles G.D. *The Canadian Guide-Book: The Tourist's and Sportsman's Guide to Eastern Canada and Newfoundland*. London: William Heinemann, 1892

Robertson, Ian Ross. Introduction. *The Master's Wife*. By Andrew MacPhail. Toronto: McClelland and Stewart, 1977

– 'Notable Prince Edward Islanders.' *Canadian Antiques Collector. A Journal of Antiques and Fine Arts* 8.1 (1973): 15–17

Robertson, Janice. 'A Dictionary of Lobster Fishing in the Eastern Kings Area.' Unpublished student essay. UPEI, Charlottetown, 1986

Rogers, Irene L. 'Island Homes.' *The Island Magazine* 1 (Fall Winter 1976): 9–13

Rogers, Stan. 'Make and Break Harbour.' *Atlantic Folk Poetry*, 12–15. Ed. Jane Everts Baird and Martha Gabriel. [Charlottetown]: Department of Education, Prince Edward Island, [1976]

Rogers, Webster. *Abegweit and Other Poems*. N.p.: n.p., n.d.

Rose, Livingstone D. 'The Lobster Ground.' *Poems and Prose*. N.p.: n.p., [1956]

Rose, Pat. 'Ghost Tales and Mysterious Lights.' *The Eastern Graphic Magazine* 3.1 (1976): 14–15

Ross, David. 'The David Ross Diary 1836–1879.' PEI Collection. UPEI, Charlottetown

Ross, Theodore. 'Potato Growing.' *The Agricultural Gazette of Canada* 2.1 (January 1915): 334–5

'Running the Lines.' *The Daily Examiner* (25 April 1903): 2–3

Rutherford, J.B., D.G. Wilder, and H.C. Frick. *An Economic Appraisal of the Canadian Lobster Fishery*. Ottawa: Fisheries Research Board of Canada, 1967

Sage, Mary Stuart. *The Lord Selkirk Settlers in Belfast, Prince Edward Island*. N.p.: n.p., [1973]

Scarratt, D.J. *Investigations into the Effects on Lobsters of Raking Irish Moss, 1970–1971*. St. Andrews: Fisheries Research Board of Canada, 1972

– 'Rocks and Rakes: Lobsters vs. Irish Moss.' *Canadian Geographical Journal* 95.2 (October-November 1977): 56–9

Sellick, Lester B. *My Island Home*. Windsor, NS: Lancelot Press Limited, 1973

Shaw, Lloyd W. *The Province of Prince Edward Island: Geographical Aspects*. Ottawa: The Canadian Geographical Society, [1940?]

Shaw, Walter. *Tell Me the Tales*. Charlottetown: Square Deal Publications, 1975

Simpson, Harold H. *Cavendish: Its History, Its People. The Development of a Community from Wilderness to World Recognition*. Amherst, NS: Harold H. Simpson and Associates, 1973

Sleigh, B.W.A. *Pine Forests and Hacmatack Clearings; or Travel, Life, and Adventure, in the British North American Provinces*. London: Richard Bently, 1853

Smith, R.E. 'Where the Speckled Trout Doth Jump.' *Prince Edward Island Magazine* 1.5 (July 1899): 171–3

Souris, P.E.I., 1910–1980: A Profile of the Town. Souris: Anniversary Committee, 1980

Springfield Women's Institute. *Springfield 1828–1953*. 1954

Stanhope Women's Institute History Committee. *Stanhope, Sands of Time.* 1984

Stewart, Deborah, and David Stewart. 'Winter Travel.' *The Island Magazine* 7 (Fall-Winter 1979): 19–24

Stewart, Geraldine. Letter. *Atlantic Insight* 3.10 (1981): 88

Stewart, Marion Lea. *Marion Stewart's Journal.* N.p.: n.p., 1976

Stilgenbauer, F.A. 'Geographic Aspects of the Prince Edward Island Fur Industry.' *Economic Geography*, 3 (1927): 110–25

Stirling, Lilla. *Jockie: A Story of Prince Edward Island.* New York: Scribner's, 1951

Sutherland, [Rev.] George. *A Manual of the Geography and Natural and Civil History of Prince Edward Island – For the Use of Schools, Families and Emigrants.* Charlottetown: John Ross, 1861

Swabey, Rev. M. 'Fox Hunting in Prince Edward Island – 1840–1845.' *Prince Edward Island Magazine* 1 (September 1899): 233–6

Sweetser, Moses Foster, ed. *The Maritime Provinces: Handbook for Travellers.* Boston: James R. Osgood and Company, 1875

Tanton, John P. 'Memories of the Past – Continued.' *P.E.I. Magazine* 1 (December 1899): 347–52

Thompson, Harold W. *Body, Boots and Britches.* Philadelphia: J.B. Lippincott, 1940

Thomson, Winnifred Conrad. *Vernor Had Vision: A Tribute to Vernor Wilberforce Jones.* Privately published, 1976

'Through Tommy Hawke's Telescope.' *Prince Edward Island Magazine* 4.11 (January 1903)

Townshend, Adele. 'For the Love of a Horse.' Unpublished play, 1985

– 'The Wreck of the Sovinto.' *The Island Magazine* 4 (Spring-Summer 1978): 36–9

– comp. 'Looking Back.' Unpublished compilation from issues of *The Eastern Graphic*, 1978–1980. 2 vols. PEI Collection. UPEI, Charlottetown

Tricoche, George Nestler. *Rambles through the Maritime Provinces of Canada.* London: Arthur H. Stockwell, [1931]

Tuck, Robert Critchlow. *The Island Family Harris.* Charlottetown: Ragweed Press, 1983

– 'Victoria: Seaport on a Farm.' *The Island Magazine* 7 (Fall-Winter 1979): 38–44

Tufts, Robie W. *The Birds of Nova Scotia.* Halifax: Nova Scotia Museum, 1961

Unidentified Diary 1896–1899. PAPEI, Charlottetown

Unidentified Diary 1941–1942. David Weale Collection. UPEI, Charlottetown

Unpublished student essays. T.K. Pratt Collection. UPEI, Charlottetown, 1972–1983

Vickerson, Lemuel. 'Diary: 1868.' Unpublished diary. PAPEI, Charlottetown

Walker, Stewart. 'Reducing Pre-weaning Pig Mortality Important.' *The Corner Post* 2.3 (April 1982): 18

Wallace, Lester. 'Hunting the Mud.' *Remembering the Farm.* By Allan Anderson. N.p.: n.p., 1977

Warburton, A.B. *A History of Prince Edward Island from Its Discovery in 1534 until the Departure of Lieutenant-Governor Ready in A.D. 1831.* St. John, NB: Barnes, 1923

Warren, S. Evangeline. *Andy the Milkman.* Devon, England: Arthur Stockwell, 1957

Watson, Lawrence W. 'Wolves in Sheep's Clothing.' *Prince Edward Island Magazine* 2 (Nov. 1900): 275–8

Weale, David. 'The Emigrant, Part II: Life in the New Land.' *The Island Magazine* 17 (Summer 1985): 3–11

– '"The Minister": The Reverend Donald McDonald.' *The Island Magazine* 3 (Fall-Winter 1977): 1–6

Weekly Recorder of Prince Edward Island. UPEI, Charlottetown

Wellington Centennial Committee. *Immaculate Conception Parish Centennial, 1875–1975.* Summerside, PEI: Alpha-Graphics, 1975

Wells, Marlene. 'The House That Fox Built.' *The Atlantic Advocate.* 65.4 (December 1974): 56–8

Wheeler, David. 'The Saint Patrick's Day Snow Storm.' *Posture* (March 1983): n.pag.

White, R.P., and H.W. Platt. *Hints on Growing Netted Gems for Processing.* Charlottetown: Charlottetown Research Station, 1980

Wightman, F.A. 'Maritime Provincialisms and Contrasts.' *The Canadian Magazine* 39.1 (May 1912): 3–7

Wilder, D.G. *Canada's Lobster Fishery*. Ottawa: Department of Fisheries, 1957
– *The Lobster Fishery of the Southern Gulf of St. Lawrence*. St. Andrews, NB: Fisheries Research Board of Canada, 1954
Willey, R.C. 'Early Coinages of Prince Edward Island.' *The Canadian Numismatic Journal* 24.8 (September 1979): 352–5

Woodman, Susan. 'Diary: January 1, 1895–December 31, 1896.' David Weale Collection. UPEI, Charlottetown
Wright, Wayne. *Wayne Wright's Prince Edward Island – A Selection of Comic Drawings*. Privately published, 1980
The Zonta Club. *A Century of Women*. N.p.: n.p., n.d.